Number is the most underestimated of the grammatical categories. It is deceptively simple yet the number system which philosophers, logicians and many linguists take as the norm – namely an obligatory distinction between singular and plural (as in *cat* versus *cats*) – is only one of a wide range of possibilities to be found in languages around the world. Some languages, for instance, make more distinctions than English, having three, four or even five different values. Adopting a wide-ranging perspective, Greville Corbett draws on some 250 languages to analyse the possible systems of number. He reveals that the means for signalling number are remarkably diverse and are put to a surprising range of special additional uses. By surveying some of the riches of the world's linguistic resources this book makes a major contribution to the typology of categories and demonstrates that languages are much more varied than is generally recognised.

GREVILLE G. CORBETT is Professor of Linguistics at the University of Surrey. He is author of *Gender* (1991), also in the Cambridge Textbooks in Linguistics series, and co-editor of *Heads in Grammatical Theory* (1993) and *The Slavonic Languages* (1993).

CAMBRIDGE TEXTBOOKS IN LINGUISTICS

General editors: S. R. Anderson, J. Bresnan, B. Comrie, W. Dressler, C. J. Ewen, R. Lass, D. Lightfoot, P. H. Matthews, S. Romaine, N. V. Smith, N. Vincent

NUMBER

NUMBER

GREVILLE G. CORBETT

UNIVERSITY OF SURREY

CAMBRIDGE
UNIVERSITY PRESS

CAMBRIDGE UNIVERSITY PRESS
Cambridge, New York, Melbourne, Madrid, Cape Town,
Singapore, São Paulo, Delhi, Tokyo, Mexico City

Cambridge University Press
The Edinburgh Building, Cambridge CB2 8RU, UK

Published in the United States of America by
Cambridge University Press, New York

www.cambridge.org
Information on this title: www.cambridge.org/9780521649704

© Cambridge University Press 2000

First published 2000

A catalogue record for this publication is available from the British Library

Library of Congress Cataloguing in Publication data
Corbett, Greville G.
Number/Greville G. Corbett.
   p. cm. – (Cambridge textbooks in linguistics)
Includes bibliographical references and index.
ISBN 0 521 64016 4 (hardback) ISBN 0 521 64970 6 (paperback)
1. Grammar, Comparative and general – Number.   I. Title.   II. Series.
P240.8.C67   2000
415 – dc21   00-023604   CIP

ISBN 978-0-521-64016-9 Hardback
ISBN 978-0-521-64970-4 Paperback

For Judith, David, Ian and Peter

CONTENTS

FIGURES

TABLES

List of tables

PREFACE

During the ten years that I have been working on this book, many people have offered data, ideas, comments and other help. It is a pleasure to record my thanks to them: Alexandra Aikhenvald, Peter Austin, Matthew Baerman, Julia Barron, Laurie Bauer, Barry Blake, Jim Blevins, Juliette Blevins, Misi Brody, Jürgen Broschart, Dunstan Brown, Gordon Brown, Wayles Browne, Wallace Chafe, Hilary Chappell, Ross Clark, Ulrike Claudi, Richard Coates, Michael Colenso, Stanford Cormack, Alan Cruse, Anna Morpurgo Davies, Alan Dench, Aleksandra Derganc, Ivan Derzhanski, Werner Drossard, Barrie Evans, Nick Evans, Roger Evans, Ray Fabri, William Foley, Michael Fortescue, Victor Friedman, Norman Fraser, Gerald Gazdar, Adele Goldberg, Ian Green, Rebecca Green, Ekaterina Gruzdeva, Tom Güldemann, Ken Hale, Shelly Harrison, Mark Harvey, Martin Haspelmath, Katrina Hayward, Bernd Heine, George Hewitt, Jane Hill, Nikolaus Himmelmann, Andrew Hippisley, Robert Hoberman, Richard Hogg, Axel Holvoet, László Honti, Jim Hurford, Don Hutchisson, Larry Hyman, Ruth Kempson, Aleksandr Kibrik, Simon Kirby, Klaus-Michael Köpcke, Antonina Koval', Ulla-Maija Kulonen, Klaus Laalo, Mary Laughren, Velma Leeding, Werner Lehfeldt, Frank Lichtenberk, Jouko Lindstedt, Elizabeth Löbel, Paul Marriott, Michael Mitchell, Arto Mustajoki, David Nash, Johanna Nichols, Almerindo Ojeda, Janez Orešnik, Barbara Partee, Frans Plank, Maria Polinsky, Tom Priestly, Robert Ratcliffe, Nick Reid, Bruce Rigsby, Jan Rijkoff, John Roberts, John Saeed, Hans-Jürgen Sasse, Wolfgang Schellinger, Harold Schiffman, Jane Simpson, Elena Skribnik, Neil Smith, Gerald Stone, Greg Stump, Roland Sussex, Dalija Tekorienė, Hannu Tommola, Larry Trask, Robert Van Valin, Nigel Vincent, Max Wheeler, David Wilkins and Dieter Wunderlich. I am particularly thankful to those who generously shared the data and insights gained from fieldwork in different parts of the world. Special thanks are due to the following colleagues and friends who have had a substantial influence on the book: Bernard Comrie, David Gil, Dick Hayward, Marianne Mithun, Edith Moravcsik and Malcolm Ross.

At different times the research reported here has been supported by the ESRC (grants R000222419 and R000238228), and by the British Academy. This support is gratefully acknowledged. Writing was facilitated by stays at: the Centre for Language Teaching and Research, University of Queensland, April–June 1991 and at the Max Planck Institute for Evolutionary Anthropology, Leipzig, June–July 1999 (made possible by Roland Sussex and Bernard Comrie respectively). Various audiences have been interested and helpful; I thank all participants, particularly those at the Australian Linguistic Institute (La Trobe University 1994), the International Summer School on Typology (Mainz 1998), the members of the Noun Phrase Group in the EUROTYP project (funded by the ESF 1990–4) and the participants in the seminar series 'Challenges for Inflectional Description' (funded by the ESRC 1996–9). Preliminary results were published in a EUROTYP working paper (1992), which is superseded by the account here.

I am also very grateful to the team at Cambridge University Press for their professionalism, in particular Andrew Winnard, Citi Potts, Peter Ducker and Robert Whitelock, to Alan Rayner for expert typesetting, and to Dunstan Brown and Matthew Baerman for welcome help during the last stages of the work.

And now a Jakobson story. Haugen (1975: 326) recalls that Jakobson told him that Tesnière's book on number *Les formes du duel en slovène*, published in Paris in 1925, was made a best-seller by potential readers who assumed it was about duelling in Slovenia. The present book may not be snapped up by a public mistakenly eager for the latest contribution to number theory. But if a few stray mathematicians read it, I hope they will find that the linguistic number systems analysed here show the elegance and complexity they are accustomed to in their area of enquiry.

ABBREVIATIONS

ABL	ablative
ACC	accusative
AG	agreement marker
AGT	agent
AOR	aorist
ART	article
ASSOC	associative
AUG	augmented
AUX	auxiliary
BENEF	benefactive
CAUS	causative
CERT	certain
COND	conditional
DAT	dative
DIM	diminutive
DIR	directional
DU	dual
EFF	effector
ERG	ergative
EXCL	exclusive
FEM	feminine
FUT	future
GEN	genitive
IMMED	immediate
IMP	imperative
IMPERFV	imperfective
INCL	inclusive
INDEF	indefinite
INDIC	indicative
INST	instrumental

List of abbreviations

INTRAN	intransitive
IRR	irrealis
LOC	locative
MASC	masculine
NEG	negative
NEUT	neuter
NOM	nominative
NOW	'now' discourse clitic
OBJ	object
OBL	oblique
PARTIC	participle
PASS	passive
PAT	patient
PERFV	perfective
PERSE	personal experience
PL	plural
POSS	possessive
PRES	present
PRET	preterite
PROX	proximate
PRV	preverb
PST	past
Q	question
QM	quantity marker
REDUP	reduplication
REFL	reflexive
REL	relative pronoun
SBST	substantivizer
SG	singular
SUBJ	subject
1	first person
2	second person
3	third person
I	gender I
II	gender II
III	gender III
IV	gender IV

1
Introduction

Number is the most underestimated of the grammatical categories. It is deceptively simple, and is much more interesting and varied than most linguists realize. This was recognized by Jespersen: 'Number might appear to be one of the simplest natural categories, as simple as "two and two are four." Yet on closer inspection it presents a great many difficulties, both logical and linguistic' (Jespersen 1924: 188). Lyons too pointed out its interest: 'The analysis of the category of number in particular languages may be a very complex matter' (Lyons 1968: 283). This book will illustrate the interest of number, and some first pointers are given in §1.1. We shall also see the challenges which Jespersen and Lyons allude to, one of the trickiest being the need to ensure that as we compare across languages we are really comparing like with like (§1.2). Hence the book is structured so as to work upwards from properties that are safe building blocks for comparison (§1.3). Finally in this introduction a few notes on presentation are needed (§1.4).

1.1 The special interest of number

Despite the significance of number, there are still surveys of linguistics where it receives a footnote's worth of attention. This is largely because there are some reasonable but incorrect assumptions about number, which are generally based on the consideration of a rather limited range of languages. In seeing where these assumptions are false we shall get an initial idea of how interesting the category really is.

> *First assumption:* number is just an opposition of singular versus plural

There are indeed languages with this basic opposition. But there are also many languages with richer systems, with a dual for two real world entities, some with a trial for three, others with a paucal for a small number. There are more exotic possibilities too, with the richest systems having five number values, as in Sursurunga. Moreover, some of the trickiest problems with number become much clearer when we look at the evidence from larger systems, that is those with more than the basic singular–plural distinction.

1

> *Second assumption:* all relevant items (nouns, for instance) will mark number

We might expect that, say, all nouns would show number. That clearly is not the case, for instance English *honesty* does not mark plural. It seems natural to say that it is an abstract noun and that for certain abstract nouns number is not relevant. But this is a parochial fact about English; there are languages where the proportion of items for which number is relevant in this sense is quite small, and others where number marking is practically always available. The possible ranges of number marking are constrained in interesting ways.

> *Third assumption:* items which do mark number will behave the same

Suppose that we carefully specify how many number values a particular language has and which types of noun mark number. Having avoided our first two false assumptions, we might assume that items would either fail to mark number or would show all the number values available. Once again, things are more interesting than that. In Maltese, for instance, just a few nouns have singular, dual, and plural, while the majority of nouns and the pronouns have only singular and plural. Or in Bayso, pronouns have two number forms while typical nouns have four.

> *Fourth assumption:* number must be expressed

If number forms are available, then surely they must be used? This is an Anglo-centric assumption and is quite false. We shall see instances where the marking of number is optional, and there are languages like Bayso where there are special forms which allow the use of a noun without any commitment to the number of entities involved. Linked to this assumption is the fact that number is usually thought of as prototypically inflectional. The inflection–derivation distinction is becoming a hot topic again in morphology and number is in fact highly problematic in this respect. This book will provide a good deal of relevant material; the presentation will be as neutral as possible in order to include the relevant data for a continuing debate in which the criteria are likely to change.

> *Fifth assumption:* number is a nominal category

So far our examples have involved nouns and pronouns. But there are languages where number is a verbal category, marking the number of events rather than the number of individuals. We return to this distinction in the next section.

The point which is emerging is that English and other familiar Indo-European languages have quite *unusual* number systems; they occupy one corner of the typological space. It is clear that to understand the category of number we need to look at a broad range of languages. Hale made a related point in a discussion of the problem of language endangerment:

> while the category of number is accessible, in an obvious sense, its surface realization across languages exhibits great diversity, and a great many individual languages fail to present the observable data which will permit us to get at the fundamental character of the oppositions involved and, thereby, to come closer to an understanding of the universal organization and inventories of the category of number. (Hale 1997: 75)

We shall see several instances of interesting systems which are essential for appreciating the full range of possibilities being found in languages which have few speakers and are clearly endangered. And the prospects for language loss are particularly serious for number. There are perhaps 6,000 languages spoken at present, of which around 250 are 'safe': they are likely to survive another hundred years at least. But these safe languages are not evenly distributed: over half of them belong to Indo-European or Niger-Kordofanian (Krauss 1992, 1993), while some families with many languages of special interest for number are hardly represented at all. It is therefore important to identify and investigate the most interesting systems while there is still time. Our 'linguistic tour' in the book will include over 250 languages. Several of these languages do not occur in the various typological samples and yet are vital for a full typology (Bayso is a good example). Hence this was a case where it was appropriate to examine as many languages as possible, rather than taking a defined sample. Many of the languages which were investigated will not be mentioned since they turned out to be similar in the relevant respects to others which are described here.

1.2 Comparing like with like

Since we shall look at a wide range of languages we must be careful to ensure that we are comparing like with like. For instance, how do we know that a language has number? Languages like English have the category of number, since we find correspondences like the following:

magazine	magazine-s
head	head-s
woman	women

There is a difference in meaning between *magazine* and *magazines* (obviously concerning the number of them), which corresponds to a difference in form. That same difference in meaning is found in *head/heads* and *woman/women*. The first member of each pair is said to be singular, and the second is plural. So when we say

3

that English has singular and plural we are referring to correspondences of meaning and form.

In many theoretical frameworks number, like comparable categories such as gender, case and person, is treated as a 'feature'. This feature is said to have certain 'values' (for number, these include singular and plural, and we have already come across others too).[1] These values of the number feature have meanings and forms associated with them. The main part of the meaning of the singular is that it refers to one real world entity, while the plural refers to more than one distinct real world entity. The formal expression of the plural in English is usually the addition of an ending, as in *magazines*, *heads*, while the singular is usually signalled (on nouns) by the absence of such a marker. But there are other ways of marking the plural too, as found in *women* and *geese*. It is the association of (a set of) meanings with (a set of) forms which allows us to talk of the singular and plural values of the feature number.

The plural may be realized in various different ways in a given language. Rather than listing all the forms on each occasion, linguists talk of 'plural forms'. Conversely, these plural forms may be used to express various related meanings, and here we may talk of 'plural meanings'. However, as a shorthand, people often talk of 'the plural' or 'the singular' when in fact just the meaning or just the form is intended. Normally the intention is clear but, particularly when comparing languages, it is important to be explicit about which we intend, for the following reason. We do not expect the form of the plural to be the same in English as, say, in Russian: even if the morphological means used are similar (mainly inflections in both languages); we anticipate that there will be phonological differences between them. Of course, we are correct (the items on the right are Russian translations of the English):

magazine	magazine-s	žurnal	žurnal-y
head	head-s	golov-a	golov-y
woman	women	ženščin-a	ženščin-y

The danger is that using the same term 'plural' for both forms and meanings may lead us to assume without question that though the forms differ the same meanings are expressed. In fact there are small but not insignificant differences between the English and Russian plural.

At this stage let us take an example where the differences are more obvious. English and Russian have singular and plural, while Sanskrit had singular, dual

---

[1] An alternative terminology has number as a 'category' and singular as a 'property' or 'feature' (Matthews 1991: 39–40). We retain 'category of number' as a wider term, to include all manifestations of number, including number words (for which see §5.1), as opposed to the category of gender, tense and so on.

and plural. Sanskrit used the dual for referring to just two real world entities, and the plural for more than two. Clearly the plural does not have the same meanings in English or Russian as in Sanskrit: it covers cases where two items are referred to in the former languages but not in Sanskrit (a general point made by Saussure 1916/1971: 161).

How then can we compare, say, the plural in different languages? The first answer must be 'with care', to ensure that we are indeed dealing with comparable things. Provided first that we can establish that in each language under consideration there is a regular correspondence of meanings and forms which allows us to demonstrate the existence of a number system, we can then compare the values in the two languages. Typically the value which includes in its meaning reference to the largest sets of referents will be called 'plural', whatever other meanings or restrictions it may have. It is therefore reasonable to compare the degree of overlap between the use of the plural in the different languages. (But we must be careful; for instance, in descriptions of Cushitic languages 'plural' is used to indicate a set of forms whose use does not always correspond to plural in most other languages, as we shall see in §6.1.1.) We shall find potentially confusing terminology for other number values too. The term 'collective' is used quite differently in different traditions. And there are subtler problems, for example where 'trial' is sometimes used of forms historically related to the numeral three but currently used for a small number ('few'). Thus although 'trial' is a possible term for the form in such languages we shall choose our terms favouring meaning and so would call this a 'paucal'.[2] The important thing in such cases is to be explicit about what is intended. As a general rule we shall give priority to meaning in our choice of terms.

The last question we need to tackle at this early stage in our investigation is: What type of category is number? The obvious answer, certainly for speakers of Indo-European languages, is that it is a nominal category, affecting primarily nouns and pronouns. In our examples above, the difference between *head* and *heads*, *golova* and *golovy* is the number of heads involved. Of course, number may be shown by verbs too in English (and Russian, and many other languages):

(1)   my dog watches television
(2)   my dogs watch television

Though number is marked on the verb here as well as on the noun, the essential difference between (1) and (2) is, of course, the number of dogs involved. This point can be seen particularly clearly in these examples:

---

[2]   Though we favour terms based on semantics, this does not entail any claim that particular number values are always used according to meaning. Thus we label the form *cat* 'singular' because it is regularly used in expressions referring to a single cat; but there are also expressions, like *more than one cat*, where the singular is out of line with the semantics.

(3) the sheep drinks from the stream

(4) the sheep drink from the stream

Though the form of the noun does not change, and the marker of number is on the verb, it still indicates the number of sheep involved. (Example (4) cannot be used in English for the situation in which *one* sheep drinks several times.) In other words, we have nominal number which happens to be expressed on the verb (usually, in English, in addition to being expressed on the noun). Number in English is largely regular: words like *dog ~ dogs* greatly outnumber those like *sheep ~ sheep* and *criterion ~ criteria*. This suggests that number is an inflectional category in English: *dog* (singular) and *dogs* (plural) are forms of the same lexical item DOG.

There are many languages which, broadly speaking, are comparable to English in this respect. But there are also many languages in which number is fundamentally different: in particular it may be not a nominal category but a verbal one. Moreover it is often highly irregular and may not be an inflectional category. Let us consider briefly what verbal number is. The following examples are from Rapanui (the language of Easter Island, one of the Oceanic languages within Austronesian: data from Veronica Du Feu 1996: 191–2 and personal communication):

(5) ruku
     'dive'

(6) ruku ruku
     'go diving'

The form in (6) implies more than one dive, but not necessarily more than one diver. Verbal plurality is indicated (by reduplication here) since the event is in a sense plural. There are other possibilities for verbal number, just as nominal number can be more complex and varied than the English data suggest, as we shall see.

1.3 Structure of the book

We begin with nominal number, since it is the part of number where we find the greatest variety. In chapter 2 we look for as many meaning distinctions as we can identify in the world's languages. We keep the nominal 'still' and see how many different number values it may have. Then in chapter 3 we hold the number value still, and see which nominals may be involved. The possible patterns of involvement in the number system are constrained by the Animacy Hierarchy, according to which, informally, the 'more animate' a nominal is the more likely it is to show number. We then allow both dimensions to vary together, that is to say, we attempt a typology of what number values are possible for what nominals (chapter 4). This integration of the two dimensions of the typology requires us to address the issues of minor numbers, associatives and distributives, among others. In chapter 5 we go on to the ways in which number is expressed, and in chapter 6 we discuss syntactic issues, mainly agreement but also including problems caused by numerals. Then we look at other ways in which the means for expressing number can be used, and see that there is a surprising range of uses, from honorific to evasive use (chapter 7). In chapter 8 we survey verbal number, covering meaning distinctions, the items involved in the verbal number system and the ways in which verbal number is expressed. In the concluding chapter we review what has been established about the category of number, draw together strands of the material particularly on the development of number systems (their rise and decline) and on the interaction of number with other categories; and then we look forward to new ideas for research into number.

1.4 Presentation

The book is designed for readers of several different types. For the student of linguistics, it is a guide to an area of obvious interest which has been neglected. And more importantly, it attempts to give a picture of the tremendous richness and diversity of the world's languages, by tackling a category where the familiar languages of Western Europe are overshadowed by the complexities of systems found elsewhere in the world. It is also intended to assist those researching particular languages or groups of languages, whether for a major research project or an undergraduate essay. Seeing familiar material analysed in a typological context can give a new perspective. This is particularly important for those areas where the terminology has become misleading, suggesting differences and similarities which do not hold. It is hoped especially that the book will prove valuable to field-workers by giving them both helpful leads for analysis and the awareness of the types of data which will enable us to understand the category of number more fully. The task in this area is urgent since, as mentioned above, many of the crucial languages are endangered. The picture presented in the book has been built up out of many small pieces, and this should be made evident; hence there are many references in the text, though where possible the detail is given in notes. There are extensive references for those who wish to go further. Since the work is organized thematically, special care has been taken so that those seeking data on specific languages can find the relevant references through the index.

The relevance of the book to typologists is evident: it is another example of the approach to typology which examines categories rather than constructions. Furthermore each chapter can be taken as illustrating a particular typological point, and so the book may be used as a hands-on introduction to typology. For morphologists, it should provide grist to the mill for those concerned with the relations of inflectional and derivational morphology (as noted in §1.1). There is also a

7

substantial amount of research in formal semantics on the nature of plurals; key references will be found in §2.5. That work is starting to connect with the wide range of number use in natural language: it is hoped that this book will be of use to semanticists for that purpose.

The orthography used in examples normally follows that of the source, to enable the reader to refer back easily, while for examples originally in a non-Roman script a standard transliteration is used. Examples are followed by glosses. These are intended to clarify the point at issue rather than being full glosses. When items are segmented in an example, this segmentation is mirrored in the gloss: *smile-s* smile-3.SG, in which the *s* is glossed as '3.SG'. Since the *s* cannot itself be segmented into constituent morphs representing third person and singular number separately, the glosses for these, abbreviations in this case, are joined by a stop. Abbreviations are listed on page xix.

2
Meaning distinctions

In this chapter we concentrate on the possible meaning distinctions in number systems. Often the situation in languages like English is taken as normal, whereas it represents only one of the possibilities. We will first consider whether number needs to be expressed; we shall see that for some languages the expression of number is in a sense optional, while in others it is a category which speakers cannot avoid. To investigate these systems we shall first consider the notion of 'general' number as a meaning distinction and base a partial typology upon it (§2.1). We then narrow our attention to the cases where number is expressed, and establish the main types of distinction within the category (§2.2). Thus §2.1 is devoted to the opposition of number and 'non-number', while §2.2 examines the possibilities within the number domain. In §2.3 we propose a typology, systematizing the material examined so far, and we go on to show that languages may simply not have a number system (§2.4); then we consider approaches to number within formal semantics (§2.5).

Our aim in this chapter is to find all the possible distinctions. At this stage we shall not be concerned about the type of nominal we look at, so long as we find those which show the greatest differentiation. Keeping any particular nominal 'still' as it were, we shall see how many different numbers it may have available, in the most favourable contexts. In the next chapter we consider the possibilities along the other dimension (holding a particular number distinction constant we shall examine which nominals can be involved in it). Then in chapter 4 we integrate the account of the possible number systems with the possible patterns of involvement of different nominals. In these chapters we concentrate on the semantic distinctions and we leave detailed consideration of the means used to express them for chapter 5. The more general typological point of this chapter is that as a first step we must cast our nets widely; a category as familiar as number proves to be remarkably varied once we examine a broad range of languages.

2.1 General number

In English we are usually forced to choose between singular and plural when we use a noun. However, there are languages for which number is less dominant, languages in which the meaning of the noun can be expressed without reference to number. We shall call this 'general number', by which we mean that it is outside the number system. Various other terms have been used: Jespersen (1924: 198) writes of the lack of 'a common number form (i.e. a form that disregards the distinction between singular and plural)'; Hayward (1979) introduced the term 'unit reference', the German tradition is to use 'transnumeral', as in Biermann (1982). We follow Andrzejewski (1960) in using the term 'general'.

Given our definition of the meaning of general number, let us analyse its place in the number systems of various languages. It is found in the Cushitic language Bayso, which at the last count had a few hundred speakers on Gidicho Island in Lake Abaya (southern Ethiopia) and on the western shore of the lake. Bayso nouns have a form which represents the general meaning, that is, it is non-committal as to number (Corbett and Hayward 1987). *Lúban* 'lion' denotes a particular type of animal, but the use of this form does not commit the speaker to a number of lions: there could be one or more than that. Other forms are available for indicating reference specifically to one or to more than one lion, when required.

The situation in which a language would have both a form outside the number system and a minimal number contrast can be diagrammed as in figure 2.1. The meaning of the noun may be expressed independently of number, as occurs with the general meaning, or it may be expressed within the number system, which at its simplest means there will be a choice of singular or plural. In Bayso these meanings all have independent forms: as we have already noted, *lúban* 'lion(s)' is the general form. For reference to one lion, especially for reference to a specific lion, the singular *lubántiti* 'a/the particular lion' is used.[1] Bayso actually has one more possibility than the system in figure 2.1, since for reference to a small number of lions, two to

---

[1] Specificity plays a role with the other numbers too; for instance, in phrases consisting of noun plus numeral, number must be marked on the noun if there is a determiner or other modifying element in the phrase, but otherwise it need not be (Dick Hayward, personal communication). Compare:

   (i) hiṇi   deelel-jaa   lama emeten
         this.PL young.woman-PAUCAL two   came.PL
         'these two young women came'

  (ii) deelel / deelel-jaa   lama emeten
         young.woman.GENERAL/ young.woman-PAUCAL two   came.PL
         'two young women came'

A subscript point (superscript in the case of 'p̓') indicates glottalization, as in *hiṇi* 'these'. In the case of obstruents, glottalization is manifested as an ejective, but in the case of sonorants, it involves a preceding or following glottal stop. The labelling of the forms (as again with *hiṇi* 'these') is difficult, since controller and target numbers do not match in Bayso; see Corbett and Hayward (1987: 11–12) and §6.1.1. In (ii) use of the paucal for the noun is possible, but so is general number, while in (i) the paucal is required.

general

singular   plural

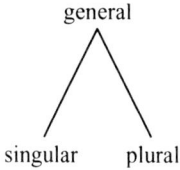

Figure 2.1 *System with separate general number*

about six, the paucal *lubanjaa* 'a few lions' is available; for more than that the plural *lubanjool* 'lions' can be used. We return to the relations of paucals to plurals in §2.2.4 and §2.3.2. Examples include (Dick Hayward, personal communication):

(1) lúban   foofe
    lion.GENERAL   watched.1.SG
    literally: 'I watched lion' (it could be one, or more than that)

(2) lubán-titi   foofe
    lion-SG   watched.1.SG
    'I watched a lion'

(3) luban-jaa   foofe
    lion-PAUCAL   watched.1.SG
    'I watched a few lions'

(4) luban-jool   foofe
    lion-PL   watched.1.SG
    'I watched (a lot of) lions'

For easy comparison with the systems which follow, let us use an artificial version of English based on Bayso. A language which distinguishes general, singular and plural allows the following contrasts:

(5) I saw dog (general: one or more)

(6) I saw dog-a (singular: exactly one)

(7) I saw dog-i (plural: more than one)

This three-way system is found in the Fouta Jalon dialect of Fula, which has over two million speakers in Guinea (and over 100,000 more in Sierra Leone and Senegal), but not in other dialects of Fula. Moreover, it is restricted to a part of the noun inventory. Fula nouns typically carry a marker which indicates number: *caa-ngol/can-ɗi* 'river/s', *gabb-ii/gabb-i* 'hippopotamus/es' (data are from Antonina Koval' 1979 and personal communications, Barrie Evans 1994 and personal communications). In most instances, when a noun is used the speaker is required to

11

indicate singular or plural number, since one or other marker is required. But some nouns have a third form, which does not have such a marker:

general	*singular*	*plural*
toti 'toad(s)'	totii-ru 'toad'	totii-ji 'toads'
nyaari 'cat(s)'	nyaarii-ru 'cat'	nyaarii-ji 'cats'
gerto 'hen(s)'	gerto-gal 'hen'	gertoo-ɗe 'hens'[2]
boofo 'egg(s)'	woofoo-nde 'egg'	boofoo-ɗe 'eggs'
biini 'bottle(s)'	biinii-ri 'bottle'	biinii-ji 'bottles'

The forms which have no suffix express general meaning, that is they are used when number is irrelevant, for instance (Koval′ 1979: 11):

(8) ko   biini   tun   waawi   marde   beere
     PARTICLE bottle only can.PERFV   preserve beer
     'only a bottle/bottles can preserve beer'

Various nouns are able to show general number; as our list indicates, those denoting animals are well represented, and nouns denoting humans are included too. Barrie Evans (personal communication) gives interesting statistics on the availability of general forms; his database includes 180 items with a general form (11.5 per cent of all nominals in the database). They are spread across about half the genders of Fula; in the human gender, around 30 per cent of the nouns have general forms; thus 70 per cent do not, yet many nouns lower in terms of animacy do have general forms. In addition, there is the interesting restriction that the form without the suffix must have at least two syllables. Compare the following examples (Koval′ 1979: 12, 22):

(9) nyaari   peɗay
     cat(s)   scratch
     'a cat scratches/cats scratch'

Here the unsuffixed form, expressing general number meaning, is used (the singular, as noted above, would be *nyaarii-ru* and the plural *nyaarii-ji*). This is not possible in the next example:

(10) pucc-u   latay
      horse-SG   kick
      'a horse kicks/horses kick'

Here the unsuffixed form would consist of a single syllable, and so the singular form must be used to express general number. A further limitation on the use of

---

[2] The symbol ɗ indicates a preglottalized *d*.

forms with general meaning is that they are usually restricted to contexts in which no agreement is required.[3] (General number in Fula will be discussed further in §4.5.5.)

Another language with a comparable system for a part of the noun inventory is Arabic. In Syrian Arabic, for example, many nouns denoting vegetables, fruits (also fruit trees), grains, flowers, some mammals, birds, insects have a form usually called the collective (Cowell 1964: 297–302). 'Collective' is a term which has been used in a bewildering variety of ways, as Gil (1996) shows. The forms we are interested in here are comparable to those we have discussed in Fula, in that they do not specify the number of real world entities involved: *baṭṭa* can be 'duck' or 'ducks'.[4] In addition Syrian Arabic has singular, dual and plural.

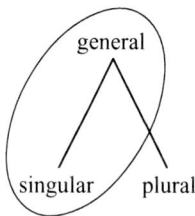

Figure 2.2 *System with general/singular versus plural*

Languages in which the general meaning is expressible by a unique form, whether regularly as in Bayso,[5] or less so as in Fula and Arabic, are not widespread. However, there are many languages in which general meaning is widely expressed, but by means of a form used also for one of the more restricted number meanings. In languages which distinguish singular and plural this offers two possibilities. The first is that the general is combined with the singular, giving a general/singular versus plural system, as shown in figure 2.2. The ellipse is used to signal that the two potential meanings share a single form. Let us consider how such a system would work. In artificial English the possibilities are these:

[3] In exceptional cases where agreement is found, it is singular, according to Koval' (1979: 12–13); however, Evans (1994) claims that both singular and plural agreements are possible. Note that in this dialect of Fula, number is not marked on the verb; thus in (9) and (10) the verb gives no information about number.

[4] Furthermore they are grammatically singular, and are not used with numerals (but see Fischer 1980: 77–80 for the earlier situation). Note that for some such collectives there can be such strong preferences that they are likely to be interpreted in neutral contexts as implying several referents (Gil 1996).

[5] Recall that we are considering in this chapter the nominals with the greatest range of possibilities; in Bayso, these are nouns. The personal pronoun has a simple singular–plural opposition. It should also be said that the Bayso system is an innovative one in Cushitic (Dick Hayward, personal communication). The type found in Arbore (discussed below) pre-dates the Bayso system in Cushitic, and is a common system world-wide.

> (11)   I saw dog (general: 'one or more' OR singular: 'exactly one')
>
> (12)   I saw dog-i (plural: 'more than one')

In this system, examples like (11) are vague; they cover the meanings of examples (5) and (6) above; (11) could be used for seeing one dog or more than one (and so this system differs from that of English); however, (12) unambiguously indicates that more than one dog is intended.[6]

A good example of this type is Japanese, as the following example shows (Bernard Comrie, personal communication; see §3.4 for references and further discussion):

> (13)   Kooen   ni   wa   inu   ga   iru   rasii.
>   park   in   TOPIC   dog   SUBJ   be   seems
>   'It seems there is a dog/are some dogs in the park.'

Without marking, *inu* 'dog' does not specify the number. There is a plural form *inu-tati* 'dogs',[7] which can be used to make clear that there is more than one dog (or the quantifer *takusan* 'much, many' could be added after *ga*). Conversely, if the speaker wishes to make clear that there is only one dog, the form *ip-piki* 'one-CLASSIFIER' can be used (in example (13) it would go after the subject marker *ga*). Similarly, in Turkish the form *ev* can mean 'house' or 'houses', while the plural form *evler* must mean 'houses' (for details see Schroeder 1999).

As we shall see, there are many languages of this type from various linguistic families. Before considering more of them, it is important to be clear on how they are defined. Languages of this type have an opposition general/singular versus plural (Turkish *ev* 'house'/'houses' versus *evler* 'houses') in which the first form does not by itself establish a number for the noun. We have to consider the form–meaning pairings available, independently of context. It does not follow that a language of this type cannot make a full number contrast. There are various possible means for making the distinction: use of numerals, especially 'one', use of an article (often the grammaticalization of the word for 'one'), and so on. But in such languages, the distinction is made 'when it matters' and not automatically, as in languages like English. The conditions 'when it matters' to specify number vary from language to language. The following characteristics may favour specifying number: being the topic as opposed to non-topic, first mention versus subsequent mention, referential versus non-referential use, human versus non-human, definite versus indefinite.[8]

---

[6] Here we could use a real variety of English: Singlish, the English of Singapore, has the forms *dog/dogs* but uses them as in (11) and (12); see Gil (forthcoming).

[7] Note that the suffix carries an implication of definiteness; it is used primarily but not exclusively with nouns denoting humans; the interaction of definiteness with number is taken up in §9.2.4.

[8] I am grateful to Nikolaus Himmelmann and Christoph Schroeder (personal communications) for suggestions here. It might seem that we just have to establish the conditions

Suppose that in a particular language it becomes established that number (plural) is to be marked where appropriate in particular circumstances, for instance, when humans are referred to. This means that all speakers treat number as mattering for human referents. A characteristic which favoured marking of number can come to favour it so much that number marking there is as good as obligatory. Then, if plural is not specified on a noun phrase with a human referent, the form with no number indication will imply singular. Number marking would have come to be obligatory for part of the system, but there could still be general number elsewhere (as we shall see in §4.5, it is common for there to be different systems in operation for different types of nominal). For instance, Smirnova (1981) shows that general/singular versus plural is a widespread system in Iranian languages, but not for nouns denoting humans; the latter have singular versus plural. And in Vai, a Northern Mande language (Welmers 1976: 45–6), there is a similar system. These reflect the tendency for number to be marked for nouns higher on the Animacy Hierarchy (see §3.1).[9]

Languages which have general/singular, for varying types of nominal, can be found widely distributed in the world. They include various West African languages in addition to Vai just mentioned (Manessy 1968), then also Sango (Samarin 1967: 134–7), Amharic (David Appleyard, personal communication) and Mangap-Mbula (Mangaaba-Mbula, Bugenhagen 1994). According to Aikhenvald (1994: 432) it is found in the majority of languages of South America. Elsewhere a particularly clear case is Even (sometimes called Lamut), a Tungusic language spoken by some 6,000 people scattered in north-east Siberia. Benzing (1955: 50) gives the following examples:

(14) zawod-la   bǝj   gurgǝ̄wci-n
      factory-LOC   man   work-3.SG
      'in the factory, a man works/men work'

under which plural can be indicated (for instance, 'a noun is marked as plural only if it denotes humans . . .'). But this runs the risk of conflating two separate issues: we must specify the nouns for which marking is possible (for which see §3.2) and, as discussed above, the pragmatic conditions under which this possibility of number marking is actually taken advantage of. For an interesting case see the analysis of Tolai, a Melanesian language of New Britain (Mosel 1982: 129–40), where general number is compared to marking by number words (§5.1); both the type of noun and the context have a role.

[9] However, a general versus plural system may affect the pronouns too. Thus in Asheninca (an Arawakan language of the central Peruvian highlands; Reed and Payne 1986), the pronouns distinguish inclusive from exclusive for the first person (the inclusive implies more than one referent), and otherwise they have a second person form and a third person (distinguishing masculine and feminine). These pronouns may take the plural marker (*-payeeni*), which is the regular plural marker for nouns. However, this marker need not be used and is infrequent. Verbal suffixes which indicate number are also used relatively infrequently. Thus we seem to have a case of general number within the pronominal system. According to Reed and Payne (1986: 325) 'plural distinctions are not an integral part of the pronoun system of Asheninca'.

(15)　tala　asi　　gurgɔ̄wci-n
　　　　here　woman　work-3.SG
　　　　'here a woman works/women work'

Benzing's translations make clear that the general/singular form of the noun, together with singular agreement, can be used for reference to one individual or more than one.[10] A last example of this type is provided by the Austronesian language, Tagalog (David Gil, personal communication). In Tagalog, a form like *aso* can mean 'dog' or 'dogs'. Plural number can be expressed primarily by means of the interesting element *mga* [maŋa], probably best analysed as a clitic. It may occur before virtually any constituent, as in:

(16)　mga　　　　aso
　　　　PLURAL　dog
　　　　'dogs'

Thus the presence of *mga* indicates plurality, but its absence leaves the possibility of singular or general meaning.

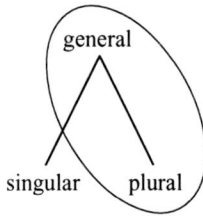

Figure 2.3 *System with general/plural versus singular*

The converse of the widespread system we have been examining would be one in which the general and plural meanings shared a form, as shown in figure 2.3. This system would allow the following contrasts in artificial English:

(17)　I saw dog-a (singular: 'exactly one')

(18)　I saw dog (general: 'one or more' OR plural: 'more than one')

---

[10] In the language isolate Nivkh, according to Panfilov (1958: 48, 52), when more than one entity is referred to, the subject and the verb may both be singular, or either one can be singular and the other plural, thus giving three possibilities. Lefebvre (1981: 76) gives examples from Quechua, in which there are four possibilities: subject and verb may each be marked as plural or have no plural marker. She discusses these in terms of the conditions under which plurality may be recovered by the hearer. There is an interesting research area here: we need to establish the languages where there are general forms and where number is simply not an issue, and to distinguish them from languages where number marking may be omitted, provided it can be recovered.

In this system, examples like (18) are vague; they cover the readings of examples (5) and (7) above; (18) could be used either for non-committal reference to a dog or dogs, or to indicate more than one.

This system does not exist in the pure form; that is, no language employs it as the normal case, forming the basis of its number system. This gap may be explained by appealing to markedness. It is generally accepted that the singular is the unmarked number as compared to the plural. When one member of an opposition is neutral with regard to the opposition, then this should be the unmarked form. Thus if one out of singular and plural can also be used as a number-neutral form (that is, having general meaning), then we would expect this to be the singular. (See §5.3.4 for zero expression, and §5.3.6 for further discussion of markedness.)

While the system of general/plural versus singular (figure 2.3) has not been found in pure form, it is nevertheless well established for sections of the noun inventories of particular languages (where the other system of general/singular versus plural is found for other parts of the noun inventory). According to Dick Hayward (personal communication) Cushitic languages normally have a form which is outside the number opposition. However, we frequently find that this general form is the same as the singular for some nouns, and the same as the plural for others, though fewer. This situation can be illustrated from the Cushitic language Arbore (Hayward 1984: 159–83). Many Arbore nouns have a general form (unit reference in Hayward's terms) which is 'semantically non-specific as to the "singular : plural" distinction' (1984: 161). We find pairs like the following:

general	plural
kér 'dog(s)'	ker-ó 'dogs'
garlá 'needle(s)'	garlá-n 'needles'

But we also find pairs in which the general form contrasts with a 'singulative'. ('Singulative' is a term relating to form; in meaning such forms are singular; 'singulative' is normally used when the singular form is derived from some other form, typically a collective or general form, and carries a number marker. It is not a significant term and we use it here only because we are quoting from sources which use it.)[11] Examples of general contrasting with singulative include:

singulative	general
tiis-in 'a maize cob'	tíise 'maize cob(s)'
lassa-n 'a loaf'	lássa 'bread'
nebel-in 'a cock ostrich'	nebel 'ostrich(es)'

---

[11] If one uses 'singulative' consistently for singular forms which correspond to a more basic plural form, then would be logical to use the term 'plurative' for plural forms which correspond to a more basic singular, as in *kér* 'dog' ~ *ker-ó* 'dogs' above, as suggested by Dimmendaal (1983: 224).

There are also some instances in which the singulative contrasts with the plural:

singulative	*plural*
heero-nté 'a flood'	heeró-n 'floods'
farr-it 'a finger/toe'	farr-ó 'fingers/toes'

Thus nouns regularly have two number forms only. For most nouns, one of these forms can be used with general meaning; but this general meaning form may be paired with a singulative or with a plural. Other nouns have singulative versus plural.

The situation found in the Borana dialect of Oromo (another Cushitic language, previously called Galla) is comparable and equally interesting. When a noun has two forms these are normally singulative and general, or general and plural (singulative and plural is very rare). Andrzejewski (1960: 68) reports that:

> the vast majority of Nouns occur normally only in their *General Forms*. The *Plural* and *Singulative Forms* are seldom used and in fact it is possible to listen to conversations among the Borana for a whole day or even longer without coming across one *Plural* or *Singulative Form*. Nevertheless, there are Nouns whose *Plural* or *Singulative Forms* I have found in common use.

This quotation makes it quite clear that the difference in forms is not simply a morphological one; in this Oromo dialect, nouns have a general form, the one normally used, which gives no information as to number. A singulative or plural form may well be available when specificity as to number is required, but this need occurs infrequently. What then is the relative importance of singulatives as opposed to plurals in Oromo? Singulative forms are very rare and, with one exception are found only with nouns denoting persons (Andrzejewski 1960: 64n). The exception is the word for 'young bull'; cattle are of great significance in Oromo culture. Thus the general form appears to coincide with the singular more often than with the plural. That is to say, nouns following the model of figure 2.2 outnumber those following figure 2.3. This is what we would expect, if the singular is indeed unmarked with respect to the plural.

Most studies of Cushitic languages have, quite naturally, been concerned to establish the forms involved, and less has been done on the interesting question of the semantics of these systems. In languages where the preponderance in use of the general form is less great, where many nouns commonly use two number forms, it would be interesting to establish when the general form retains its general meaning and when, by regular contrast with either a singulative or a plural form, it becomes restricted in meaning to singular or plural. (There is further discussion of general number in §3.4, §4.5.3, §4.5.4 and §4.5.5.)

Before going on to the last system in our typology, it is perhaps worth making it quite clear how these systems differ from that of English. Of course, it is possible in English to use the singular, the unmarked number, for more general reference, as in: *the lion is a noble beast.* Here we are not referring to one lion, but to lions more generally, so this usage is sometimes called 'generic'. We can also say *lions are noble beasts.* Hence in this type of expression, number is not particularly important.[12] But in most contexts we are forced to choose singular or plural, and the choice is significant. Imagine that I can see three lions in the garden. If I then say *there's a lion in the garden*, this is true but misleading, since the use of the singular in English implies that there is exactly one lion in the garden.

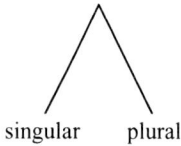

Figure 2.4 *System with singular versus plural*[13]

This leads us to the last possibility in our typology, and English is a good example of this. This is a system in which number must normally be expressed: there is no way of expressing general meaning (except by circumlocution), no forms outside the number system. We have the picture in figure 2.4. Let us consider our examples again, this time in normal English:

(19) I saw a dog (exactly one)

(20) I saw some dogs (more than one)

There is no form which would be appropriate for the readings of both (19) and (20). Indeed, this situation is taken by many people, including large numbers of linguists, to be completely normal and yet, as we have seen, there are many languages which employ rather different systems.

2.2 Number values

Having established the place of general number as outside the number system, we now turn to the distinctions which may be drawn within number. We shall look at that part of the system in a given language which is of greatest interest in terms of

---

[12] Nevertheless, *the lion / lions / a lion* are not interchangeable in such uses; see Rusiecki (1991) for an interesting discussion of the differences.

[13] Since English does not have general number, whether expressed by a unique form as in Bayso or by a form shared with another as in Japanese, the top node is unlabelled, leaving the opposition between singular and plural.

the distinctions available. This is often the personal pronoun, though sometimes particular classes of noun show greater possibilities. We return to relation between the different values and the different nominals in chapter 3.

2.2.1 The plural

The simplest system, and a common one, has an opposition:

> singular   plural

The singular–plural opposition is the primary one, on which all systems are built. Plural here refers to more than one real world entity. Quirk et al. (1985: 297) observe that English 'makes the division after "more than one"' (*one and a half days*) unlike languages like French where plural implies 'two or more'.

2.2.2 The dual

The dual refers to two distinct real world entities. If a dual is added to our previous system, we have another common system:

> singular   dual   plural

Examples can be found all over the world, for instance, in Upper Sorbian, a West Slavonic language (Stone 1993a). Some of the forms are given in table 2.1.

Table 2.1   *The dual in Upper Sorbian*

singular	dual	plural
ja 'I'	mój 'we two'	my 'we'
ty 'you'	wój 'you two'	wy 'you (all)'
hród 'palace, castle'	hrodaj 'two palaces/castles'	hrody 'palaces/castles'
dźěłam '(I) work'	dźěłamoj '(we two) work'	dźěłamy '(we) work'

It is important to note that the introduction of the dual has an effect on the plural. More generally, a change in system gives the plural a different meaning; if the system is singular–dual–plural, the plural is for three or more real world entities, as noted by Saussure (1916/1971: 161). The dual has long fascinated linguists, a notable early example being Humboldt (1830); see Plank (1989) for illuminating discussion and references. Some Indo-Europeanists speculated on the reasons for what seemed its inevitable loss, unaware of the fact that in many languages from other families around the world it is thriving.[14]

---

[14] For a discussion of semantic distinctions within the dual see Rukeyser (1997); for the related question of special forms for kin dyads in Australian languages see that reference, Dench (1987) and McGregor (1996). The dual's poetic functions in Slovene are considered

2.2.3 The trial

Just as the dual is for two, the trial is for referring to three distinct real world entities. Adding it in to systems like those just discussed gives the following system of number values:

> singular dual trial plural

Such a system is found in Larike, a Central Moluccan language with 8,000–10,000 speakers on the western tip of Ambon Island, Central Maluku, Indonesia. Central Moluccan forms part of the Central Malayo-Polynesian subgroup of Austronesian; the data are from Laidig and Laidig (1990). Larike distinguishes singular, dual, trial and plural in its free pronouns (though there are no third person pronouns for non-human referents):

(21)   Duma   hima   aridu   naʔa
      house   that   1.TRIAL.EXCL   own.it
      'We three own that house'

It also makes these distinctions in its various series of pronominal affixes:

(22)   Kalu   iridu-ta-ʔeu,   au-na-wela
      if   2.TRIAL-NEG-go   1.SG-IRR-go.home
      'If you three don't want to go, I'm going home'

These affixes work on an agent–patient basis, hence the person–number affixes in (22) are agent markers.

It is interesting to note that the dual and trial forms originate from the numerals 'two' and 'three', and that the plural comes historically from 'four'. Such developments are fairly common in Austronesian languages (see §9.1.2 for explanation). However, as we shall see, there are descriptions of other languages where forms labelled 'trial' in the literature were once semantic trials but are now paucals, appropriate for use not only of three, but also of a small group greater than three. This shows again the need for care in the use of terms. The Larike trial is a genuine trial: 'it should be stated explicitly that Larike trials are true trial forms. In other words, they represent the quantity three, and are not used to refer to the more vague notion of several, as is a paucal or limited plural' (Laidig and Laidig 1990: 92). The Larike trial is 'facultative', a distinction to which we return in §2.3.3 below. Ngan'gityemerri (a Daly language with two dialects, Ngan'gikurunggurr and Ngan'giwumirri, and with 100 speakers, 300 miles SW of Darwin, Australia) also has a trial, strictly for three (Nicholas Reid 1990: 118–119 and personal

by Lenček (1982) and in Old English by Bragg (1989); the special development of the Icelandic dual is examined by Guðmundsson (1972). The dual will feature significantly in chapter 7, and its loss will be taken up in §9.1.2.

communication) as has Marrithiyel, another Daly family language (Ian Green 1989: 136–9). It occurs too in Anindilyakwa, the language of Groote Eylandt (the large island in the Gulf of Carpentaria, Northern Territory, Australia, about 1,000 speakers).[15] In traditional Anindilyakwa it would have been more correct to call the form a paucal since it could be used for three to five, and not just for three; however, younger speakers, who have been through school, tend now to use it as a strict trial for three only (Velma Leeding 1989: 225 and personal communication).[16]

We have seen languages with genuine trials, appropriate just when referring to three entities. There is a question as to whether there are also languages with quadrals (for reference to four entities). However, having raised the issue of paucals, we shall first continue the analysis of these, and only then return to the question of quadrals.

2.2.4 The paucal

The paucal is used to refer to a small number of distinct real world entities. It is similar to the English quantifier 'a few' in meaning, particularly in that there is no specific upper bound that can be put on its use. (Its lower bound, like that of the plural, will vary according to the system in which it is embedded.) As noted earlier, Bayso has a paucal, with singular and plural, giving the following system (in addition to general number):

singular   paucal   plural

The paucal is used in Bayso for reference to a small number of individuals, from two to about six. Bayso has this system in nouns, as we saw in §2.1, but not in its pronouns (§4.5.4).[17] The paucal is also found in Avar, but as a minor number there (§4.2.3).[18]

---

[15] The trial is also facultative in Ngan'gityemerri, Marrithiyel and Anindilyakwa. For other languages with trials we do not have enough information to know whether they are facultative or obligatory; it may be that trials are always facultative.

[16] A clear inflectional trial is reported in Lenakel and other Tanna languages, which are part of Oceanic (Lynch 1977); Lynch is specific about the trial 'marking three only' (1986: 262). For evidence on the use of the trial in languages of Victoria and in Arabana see Hercus (1966); it is suggested (1966: 337) that the forms there originally meant 'a group of people standing or sitting together or associated with each other in some way'.

[17] Walapai (Hualapai), a Yuman language of north-western Arizona appears to have singular–paucal–plural for nouns, pronouns and verbs (Redden 1966: 149–50, 159); Pilagá, a Guaykuruan language of Argentina, has this system for classifiers, but the full number system includes a dual (Vidal 1997); Kayapó, a Jê language of Brazil, may have singular–paucal–plural in its pronoun system (Wiesemann 1986: 361, 368) but this requires further investigation.

[18] The term 'restricted plural' may be found in place of 'paucal'. Sometimes the term 'paucal' is used for forms that are required with lower numerals. For instance, in constructions with

Systems with just a paucal in addition to singular and plural are rare. It is much more common to find it with a dual too, giving this system:

singular   dual   paucal   plural

Here the meaning of the paucal changes to exclude two. This system is found, for instance, in Yimas, a Lower Sepik language with 250 speakers in the Sepik Basin of Papua New Guinea. The paucal is found in the pronoun and in the pronominal affixes on the verb. 'The paucal expresses a set of a few; more than two and usually less than seven, but the exact number varies quite widely according to context. Prototypically, however, it refers to a class of three to five individuals, and is always restricted to humans' (Foley 1991: 216). The restriction to humans is specific to Yimas, of course. The related language Murik formerly had this four-way number system for pronouns, nouns and agreeing adjectives (Foley 1986: 221–2). Another language with the system is Meryam Mir (Trans-Fly family) spoken in the eastern Torres Strait islands, but being squeezed out by Torres Strait Creole (Piper 1989). It too distinguishes singular, dual, paucal and plural (through complex morphology).

Dual and paucal are found in Fijian; for Boumaa Fijian, a dialect mutually intelligible with Standard Fijian, Dixon states that there is no fixed paucal–plural boundary, except that plural must be more than paucal. He points out a good example of its use in one of his texts:

> It is an announcement about village work, which every adult person must do each Tuesday. The message is called out, by Suliano, three times, each in a different part of the village; it should reach the ears of one-third of the villagers each time. Suliano uses the paucal second person pronoun in addressing his listeners – you (*dou*, 2pa) listen, our (*odatou*, 1incpa) people in this part of the village. Then he says: I'm calling out the tasks of you (*omunuu*, 2pl), the women, for today because this is our (*oda*, 1incpl) day for village work. (Dixon 1988: 52; 'inc' = inclusive, 'pa' = paucal, 'pl' = plural)

Here the paucal is used for about twenty people, one-third of the adult villagers, and the plural for them all (about sixty). Schütz (1985: 251) also discusses the

---

the numerals '2', '3' and '4' in Russian, when they are in a direct case form, a special form of the noun is required, almost always the same as the genitive singular, but unique at least in terms of stress for a few nouns, for example *dva časá* 'two hours, two o'clock' (the genitive singular is *čása*). However, this special form depends entirely on the presence of the numeral, it is not part of the number system. This is shown by that fact that it is not possible to say *časá* meaning 'a small number (2–4) hours'. Hence the use of 'paucal' is inappropriate here. The use of the genitive singular is taken up in §6.7.1.

paucal in Fijian, and says that it can be used for three and for twelve. Some consultants put the limit at fifteen, others put it higher. He points out that contrast is more important than the specific number, and mentions a text in which approximately thirty people are referred to sometimes with the paucal and sometimes with the plural. Andrew Pawley (personal communication) also says that its range varies considerably according to the situation.[19]

This system (with dual and paucal) is found widely in other Oceanic languages besides Fijian, for instance in Paamese, spoken in Vanuatu. The factors governing the choice of paucal and plural have been well described:

> The basic factor that is involved is the absolute size of the group being referred to. Intersecting with this parameter however is the question of relative size, i.e. whether the group being referred to is contrasted with some larger group within which it is subsumed. When the absolute number is low (say between three and about half a dozen), the paucal is generally used, whether or not there is any contrast with a larger group. (However, the plural will still very occasionally be used even with these low numbers when there is no such contrast.)
>
> When the absolute number is in the middle range (say, between about half a dozen and a dozen or so), the most significant parameter is that of relative number. For instance, one's own patrilineage will be referred to paucally when it is contrasted with the village as a whole, which will be plural. On the other hand, the patrilineage will be expressed in the plural when contrasted with the nuclear family, which will be in the paucal.
>
> As the absolute number increases over the middle range, relative number again becomes less significant, and the plural is generally used for all numbers over a dozen. (However, even with very large numbers, the paucal is occasionally used when the contrast in number is expressed. So, while the entire population of Paama will normally be expressed in the plural, even when contrasted with the country as a whole, it has been heard referred to paucally.) (Crowley 1982: 81)

Staying within Oceanic, the singular–dual–paucal–plural system also occurs in Manam, spoken on islands off the north coast of Papua New Guinea (Lichtenberk 1983: 108–9), and in Ambrym, which has around 400 speakers on the island of

---

[19] For the system in Wayan (a local language within the Fijian subgroup with 2000 speakers on two islands at the western margin of Fiji) see Pawley and Sayaba (1990: 152, 156).

Ambrym in the New Hebrides (Paton 1971: 12–13). This paucal is clearly a trial in origin, but is now used for small groups of persons. There are numerous instances of former trials becoming paucals, for instance in Kwaio, Sa'a, Langalanga and Lau, all Malaitan languages spoken in the Solomon Islands (Simons 1986: 33).[20]

It is found in Australian languages too, in Ungarinjin (Rumsey 1982) and in Murrinh-Patha, a Daly family language of north-west Australia. As I. Green (1993, chapter 6) points out, there have been two slightly different assessments of its paucal (which is found in the verb paradigm and in the free pronouns). Walsh (1976: 150) says the paucal is for 'no less than three individuals and up to about ten individuals', while Street (1987: 49) gives its range as three to approximately fifteen. This suggests again that its use varies from context to context.

Table 2.2 *Independent pronouns in Lihir*

	singular	dual	trial	paucal	plural
1 exclusive	yo	gel	getol	gehet	ge
1 inclusive	—	kito	kitol	kitahet	giet
2	wa	gol	gotol	gohet	go
3	e	dul	dietol	diehet	die

The paucal has been found in a more complex system too, with four other values, possibly in this configuration:

> singular   dual   trial   paucal   plural

This system in question is found in Lihir, an Oceanic language spoken on a group of tiny islands off New Ireland (PNG). It is a member of the New Ireland Network, but does not belong to the same branch as Sursurunga and Tangga to be discussed below (Ross 1988: 258). The data are from Malcolm Ross (unpublished fieldnotes), from the dialect spoken on Lihir Island itself. As table 2.2 shows, five numbers are distinguished in each person, the only gap being the logically necessary one in that the first person singular cannot be inclusive. The same distinctions are found in the set of possessor suffixes (used on inalienables). The problem here is not the paucal, whose status is sure, but the 'trial', whose usage is not known. (If it is a paucal, giving the language a paucal and a greater paucal, then it would have a system like Sursurunga, discussed in §2.2.5 below.) Whether we have a trial or two paucals, Lihir is of considerable interest as a language with the maximum number of number values.

---

[20] The dual is less prone to this development. However, Blanc (1970: 45) notes that the former dual can be used for a small number in Arabic dialects, which suggests that a development of dual to paucal is possible.

Table 2.3 *Lihir number markers (Malcolm Ross, personal communication)*

Lihir number markers		Proto-Oceanic numerals		Lihir numerals	
-l	dual	*rua	two	lo	two
-tol	trial	*tolu	three	laktul	three
-het	paucal	*pati	four	burut	four

The origin of the forms can be traced back around 3,500 years to the Proto-Oceanic numerals, as given in table 2.3. Note that it is not only the paucal whose origin is obscured; comparison with the modern numerals shows that the origin of the dual and trial is no longer clear either. Such examples refute any suggestion that larger number systems might be no more than the use of numerals: in Lihir the number markers and numerals are evidently distinct.

We have seen that the paucal may be found in different systems, and the lower bound on the number of entities referred to varies accordingly.

2.2.5 The question of quadrals

We now consider whether there are languages with the following system:

> singular dual trial quadral plural

Such languages would have a quadral, a set of forms specifically for the quantity four. If such languages exist, they are rare and all the claims come from within the Austronesian family. A well-documented suggested case is Sursurunga (Hutchisson 1986, and personal communications), which has some 4,000 speakers in southern New Ireland. It is one of the South New Ireland/West Solomonic languages, which form part of the New Ireland Network, that being a branch of Melanesian, within Oceanic, in turn part of Austronesian (Ross 1988: 258). The forms labelled quadral are restricted to the personal pronouns, but are found with all of them, the first person (inclusive and exclusive), the second and the third.

We retain the term 'quadral' in table 2.4 and in this section, while we give the reasons why it should be replaced for Sursurunga (as indeed should 'trial'); in later references to Sursurunga we replace it. Here is an example of a quadral form in use:

(23) gimhat   káwán
     1.EXCL.QUADRAL   maternal.uncle:nephew/niece
     'we four who are in an uncle-nephew/niece relationship'

Besides being used of four, the quadral has two other uses. First, plural pronouns are never used with terms for dyads (kinship pairs like uncle–nephew/niece in (23))

Table 2.4 *Emphatic pronouns in Sursurunga*

	singular	dual	trial	quadral	plural
1 exclusive	iau	giur	gimtul	gimhat	gim
1 inclusive	—	gitar	gittul	githat	git
2	iáu[21]	gaur	gamtul	gamhat	gam
3	-i/on/ái	diar	ditul	dihat	di

and the quadral is then used instead for a minimum of four, and not just for exactly four (Hutchisson 1986: 10). The second additional use is in hortatory discourse; the speaker may use the first person inclusive quadral, suggesting joint action including the speaker, even though more than four persons are involved. These two special uses account for most instances of the quadral. If our terminology is based on meaning, the term 'quadral' is hardly appropriate, when in the majority of its uses the forms are not restricted to denoting foursomes. The forms might be better designated 'paucal'.

Let us consider the rest of the system in more detail (examples and judgements from Don Hutchisson, personal communications). The dual is used quite strictly for two people (if there are two it must be used, and if it is used it indicates two). It is also used for the singular when the referent is in a taboo relationship to the speaker. This is a special use (of the type to be discussed in §7.1) which does not alter the fact that its main use is as a regular dual. The trial will be used for three. But, it is also used for small groups, typically around three or four, and for nuclear families of any size. It is therefore not strictly a trial, rather it could be labelled a paucal (an appropriate gloss would be 'a few'). We saw earlier that the trial frequently develops in this way. The quadral, as we have noted, is primarily used in hortatory discourse and with dyad terms; but otherwise it is used with larger groups, of four or more (an appropriate gloss would be 'several'). This too would qualify as a paucal; we therefore have two paucals, a (normal/lesser) paucal (traditionally trial) and a greater paucal (traditionally quadral).

The next example is particularly helpful for distinguishing the use of the two forms. It is from a letter to Don Hutchisson written in 1976:

(24) Iau   lala   hol   pas   gamhat   kabin   ngo
     1.SG   greatly think about   2.QUADRAL   because that

---

[21] *á* is used to indicate schwa (ə); this is the preferred form according to Hutchisson (personal communication), rather than '*a*, as in Hutchisson (1986: 20fn7). Other changes from the 1986 paper, like *-hat* for *-at* in the quadral, are based on personal communications.

iau	lu	mákái	málálár	gamtul	mínái	i
1.SG	HABITUAL	see	photo	2.TRIAL	here	in

rum
house

'I am thinking about you [QUADRAL] all the time because I often see the picture of you [TRIAL] here in my house'

The family consists of four members; the quadral is used first (perhaps to stress that all four are included), but then the writer moves to the trial, more normal usage for a small group. The entire family is intended in each case.

The next example is from a village meeting:

(25)
Gamhat	til	main	gam	han	suri	tártár
2.QUADRAL	from	here	2.PL	go	PURPOSE	chop

on	á	kakau	káián	Himaul	viles,	honin
it	TOPIC	cacao	its	Himaul	village	today

dihat	má	lu	tangkabin	sirai
3.QUADRAL	EMPHATIC	HABITUAL	begin	selling

má . . .
now

'You all from here (i.e. from this village) went to slash (for burning, then planting) Himaul village's cacao, which already they (i.e. people from Himaul) have begun to sell . . .'

This is hortatory discourse, so the initial quadral form is quite expected. But then the plural occurs for the subject/agent, soon after the quadral which was used to define the group the writer is referring to. The people from Himaul are also referred to with a quadral.

As an example of a plural, here is the beginning of a description of how to build a cook house.

(26)
Ngo	gim	nem	i	longoi	pal,
when	1.PL.EXCL	want	OBJ	make	cook.house

gim	han	urami	bos	gim	ái
1.PL.EXCL	go	up.to	jungle	1.PL.EXCL	TOPIC

tan káláu	mái	tan wák.
males	and.TOPIC[22]	females

---

[22] *mái* is a contraction of *má* 'and' and *ái* topic marker.

'When we (i.e. Sursurungas) want to build a cook house, we go up to the bush, that is we men and women.'

Here Hutchisson believed a quadral would not be used, since the group (Sursurungas in general) is too large. Similarly in the following example:

(27) Má   máhán a   kis   main si   git   arwat
      and war   3.SG exist here to   1.PL.INCL   enough

      mai   a   hit   á   bet.
      with   3.SG seven RELATER   year

'And the war was here among us (i.e. in this area) for seven years.'
(From a story about World War II.)

Use of the quadral in this example would limit the area being referred to, say to a single village or a small group of villages, or it would limit the group, say to those alive during the war and affected by it directly. Hence the plural, as we would expect, is for numbers of entities larger than are covered by the quadral; however, there is no strict dividing line (certainly not at the number five).

If we use semantic labels, as we have done in the rest of the chapter, we should not call the forms trials and quadrals. Both have functions we have seen with paucals elsewhere. We may therefore represent the system in Sursurunga like this:

singular   dual   paucal   greater paucal   plural

The system is no less interesting since it has a well documented five-valued number category.

Another language with five values is Sursurunga's close relative Tangga (Capell 1971: 260–2; Beaumont 1976: 390; confirmed by Malcolm Ross, personal communication; note that Capell and Beaumont used the term 'quadruple'). Here we know that there are five forms, but we do not have such detailed information as we have for Sursurunga. Yet it seems clear that the forms which have the numeral 'four' as their source are not quadrals but rather paucals (Malcolm Ross, personal communication citing Maurer 1966; this is also Schmidt's view given in Capell 1971: 261). Unfortunately, as with Lihir, we have no information on whether Tangga has a genuine trial or whether it has two paucals.

The third language which has been claimed to have a quadral is more distantly related; it is Marshallese, a member of the Micronesian group within Austronesian, with some 20,000 speakers on the Marshall Islands. It has five number forms for the first, second and third person pronouns (Bender 1969: 8–9). We shall return to it when we discuss facultative numbers in §2.3.3. As in Sursurunga, the form which has been called the quadral has an additional use: with groups of more than four it is often used rhetorically to give an illusion of intimacy (Bender 1969: 159). Again, then, it appears that this may not be strictly a quadral; we shall therefore treat it as a paucal. Byron Bender (personal communication) has no evidence for any comparable extension to the trial, so we shall treat Marshallese as having singular, dual, trial, paucal and plural.

These are the three best claims for quadrals. There are several false trails in the literature, that is, suggestions of other Austronesian languages with quadrals, which turn out in fact to have four number values not five. In such cases, the plural may have a form in which the numeral four can be reconstructed. We return to the development of such forms with plural meaning in §9.1.2; their existence as plurals suggests that there might have been instances of the quadral number since lost. Or it may be that once the numeral four becomes grammaticalized as a number value, it is inevitably used for groups larger than four. We have found no clear case of a quadral, by which we mean a grammatical form for referring to four distinct real world entities in the way that trials refer to three.

2.2.6 Greater numbers

Languages may have a secondary split into normal and 'greater' (sometimes termed 'lesser' and 'greater') within certain number values. The two which may be split are the paucal and the plural. There are relatively few known cases of split numbers and the account here is tentative.

Consider first the paucal. It is rare to find a split in the paucal, but that is exactly what we found in Sursurunga (§2.2.5). Either set of forms (those labelled 'trial' and those labelled 'quadral') would independently be reckoned a paucal on semantic grounds. We therefore treat them as a paucal and a greater paucal.

Splits within the plural are more common. Claiming such a split, into greater and normal plural, implies that both would independently count as plural. Since even the lesser is a plural (used where languages with just one plural would use it), we shall call it simply 'plural'.[23] The 'greater plural' typically implies an excessive number, sometimes called 'plural of abundance', or else all possible instances of the referent, sometimes called the 'global plural'. We shall use 'greater plural' to cover the different types (abundance, global). The evidence is limited, but it comes from a variety of languages and sources, sufficient to indicate that there is an interesting phenomenon that deserves study. More examples with careful descriptions of their meanings would be welcome. Again the definition is a semantic one. There are many instances of nouns taking more than one plural marker (these are 'double plurals', for which see §5.3.6). We are concerned here only with instances

---

[23] It may be objected that 'plural' is different if in opposition to a 'greater plural' as compared to when it is the only plural. But this is also true, as noted earlier, of 'plural' in a system with a dual and 'plural' in a system without. An advantage of avoiding 'lesser plural' is that this term is sometimes used for 'paucal'.

where the different plural forms have different meanings. (For instances where the ordinary plural is used with this effect see §7.3.2.)

Banyun

A potentially interesting case of a language with a greater plural is Banyun, a language of the West Atlantic branch of Niger-Kordofanian, spoken in Senegal and Guinea Bissau. There is a little information in Sauvageot (1967: 227–8). Nouns typically have singular and plural, distinguished by prefixes of the type shared by many Niger-Kordofanian languages:

(28)   bu-sumɔl   i-sumɔl[24]
       SG-snake   PL-snake
       'snake'   'snakes'

In addition there is a greater plural (which Sauvageot calls 'unlimited'), in this case *ba-sumɔl* 'snakes', which Sauvageot suggests is used when the number cannot be counted or the speaker feels it unnecessary. There are various prefixes available to signal the greater plural; they are not equivalent in that one of them, *ti-* as in *ti-sumɔl* 'snakes (unlimited)' implies more than *ba-* as in *ba-sumɔl*. Noun phrase modifiers such as adjectives agree, distinguishing the various singular, plural and greater plural classes.[25] (A similar distinction is reported in Senufo, see discussion of Sauvageot's paper, 1967: 236.)

Fula

Related to Banyun, since both are members of the West Atlantic branch of Niger-Kordofanian, is Fula, which is widely spoken across west and central Africa (the Fouta Jalon dialect was discussed in §2.1 above). Here some nouns have two plurals 'one to imply a normal number of items and the other to imply a very large number of items' (Evans 1994: 21.6), for example, as shown in table 2.5. In the

Table 2.5 *Plural forms in Fula*

singular	plural	greater plural	gloss
ngesa	gese	geseeli	field
wuro	gure	gureeli	herd

[24] Sauvageot calls this the 'limited plural'; this term is confusing because it too has been used as a synonym for 'paucal' (for instance, by Capell 1976: 15; see also the quotation from Laidig and Laidig 1990: 92 in §2.2.3). We shall therefore avoid the term 'limited plural'.

[25] The existence of different agreement markers distinguishes Banyun from several languages with a greater plural.

second example, *gure* 'herds (plural)' might be the herds of one man, his flock of sheep, his goats and his cows. This is a case, however, where there is insufficient evidence to know whether we really have two plurals or a paucal and a plural.

Arabic

In Arabic too, there are nouns with two plural forms, and in describing Syrian Arabic Cowell (1964: 369) gives helpful pointers to their status. Recall first from §2.1 that some types of Arabic noun have a general ('collective') form, for instance *dəbbān* for which, given real world considerations, the natural gloss is 'flies'. If it matters to specify one fly, then there is the singular *dəbbāne*; there is a corresponding dual *dəbbāntēn* and a plural *dəbbānāt*. It would appear that anything one might want to say about flies is provided for. But this is one of the instances where there is a fifth form *dababīn* 'many flies'. Cowell treats this as the plural of the collective. Such plurals may function, in his terms, as 'plurals of abundance' (for a formal approach to the semantics see Ojeda 1992a).

This is an instance of a recurring phenomenon, namely the formation of a plural whose predictable function is not required, and which takes on a different one. In Arabic, there is no obvious function for the plural of a collective when there is an ordinary plural available; where the 'extra' form exists, it may take other functions: one is the 'sort' reading as in English (§3.7.2), and another is the 'abundance' reading, so *dababīn* can mean 'various flies' or 'many flies'. When there is a plural of abundance (only certain of the nouns with collective forms have them) this may affect the meaning of the normal plural (sometimes then called the 'plural of paucity' so that the use of the latter implies that the entities referred to are few and are individually discriminated. However, this is not always the case.

Thus some Arabic nouns have two plurals; the relations between them vary. The existence of the greater plural may as it were 'push down' the ordinary plural into the position of a paucal (for the situation in Classical Arabic see Wright 1967: 234; the analysis is not uncontroversial, for discussion see Ratcliffe 1998: 79–81).

Hamer

In Hamer (or Hamar), it has been claimed by Lydall (1976, 1988) that a distinction can be drawn between a plural for a particular number ('particular plural', our 'plural') and plural for all instances ('global plural', a type of 'greater plural'). Hamer is a South Omotic language, which has about 15,000 speakers in the south-west corner of Ethiopia. Nouns have a general form, which, as in languages already discussed, stands outside the number system. Thus *k'úli* means 'goat' or 'goats'. This should be contrasted with the singular forms (Lydall 1988: 81–2), for which see table 2.6. The singular formed with the suffix *-tal-a* is for the male (of animates) and for the 'minor' singular of inanimates, used for something which is

Table 2.6 *Number forms in Hamer*

general form	singular	plural (particular plural)	greater plural (global plural)
k'úli 'goat(s)'	k'últa 'he-goat' k'úllo 'she-goat'	k'úlla 'the goats'	k'últono 'all goats'
goiti/goin 'path(s)'	goita 'path (little used)' goinno 'main path'	goinna 'the paths'	goitino 'all paths'

'small, minor, individual, infrequently used, or seldom found' (Lydall 1988: 79). The *-no* suffix, on the other hand, is used with certain nouns for a female (animate nouns) or, with inanimate nouns, for the 'major' singular, used for large and major things.[26]

The contrast between the number forms in the table, according to Lydall, is between a particular number of items, and all items.[27] Unfortunately Lydall gives little more information on the choice. In particular, it would be good to know how different this system is from those where there is an interaction of number with definiteness (for which see §9.2.4).

Kaytetye

Kaytetye is an Arandic language (part of Pama-Nyungan) spoken in Central Australia. Information is from Harold Koch (personal communication; see Koch 1990 for some of the morphology, and for textual examples see Koch and Koch 1993). The pronouns distinguish singular, dual and plural. Nouns need not mark number: marking is most likely for nouns denoting humans and least likely for those denoting inanimates. In addition to having the three-way distinction of the pronouns, nouns split the plural into a normal plural marked with the suffix *-amerne*, and a greater (global) plural ('all the X in the universe of discourse'), marked with the suffix *-eynenge*. Both plurals can serve as antecedents for the single set of plural pronouns. Kaytetye then is a clear instance of a language with a greater plural alongside the normal plural. (Kaytetye is also interesting in respect of facultative number, a topic we discuss in §2.3.3 below.)

---

[26] In the case of inanimate nouns, for single syllable nouns, and two-syllable nouns which end in a consonant, major singular and global plural will be identical in form (Lydall 1988: 80): *nu* 'fire' gives *nuno* 'large/main fire' (major singular) or 'fire considered as a whole' (global plural). In addition there is *nuta* 'small fire' and *nuna* 'the (particular) fires' (particular plural).

[27] As a curiosity, Larry Trask points out (personal communication) that there is a celebrated fictional example. J. R. R. Tolkien, in *The Lord of the Rings* invented a number of languages, including the elvish language Quenya. This language distinguishes a global plural from the ordinary plural: *el* 'star', *elen* 'stars', *elenath* '(all) the stars'.

Mokilese

Mokilese is a Micronesian language with around 400 speakers on Mokil Atoll (East Caroline Islands) and up to 1 000 speakers on Ponape. It has a greater plural in the personal pronouns (called the 'remote plural' by Harrison 1976: 88–9) as illustrated in table 2.7. *Ngoahi*, and *koawoa* are emphatic forms. Note that the plural is formed by the addition of *-i* to the dual; in fact the plural represents a former trial, and the old plural survives as the greater ('remote') plural (Sheldon Harrison, personal communication); these survivals are the key to understanding the otherwise surprising plurals of several related languages (see §9.1.2). The possessive suffixes, which attach to nouns, also have remote plural forms (for remote plural possessors). Determiners do not have distinct remote plural forms (they have only a singular–plural opposition); and nouns mark number only through demonstrative suffixes.

Table 2.7 *Mokilese personal pronouns (Harrison 1976: 88)*

	singular	dual	plural	greater plural (remote plural)
1st person exclusive	ngoah, ngoahi	kama	kamai	kimi
inclusive	—	kisa	kisai	kihs
2nd person	koah, koawoa	kamwa	kamwai	kimwi
3rd person	ih	ara, ira	arai, irai	ihr

The column headed 'plural' gives the normal plural forms. The remote plural forms are little used:

> The remote pronouns refer to groups of people, usually large, and most of which are probably not directly present when being discussed. Thus, *kihs* 'we' refers to the speaker, the hearer, and a large group of people not present at the time of the conversation. Similarly, *kimi* 'we' refers to the speaker and to a group of others not present; *kimwi* 'you', to the hearer and others not present, and *ihr* 'they' to a group of people not present.
>   Since *kihs*, for example, commonly refers to very large groups of people, it is often used to refer to all the people of Mokil, or to the whole human race. (Harrison 1976: 89–90)[28]

The plural would be for smaller but more significant groups, the remote for larger, amorphous groups, who are not main protagonists in what is being related. Remote pronouns may also be used in generic sentences.

---

[28] This account shows that the forms we have labelled 'greater plural', Harrison's 'remote plural', can be used both in the 'abundance' sense and in the 'global' sense.

Mele-Fila

A particularly interesting five-member system including a greater plural is found in Mele-Fila, an Eastern Oceanic language spoken on Vanuatu. The data are from Ross Clark (personal communications). In Mele-Fila, the article makes a three-way distinction which, were it the only number system, we would treat as singular–paucal–plural. The forms are in table 2.8, with the noun *nuaane* 'old man'. The underlying form of the plural article is /a/, but before nouns of more than two morae, the form is zero.

Table 2.8 *Number contrasts in Mele-Fila (data from Ross Clark)*

article distinctions	singular	paucal		plural	
article plus noun ('old man')	t-nuaane	ru nuaane		nuaane	
pronoun distinctions	singular	dual	plural		greater plural
pronoun	aia	raaua	raateu		reafa
'constructed' number	singular	dual	paucal	plural	greater plural

The pronoun makes four distinctions rather than three, and the relation to the article is not straightforward. Let us consider the pronoun on its own first. It has singular and dual forms, and then the remaining space is divided between a plural and a greater (global) plural. For the singular, the match between article and pronoun is clear. However, the dual pronoun is appropriate only for some cases where the paucal article would be used. On the other hand, the pronoun *raateu* covers the remaining area of the paucal article, but splits the range of the plural article, the part left over being covered by *reafa*. If we put the two systems together we have five number distinctions, as in the last line of the table. Systems where different syntactic elements combine to give the full range of distinctions will be termed 'constructed number' systems; these will be discussed in more detail in §5.7.

Other languages claimed to have a greater plural include Zulu (Doke 1992: 79–80), Setswana (for nouns denoting animals, Cole 1955: 82), Miya (Schuh 1989: 175n3) and Breton (Trépos 1957: 266–7). It is noticeable that splits in the plural are more frequent for nouns than pronouns, and it may well be that it is usually only for limited groups of nouns, the extreme case here being Tigre, which has just one noun with a greater plural (*nälät* 'kind of deer', Palmer 1962: 39). However, we have also seen a split within the pronoun system, as in Mokilese.

35

2.2.7 Composed numbers

These are a rare phenomenon. Occasionally we find one number built as it were on another. Recall that we are making semantic distinctions here; using the form of one number as the base for building another is not unusual; it is also common to add number morphology 'to itself' as it were, typically adding plural morphology to an existing plural (giving a 'double plural', §5.3.6). But to base one number semantically on another is rare. Here is an instance from the Celtic language Breton, rightly reputed to have one of the most complex number systems (data from Ternes 1992: 417; compare Trépos 1957: 226–8, 265–6; Hemon 1975: 42; Ternes 1970: 191–2, 200–1; Denez and Urien 1980):

(29) lagad   daou-lagad   daou-lagad-où
      eye.SG   DUAL-eye   DUAL-eye-PL
      'eye'   '(two) eyes'   'pairs of eyes'

First note that the dual is largely lost in Celtic,[29] but Breton has a new, quite recent dual. It is clearly from the numeral *daou* 'two', but it is a genuine dual; it is obligatory with those nouns which have it (nouns denoting parts of the body and items of clothing that occur in pairs), and when emphasis on two referents is required the numeral is used together with the dual (Ternes 1992: 416–17). To this dual, plural morphology can then be added, and the meaning is then a plurality of duals. The ordinary plural of *lagad* is *lagad-où* 'eyes'; note, however, that this is a restricted phenomenon; the same possibilities are not generally available to Breton nouns.

Breton can also 'compose' plural on plural (Ternes 1992: 415):

(30) bugel   bugal-e   bugal-e-où
      child-SG   child-PL   child-PL-PL
      'child'   'children'   'groups of children'

In this example the first plural formation is highly irregular, and the second is a common one. The possibility of composing plural on plural is not freely available.[30]

---

[29] Though see §6.7.1. Breton also has nouns which take what looks like plural morphology but which are interpreted as duals, such as *maneg* 'glove', *manegoù* '(pair of) gloves' (Greg Stump, personal communication). For the plural, a second plural marker is added (an *-où* with the second marker *-ier* gives *-eier*), hence *manigeier* 'gloves'. This is not a composed form however: it does not mean 'several pairs of gloves', but merely 'gloves'. It can be used, for instance, for three gloves.

[30] A similar effect is found in Finnish, but in numeral phrases (data from Hurford forthcoming):

(i) kolme-t   suka-t
     three-PL   sock-PL
     'three pairs of socks'

Moreover the meaning of the form with two plural markers varies from noun to noun, and according to dialect (Stump 1989: 270–1).[31]

A very interesting and tricky example is Warekena (of Xie), an Arawakan language with some twenty older speakers in Brazil and around 200 in Venezuela. The data are from Alexandra Aikhenvald (1998: 300–4 and personal communications). Number is not required on nouns, but various plural markers are available (so this is a general/singular versus plural system). And once a referent is established as plural, plural marking is not repeated.

Let us look at the plural markers. First there are *-pe* and *-ne*, with *-ne* being used for nouns denoting animate non-humans and a few others, and *-pe* for the rest (human and non-human): *neɹima-pe* 'cousins' (ɹ is a lateral flap), *ʧinu-ne* 'dogs', *muɹupa-pe* 'canoes'. Then there is an 'emphatic plural' for 'very many' namely *-nawi*, as in *atapi-nawi* 'a great many trees'. It does not differentiate according to animacy and is used for larger numbers of entities than is *-pe*. And then, for particular emphasis on plurality, two plural markers can be used together: *-pe-nawi*. This gives:

(31)   abida-pe   abida-nawi   abida-pe-nawi
       pig-PL   pig-GREATER.PL   pig-PL-GREATER.PL
       'pigs'   'very many pigs'   'very many pigs indeed, too
                                              many to count'

Note that *-pe* rather than the expected *-ne* is used for this noun. We might think that *-pe* is really a paucal, but according to Alexandra Aikhenvald (personal

---

Normally the numeral stands in its singular form (the singular of *kolmet* 'three' would be *kolme*) and takes a noun in the singular. In the construction in (i), with the numeral and noun in the plural, the meaning is 'three groups of socks', and the natural group here is a pair.

[31] Comparable examples were recorded in Khamtanga (Chamir), a dialect cluster belonging to the Agaw group within Cushitic, by Reinisch (reported in Appleyard 1987: 252):

(i)   ieferā̀   iefīr   iefīrt
      child.SG   child.PL   child.PL.PL
      'child'   'children'   'crowds of children'

(ii)   lálā   lal   lálāle
      bee.SG   bee.PL   bee.PL.PL
      'bee'   'bees'   'swarms of bees'

Appleyard was working a century after Reinisch, and though he found similar forms, they were preserved as alternative plurals – his informants did not differentiate them semantically. It may be that dialect differences explain this; but it may also be that the distinction was lost in the intervening period. The point is that a plural of a plural is itself a plural; it would not be surprising if such a distinction, probably available for only a limited part of the noun lexicon, should be lost. Composed numbers are also reported in Arabic (Wright 1967: 190–1, 231–2, discussed in Ojeda 1992a).

communication) it can refer to quite large groups. If we treat *-pe* as a plural, then that makes *-nawi* a greater plural. What then of forms with both *-pe* and *-nawi*? The analysis is not as easy as with Breton, where the existence of the dual makes the distinction between a composed number (a plurality of pairs) and a vague greater plural clear. We should therefore be cautious about claiming that Warekena has a composed number (for a plurality of plurals), but it is a possible position. The alternative would be to claim that it, remarkably, has two greater plurals. In any case, the evidence that is beginning to emerge about Amazonian languages such as Warekena will be of special importance for understanding number systems.

2.3 Number systems (the Number Hierarchy and associated problems)

Having seen the ranges of number values, we would like to be able to predict the possible number systems which natural languages can have.[32] The main claim in the literature is the Number Hierarchy, which is often taken as unproblematic, yet which cannot account for some of the systems we have discussed. We shall first see why this is so (§2.3.1), then consider an alternative proposal (§2.3.2), and finally see how this alternative is also able to account for facultative numbers (§2.3.3).

2.3.1 The Number Hierarchy

A Number Hierarchy has been proposed, along the following lines:

> singular > plural > dual > trial

Most of this can be derived from Greenberg's universal 34 (1963: 94):

> No language has a trial number unless it has a dual. No language has
> a dual unless it has a plural.

In addition to the positions derivable from Greenberg, the hierarchy is usually quoted with the singular in the first position. The logic of doing so is that just as the dual is more marked than the plural, so the plural is more marked than the singular. It might be argued that, in a sense, languages like Japanese (§2.1 above) have a plural without having a singular, and so the singular should not be included in the hierarchy. The view taken here is that such languages give the possibility of not specifying number (and using the form with no marker, the general form), but if number is specified, then there is a singular–plural opposition. The Number Hierarchy, then, is concerned only with the cases where number is specified.

---

[32] When checking grammars for counter-examples and confirming examples for such claims, it is important that the grammatical system as a whole should be considered; occasionally single lines are quoted from grammars, apparently suggesting quite exotic number systems, which prove to be rather more ordinary when the grammar and the examples are studied carefully.

A few points need to be clarified about the presentation of such hierarchies. The ordering of positions is crucial; the claim is that, for instance, the presence of a trial implies the presence of a dual. This differs from the way we presented the different systems above, where we ordered the number values simply from smaller to larger (for instance, singular, dual, plural). Though the ordering matters, the use of '>' or '<' is not important. We shall use '>' since there are more plurals than duals. This is true in three senses: in the sense of Greenberg's claim, that more languages have plurals than have duals; also in the sense that for languages which have both, speakers use the plural more frequently than the dual, and they also use the singular more frequently than the plural (see §9.3.2 for statistics); and third, for languages which have both values, there will be as many or more nouns with the plural as compared to the dual (§4.1). Those who prefer the use of '<' reflect the idea that the value to the right is the more marked.

There are two problems with the Number Hierarchy, which we will address in turn; the first is the problem of the systems with paucal number and the second is that it makes the wrong predictions when facultative number is involved.

2.3.2 Possible systems of number values: incorporating the paucal
The first problem with the Number Hierarchy is that it does not account for systems which include a paucal. Foley (1986: 133) and Croft (1990: 96–7) suggest this modified hierarchy (changed to our notation):

> singular > plural > dual > paucal/trial

This would account for systems like the following:

singular	plural	(Russian)		
singular	dual	plural	(Upper Sorbian)	
singular	dual	trial	plural	(Larike)
singular	dual	paucal	plural	(Yimas)

However, it does not allow for systems which include the paucal in a different combination:

> singular   paucal   plural   (Bayso)

Lihir would also be a problem. We must allow for the paucal to be an option at more than one point, which makes it clear that no straightforward hierarchy will be adequate.

To make progress here we need to draw a distinction between 'determinate' and 'indeterminate' number values. These terms are to differentiate situations where, given the knowledge of the real world which the speaker has, we can determine that only one form is appropriate (determinate number) from those where we cannot

39

(indeterminate). Thus in a language with an obligatory dual, this would be an instance of determinate number, since to refer to two distinct entities only the dual is appropriate. The determinate numbers are basically the numerical ones: plural, dual, trial. Use of determinate number values is agreed across speakers (different speakers agree that, say, the dual is appropriate for referring to two referents),[33] it remains constant for the same speaker across different occasions, and it does not vary according to the referent (thus elephant-DUAL refers to two elephants just as ant-DUAL refers to two ants). The indeterminate number values are the paucal (and greater paucal) and the greater plural. These may vary across speakers (there is no clear dividing line between paucal and plural, recall the discussion of Murrinh-Patha in §2.2.4), for one speaker across occasions, and can vary according to the referent (elephant-PAUCAL may typically refer to fewer real world entities than ant-PAUCAL). While the determinate numbers can be defined in terms of numerals, the indeterminates correspond to other quantifiers: 'a few', 'many', 'all'.

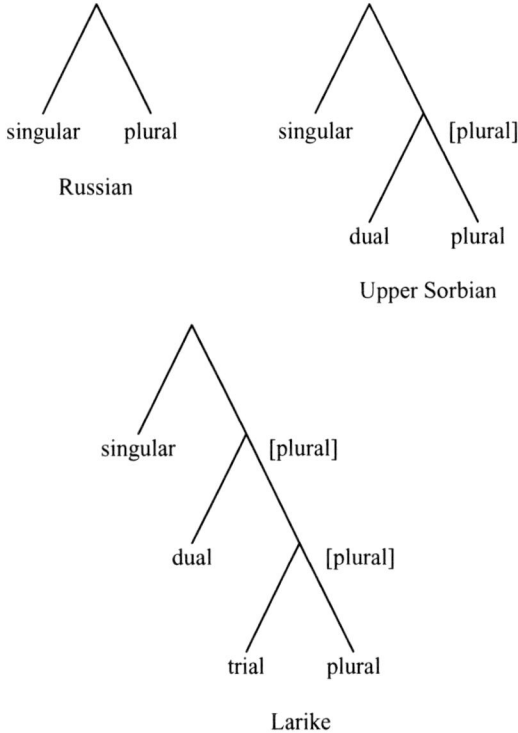

Figure 2.5 *Illustration of possible number systems*

---

[33] This statement must be qualified when facultative numbers are discussed.

How then are number systems constrained? First, a language may take any number of the determinate number values, in the order given (i.e. in accord with the old hierarchy, §2.3.1). However, this should be seen as adopting a series of binary choices, and choices in addition to the selection of the plural should be seen as removing a part from the range of the plural and hence dividing the plural. This gives the possibilities shown in figure 2.5. We have chosen to arrange the branches with the values for larger numbers of entities to the right. '[plural]' indicates what the value would be at that point if no further choices were made; this will be relevant when we consider facultative number. Recall that the meaning of 'plural' will vary according to the system of which it is a part.

In addition to the determinate number values, languages may further divide up the plural space by taking an indeterminate number value. Most commonly only one is selected. Some of the possibilities which result are given in figure 2.6.

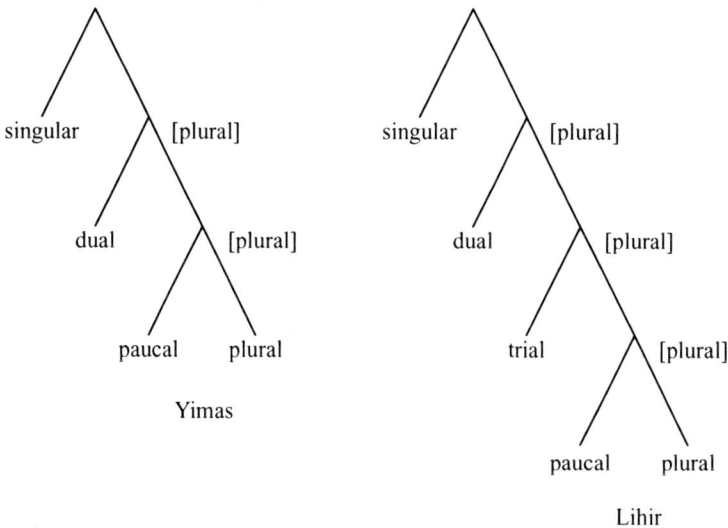

Yimas   Lihir

Figure 2.6 *Possible number systems including an indeterminate value*[34]

While it is more common for just one indeterminate value to be selected, two is possible, as figure 2.7 illustrates (page 42). Mele-Fila is perhaps the less surprising, in that it takes two indeterminate values of different types. Sursurunga has two paucals. It is tempting to try to add further constraints in order to bring the systems permitted into closer match with those so far recorded. This would be premature since we are still short of data on the larger systems; it is to be hoped that highlighting these examples will encourage others to report on large number systems with indeterminate values included.

[34] We develop the representation of the systems of Larike, Marshallese and Bayso in §2.3.3.

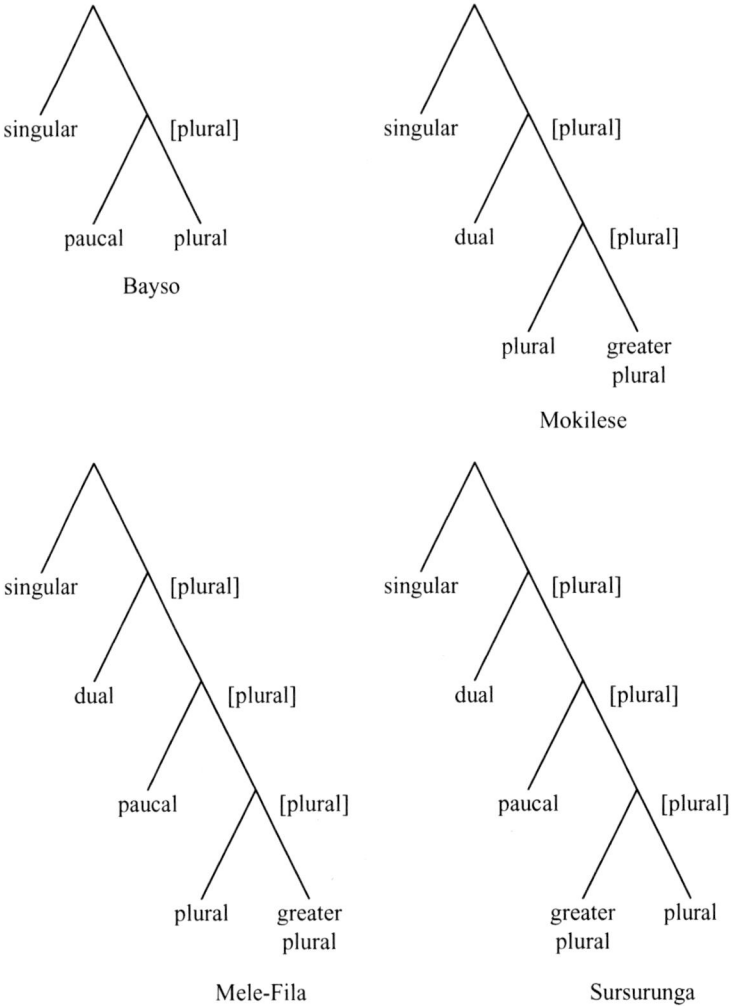

Figure 2.7 *Number systems with two indeterminate values*

We have now set out a typology of possible number systems. As we shall see shortly, this same typology imposes further constraints on the number system.

2.3.3 Facultative number

We have considered how number systems vary according to how many number values they have, that is, how many different numbers of real world entities may be referred to by different means. But they may also differ in a more subtle way, according to whether the use of particular values is obligatory or 'facultative' (Greenberg 1966: 28). In §2.1 we looked at languages where the expression of number as a whole is not required. Here, however, we are concerned with particular values which may be facultative, even though the category of number is being expressed. For instance, in Ngan'gityemerri (see §2.2.3) there is singular, dual, trial and plural. The dual must be used to refer to two entities, the plural must be used for four and more. For three entities, the trial is used when the fact of there being three is salient (for example, at the first mention in discourse) but otherwise the plural is used for three. Recall that the trial is strictly for three, and is not a paucal (Reid 1990: 118–19 and personal communication). The trial is similarly facultative in Marrithiyel (I. Green 1989: 136, 138) and in Anindilyakwa (Velma Leeding, personal communication). Thus number must be expressed (in the sense that there are no general forms for avoiding it) but where it is expressed the use of the trial is facultative.

Consider now the systems with singular–dual–plural. The use of the dual may be obligatory, as in Sanskrit: 'The dual number is in regular use and of strict application, the plural practically never referring to two objects' (MacDonell 1927: 180); 'In Sanskrit, if there are two of something, whatever it is, the structure gives you no option but to use the Dual' (Diver 1987: 103). Or it may be facultative, as in the South Slavonic language Slovene. Here we do not find the same degree of choice as with the Ngan'gityemerri trial, but the important point is that the dual is not obligatory in the way that the plural is in Slovene:

> Normally, dual forms are used in pronouns and in verbal forms whenever two actual referents are involved, be they explicitly mentioned or only implicit. However, in non-pronominal noun phrases with, for example, body parts that come in pairs like 'eyes' and 'feet', dual forms tend to be used only when the quantifiers 'two' or 'both' are explicitly stated in the context, and are replaced by the plural when this quantifier is unstated, even if a pair of referents are obviously implicit. (Priestly 1993: 440–1)

Priestly gives the following example:

(32) nóge   me   bolijo
      foot.PL   1.SG.ACC   hurt.PL
      'my feet hurt'

This is a fully appropriate utterance for a normal biped. It is assumed that two feet are referred to, and the dual is not required. We return to the difference between pronouns and nouns in §4.1. For present purposes, the important point is that nominals express number obligatorily in Slovene; however, for referring to two entities, the use of the dual is not obligatory (see §9.3.2 for statistics on its use). The dual was obligatory in Classical Arabic, but is facultative in modern Arabic dialects (see Blanc 1970: 42–3 and references there; and see Cowell 1964: 367 for Syrian Arabic), as it was too in Classical Greek (see Diver 1987 for interesting statistical data). Just as the plural is different in English (no dual) and Sanskrit (with dual), so it is different in Sanskrit (with an obligatory dual) and Slovene (with a facultative dual). A plural in Slovene may be used for reference to just two real world entities.

Let us now consider how this relates to the Number Hierarchy, repeated here for convenience:

$$\text{singular} > \text{plural} > \text{dual} > \text{paucal}$$

If we have a system in which use of the plural is not required, then the less marked number, the singular, is used (as discussed in §2.1 above). If we have a system in which the dual is facultative, then in its place the less marked number, the plural, is used. It appears that the hierarchy is making useful predictions, based on markedness. Unfortunately this is only apparent here. Consider again Ngan'gityemerri: it has a trial which is facultative and so we would predict that the less marked dual could be used in its place. But of course this is not the case, the plural is used. This is what is expected if, as discussed earlier, the system is viewed as a set of binary choices (see figure 2.8).

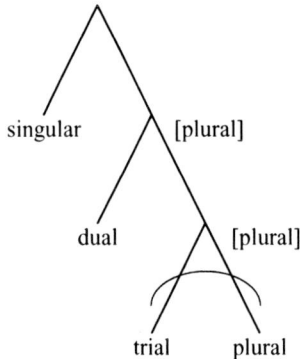

Figure 2.8 *The facultative trial of Ngan'gityemerri*

The point is that the last choice is facultative. If it is removed, as by the arc in figure 2.8, then Ngan'gityemerri has another possible system, singular–dual–plural, and the plural covers the area otherwise covered by trial and plural. In Slovene, the situation is as in figure 2.9.

If the dual–plural choice is not taken up, then the system reverts to a straightforward singular–plural system. It is tempting to suggest that facultative number can

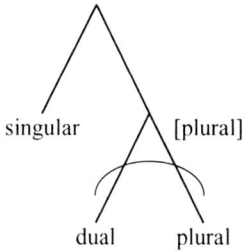

Figure 2.9 *The facultative dual of Slovene*

only affect the 'last choice' of number, as in the examples so far. However, there are three languages which show the situation is rather more interesting.

The first is Larike, which we considered earlier as an example of a language with a genuine trial. Unlike Ngan'gityemerri, it is not only the trial which is facultative, the dual is as well:

> The Larike plural forms may also be used when referring to quantities of two or three. Thus, in spite of the fact that duals and trials are used to specifically denote twos and threes, plural forms can still be used with the meaning of two or more. In these situations, the choice of whether to use plural versus dual or trial forms depends upon the speaker's desire to specify or focus upon the number of the referent nouns. Although the plural forms are probably most frequently used (even when referring to twos and threes), duals and trials are also quite common, and are often heard in routine conversations as well as in more formal language contexts. (Laidig and Laidig 1990: 93)

We represent this system in figure 2.10.

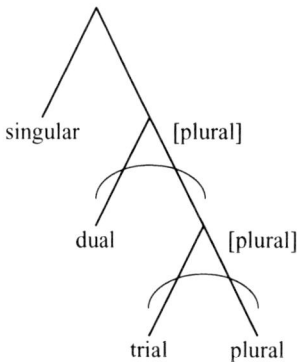

Figure 2.10 *The facultative numbers of Larike*

The second is Longgu, an Austronesian language (Cristobal-Malaitan sub-group) spoken on the north-eastern coast of Guadalcanal, Solomon Islands (data from Hill 1992). Longgu independent pronouns distinguish singular, dual, paucal and plural. The range of the paucal is not fully established, but Hill gives examples of its use referring to five people. There are also 'subject pronouns', which form the first element of a verb phrase and cross-reference the person and number of the subject noun phrase (Hill 1992: 92). These subject pronouns also distinguish four numbers. However, they do not necessarily match the number of the subject; they may match it or, in the third person, the plural may be used where the dual or paucal would be expected. This use of the plural occurs 'when the number of the subject has been established' (Hill 1992: 130) whether by a noun phrase or by a subject pronoun in a previous clause. For example:

(33) m-*arua*   goni   pilu   na,   *ara*   goni-a
      CONJ-3.DUAL   build fence PERFV   3.PL   build-3.SG.OBJ

      pilu-i   liva'a-na   pilu   ni   boo-i   m-*arua*
      fence-SG   like-3.SG   fence LIG   pig-SG   CONJ-3.DUAL

      na'i-a   i   ei
      put-3.SG.OBJ   LOC   there

      'and they both built a fence, they built a fence like a pig fence and they both put it there' (Hill 1992: 131)

The first subject pronoun *arua* is dual, and shows that there are two referents; the second clause partly repeats the first, and here the plural *ara* is used, rather than the dual. In the third clause, which involves a new event, the dual is again used. There is a similar usage with the paucal and, according to Deborah Hill (personal communication), replacement by the plural is more likely to occur with the paucal than with the dual. We represent this system in figure 2.11.

The more important use of number is its referential use with independent pronouns, where this facultative use does not apply; facultative use is restricted to subject pronouns, which we might argue are like agreement markers. However, we would expect the constraints we have developed to play a role here too, and indeed they do, in that the singular–plural choice is not affected, while the other two choices are. It is interesting too that the paucal is more likely to be replaced by the plural than is the dual.

The third language which requires us to weaken the constraint that only the last number choice can be facultative is Marshallese. Recall from §2.2.5 that the first, second and third person pronouns all have five number forms (Bender 1969: 8–9): singular, dual, trial, paucal (Bender's 'quadral') and plural. The dual, trial and

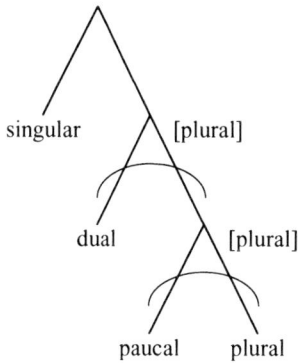

Figure 2.11 *The facultative numbers of Longgu*

paucal are all formed from the plural by the addition of regular suffixes and they are treated syntactically as singular (Bender 1969: 5). However, the important point is that according to Bender the use of these forms (dual, trial and paucal) is optional (1969: 5). Thus we have three facultative number choices. The system is given in figure 2.12.

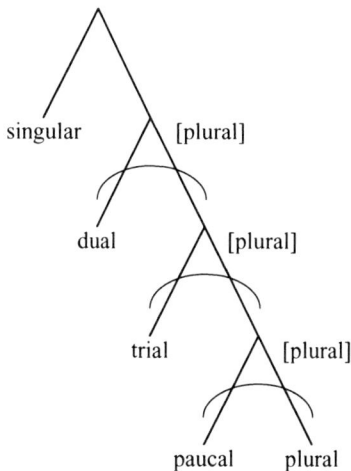

Figure 2.12 *The facultative numbers of Marshallese*

A pattern is emerging. We cannot restrict facultative number values to 'the last choice'; rather we must say that if there is facultative number it must involve 'the last choice'. It may involve other numbers, working up from the last choice. Thus it may affect the dual–plural choice in Larike, because it also affects the trial–plural choice; similarly it may affect the dual–plural choice in Longgu, because it also

47

affects the paucal–plural choice. And it may affect the dual–plural choice in Marshallese because it affects the trial–plural choice, which is in turn possible only because the paucal–plural choice is affected. We claim that there could not be a language which was, say, identical to Longgu except that it had the possibility of the plural being used for the dual but not for the paucal.

Furthermore, if there is a difference in the probabilities of use of different facultative values, then the last choice will be the 'most facultative' – the one most likely not to be taken. We saw this in Longgu, where the paucal–plural choice is the more likely not to be used (and so the plural is found) and the dual–plural choice is more likely to be used. We claim the opposite situation will not be found. Thus for Marshallese we would predict (there is no evidence about this) that the dual would be used more than the trial and the trial more than the paucal (as a proportion of the instances when each could be used, and not just as a matter of overall frequency).

Before leaving facultative number, we should consider how it differs from general number. Facultative number is found where marking of number is required, but not all number distinctions are obligatory. Thus languages like Slovene have a facultative number value, the dual, but no general number. Conversely, Bayso (discussed in §2.1) has general number, but no facultative number, as shown in figure 2.13. In Bayso the choice is to mark number or not, and within number the appropriate value is selected.

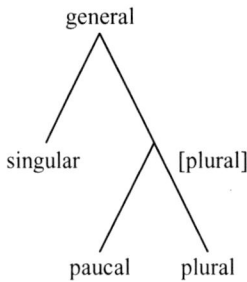

Figure 2.13 *System with separate general number (Bayso)*

Languages like Kaytetye are also important here (figure 2.14). Besides the plural markers (discussed in §2.2.6), nouns have a dual (in -*therre*) and a singular, which has no ending. Marking of number on nouns is not required. However, if number is marked, it must be the appropriate number. Specifically, the plural is not used for two referents. Thus the choice is to mark number or not to mark number; the dual–plural opposition is not facultative. This means that the unmarked form should be seen as a general form (outside the number system) and as a singular. Number need not be marked, but if it is marked there is no facultative opposition

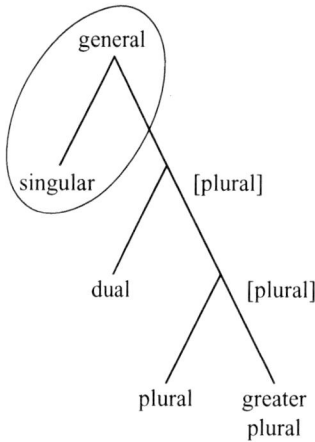

Figure 2.14 *System with shared general number (Kaytetye)*

within it. Harold Koch (personal communication) states that in this respect the system is like that of many Australian languages (see for example Wambaya; Nordlinger 1998: 72–6). Such systems are represented in figure 2.14. Here then there is general number, but it shares forms with the singular.[35] However, once within the number system, the appropriate value must be used – the plural is not used in place of the dual.

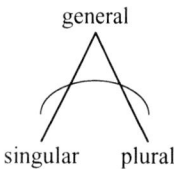

Figure 2.15 *General number (first attempt)*

The limiting case is the system with just two numbers, singular and plural. If the use of the plural were facultative then the effect would be that the use of number as a whole would be facultative (this is the situation in Japanese, for instance). In analysing such systems, we could consider treating the singular–plural distinction as facultative, as in figure 2.15. This initially attractive solution fails. General and singular regularly share a form, in language after language. The unique general form is rare. Hence we would be predicting use of a form which is rarely available. A

---

[35] This sharing with the singular is something we have seen before. And in Bayso, where there are unique forms, the agreements taken by general forms are as for the singular.

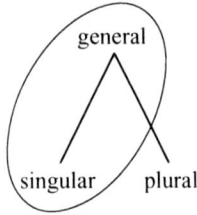

Figure 2.16 *System with general/singular versus plural*

more helpful representation of the system that we used earlier, given again as figure 2.16. This figure makes clearer a second type of problem with the other proposal: if we try to claim that the plural is facultative, then we get exactly the wrong pattern of overlapping: it is not consistent with the patterns found with the clear facultative numbers, in which it was precisely the plural that was used in place of facultative numbers (dual or trial). We should accept that the systems with general/singular forms are more radically different than figure 2.15 suggests: here it is the whole category of number which is optional (these systems are discussed further in §3.4 and §4.5.3). Therefore the position taken here is that such systems have general number (the choice is whether to express number or not); facultative number then occurs within systems where number is to be marked, but where a particular choice or choices need not be taken.

2.4   Languages without number

Linguists have claimed that all languages have number; that appears a reasonable claim, but when we look far enough we find counter-examples. Pirahã is the only remaining member of the Mura family and was spoken in 1997 by some 220 people along the Maici River (Amazonas, Brazil); it has been described by Everett (1986) on the basis of fourteen months of intensive contact with the Pirahã, and updated (1997) after five years of fieldwork. He states (1986: 217): 'there are no plural forms in Pirahã'. This holds even for pronouns, whose free forms are as in table 2.9 (1986: 280).

Table 2.9   *Personal pronouns in Pirahã (Everett 1986: 280)*

1st person	ti
2nd person	gíxai
3rd person	hiapióxio

He adds: 'There are no special plural forms for these pronouns.' This means that *hiapióxio* (third person) can be plural or singular, as this example shows (1986: 282):

(34) hiapióxio soxóá   xo-ó-xio
      3   already   jungle-LOC-DIR
  (i) 'He already went to the jungle' or
  (ii) 'They already went to the jungle'

There are ways of expressing what in other languages would be plurality, by conjoining, for instance (1986: 281):

(35) ti gíxai pí-o   ahá-p-i-í
      1   2   also-OBL go-IMPRFV-PROX-
                                     COMPLETE.CERTAINTY
      'You and I will go (i.e. we will go)'

There are other means for expressing the notion of plurality: the associative/comitative postposition *xigí* and various quantifiers. But this does not mean that the language has a number category; after all, English can express duality through the use of *two* and *both*, but this does not mean that English has a dual. The grammar of English does not need to refer to a value 'dual'. Similarly in Pirahã, from Everett's description, the grammar has no need to refer to a value 'plural'. We conclude that Pirahã appears to have no number category.[36]

Kawi (Old Javanese) is reported to have been similar to Pirahã in this respect, in not having plural nouns or pronouns, though number could be indicated by quantifiers such as 'many' and 'all' or by conjoining pronouns (Becker and Oka 1974: 232); Classical Chinese too seems to have lacked number (Norman 1988: 120–1; Goddard 1995: 119n2). (Another suggested case is Acehnese; this will be discussed in §3.2.4.3 since it has number just in the first person.)

2.5 Approaches in formal semantics

A concise overview of work on number within formal semantics can be found in Link (1998), who shows how the study of plurals relates to different movements in linguistic semantics, and also provides a substantial bibliography. There is a good deal being done, including several monographs (Ojeda 1993, Schein 1993, Lasersohn 1995 and Schwarzschild 1996). Some work in this area appears highly technical, with perhaps a tenuous link to research on natural language. But there are signs that the two are coming closer together. Partly this is due to a growing awareness of the 'precision problem':

---

[36] It might be asked whether this is equivalent to having a language in which all nominals have general number. General number, in my view, suggests that there is an opposition of number, which the general form is not involved in, hence without any category of number there are no general forms.

> Over the years it has become evident that a typical difficulty in studying plurals is the fact that plural terms are notoriously vague in their reference; in this way they serve the overall efficiency of language in a remarkable way. Formal representations, on the other hand, are typically calibrated for a high degree of precision. The problem here is to come up with representations that are optimally tuned to this empirical level of accuracy. (Link 1998: 21)

Link gives the following illustration:

(36)   The Romans built the aqueduct. They were excellent architects.

The point is that not all the Romans built the aqueduct, equally not all Romans were excellent architects. And those Romans who did the building were not exactly the same Romans as those who were excellent architects. A challenge for those in formal semantics is representing the vagueness of natural language rather than giving representations which are overprecise.

A second way in which the two areas of research are becoming closer has been through the interest of formal semanticists in distributivity, a notion which can be seen in the following contrast:

(37)   Five boys laughed

(38)   Five boys moved the piano

(37) has a distributive reading: each of the boys laughed, while the natural reading of (38) is not distributive: it is not the case that each boy moved the piano. Work on this topic has started to draw on cross-linguistic research because languages vary in the ways in which they mark different types of distributivity (see for instance Gil 1988, 1995 and Link 1991; we take up a part of this topic in §4.4). Similarly, variation in the types of quantifiers found in different languages is examined in Bach et al. (1995). A third area of convergence is the growing interest of formal semanticists in instances where number is not obligatorily encoded: there is general number as discussed in §2.1 and mass nouns to be discussed in §3.6. Examples of work which consider cross-linguistic differences in this general area are Krifka (1995) and Chierchia (1998a).

2.6   Conclusion

The typology of number must be much more elaborate than is generally thought, which illustrates well the typological point with which we began the chapter, namely the need to cast the net widely at the beginning of the investigation. We have first approached number from the semantic point of view, investigating the meaning distinctions on which number systems are based. We saw that there is a primary distinction between languages which have general number, and so can refer to entities without specifying number, and those which cannot. Then we narrowed our focus to the values available when number is specified and found considerable variety, with some languages having five number values in their systems. (Languages like English occupy a relatively undistinguished corner of the typology, having obligatory number and a simple singular–plural distinction.) There are further number systems, such as 'inverse' and 'augmented', but as we shall see in chapter 5 these relate to the formal side of number, and do not lead to additional semantic distinctions. To give a typology of the possible systems we considered the Number Hierarchy, but replaced it with an analysis based on binary branching structures. There were two main arguments in favour of this: the way they allow us to include the paucal and greater plural in our typology, and the convincing account they make possible for facultative number. We shall see further evidence in their favour in subsequent chapters (see, for instance, §4.2.1 for an instance of dual and plural patterning together). We have concentrated on the areas of greatest richness, looking now at pronouns, now at particular types of noun. We still need to address the question of different systems coexisting in the same language. In the next chapter we consider the minimal case, where some nominals are involved in the number system and some fall outside it, and we see that there is a typology of the possible distributions of number values over types of nominal. Then in chapter 4 we put the two typologies together, and consider which values are found for which types of nominal. Thus we shall discuss cases where a language has more than one number system operating and account for the possibilities found.

3
Items involved in the nominal number system

In the last chapter we focused on number values. We therefore kept the noun or pronoun 'still' in order to see which number values were available to it. Now we take the opposite approach: we keep the number value still and see which nominals can take it. We want to know why the values singular and plural are straightforwardly available to the noun *friend* (*friend ~ friends*) but not to the noun *friendliness*. More generally, we will ask which nominals are involved in the number system of a particular language, looking mainly at the basic singular–plural opposition (we shall integrate further number values in chapter 4). And though we shall examine languages of very different types we shall see that there is a clear pattern, which we shall capture in terms of an animacy hierarchy. Since hierarchies play such an important role in modern typology, the investigation of a hierarchy will be our main typological point in this chapter.

The world's languages show greater variety than we might have expected in terms of which nominals have a number opposition. Consider the following Warrgamay example (Queensland, Australia), given by Dixon (1980: 266–8):

(1)   yibi-yibi   ŋulmburu-ŋgu   wurrbi-bajun-du
       child-REDUP.ABS   woman-ERG   big-VERY-ERG

       buudi-lgani-y   malan-gu
       take-CONTIN-UNMARKED.TENSE[1] river-ALLATIVE

       'the very big woman/women is/are taking the children to the creek'

This example indicates that a noun can indicate number in Warrgamay, as in *yibi-yibi* 'children', but this is extremely restricted (Dixon 1981: 35) and forms like *ŋulmburu-ŋgu* 'woman' are usual; in fact Dixon (1980: 267) says that a noun in this language 'is not normally specified for number' and suggests that this is the typical situation in Australia (1980: 22). Note especially that the verb in (1) does not

---

[1] *-l-* and *-gani-* together indicate continuative and *-y-* indicates unmarked tense, hence the gloss 'is/are taking' (Dixon 1980: 268).

determine number either. For the pronouns we turn to Dixon (1981: 39–40). The first and second persons, singular, dual and plural, and the third dual and plural are 'strictly specified for number' and are available only for reference to humans (and occasionally tame dogs). The form filling the third singular slot can range over all persons and all numbers (it can have non-human as well as human reference) but its basic sense is third person singular. Thus the word for 'woman' is not normally specified for number, while in English it must be. Yet the personal pronouns are. Could there be a language in which the word for 'woman' specified number but the first person pronoun did not? We shall see in §3.1 that according to the Animacy Hierarchy this is predicted to be impossible. We shall then look at the types of nominal which may be distinguished in terms of their participation in the number system (§3.2). Next we ask what 'participating in the number system' means; more concretely are nouns like English *sheep* problematic in terms of the claims being made (§3.3)? We then consider instances like *yibi-yibi* 'children' in (1) above, in other words where plural forms *can* but *need not* be used (§3.4). The Animacy Hierarchy also provides insight into the forms of number marking: in English we have, for instance, *I* ~ *we*, *woman* ~ *women*, but *cat* ~ *cats*, *book* ~ *books*, and so on. We do not expect to find a language in which 'I' and 'woman' have regular plurals, while 'cat' and 'book' are irregular (§3.5). Moreover, forms which are morphologically equivalent may be semantically different; thus *mines* and *wines* are morphologically similar, but number has different effects here. To approach this, we first discuss the count–mass distinction in §3.6, and go on to a general consideration of semantic effects in §3.7.

3.1   The Animacy Hierarchy

Smith-Stark suggested that plurality 'splits' a language if 'it is a significant opposition for certain categories but irrelevant for others' (1974: 657). The type of evidence he produced concerned marking of the noun phrase for number (usually by marking on the noun itself) and agreement in number (mainly verbal agreement but with some instances of agreement within the noun phrase). He claimed, for instance, that in Georgian if the subject is plural and denotes an animate the verb will be plural, if it denotes an inanimate then the verb will be singular. Thus Georgian nouns are split, and the division is between animates and inanimates. Various languages make the split at different points, according to a hierarchy based on animacy. Smith-Stark was inspired by work by Silverstein, presented in 1973, later published in revised form (Silverstein 1976). As Cedric Smith-Stark has pointed out (personal communication) the hierarchy is prefigured in Forchheimer (1953: 12–13); even earlier, part can be found in de la Grasserie (1886–87: 234–7); for other precursors see Plank (1987: 181). The hierarchy presented by Smith-Stark is clearly akin to what others have termed the Animacy Hierarchy or the Topicality

Hierarchy (see Comrie 1989: 185–200; Allan 1987: 57 gives a slightly different version and calls it the personal hierarchy). See also Nichols (1992: 143–52, 160–2) for discussion and further data.

Smith-Stark's paper (1974) was a major step forward in our understanding of number systems; he provides a good deal of data to support his claim, and notes some problematic cases too. On the other hand, the paper is confusing in places, and some relevant data are missing (that is still true, since it has not been followed up as well as it deserved). We will therefore not follow his exposition closely but the major ideas of the paper will be covered: the hierarchy and the different positions on it (taken up in §3.2); the types of evidence, namely number marking and agreement (Smith-Stark expected all to be regular, but this is not how it turns out, §3.3); obligatory versus optional expression of number (§3.4) and the correlation of different morphological means of marking number with the positions on the hierarchy (§3.5). We also consider a type of regularity not discussed by Smith-Stark, namely the correlation of different meanings of number values with positions on the hierarchy (introduced in §3.6 for discussion in §3.7).

3.2 The hierarchy positions

The evidence varies from instances where it gives very clear support for the division between two positions on the hierarchy to those where it is less secure. We will start from the clearer cases, rather than working our way down the hierarchy from the top. The version of the Animacy Hierarchy justified by the latest data is given in figure 3.1; we shall point out at relevant points below where it differs from that of Smith-Stark.

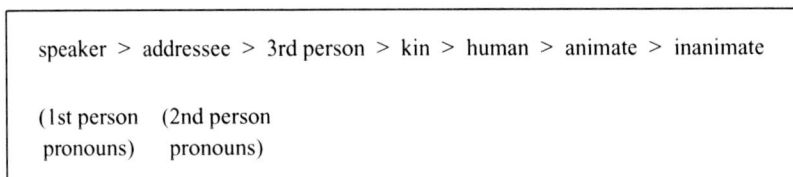

---

speaker > addressee > 3rd person > kin > human > animate > inanimate

(1st person   (2nd person
pronouns)   pronouns)

Figure 3.1 *The Animacy Hierarchy*

The basic claim, which we shall develop in chapter 4, is as follows:

> I. *Constraint of the Animacy Hierarchy on the singular–plural distinction*
> The singular–plural distinction in a given language must affect a top segment of the Animacy Hierarchy.

Languages which are claimed to be possible and impossible are represented in figure 3.2 (where A–F are hypothetical languages and ■ indicates a number distinction, singular-plural in this case). Languages A and B are both in accord with the con-

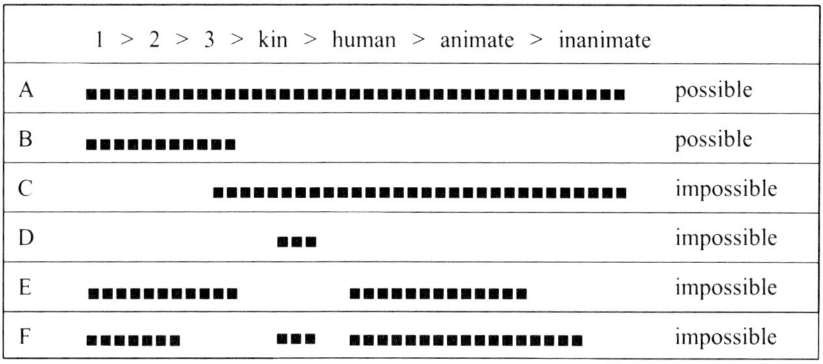

1 > 2 > 3 > kin > human > animate > inanimate		
A	■■	possible
B	■■■■■■■■■■■	possible
C	■■■■■■■■■■■■■■■■■■■■■■■■■■■■■■■	impossible
D	■■■	impossible
E	■■■■■■■■■■■ ■■■■■■■■■■■■■	impossible
F	■■■■■■■ ■■■ ■■■■■■■■■■■■■■■■■	impossible

Figure 3.2 *The effect of the Animacy Hierarchy on number systems*

straint of the hierarchy; it does not matter that in A the number distinction has a large range and in B a small range (we shall see examples of both in this chapter). Languages C and D are both claimed to be impossible, because the range of number differentiation, whether large or small, does not involve a top segment. E and F are both impossible because although the top of the hierarchy is involved, we do not find a single segment: it is the breaks in the range which make these systems impossible.

3.2.1 Human versus non-human

This split is well represented. In Slave (an Athabaskan language spoken in parts of the Northwest Territories, British Columbia and Alberta, Canada) the pronouns distinguish singular and plural. For certain nouns there is a suffix -*ke*, which is a 'plural or group marker' (Rice 1989: 247). It is attached optionally after other modifiers, provided the noun denotes a human (kin or not) or a dog (see §5.3.5 for discussion of such phrasal affixes). Examples are from the Hare dialect of Slave:

(2) se-ya   se-ya-ke
     1.SG-son   1.SG-son-PL
     'my son'   'my sons'

(3) t'eere   t'eere-ke
     girl   girl-PL
     'girl'   'girls, group of girls'

(4) lį   lį-ke
     dog   dog-PL
     'dog'   'dogs'

The use of -*ke* is optional. If the noun phrase functions as the subject, -*ke* may appear in suffixal position, or it may appear as a prefix on the verb, or it may occur on both. Here then the break is between human and animate, with just dogs being treated as 'honorary humans'. This situation is common in North America:

> In the vast majority of North American languages . . . only certain nouns have plural forms. In most of these, only nouns referring to human beings have plurals, or only some nouns referring to humans, often kin terms. (Multiple animals that are considered 'sentient beings,' such as pets or characters in legends, are also often referred to by plural nouns.) The plurals that do exist are used only on some occasions, not every time multiple participants are discussed. (Mithun 1988a: 212)

Elsewhere in the world, a similar division can be found. Thus in Mayali, a Gunwinjguan language of western Arnhem Land, Australia, number is normally marked on the verb for nouns denoting humans 'and a few other higher animates like spirits' (Evans 1995: 213; examples are from §7.5.5 in Evans forthcoming):

(5) Abanmani-na-ng   bininj
     1.MIN/3.UNIT.AUG-see-PAST.PRFV   man
     'I saw the two men'

The pronominal prefixes on the verb mark subject and object, thus 1/3 indicates first person acting on third. Here the first person is 'minimal' (singular) and the third person is 'unit augmented', indicating a dual object (augmented systems will be discussed in §5.6). Since the object is human, its number is coded on the verb in (5). This is not the case with non-human objects:

(6) Duruk   ginga   ba-bayeng
     dog   crocodile 3.MIN/3.MIN-bite.PAST.PRFV

     ba-ngune-ng   na-wern-gen
     3.MIN/3.MIN-eat-PAST.PRFV MASC-many-GEN

     'The/a crocodile has eaten all the dogs / the many dogs'

In (6), the verbs have the default minimal (singular) form for the object, even though there is more than one dog involved (as shown by *na-wern-gen* 'many', which agrees in gender (masculine) with *duruk* 'dog'; the genitive marker on 'many' is found in various expressions of number and extent); since dogs are not human, the number is not coded on the verb.[2]

---

[2] Human versus non-human is one of the factors determining number agreement in Turkish according to Schroeder (1999: 111–25).

Thus the split comes between human and non-human for coding by pronominal affixes. Note that in (5) there is no number marker on the noun, even though two men are involved. This shows that for marking on nominals, the split is somewhat higher: pronouns mark number, and a small number of nouns in the kin and human categories, but not all, as (5) demonstrates (Evans §5.3 and §6.1 in forthcoming). Another example, from quite another part of the world, is Manchu, a Tungusic language of northern China, where number is marked on pronouns and on most nouns denoting humans (Doerfer 1963: 182; Sunik 1997: 167).

3.2.2 Animate versus inanimate

There is also good evidence for a split between animates and inanimates. One language which shows this is Marind, which belongs to the family of the same name and has about 7,000 speakers in southern Irian Jaya. The data are from Drabbe (1955: 18–20), also discussed in Foley (1986: 78, 82–3). Drabbe describes four genders, which we designate I–IV in the examples:[3] gender I is for male humans, gender II for female humans and animals, while inanimates are divided between genders III and IV. First we see examples of genders I and II:

(7) e-pe   patur   e-pe   akek   ka
     I-DEF   boy   I-DEF   light.I be
     'that boy is light (not heavy)'

(8) u-pe   kivasom u-pe   akuk   ka
     II-DEF   daughter II-DEF   light.II be
     'that daughter is light'

The agreement is prefixed on -*pe* 'the' but infixed in the adjective *ak-k* 'light'; *ŋat* 'dog', an animate so in gender II, behaves like *kivasom* 'daughter'. In the plural, the forms are as follows:

(9) i-pe   patur   i-pe   akik   ka
     PL-DEF   boy.PL   PL-DEF   light.PL be
     'those boys are light'

(10) i-pe   kivasom i-pe   akik   ka
     PL-DEF   daughter PL-DEF   light.PL be
     'those daughters are light'

Thus the plural agreement forms are the same for genders I and II. There are a few nouns in these genders, almost all denoting humans rather than animals, which have a distinct plural form, thus *anum* 'man' has the plural *anim*. Most however do

---

[3] A single noun, denoting an inanimate, is outside these genders.

not change morphologically. For genders III and IV, these are the forms (the adjective here distinguishes gender III from gender I):

(11) e-pe   de   e-pe   akak   ka
      III-DEF   wood   III-DEF   light.III   be
      'that wood is light' or 'those pieces of wood are light'

(12) i-pe   beha^u i-pe   akik   ka
      IV-DEF   pole   IV-DEF   light.IV   be
      'that pole is light' or 'those poles are light'

Nouns of genders III and IV, those which are 'below' animals, have no distinct plural forms and no distinct plural agreement forms. (Note that the gender IV marker is the same as the plural marker for genders I and II.) Here then the split between animate and inanimate is clear. Similarly in Mundari, a Munda language of east India, verbs agree in number down as far as animate nouns, but not with inanimates (Bhattacharya 1976: 191–2).

3.2.3   Kin (and rational)

'Kin' is a position for which the evidence is weaker. In Kobon, a language of the East New Highlands family spoken in the Kaironk Valley of Papua New Guinea, number (singular, dual and plural) is distinguished on personal pronouns (all three persons), and on nouns denoting kin (Davies 1981: 147–8, 154).[4] And in Kalkatungu, a language of western Queensland with no known remaining full speakers, pronouns (free and bound) and demonstratives distinguish singular, dual and plural. There is a dual and a plural marker for nouns; both are 'common' with kinship nouns, are part of the number system of demonstratives, but are 'rarely used' with other nominals (Barry Blake 1979: 31–2, 34–7, 80–1 and personal communication).

A good case is provided by Maori. Here number marking on pronouns is obligatory (we return to this in §4.1). Then there are the nouns in table 3.1 which mark number, also obligatorily (Bauer 1993: 353–4, 371, 593). While the list is not exclusively of kin terms, it is close to being so. Note the interesting way in which the plural is formed in all but the last example, namely by reduplicating the antepenultimate vowel.

Smith-Stark also included a position 'rational' between kin and human. This is a split within the human category, dividing the vast majority of nouns denoting humans (then called 'rational') from those for infants ('human non-rational'). He claims that there can be a division at that point, but cites only Tamil as an example.

---

[4] This was noted in Barlow (1992: 60); there are other means of marking number, notably verb agreement: here the split is lower on the hierarchy (Davies 1981: 149).

Table 3.1 *Complete list of nouns with plural form in Maori*

singular	plural	gloss
matua	maatua	parent
tangata	taangata	man
teina	teeina	younger sibling (same sex)
tuahine	tuaahine	sister (of male)
tuakana	tuaakana	older sibling (same sex)
tupuna	tuupuna	ancestor
wahine	waahine	woman, wife
whaea	whaaea	mother [some speakers only]
tamaiti	tamariki	child

He cites grammars giving a distinction between neuter nouns and others in Tamil, with the neuters frequently not expressing number. Nouns denoting humans are in the masculine and feminine genders, but the words for 'child' and 'infant' are neuter – they take neuter agreements. Harold Schiffman (personal communication) confirms that *koṛande* 'baby, infant'[5] is indeed treated differently from other nouns denoting humans. These latter must be marked for plurality when appropriate; for other nouns, including non-human animates, plural marking is optional, and this is the case with *koṛande* 'baby, infant'. So far the evidence is restricted to Tamil. Even in the related language, Kannada, the situation is different. Here number marking is obligatory down to nouns denoting humans, and for those denoting non-humans it is optional (Sridhar 1990: 197, 205, 244). Though *magu* 'child/infant' is neuter, it takes number marking obligatorily (Shikaripur Sridhar, personal communication). Thus the division for number marking is human ~ non-human and not rational ~ non-rational in Kannada. The 'demoting' of children from human to non-human animate in Tamil does not justify setting up a separate position on the hierarchy any more than the 'promoting' of dogs to human in Slave justifies setting up a position 'canine' above animate but below human. The main hierarchy positions 'human', 'animate' and 'inanimate' cover many hundreds of nouns. The occasional leakage of one or two nouns at the border of these categories is understandable, but should be seen as the special treatment of individual items rather than evidence for separate hierarchy positions.

3.2.4 Pronouns

This too is an area where the situation is less clear. First there is the question of whether *we* and other first person plural pronouns are really the plural of *I* and

---

[5] *ṛ* is used for the retroflex frictionless continuant.

equivalents. This is something to which we shall return in §3.7.1; for now we shall assume the conclusion there, that we should treat them as plurals. The data on pronouns presented by Smith-Stark are sketchy in places, and descriptions of relevant languages often appear contradictory: a common difficulty is that one researcher describes, say, the free pronouns while another describes person agreement markers (and naturally we should aim to give descriptions of whole systems). There are good grounds for saying that pronouns may behave differently from nouns in respect of number; it is also fairly clear that first and second pronouns on the one hand can differ from the third person on the other. The trickier question is whether there are good grounds for separating first from second person pronouns in terms of number marking.

3.2.4.1 The position of the third person

We used the divide between pronouns and nouns to introduce the chapter; Warrgamay showed a split here. Not all languages have third person pronouns and if such pronouns are found they may be restricted in the type of antecedent for which they are appropriate (they may be restricted to humans, for instance). The evidence we have already seen suggests that there are languages in which all personal pronouns, including the third person pronoun, can be distinguished from nouns in terms of their number behaviour. This suggests we need a position on the hierarchy, between addressee and kin. Smith-Stark did not include third person pronouns on the hierarchy. He suggested: 'Whenever there is a split in the lexical nouns, the split in the third person pronoun (if there is one) will be at the same place or lower down in the hierarchy' (1974: 664). This means that if, say, nouns have a split between human and non-human animate, the third person pronoun may follow this split, or may mark plurality for antecedents lower on the hierarchy than this. The logic of this position, where the third person pronoun may or may not behave like the nouns, would be that it should have a separate position on the hierarchy, which is the line we have adopted. In fact the hierarchy may be seen as a combination of three complementary hierarchies, a Person Hierarchy (1st > 2nd > 3rd), a Nominal Hierarchy (pronouns > nouns) and an Animacy Hierarchy proper (human > animate > inanimate); this follows ideas in Comrie (1989: 197–9) and Croft (1990: 112–13).

The difficulty with the third person pronoun arises because it can be viewed in two ways, and the difference is often not made explicit. We may view it in terms of its form, and ask whether it has singular and plural forms. This is the consistent thing to do, if we are similarly interested in whether nouns of different types have two distinct number forms. Or we can view it in terms of use, and ask whether it can be used in both singular and plural, when the antecedent is a noun phrase headed by a noun denoting humans, non-human animates, and so on. But this is relevant to the number properties of the nouns rather than that of the pronoun. It raises the question we shall treat in §3.3, namely that of the tests we are using (a question which till now we have glossed over).

Table 3.2 *Personal pronouns in Igbo*

	singular	plural
1st person	m	anye
2nd person	e	anu
3rd person	ɔ	ha

Returning then to the supporting evidence for a separate position for the third person pronoun, we should consider Igbo, a Niger-Kordofanian language (Carnochan 1962). The pronouns have the forms shown in table 3.2. In contrast, nouns do not alter their form to mark number. However, most of them can serve as the antecedent for the singular or plural pronoun. Thus the formal possibilities give us grounds for distinguishing all pronouns (including the third person) from nouns, and the third person pronoun would give us a test for making a different distinction in the nouns. In Usan too (Adelbert Range, Papua New Guinea), the personal pronouns mark number in all three persons but nouns do not (Reesink 1987: 53, 57).

Another instance where there is a split between pronouns and nouns is Central Pomo, a Pomoan language of Northern California (Mithun 1988b and personal communication). Here the distinction is a little more subtle. Personal pronouns of all three persons have distinct singular and plural forms. Where nouns are concerned, number marking is possible only on certain nouns denoting persons. The difference between pronouns and those nouns which can mark number is as follows. Number is marked obligatorily on personal pronouns, provided they refer to persons. The third person pronoun is *mu:l* 'that, he, she, it'. 'They' of persons is *mu:tuya*, but for non-persons only *mu:l* is available. But for those nouns which potentially have number marking (some of those denoting humans) it is not obligatory. Thus there is a split between the pronouns (marking obligatory for humans) and the nouns (marking not obligatory for the minority which have it). The question of obligatory and optional marking is taken up in §3.4.

3.2.4.2 First and second persons versus third

There is regularly a difference in the behaviour of third person pronouns, as opposed to other persons, so we might expect to find that reflected in number marking. Examples are not so frequent, however. A language which does appear to have a clear split between second and third persons in the pronominal system is Asmat, which belongs to the family of the same name, probably a part of the Trans New Guinea phylum (see table 3.3). The Tupi language Guaraní is a comparable

Table 3.3 *Personal pronouns in*
Asmat (Voorhoeve 1965: 143)

	singular	plural
1st person	no	na
2nd person	o	ca
3rd person	a	

example, though in addition it has an inclusive–exclusive distinction in the first person (Gregores and Suárez 1967: 131–2, 141; Croft 1990: 111).

3.2.4.3 First person versus second

This is the part of the hierarchy where the data are least clear. Smith-Stark offers three languages to support a split of first person from the rest, but he discusses only one of them in the text. This is Kwakiutl, now usually called Kwak'wala, for which he cites Boas (1911b: 444, 550); there is a fuller account in Boas (1947: 251–5). The pronouns distinguish five forms: first person only, inclusive (first plus second), exclusive (first plus third), second and third. The inclusive and exclusive each contain the first person form, but with an addition. So this situation could be interpreted as marking number only in the first person. Perhaps rather we should say that the real distinction is of inclusive and exclusive (which imply plural somewhat in the way that distributive can, as we shall see in §4.4.1) There are other markers of plurality in Kwak'wala, but these are later developments. Thus an earlier stage of Kwak'wala might be taken to support the claim of a split between first person pronouns and all other nominals.

Another candidate for a split in the first person only, not discussed by Smith-Stark, is Acehnese. It has around one and a half million speakers, mainly at the northern tip of Sumatra, and is closely related to the Chamic subgroup of Austronesian. The relevant information is from Mark Durie (1985 and personal communication). Durie claims that Acehnese has no inflectional morphology and that: 'it does not mark for gender, case, person or number' (1985: 29). 'Nominals are not marked for case, number or gender. Plural can sometimes be suggested by reduplication . . . but this is only an expression of emphasis which in context may indicate plural; it is not a plural inflection. It is more usual not to mark plural in any way' (1985: 107). With nouns the picture is clear; there is no plural marker. Plurality may be indicated by reduplication, but this is indirect, since reduplication is used for emphasis. There are also quantifiers available. Let us turn to the personal pronouns (Durie 1985: 116–25). In the second person there are the forms *kah* (familiar), *gata* (neutral) and *droe'=neu(h)* (polite; here′ indicates that the preceding syllable is stressed and = indicates a clitic boundary). All these can be used of one person or of more than one, though there are ways of emphasizing plural reference if required, for instance by the use of *dum* 'all'. With the third person too, pronouns vary according to politeness but they are non-specific as to number. It is the first person which is of greatest interest. There is a familiar pronoun *kee* which is only singular. Then there are various polite pronouns: *ulôn, lôn, ulông, lông, ulôntuwan, lôntuwan*, all of which are non-specific as to number. In addition there are three pronouns (all neutral in terms of politeness) *geutanyoe* and *tanyoe* (first and second person, or 'first person inclusive') and *kamoe* (first person exclusive).

It is therefore a nice question, whether Acehnese has number at all. I would suggest that the existence of the inclusive forms like *geutanyoe* and *tanyoe* would not be sufficient to claim the language has number, since such forms imply number secondarily. The existence of *kee* (first person, only singular) is trickier: it functions alongside pronouns which are non-specific as to number but also, of course, in opposition to the inclusive and exclusive pronouns. Like them it has related clitic forms. It is at the least the germ of a number system, and the opposition is indeed exactly where it would be predicted, in the first person singular. If we conclude that Acehnese has no number, and that the existence of *kee* (first person, only singular), as opposed to *kamoe* (first person exclusive, only plural) is insufficient to suggest otherwise, then it is another interesting case to be added to those in §2.4. On the other hand, the facts that *kee* is for one person, and *kamoe* more than one, that both have clitic forms, and that the opposition occurs exactly where predicted, may make us lean towards saying that this is an instance of a minimal number system, with number in the first person only.

It should be clear by now that it is difficult to find clear cases of extant systems with an unarguable split of first person pronouns versus the rest. Possible leads are provided by Členova (1973: 174–5) and Forchheimer (1953: 65–7). A good place to look appears to be the languages of Papua New Guinea. For these, interesting data can be found in Foley (1986: 66–74); sometimes the sparse inventories of pronouns are bolstered by fuller sets of distinctions within the verb inflection. Foley (1986: 70, following Piau 1985) gives the example of Kuman, of the Chimbu family, which has the pronoun inventory given in table 3.4. In this language the bound pronouns have many more forms, filling out the distinctions of number. Nevertheless, the forms of the personal pronouns given in table 3.4 are at least suggestive, showing a distinction only in the first person. Since the evidence is not clear-cut, it would be good to have data from more languages.[6] We shall examine an additional type of evidence in §4.1. Overall, then, the available evidence, though not conclusive, suggests splitting first and second persons, with the first person ranked higher.

---

[6] See also Berik, a language of Irian Jaya, where the pronouns make the same distinctions as Kuman but where number (dual and plural) is marked on the verb (Westrum and Wiesemann 1986).

Table 3.4 *Personal pronouns in Kuman (Foley 1986: 70)*

	singular	plural
1st person	na	no
2nd person	ene	
3rd person	je	

In this section we have seen instances where the split involves the possibility versus impossibility of the plural, and others where the opposition is instead obligatory versus optional use of the plural, a point we return to in §3.4. We have marshalled a good deal of evidence in support of the hierarchy and justified all the separate hierarchy positions in figure 3.1. Of course, we should give closer attention to possible evidence against; the next section will address that.

3.3   Marking and agreement

At the beginning of the chapter, when we looked at the plurality split in Warrgamay we examined the markers on the nominals involved; in Marind (§3.2.2) we looked primarily at agreement. And in Mayali (§3.2.1) we saw that the split came at different points depending on the test we chose: marking on nominals or pronominal affixes on the verb. We should now consider the basic question of how we decide whether a particular nominal counts as showing a singular–plural distinction or not, and hence whether it is in accord with the requirement of the Animacy Hierarchy. To take a specific instance: in English, if we look at marking on the noun the split comes low on the hierarchy, within the inanimates; we have *friend ~ friends*, but no number distinction for *friendliness*. As expected, then, animates, being higher on the hierarchy, typically have singular and plural (for example, *dog ~ dogs*). What then of *sheep*? It looks like a counter-example, since it has only the form *sheep*. If, however, we look at agreement, then it is regular:

(13)   This sheep has been cloned.

(14)   These sheep have been cloned.

The noun *sheep* does not mark number and in that respect it is irregular. On the other hand, its agreements are regular. It will not do to 'play fast and loose' with the criteria, choosing whichever suits us in a particular case. We should rather investigate the criteria, and see what the relations between them are. The major distinction is between morphological expression of number (a marker, typically on the noun itself) or syntactic expression (by agreement, which we shall take in the broader sense, to include determining the form of personal pronouns, see §6.1). In English at least, for a given noun, the different types of agreement will be typically consistent (that is, if it can take a plural attributive modifier, as in *these sheep*, it will head a noun phrase which takes a plural verb and plural pronouns). We consider cases where the agreement facts are more complex in §6.2.

Generalizing from the case of English *sheep*, we need to consider what different combinations of results are possible.[7] We might suggest that there will always be one test (the morphological test or the syntactic test) according to which a given language will conform to the hierarchy. I suggest rather that the syntactic test (agreement), will always match the hierarchy as well as or better than the morphological test (we shall suggest why in §3.6). That is to say, while we have exceptions of the '*sheep*-type' we shall never find the converse. Imagine a new lexical item *peesh* (a cloned sheep). It could not be the grammatical reversal of sheep:

(15) This peesh has been fed. [Hypothetical]

(16) This peeshes has been fed. [Hypothetical, claimed impossible][8]

The claim is this:

> *II   The relation of number marking and agreement to the Animacy Hierarchy*
>
> Lexical items may be irregular in terms of number marking with respect to the Animacy Hierarchy and regular in terms of agreement, but not vice versa.

A further claim, which depends on the Agreement Hierarchy (§6.2), is that the different positions moving rightwards along that hierarchy will give increasingly regular results. At first sight, the hypothetical system which is claimed to be impossible looks rather like that which is found in Miya, to be discussed in §3.4 below. The difference is that in Miya noun marking and agreement behave differently, but both in accord with the Animacy Hierarchy. In other words, in Miya the two tests conform to the hierarchy equally well.

---

[7] Smith-Stark suggested four main mechanisms for marking plurality (1974: 657) 'verb–argument concord, noun–modifier concord, direct marking of a noun, and direct marking of the noun phrase'. He appears to expect regularity in respect of each, though he points out counter-examples. Almost all the examples he discusses involve noun marking and verb agreement; there is a short section on 'noun–modifier concord' and no section on marking of the noun phrase (there are some data in his table 1 however). We shall cite Taiap as an example of noun phrase marking in §3.5.

[8] These examples are considered within a discussion of number in terms of the distinction between contextual and inherent inflection in Corbett (1999).

There are three further problems we should deal with, each from English, whose behaviour in this respect is truly exotic. The first is seen in examples like this:

(17)   We observed three elephant in the game park.

This example and (18) are from Keith Allan (1976), who also gives several textual examples. In such instances, *elephant* and similar nouns are not pluralized, and hence appear exceptional. They differ from *sheep* in that they may be morphologically regular in some circumstances, but take a zero plural in others. This behaviour is limited to: 'the set of animals and birds hunted – in times past if not at present – for food or sport (i.e. for trophies like feathers, skins, tusks, etc.)' (K. Allan 1976: 103). Allan points out that for some nouns this use is appropriate only in the context of hunting or – surprisingly – conservation. And nouns vary in the likelihood of taking plural marking, from those where it is most likely, such as *hyena*, to those where it is least likely, like *teal*.[9] In terms of number marking, these nouns do not conform to the Animacy Hierarchy. However, agreements are regular:

(18)   The elephant are downwind of us.

Thus again English conforms to the hierarchy, only partially in respect of morphology but fully in respect of agreement.

The second problem concerns nouns like *committee*, which permit singular and plural agreements. This is an additional possibility: since such nouns can take singular and plural forms, and singular and plural agreements, the ability to take plural agreement when singular in form is in addition to any requirement of the Animacy Hierarchy. We discuss such nouns in §6.2. Note, however, the interesting animacy effect: *committee* (a group of humans) is more likely to take plural agreement than *herd* (a group of animals), while *forest* (a group of trees) does not take plural agreements. They conform to the hierarchy in this respect.

And third, English appears to be a counter-example in a striking way: the second person pronoun *you* has only this form in some varieties. This formerly

---

[9] There is clearly something odd about hunting (linguistically as well as otherwise). According to Gawełko (1985: 140–1) French uses the singular in expressions like:

(i) Ils   sont   partis   chasser   le   canard
    they   are   gone   hunt   the   duck
    'They have gone to hunt duck'

He claims that in similar examples Romanian uses the plural, while Polish uses the singular where one catch is sufficient (as with fox or bear) but the plural where it is not, in cases such as ducks. For interesting detail on the factors determining the plural forms of nouns for fish, see Coates (1980), and for a questionnaire investigation of the use of plural marking with nouns like *deer* see Reid (1991: 130–65). There are interesting examples of nouns of this type in Hirtle (1982: 20–3).

plural form came to be used for the singular too as a result of being used as a polite form of address (we consider similar instances in §7.1 and a related phenomenon in §9.1.2). However, when we turn to the agreement facts, we find that *you* conforms:

(19) you can do that yourself

(20) you can do that yourselves

The reflexive pronoun, which shows agreement within the clause, demonstrates that even *you* distinguishes singular and plural. Moreover, in many varieties of English there are forms such as *y'all*, *you guys*, *you'uns* and *yous*, which suggests that a new plural is gaining ground, though the distribution of these forms tends not to be that of a simple second person plural.

We have seen that a number split according to agreement may conform to the Animacy Hierarchy when a split according to morphology does so less strictly (as in English), but we do not find the converse. The question remains as to the relation between morphology and agreement, when they provide evidence for splits at different points on the hierarchy: can we predict which one will make the split at the higher point? Since some of the best examples involve optionality, we shall discuss that topic in the next section and then return to the question of splits which differ according to whether we look at agreement or morphology.

Once we have made the general claim that agreement will be at least as regular with respect to the Animacy Hierarchy as is number marking, some tentative claims can be made here, putting down markers for topics to be covered later in the book. First, the claim will prove relevant to the question of minor number in languages like Maltese (§4.2). These have additional number marking for a small number of nouns, which can be seen as the mirror image of English *sheep*. There could not be a language (otherwise like Maltese) in which instead the verb had special number agreement forms for a small number of nouns. Second, inverse number systems (as in Kiowa, §5.5) can have inverse for number marking on the noun, which in a three-number system gives an otherwise unattested system, and non-inverse for agreement on the verb. The reverse system cannot exist. And third, when there are constructed numbers (§5.7), then the system of noun marking can give an otherwise 'illegal system', but the system of agreement will always be an otherwise attested system.

Two points deserve highlighting here. First that conformity to the Animacy Hierarchy may vary according to the criterion. Number marking on the noun may allow various types of exception (as in English) where agreement conforms to the hierarchy. The second point is that descriptions often tell just part of the story: sometimes there is careful description of part of the system (say the number markers on nouns) while another part is almost ignored. For many languages there is a good deal to be done to find out how they really indicate number.

3.4 Optionality

We find cases where some nominals *must* be involved in the number system, while the others cannot be, but we also find cases when some nominals *may* be involved and the others cannot. For example, various Oceanic languages use personal pronouns as determiners within the noun phrase. According to Andrew Pawley (1977 and personal communication), they are more likely to mark plurality for noun phrases referring to humans than for non-humans, and for animates rather than inanimates.[10] There are examples of optional marking from different parts of the world: in Comanche, a Uto-Aztecan language with a small number of speakers in Oklahoma (Charney 1993: 49–52), there is dual and plural marking which is obligatory when humans are involved, optional for animates, and seldom found with inanimates; in Kannada, as noted earlier, number marking is obligatory down to nouns denoting humans, and for those denoting non-humans it is optional (Sridhar 1990: 197, 205, 244); finally, in Bengali, according to Masica (1991: 225–6), number is obligatory for pronouns; plural suffixes on other items are optional.[11]

We can see that the Animacy Hierarchy operates like similar typological hierarchies (such as the Agreement Hierarchy discussed in §6.2) in that the condition should be stated as a monotonic decrease in the likelihood of a particular outcome, in this instance that of number being distinguished. This is a more general formulation which includes the effect of constraint (I) above:

> III *General constraint of the Animacy Hierarchy on number differentiation*
> As we move rightwards along the Animacy Hierarchy, the likelihood of number being distinguished will decrease monotonically (that is, with no intervening increase).

This formulation holds equally well for two different situations: first, languages where there is a sharp cut-off between cases where number must be distinguished and those where it cannot; and second, languages where the difference is a matter of optional marking as opposed to no marking. The direction is never reversed: that is, we never find languages for which number *may* be distinguished at a high point on the hierarchy and *must* be distinguished lower down (for the same type of marking).

Having established that degrees of optionality are relevant to the Animacy Hierarchy, we can make progress on two outstanding issues: the first is the question

---

[10] Specifically for Kilenge, Kabana, Lusi and Kove (West Oceanic languages of New Britain) see Goulden (1996: 115).

[11] Lucy investigates Yucatec (a Mayan language with 350,000 speakers in south-eastern Mexico) in which number is optionally marked for relatively few (primarily animate) nouns (1992a: 43–61). He uses the contrast in number marking as compared with English for a psycholinguistic investigation of the question of linguistic relativity. This is a topic which he also discusses elsewhere (Lucy 1992b: 50–9); for further discussion see Mufwene (1995).

of different splits according to different criteria, and the second is the place of general number.

Consider first the interesting case of the Austronesian language Muna (a member of the Western Malayo-Polynesian branch), spoken on Muna, an island off the southeast coast of Sulawesi, Indonesia (van den Berg 1989: 51–2). Here we should look at verb agreement. Plural pronouns and plural nouns denoting humans take plural agreement:

(21) ihintu-umu o-kala-amu
      2–PL   2–go-PL
      'you go'

Nouns denoting inanimates, even when carrying a plural marker (as in (22)), take singular agreement:

(22) bara-hi-no   no-hali
      good-PL-his   3.SG.REALIS-expensive
      'his goods are expensive'

That leaves non-human animates, and it is these that show optionality. They may take a singular or a plural verb:

(23) o   kadadi-hi   no-rato-mo/do-rato-mo
      ART   animal-PL   3.SG.REALIS-arrive-PF/3.PL.REALIS-arrive-
                                                          PERFV
      'the animals have arrived'

In Muna, the data available suggest that noun marking and agreement are in accord with the Animacy Hierarchy; however, the cut-off point for agreement is higher than that for marking on the noun.[12]

---

[12] Compare this with the situation found in Ngalakan (Merlan 1983), a language of the Gunwinjguan group, which had around twenty-five speakers in the late 1970's, at Bulman and Ngukurr in Arnhem Land, Australia. Here too, marking of number on the verb is sensitive to position on the hierarchy:

> 'in Ngalakan explicit non-singular marking on the noun is limited; nouns not explicitly marked as non-singular can be cross-referenced as non-singular, but this possibility is limited almost entirely to human and sometimes animate nouns. Non-singular reference of inanimate NPs is generally not explicitly marked in the verb, and is largely to be understood from the larger context of discourse.'(Merlan 1983: 90)

In Ngalakan marking on the verb extends further down the hierarchy than marking on the noun, which is the converse of the Muna situation. Note however that this depends on how the verbal affixes are to be interpreted. If they are treated as the arguments of the verb in this language, then we can say that number is differentiated best for pronouns, which is entirely as expected.

Table 3.5 *The demonstrative*
'this' in Miya

	singular	plural
masculine	nákən	níykin
feminine	tákən	

An extremely interesting and rather surprising instance of a number split is found in the West Chadic language, Miya (Schuh 1989, 1998: 193n6, 197–8, 243–4)[13], since the split involves optional number marking, and obligatory versus excluded agreement.[14] Nouns are of two genders, masculine and feminine; males are masculine, females feminine, and non-sex differentiables can be of either gender. Agreement targets (and many different items agree) have three agreement forms: masculine singular, feminine singular and plural. This may be illustrated by one of the demonstrative pronouns, as shown in table 3.5. In addition there is a distinction according to the Animacy Hierarchy: the nouns above the split are those which denote 'humans, most (if not all) domestic animals and fowls, and larger wild animals' (Schuh 1998: 197). The remaining nouns form the second group. The higher group nouns must be marked for plurality where appropriate:

(24) təvam   tsə́r   cf.:   *'ám   tsər
      woman.PL   two   woman.SG   two
      'two women'   *'two women'

For the lower group, the inanimates, on the other hand, marking is optional:

(25) zəkiyáyàw   vaatlə   cf.:   zəkiy   vaatlə
      stone.PL   five   stone.SG   five
      'five stones'   'five stones'

The higher group, when plural, take plural agreements:

(26) níykin   dzáfə   níykin   təmakwìy
      this.PL man.PL   this.PL sheep.PL
      'these men'   'these sheep'

---

[13] The basic analysis was given in Schuh (1989); the presentation of forms is slightly different in Schuh (1998) and we follow the more recent version here.

[14] Number is involved in agreement and hence is relevant to syntax. By almost any definition the language has inflectional number. And yet, as we shall see, number is an optional category for inanimate nouns. For discussion with regard to the inflectional/derivational problem see Corbett (1999), and on this compare Beard (1982), van Marle (1996) and Baayen, Lieber and Schreuder (1997).

The others, however, even if they are marked as plural, do not take plural agreement; they take agreement according to their gender in the singular:

(27) nákən   víyayúwawàw
     this.SG.MASC fireplace.PL (*vìyayúw* 'fireplace' is masculine)
     'these fireplaces'

(28) tákən   tlərkáyayàw
     this.SG.FEM   calabash.PL (*tlə́rkáy* 'calabash' is feminine)
     'these calabashes'

Thus there is a clear split. Marking of number is obligatory for humans and some animates but optional for the remainder. Agreement in number with the higher group of nouns is obligatory, but plural agreement with the lower group is impossible. And, most interestingly, agreement with such nouns does occur, but in gender and not in number. This shows that there is an agreement rule for these lower nouns where we might have expected to find number agreement, but where the latter fails to occur. In Miya, then, agreement in number and number marking differ, with number marking being possible lower down the hierarchy than is agreement in number (see table 3.6). We see that for the relevant part of the hierarchy

Table 3.6 *Number marking and agreement in Miya*

		animate		
hierarchy position	human	higher	lower	inanimate
number marking	obligatory	obligatory	optional	optional
number agreement	obligatory	obligatory	excluded	excluded

there is a split within the animate position, and that number marking and number agreement behave differently. This is the converse of Muna, where plural marking extended further down the hierarchy than did agreement. These instances where there is an obligatory use of number at one point on the hierarchy and optional use at a lower point can be seen as cases where there are somewhat different systems at different points on the hierarchy. There are examples where there are more dramatically different number systems at different points on the hierarchy: the number values available may differ according to the point on the hierarchy. We shall consider such cases in the next chapter (§4.5).

The second issue on which we can now make progress is how languages with general number fit into the overall typology. Consider again languages like Japanese (§2.1) which have general number and singular on the one hand, identical in form, as opposed to the plural on the other. This means that the plural can be used 'when it matters', to mark clear plurality, while the other form may indicate either that the noun is singular or that number is not important. This is a type of optional marking. In chapter 2 we examined whichever type of nominal provided the greatest choice of number values for a given language: when we looked for general number, the type of nominal was usually a sort of noun.[15] Though often the descriptions are not as explicit as we might hope, we normally find a split in these languages (sometimes quite high on the hierarchy) above which number is distinguished, and below which there is a system of the type general/singular versus plural. Thus in Japanese 'the grammatical number of a noun is not normally made explicit' (Sugamoto 1989: 276) 'but the pronouns have lexicalized grammatical number' (see also Martin 1975: 143–54; Xolodovič 1979; Ikari 1989; Downing 1996: 200–9). Downing (1996: 205) gives a summary table, shown here as table 3.7, of the effect of referent type and noun phrase type on the use of plural markers. This table shows the factors which influence the choice between marking plurality or not marking it; the Animacy Hierarchy is clearly a major influence but not the only one (and Japanese provides good evidence for splitting pronouns from other nominals).

Table 3.7 *The use of plural markers in Japanese*

	referent type:	human	other animate	inanimate
	pronoun	required	required	required
NP head type	proper noun	required	rare	impossible
	common noun	possible	rare	impossible

We noted in §2.1 that general/singular versus plural is a widespread system in Iranian languages, but not for nouns denoting humans, which have singular versus plural (Smirnova 1981). The Northern Mande language Vai has a similar system (Welmers 1976: 45–6). A further example is the Cushitic language Qafar (Dick Hayward, personal communication); the personal pronouns are restricted to use for humans, there is a singular–plural opposition and it is obligatory. For nouns denoting humans too, the plural is used for referring to more than one. But for other animates and nouns lower on the Animacy Hierarchy, the plural is optional; in other words there is a general/singular versus plural system. In these languages, then, there is a singular–plural system operating for some top segment of the Animacy Hierarchy (not the same segment in every case), and a general/singular versus plural system operating for some lower part of the hierarchy, that is,

---

[15] But recall the discussion of Asheninca (§2.1 n9), where pronouns also have general/singular versus plural.

number is an obligatory category higher on the hierarchy and an optional category at a lower point.

Thus once optionality is taken into account, we have examples which show that the possibilities for marking on the noun and for agreement may be different. We have also seen how languages with general number fit into the general typology.[16] For them, the optionality produced by general number occurs at positions lower on the hierarchy than those for which number marking is obligatory. In this they follow the wider regularity that obligatory marking of a particular number value (plural in the cases discussed) will be found higher on the hierarchy than optional marking.

3.5 Morphological effects

The hierarchy helps us understand further patterns in number marking. These are not exceptionless, but they are often found.

Consider first the different means used to mark number (the possibilities will be dealt with in more detail in chapter 5). Suppose a language marks the plural in different ways for the same syntactic position. For instance, within the noun phrase number may be marked partly morphologically and partly by means of number words. Then, we claim, the morphological means, direct marking of the noun or pronoun, will occur for the items higher on the hierarchy. For instance, in Taiap (a language whose affiliation is still open to debate, spoken in the 1980s by eighty-nine speakers in the village of Gapun, between the Sepik and Ramu rivers in Papua New Guinea; Kulick and Stroud 1992), pronouns have distinct singular and plural forms, and a few nouns denoting kin and other humans have special plural morphology; for all other nouns the marking within the noun phrase relies on various plural words. Thus morphological marking occurs at the top of the hierarchy while the use of number words is found lower down.

Next let us take languages where the system of number marking is a morphological one, but there is irregularity within it. Smith-Stark suggests that we are likely to find irregularity precisely with the items high on the hierarchy. To a degree this is quite true. In English, the personal pronouns are at the extreme of irregularity,

---

[16] We are concerned with whether or not number is *available* to nominals of particular types, considering obligatory versus optional versus excluded. A further set of research questions concerns the *use* of number for different types of nominals which are the same in terms of availability. Thus if there are different types of nominal in a language for which number is optional, we might ask whether the Animacy Hierarchy would have any further effect. In Nigerian Pidgin English, according to Tagliamonte, Poplack and Eze (1997), number marking on nouns is optional; however, a major factor in the choice is the type of noun: those denoting humans are considerably more likely to mark number than those denoting non-humans; this is an effect of the Animacy Hierarchy, which goes beyond the original claims. It is interesting that the majority of the speakers investigated had Igbo as their first language (see §3.2.4.1) and Tagliamonte et al. suggest that this is significant (see also §9.1.1, n5).

since they show suppletion. Other irregular nouns, as Smith-Stark points out, include nouns denoting humans (*man/men, woman/women, person/people, child/children*), other animates (*mouse/mice, louse/lice, ox/oxen*) but also inanimates like *foot/feet, tooth/teeth*. As we shall see (§5.3.6) there are interesting frequency effects here. These help to explain why we find greater irregularity at the top of the hierarchy (though this pattern may be distorted by other factors). One explanation lies in the development of number systems: if only some nominals have number it will be those at the top of the hierarchy; if lower nominals then develop number this will be a later development, and so they will simply have had a shorter period in which to develop irregularities. In addition, it is well known that more frequent items preserve irregularities which are regularized elsewhere, and some of the items listed above (particularly the pronouns) are extremely frequent. But there is a more subtle effect: items which occur more frequently in the plural than in the singular are more likely to be irregular in the plural (which helps to explain several of the English cases; see §5.3.6n24, and for Russian data for comparison see §9.3.3). English also has many borrowings with exceptional plural morphology, such as *criterion/criteria*; Smith-Stark ignores these and they clearly come lower on the hierarchy than many regular nouns.

A nice example of a regular–irregular split in accord with the hierarchy is found in Turkish, where the third person pronoun has regular plural morphology, like the majority of nouns, but the first and second person pronouns are irregular (Kornfilt 1997: 281); Moravcsik suggests that if just one of the personal pronouns forms its plural inflectionally it must be the third person (Moravcsik in forthcoming §3.1.6). It is certainly common to find irregular personal pronouns, however regular or irregular the morphology of nouns. We should not assume, however, that personal pronouns are always suppletive or otherwise irregular. They can be regular (Myrkin 1964: 79–80). Mandarin Chinese is a good example (Chappell 1996: 470–1; see also Iljic 1994 for a different account of *-men*, he considers it a collective marker): the pronouns include those given in table 3.8. Chappell points out that *-men* is spreading to nouns, those for occupations and professions, not for inanimates: *xuésheng* 'student', *xuéshengmen* 'students', *lǎoshī* 'teacher', *lǎoshīmen*

Table 3.8 *Pronouns of Mandarin Chinese (Chappell 1996: 471)*

	singular	plural
1st person	wǒ	wǒmen (exclusive)
2nd person	nǐ	nǐmen
3rd person	tā	tāmen

'teachers'. Similarly, in Sierra Popoluca, a Mixe-Zoque language of southern Mexico, the plural pronouns have regular plural markers (Elson 1960: 219). Another good example is Miskitu, a Misumalpan language of Nicaragua and Honduras, where pronouns mark person and plurality is supplied by a plural word (T. Green 1992); see §5.1. Pronominal prefixes may show similar regularity, as the data in table 3.9 from Barbareño Chumash, a language of California, show (Marianne Mithun, personal communication; note that the initial *š* in the third dual is the result of regular sibilant harmony).

Table 3.9 *Pronominal prefixes of Barbareño Chumash*

	singular	dual	plural
1st person	k-	kiš-	kiy-
2nd person	p-	piš-	piy-
3rd person	s-	šiš-	siy-

Thus, contrary to what most linguists expect, pronominal forms can be fully regular;[17] this has implications for the discussion of the meaning of plural pronouns (§3.7.1 below). However, they are frequently irregular, and this fits with the trend (no more than that) for number marking to be less regular for items higher on the hierarchy than for those lower down (for further examples see Stebbins 1997: 35–7).

We should now consider the case where there are simply different morphological forms available. We find variations on this theme in the Uto-Aztecan family. We shall look at Eastern Huasteca Nahuatl, a Uto-Aztecan language spoken in Hidalgo, northern Veracruz and northern Puebla (other dialects of Nahuatl differ in their number system). In this dialect, nouns denoting humans and animates form the plural in *-meh*, inanimates in *-tinih* (both with various adjustments). Nouns denoting abstracts and masses of objects (both within the inanimate category) do not form a plural, for instance *eλ* 'beans', *miak esλi* 'much blood', *miak λamanλi* 'many things', none of which has a plural marker (the *λi* is the absolutive marker). Table 3.10 shows that the different types of plural marking are distributed according to the hierarchy. A related language, Pipil, shows a more complex system, again with different markers distributed at least in part according to the noun's position on the hierarchy (Campbell 1985: 51–4). For the parent language of both, Proto-Uto-Aztecan, Hill and Hill (1996) reconstruct a system in which

---

[17] Another language with regular forms of pronouns is Golin, a Chimbu language of Papua New Guinea (Bunn 1974: 55; Foley 1986: 70).

Table 3.10 *Plural forms in Eastern Huasteca Nahuatl
(Kimball 1990: 200)*

	singular	plural	gloss
human and animate	siwa·ƛ	siwa·meh	woman/women
	a·škanelih	a·škanelimeh	ant/ants
inanimate	šo·čiƛ	šo·čitinih	flower/flowers
	ša·loh	ša·lohtinih	jar/jars

nouns denoting humans used reduplication to form the plural, those denoting
non-human animates had a suffixed plural, while inanimates had no plural. (For
the complex situation in another Uto-Aztecan language, Tohono O'odham, see
Hill and Zepeda 1998.) As a further example, from the other side of the world,
Drossard (1982: 166–9) shows how in Nakh-Daghestanian languages the different
plural markers including the oblique plural markers are distributed at least in part
according to the hierarchy (the complexity of these markers is introduced in
§5.3.3). While there are such cases of the different morphological markers being
distributed according to the hierarchy, this often does not occur. Thus in many
Indo-European languages we find declensional classes including nouns from
different parts of the hierarchy.

Before leaving morphology, it is worth asking about the nouns at the bottom
of the hierarchy, those which do not distinguish number. If a noun has only one
form, which will it be? English typically uses a form like the singular (as in
friendliness), but this is not always the case, either in English or cross-linguistically (English has words like *oats, outskirts*). We shall consider this further in
chapter 5, since that chapter is about the expression of number, and we shall
look there at larger systems, rather than concentrating on the singular–plural
opposition.

3.6 Count and mass

We now turn from the morphological to the semantic effects of the Animacy
Hierarchy, and to do that we need to consider the count–mass distinction. This is a
complex problem, on which there is a substantial literature;[18] for our purposes only

---

[18] There are some fine observations in McCawley (1975); a tradition maintained in Mel´čuk
(1979) on Russian, and Mufwene (1980, 1981, 1984). See Langacker (1991: 76–81) for discussion within the Cognitive Grammar framework.

    Philosophers have long been concerned about the count–mass distinction; a convenient
way in to the literature is the volume edited by Pelletier (1979) which has an introduction,
eighteen other papers and a bibliography. It is notable that only English is discussed. A
survey of work in formal semantics can be found in Krifka (1991); see also Bunt (1985)

the essentials are required. The difficulties with the concept have arisen in large part through the mixing of linguistic levels.

The distinction is clearly relevant in **semantics** (here we shall take ideas from Jackendoff 1991, though some of them can be found in several places in the extensive literature). Consider these examples:

(29)   There was water all over the floor

(30)   ??There was a book all over the floor

The sorts of noun phrase which are felicitous in the context of (29), like *water*, are termed 'mass', and those which are infelicitous, like *a book*, are 'count' or 'countable'. Clearly the latter are amenable to counting, hence the term. There is a conceptual distinction here. If we take the referent of *a book* or *a car* and divide it, what remains is no longer a book or a car. However, if we take *water*, and divide its referent, we are still left with water. Thus *a book* may be said to be 'bounded', while *water* is not (this does not entail that it has no boundaries at all, rather that they are not in view or not of interest). If we now consider a bare plural in the same semantic environment, there is an interesting effect:

(31)   There were books all over the floor

Here the plural noun phrase patterns with the mass noun phrase; we may treat the referent of *books* as unbounded, but we wish to distinguish it from the referents of mass noun phrases. The point is that the referent of *books* comprises distinguishable individuals, while that of *water* does not. Jackendoff uses a feature 'internal structure' to distinguish the two cases (again having no internal structure is a matter of human conceptualization, not a matter of physics). These two features give rise to four possibilities, as shown in table 3.11. This approach distinguishes count from mass, while drawing the parallel between mass and bare plurals (both are treated as −bounded); it brings out the special position of *committee* and similar examples (discussed in §6.2), and it makes a link to verbal semantics (Jackendoff follows the tradition of treating the distinction between count and

and Higginbotham (1995); a recent paper which includes cross-linguistic evidence is Chierchia (1998b). A psycholinguistic approach can be found in the work of Prasada (1996). Children's acquisition of the count–mass distinction has been investigated by Gathercole (1985, 1986; the second paper gives a helpful account of different approaches to the count–mass distinction, and uses acquisition data to evaluate them), Gordon (1985a, 1988), Levy (1988) and Soja, Carey and Spelke (1991). Markman (1985, 1989: 168–74) is also concerned with children's acquisition of the distinction and suggests a link between superordinate categories and mass terms, but Takatori and Schwanenflugel (1992) claim this is less clear when a sufficient cross-linguistic sample is considered. Whorfian speculations on the difference between mass and count in English and Chinese are given in Scollon and Scollon (1991).

Table 3.11 *Semantic categories of noun phrase (based on Jackendoff 1991)*

feature values	category	examples
+ bounded, − internal structure	individuals	*a book, a pig*
+ bounded, + internal structure	groups	*a committee*
− bounded, − internal structure	substances	*water*
− bounded, + internal structure	aggregates	*books, pigs*

mass in the object system as parallel to temporally bounded and temporally unbounded in the event system).[19]

While semanticists have written at length about count and mass, there has been relatively little on whether the conceptualization of the distinction might vary from language to language. There is tantalizing evidence of linguistic differences even between relatively closely related languages, but less on whether these differences reflect conceptual differences. Thus there has been interesting work on the treatment of fruit and vegetables in Slavonic. Simplifying a little, we may say that Russian *kartofel'* 'potatoes', *vinograd* 'grapes', *kljukva* 'cranberries', *gorox* 'peas', *izjum* 'raisins', and many more like them, do not distinguish singular and plural (in some cases there are derived forms which do). On the other hand, *frukt* 'fruit' has singular and plural forms. Russian then sets the boundary for number-differentiability somewhat higher than English, and indeed a little higher than some other Slavonic languages. (For the interesting detail, see Mel'čuk 1979, 1985: 257–64; Ivić 1982; Polivanova 1983; Jarvis 1986; Wierzbicka 1988: 503–6.) In Jackendoff's terms, the question is how large the component parts of a substance have to be before they are treated as individuals (for speakers of English a pea is large enough, but not for a speaker of Russian). However, whether this has any conceptual reflection is yet to be established. Within Germanic too there are interesting differences; see Behrens (1995) for comparisons between English and German (and also Hungarian);[20] for a survey of usage in Daghestanian languages see Kibrik (1992, forthcoming).

---

[19] For further discussion of the parallel 'count : mass :: perfective : imperfective' see, for instance, Langacker (1987), Brinton (1991), Herweg (1991), Mehlig (1996) and references there; Rijkhoff (1992: 75–104) goes as far as treating count and mass as part of what he calls 'nominal aspect'.

[20] We have considered the question of whether items like peas count as separate entities or not. There is a more restricted but still intriguing question as to when items like ears or boots are one item or two. Are we dealing with the hearing organ or two ears, footwear or two shoes? In several Uralic languages nouns denoting paired body parts have unusual behaviour. For instance in Hungarian (Edith Moravcsik, personal communications):

The final relevant point on the semantics of the count–mass distinction concerns 'recategorization':[21]

(32)   I'd like a coffee please

Here something usually treated as unbounded (mass) is treated as bounded (count). The converse is found in the unfortunate:

(33)   There was dog all over the road[22]

As we shall see in §3.7.2, these recategorizations are better understood in the light of the Animacy Hierarchy. The importance of recategorization is emphasized by Allan in a significant paper on the count–mass distinction in **syntax**. He shows how in English a very substantial portion of the noun inventory can be used in count and mass contexts (1980: 546–7):

(34)   Hetty likes to gorge herself on cake.

(35)   Whenever Hetty gobbles down a cake, her diet 'starts tomorrow'.

(36)   Small farmers in Kenya grow corn rather than wheat.

> (i)   Fáj   a   fül-em.
>   hurts   DEF   ear-1.SG.POSS
>   'My ear hurts.'
>
> This could be used for one ear, or for both ears. To specify one ear one could say:
>
> (ii) Fáj   az   egyik   fül-em.
>   hurts DEF   one.of.them   ear-1.SG.POSS
>   'One of my ears hurts.'
>
> The following would also normally be used of one ear:
>
> (iii) Fáj   a   fél-fül-em.
>   hurts DEF   half-ear-1.SG.POSS
>   'One of my ears hurts.'
>
> For further information on this usage in Uralic see Bergsland (1956) and Honti (1995). The phenomenon is not restricted to Uralic however. It is found in the Tungusic language Udihe (Nikolaeva 1999: 69). Farrell (1996) gives examples from Brazilian Portuguese, like *sapato* (singular) 'pair of shoes'; he also provides instances of *chave* 'key', used for 'set of keys' and *dente* 'tooth' used for 'teeth', showing that the phenomenon is not restricted to pairs. Cowell (1964: 371) gives a nice opposition in Syrian Arabic, where '(pair of) shoes' is singular but '(pair of) gloves' is plural. Finally, though almost all the examples are for inanimates, in Dutch a mother can say: *Ik heb een tweeling* literally 'I have a two-ling (SG)', that is 'I have twins' (Melissa Bowerman, personal communication).
>
> [21] There are various terms: Lyons (1968: 282) talks of 'secondary recategorization', while Quirk et al. (1985: 248) use 'reclassification'.
>
> [22] (32) is sometimes said to result from the operation of the 'universal packager' and (33) from the 'universal grinder'; it appears that the terms are due ultimately to Victor Yngve (Jackendoff 1991: 24n11).

(37)   *Triticum aestivum ssp. vulgare* is a wheat suitable for high altitudes.

(38)   There's not enough table for everyone to sit at.

(39)   We need a bigger table.

He claims, therefore, that the traditional view labelling nouns as count or mass in the lexicon is inadequate; the distinction should be one relating to noun phrases rather than to nouns. In other words, it is substantially a matter of syntax. In English, this will concern determiners, articles and quantifiers in particular.[23] Of course, it is not the case that all nouns occur equally frequently in all environments, and so we come to the third linguistic level involved, that of the **lexicon**: 'Even though countability is characteristic of NP's, not of nouns, it is nonetheless a fact that nouns do show countability preference – insofar as some nouns more often occur in countable NP's, others in uncountable NP's, and still others seem to occur quite freely in both' (Allan 1980: 566). When the full set of environments is considered, Allan distinguishes not simply count from mass, but eight different grades between these two extremes, which may be represented by these typical nouns (1980: 562), running from 'most count' to 'least count':

car, oak, cattle, scissors, mankind, admiration, equipment, Himalayas

The tests are in part, of course, specific to English, but there is evidence that a binary count–mass distinction is in general a simplification.

At what level then does the Animacy Hierarchy apply? When earlier we used the test of marking on the noun (morphology), this relates to the lexical level. We might have expected a very disparate picture here, but as we saw, despite the idiosyncrasies[24] there are considerable regularities at this level (that is, the countability preferences of nouns are partially constrained by the Animacy Hierarchy). When we used agreement as the test, this still involves the features of the specific lexical item, but in relation to syntax, where we find greater regularity (but not necessarily full regularity). And more generally, as our tests move away from the lexical level and closer to semantics so we may expect greater regularity. An important point to retain is that the terms 'count' and 'mass' are useful, but we need to be clear about the level to which we are applying them.

---

[23] For discussion of the count–mass distinction in further languages see Gil (1987), Hao (1988) and Löbel (1993, 2000).

[24] These are indeed considerable: Plungjan (1997) shows that the relations between Russian *vremja* 'time' and its plural *vremena* deserve an article to themselves (the plural is possible only in certain uses) and Plungjan and Raxilina (1995) investigate how number depends on the semantics of the noun. Another set of surprises is revealed by Rogers (1997) who shows that English and German nouns which are apparent translation equivalents have very different distributions in their use of singular and plural.

3.7 Semantic effects

Number values, such as 'plural', may take subtly different meanings in different contexts: the singular–plural distinction is somewhat different in *cat ~ cats, wine ~ wines* and *I ~ we*. These meanings are determined by a range of factors: since the place of the head (pro)noun on the Animacy Hierarchy is one of them, this is an appropriate point to tackle the problem. First we should separate out 'special' or 'affective' uses. Consider this utterance by an irate father, who knows that exactly one of his children has exactly one motorbike:

(40)   Who's been mending motorbikes in the kitchen?

This use of the plural (the intensificative) is one of the several types of use where the noun has a normal number marker, regularly used with a standard interpretation, which is 'pressed into' use for other, usually emotive, purposes. These special uses are easier to isolate in languages with more than a simple singular–plural opposition, in that for a given use there is normally only one number value available, usually the plural (thus in a language with a dual one cannot complain about *motorbike-DUAL* in sentences like (40) above). Such special uses will be considered in chapter 7. The meanings to be discussed in this section, on the other hand, are more general and are typically available for all number values. We shall consider the different uses in the order of the positions on the Animacy Hierarchy which are most often affected.

3.7.1   Pronouns and associative meaning

It is often suggested that the use of number with pronouns, especially the first person, requires special treatment. For example:[25]

> Traditional terminology is rather misleading in the way in which it
> represents the combination of the categories of person and *number*. It
> is clear, for instance, that *we* ('first person plural') does not normally
> stand in the same relationship to *I* ('first person singular') as *boys,
> cows*, etc., do to *boy, cow*, etc. The pronoun *we* is to be interpreted as
> 'I, in addition to one or more other persons'; and the other persons
> may or may not include the hearer. In other words, *we* is not 'the
> plural of *I*': rather, it includes a reference to 'I' and is plural. (Lyons
> 1968: 277)

It is certainly the case that *we* is generally used with the meaning of an associative plural ('I and associate(s)'), but it can also be used as an ordinary plural, when

---

[25] For other discussions of pronouns see Mühlhäusler and Harré (1990) and Goddard (1995).

people in chorus say *we pray, we solemnly swear*, and so on. With the second person, the uses are more balanced, in that *you* (plural) can be used to multiple addressees or to one addressee (involving also his or her associate(s)). A coach may say *I hope you win* to an entire team, and equally the mother of one player might say the same to her child (meaning 'you and your associates/fellow team members'). This associative use is not restricted to pronouns, however. As we shall see, there are numerous instances of its use with nouns. At first sight these are problematic for our account of the Animacy Hierarchy, as will be discussed in §4.3. For present purposes the important point is that associative meaning is not restricted to pronouns. However, it is found precisely at the top of the hierarchy, being extremely likely with the first person, less so with the second, and possible in different languages down to varying points in the human category[26] (there are also special associative forms and the interesting question of where they occur is tackled in §4.3.3). Thus the associative meaning is in competition with the 'ordinary numbers', and is prevalent at the top of the Animacy Hierarchy. Finally the argument that the first person does not really have a plural is sometimes bolstered by appeal to form; frequently pronouns have suppletive forms and it is claimed that pairs like *I* and *we* are not really pairs at all. However, we saw in §3.5 that there are languages in which the plurals of the pronouns are formed by regular means. We conclude that associative and ordinary plural readings are both available for the upper part of the Animacy Hierarchy, with associative reading gaining in likelihood towards the top of the hierarchy.

3.7.2   Recategorization effects

In §3.6 we saw how noun phrases headed by nouns which we expect in typically mass environments may occur in count environments (*I'd like three coffees, please*) and vice versa (*There was dog all over the road*). We should consider these effects here for two reasons: first they might appear to be counter-examples to the requirements of the Animacy Hierarchy, and second, they actually are congruent with it in a way which is often ignored.

Consider first why these might be considered counter-examples. Instances like *three coffees* are sometimes referred to as cases of 'unit plural'. Such plurals are found largely with inanimate nouns. If the unit plural were analysed as an additional number value at this point on the hierarchy this would be problematic,

---

[26] As we shall see in §4.3.1 associative use may be found with proper nouns, a category which is not distinguished on the hierarchy. Proper nouns can have ordinary plurals (*there are three Karens in the class*). They can also be used in the plural either for members of the class typified by the name-bearer (*three Jeremiahs* for three people prophesying gloom and doom, or for the products of the name-bearer, as in *three Monets*). While such examples catch the attention, it is important to note that there is nothing special about the plural here: the singular can be used in exactly the same way: *a Jeremiah, one Monet* (see Quirk et al. 1985: 1564; Honti 1997: 11).

because it does not occupy a top segment of the hierarchy. However, though we more easily notice the plural, what is really going on is recategorization from mass to count. Together with examples using the plural we find others like: *I'd like a coffee*, where the singular is used; this has a 'unit reading' and *coffees* is simply the plural of that. Thus 'unit plurals' are not a problematic number; rather they are instances of nouns which typically head mass noun phrases occurring instead in count noun phrases.[27] This reading, the '(conventional) unit' or 'portion' reading is commonly found (and as we shall see below it is available in the dual too in languages with a dual). It occurs typically with nouns which do not normally mark number (they are at a position on the hierarchy below the number split).

There is a closely related recategorization found with abstracts, the 'instance' reading, as seen in *a great injustice, a difficulty, small kindnesses, home truths* (Quirk et al. 1985: 1564). This reading is found with the items placed lowest on the Animacy Hierarchy. The other similar recategorization gives the 'sort' (sometimes 'type', 'kind', or 'variety') reading as in: *she offered three wonderful wines during dinner, he sells only three books, but they are all best-sellers.*[28] The last example

---

[27] There are some unusual effects to do with quantity, which deserve further study (see §7.2). In Syrian Arabic (Cowell 1964: 370) nouns denoting masses may take the plural for a batch or indefinite quantity: thus a milkman might bring milk (plural) but a waiter would bring milk (singular).

[28] Recategorizations typically take the expected number forms (that is, those of the 'normal' number forms if they are available or, for nouns which are otherwise outside the number opposition, the forms that would be expected by the normal processes. English *wines* 'sorts of wine' is the plural one would expect, and equally *dog* (as in *dog all over the road*) is the expected singular. For a rare case of a special mass form see §4.5.2. And David Gil (personal communication) points out that there can be special morphological forms for the plural instances too. In a very colloquial register of Modern Hebrew, for a small class of nouns of low countability preference denoting foodstuffs, there are two alternative plural forms. These vary systematically with regard to their meaning. The first plural, which is identical in form to the normative plural, is used for the sort reading, and the second, which is very restricted stylistically, is used for the portion reading. It differs formally by lacking an expected stress shift and any internal stem changes, as shown in the table.

Table i *Recategorizations in Colloquial Modern Hebrew* (David Gil, personal communication)

singular	plural (sort reading)	plural (portion reading)
sukár 'sugar'	*sukarím* 'kinds of sugar'	*sukárim* 'sachets of sugar'
rések 'puree'	*rsakím* 'kinds of puree'	*résekim* 'portions of puree'
yáyin 'wine'	*yeynót* 'kinds of wine'	*yáyinim* 'cups of wine'

Recategorization typically does not involve new morphology, but in these limited instances it does. For the complexity of number formation in Modern Hebrew more generally see Schwarzwald (1991).

shows that this reading is not restricted to nouns which normally occur in mass environments. Nevertheless it is the case that they are easiest with nouns low on the hierarchy, and as we move higher up the hierarchy, so we need more context to make the sort reading natural.

More generally, the lower the position on the hierarchy, the more readily available are recategorization readings (since the 'normal' singular–plural opposition is typically not required). As we move up the hierarchy, so recategorization becomes progressively more difficult, requiring more and more special circumstances. The same is true of the recategorization count to mass (*dog all over the road*), which also becomes more difficult the higher we go up the hierarchy.

Thus the different readings of singular and plural (and of other number values) vary in how likely they are according to the position on the hierarchy of the head nominal. At the very top, associative readings are more likely; in the middle of the hierarchy, normal number readings are most natural, and as we approach the bottom of the hierarchy so recategorizations become increasingly natural. The likely interpretation of a number form depends in part on the position of the head noun on the Animacy Hierarchy. The typical distribution of these different uses is given impressionistically for English in figure 3.3.

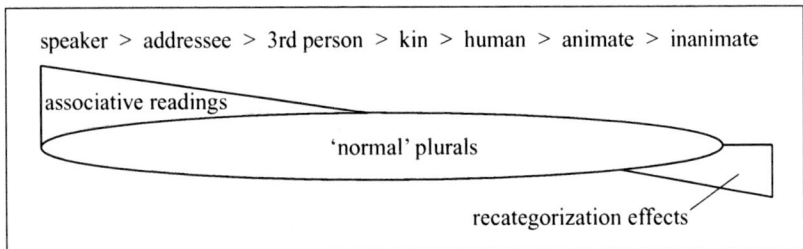

speaker > addressee > 3rd person > kin > human > animate > inanimate

associative readings

'normal' plurals

recategorization effects

Figure 3.3 *Different uses of the plural in English*

Before leaving recategorization, there are two final points of interest. It was stated that a diagnostic for distinguishing recategorization from special uses of number is that in languages with additional number values besides singular and plural these will typically be available for recategorization and not for special uses. We can illustrate this from Slovene, which has singular, dual and plural:[29]

(41) Sir-a,   ki   ste   nam   ju
      cheese-DUAL   REL   AUX   1.PL.DAT 3.ACC.DUAL

---

[29] The Slovene data are from Janez Orešnik and Milan Dolgan (personal communications). The *ju* is a resumptive clitic in the relative clause.

ponudil-i,	bomo	kupil-i
offer.PAST.PARTIC-PL	FUT.1.PL	buy-PL

'The two cheeses that you have offered to us, we will buy'

As in English, this can potentially have a sort reading (two types of cheese) or a unit reading (two units of cheese). The Slovene equivalent of (41), when an affective use is intended, may not have a dual (§7.3.2). Central Alaskan Yup'ik (to be discussed in more detail in §4.3.3) also has singular, dual and plural. Again, all numbers allow recategorization: for instance *uquq* (SG) 'oil', *uquk* (DUAL) 'two sealpokes or jars of oil', *uqut* (PL) 'three or more sealpokes or jars of oil'. Besides this unit reading, the sort reading is also available (Marianne Mithun and Elizabeth Ali, personal communication).

Once these different recategorizations are taken into account, we find that there are languages for which every or virtually every nominal has a singular–plural opposition, that is, the language has the opposition at all points on the Animacy Hierarchy. In Central Alaskan Yup'ik there are very few nouns which have singular forms only. One example is *meq* 'water' (while abstract nouns with meanings like 'happiness' are generally not used). Relatively few nouns are defective in terms of number in other ways (see §5.8.2 for further discussion). Or consider the Algonquian language Ojibway (Richard Rhodes 1990: 153–4, and personal communications). Nouns which might be expected not to have a plural do in fact form plurals freely, interestingly with the unit reading and not with the sort reading. Thus *mkwam* 'ice' or 'piece of ice', *mkwamiig* (plural) 'pieces of ice'. Rhodes is unable to find a noun that cannot be pluralized in Ojibway. (Note that there are few pure noun stems: most are analysable. Abstract nouns are rare; where we might expect to find one a relative clause is more likely to occur: not 'love' but 'their loving each other'.) And for Miya, which we discussed earlier, Schuh (1998: 199) states that: 'any noun in Miya has the potential of bearing plural morphology'. Nouns which normally occur in non-count contexts, if morphologically pluralized 'have the meaning of "many instances of/types of . . ."' These three illustrations from languages belonging to very different families and types show that languages can have a number opposition for (almost) all nominals.

3.8 Conclusion

In this chapter we kept the number values 'still', by concentrating on the singular–plural opposition, and looking at which nominals can be involved. We found languages in which very few nominals can distinguish number right through to those just discussed where all nominals have singular and plural. This variation is constrained by the Animacy Hierarchy. We saw how it constrains both the obligatory and the optional use of number and noted how different tests – marking on the noun as opposed to agreement – vary in their results in predictable ways. More generally, we saw how the hierarchy allowed us to investigate and understand the wide variation across languages which we encountered. In this way we were using one of the standard techniques of typology.

The effect of the Animacy Hierarchy has a theoretical consequence which is often ignored. It is widely assumed that number is an inflectional category. In that case, for many languages, it is necessary to say that it is so for some, but not all, nominals (while inflectional categories are usually assumed to be available for all candidate stems in a given language). The implication of the interaction of number with the Animacy Hierarchy is that the status of number as an inflectional category is less straightforward than generally imagined.

So far our discussion has been largely restricted to singular and plural. Other values of the number category add whole layers of complexity: it is not the case that, for example, in a singular–dual–plural system what is true for the plural will be true for the dual. They can vary independently. We shall face these additional complexities in the next chapter.

4
Integrating number values and the Animacy Hierarchy

In chapter 2 we investigated number values, finding up to five in certain languages. While we were trying to find all the possible systems, we looked at whichever type of nominal, whether pronoun or noun, was most promising in a given language. Then in chapter 3 we asked which nominals can be part of the number system, and to do so we concentrated on the basic singular–plural opposition. Ideally we would like to integrate these two dimensions of variation, to achieve a typology which predicts the possible patterns of values available at different points on the Animacy Hierarchy. With this goal, we begin with the strongest hypothesis: the Animacy Hierarchy constrains the distribution of all number values. We shall see that this claim needs some elaboration but that, perhaps surprisingly, it is basically true (§4.1). We examine potential counter-examples: minor numbers (§4.2), associatives (§4.3) and distributives and collectives (§4.4). Then we examine languages with different systems at different points on the hierarchy (§4.5).

The chapter illustrates an important approach in typology and the type of challenges which arise. Having established the basics, that is, the number values which languages may have and the patterns of values available for different nominals, we now combine those two elements to construct a complete typology. At several points we find that we 'run out' of languages: the critical combination of factors may be rare or non-existent (or has not yet been found). Here we have to balance the need to respect our data, with its variety and it limitations, and the desire to propose a typology which is adequate (covers the data), explicit, restrictive and falsifiable. Clearly if our typology does not cover the available data it is of little interest (similarly if it is not explicit enough for us to know exactly what it does cover). The opposite danger is that a typology can be so wide that it simply allows for any conceivable language. Given the dearth of information about some types of number system it is optimistic to hope that the typology presented here is right in all respects; however, it should be clear how it can be falsified, which will encourage others to find the crucial languages and so take the typology forward.

4.1 Extending the Animacy Hierarchy to other number values

Our main question is how the distribution of nominals is constrained in languages where number has more structure than a simple singular–plural opposition. A natural and quite restrictive suggestion is that each number choice is also subject to the Animacy Hierarchy. We repeat the hierarchy for convenience in figure 4.1. Just as the singular–plural choice is subject to the hierarchy, so we

---

speaker > addressee > 3rd person > kin > human > animate > inanimate

(1st person (2nd person
pronouns)   pronouns)

Figure 4.1 *The Animacy Hierarchy*

would expect a dual–plural division to be similarly constrained. That is to say, the nominals which have a dual must represent some top segment of the hierarchy. For instance, if nouns denoting humans have a dual, so will personal pronouns and nouns denoting kin. In a language with dual and plural we should ask whether the 'splits' which they induce will be the same. It is certainly the case that there are languages for which that is the case, languages in which a nominal which has a dual will also typically have a plural and vice versa. For instance, Mansi, Sanskrit and Slovene all have plurals for the majority of nominals, extending down to include many inanimates. And typically a noun with a plural will also have a dual. We may represent the Mansi (or Sanskrit) situation as in figure 4.2

---

                1 > 2 > 3 > kin > human > animate > inanimate

range of plural ■■■

range of dual   ■■

Figure 4.2 *Range of plural and dual in Mansi*

(we return to Slovene below). In this figure and similar ones the singular is taken as given, being implied by the opposition with the plural. For nouns at the bottom of the scale, those which are not number-differentiable, the form may be as that of the singular, or indeed as that of some other number value, as we shall see in §5.8.1. Figure 4.2 shows that in Mansi the range of the dual (the nominals which have the dual, plotted against the Animacy Hierarchy) is as that of the plural. We might expect that this would always be so, allowing for what we established clearly in the last chapter, namely that the range will vary substantially from language to language. However, this expected identity for dual and plural is not always found.

This is shown rather dramatically by Arapesh, which is spoken on the coast of Papua New Guinea between the villages of Dagur and Matapau. In Arapesh, pronouns and nouns typically distinguish singular and plural (Fortune 1942: 45). But just the first person pronoun has singular versus dual versus plural.[1] This is represented in figure 4.3. Arapesh then has different systems at different points on the

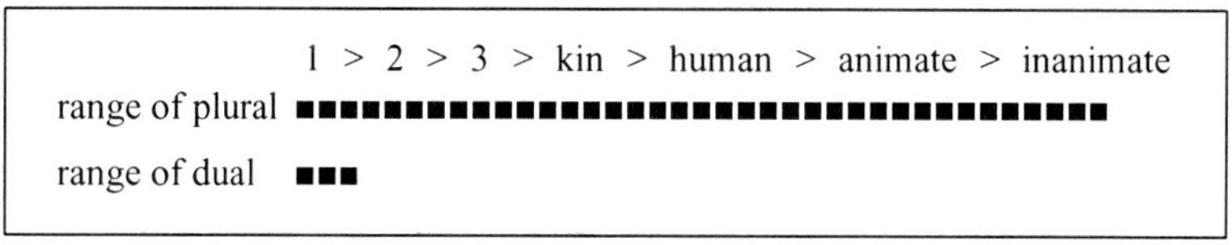

```
              1  >  2  >  3  >  kin  >  human  >  animate  >  inanimate
range of plural  ■■■■■■■■■■■■■■■■■■■■■■■■■■■■■■■■■■■■■■■■■■■■■■■■
range of dual    ■■■
```

Figure 4.3 *Range of plural and dual in Arapesh*

hierarchy. The range of the plural (i.e. of the singular–plural distinction) and the range of the dual (the plural–dual distinction) are very different. Another interesting case is Maori, where the pronouns show an obligatory distinction of singular, dual and plural. Just nine nouns, mainly denoting kin, show number (Bauer 1993: 368, 371; see also §3.2.3 above). These nouns have only a singular–plural split, as represented in figure 4.4. The difference in ranges is much less marked

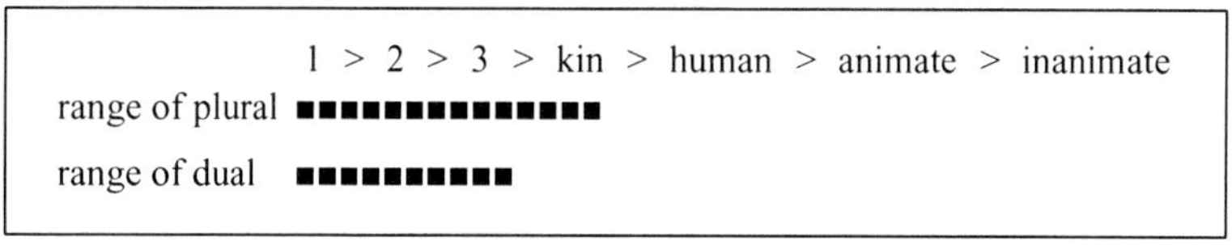

```
              1  >  2  >  3  >  kin  >  human  >  animate  >  inanimate
range of plural  ■■■■■■■■■■■■■■■
range of dual    ■■■■■■■■■■■
```

Figure 4.4 *Ranges of plural and dual in Maori*

than in Arapesh, but the basic pattern is the same. Though the ranges of plural and dual differ, in both languages the range of each number value involves a top segment of the Animacy Hierarchy (we established this requirement for the plural in chapter 3). This suggests how our findings from chapter 2 and chapter 3 fit together. As we shall see when we look at further examples, the basic patterns in figures 4.2 and 4.3 are the only possible ones (figure 4.4 is essentially like 4.3 in the important respect).

Let us abstract away from the exact range of plural and dual in these languages. We can then see that there are two possible patterns, which are allowed for by the following constraint:

---

[1] There is no inclusive–exclusive distinction to complicate matters here. Nivkh also has a dual just in the first person, and it does have an inclusive–exclusive distinction (Panfilov 1976).

I   *Constraint on ranges for different number values*
Given a language with more than one number opposition,

either: (a) the ranges of one number value and that of the next choice of
number value (according to the scheme in §2.3.2) are identical
(both involving a top segment of the Animacy Hierarchy);

or: (b) the lower choice of number value has a smaller range than the
higher choice (both involving a top segment of the Animacy
Hierarchy).

In our examples, the number value we measure from is the plural, and the lower
choice is the dual. Our constraints predict that there cannot be a language as represented in figure 4.5. In the hypothetical language shown there the lower choice
number value (the dual) has a greater range than the higher choice value (the
plural). This we claim is impossible.

```
                    1 > 2 > 3 > kin > human > animate > inanimate
range of plural  ■■■■■■■■■■
range of dual    ■■■■■■■■■■■■■■■■■■■■■■■■
```

Figure 4.5 *Impossible pattern of ranges of number values*

Let us look at more complex cases, starting with Yimas (William Foley 1986: 74,
86–7, 132–3; 1991: 216–25; and personal communications). As we noted in §2.2.4,
the personal pronouns have four numbers: singular, dual, paucal and plural. The
marking is complex. The important point here is that nouns are restricted to singular, dual and plural. These number values extend roughly to the same point as in
English, with a small number of interesting differences.[2] However, paucal marking
is found only on pronouns and/or pronominal affixes.[3] The Yimas picture is as in
figure 4.6. This is within the constraint (I); the first and second choice values have
the same range (as in clause (a)), but the third choice has a smaller range than the
second in Yimas (clause (b)).[4] All involve a top segment of the hierarchy. Now
compare the situation in Manam (introduced in §2.2.4), shown in figure 4.7. In

[2] Thus 'mosquito' is not countable, it appears only as a grammatical singular and one
cannot say 'three mosquitoes' for instance. Mosquitoes in that area tend to come in large
numbers. *Awt* 'fire' is also uncountable, but is grammatically plural (Foley 1991: 163–4).

[3] The paucal is restricted to humans. For quite separate reasons we do not find third person
paucal marking on the verb indicating the number of an overt noun phrase headed by a
noun.

[4] In the related Lower Sepik language Chambri the system is slightly different (William
Foley, personal communication). Here the paucal is preserved also on around half a dozen
nouns denoting kin and other humans, that is, it extends slightly further down the hierarchy than in Yimas.

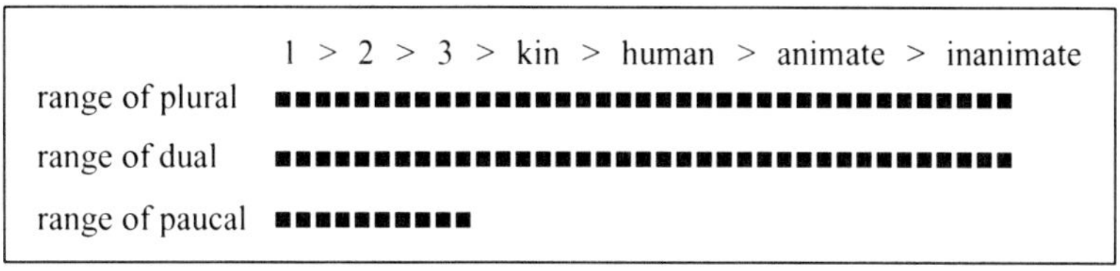

```
                1 > 2 > 3 > kin > human > animate > inanimate
range of plural ■■■■■■■■■■■■■■■■■■■■■■■■■■■■■■■■■■■■■■■■■■■
range of dual   ■■■■■■■■■■■■■■■■■■■■■■■■■■■■■■■■■■■■■■■■■■■
range of paucal ■■■■■■■■■■■
```

Figure 4.6 *Ranges of number values in Yimas*

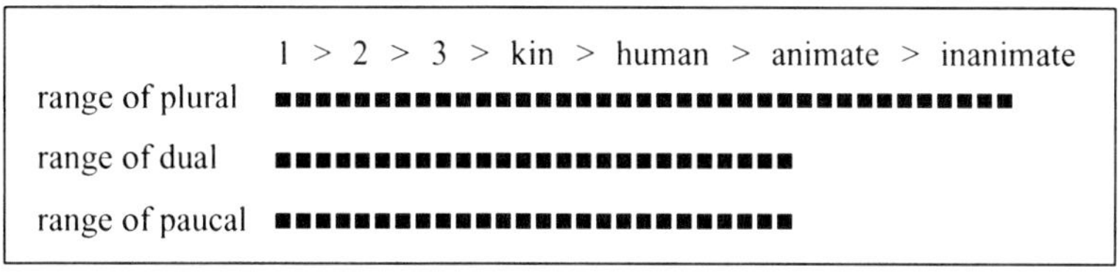

```
                1 > 2 > 3 > kin > human > animate > inanimate
range of plural ■■■■■■■■■■■■■■■■■■■■■■■■■■■■■■■■■■■■■■■■■■■
range of dual   ■■■■■■■■■■■■■■■■■■■■■■■■■■■■■■■■■
range of paucal ■■■■■■■■■■■■■■■■■■■■■■■■■■■■■■■
```

Figure 4.7 *Ranges of number values in Manam*

Manam (Lichtenberk 1983: 109–10) the dual and paucal are available only for humans and for 'higher animals': pigs, dogs, birds, and some other large animals recently introduced into Papua New Guinea. In Manam the second choice value, the dual, has a smaller range than the plural, but the paucal patterns with the dual. This too fits within the constraint.[5]

A further way in which values other than the plural need not simply follow the plural is shown by Slovene. At first sight, Slovene is unproblematic, since pronouns and those nouns which have a plural also have a dual; in other words the range of the dual matches that of the plural. But recall that in §2.3.3 it was stated that the Slovene dual is facultative. That was a simplification:

> Normally, dual forms are used in pronouns and in verbal forms
> whenever two actual referents are involved, be they explicitly
> mentioned or only implicit. However, in non-pronominal noun
> phrases with, for example, body parts that come in pairs like 'eyes'
> and 'feet', dual forms tend to be used only when the quantifiers 'two'
> or 'both' are explicitly stated in the context. (Priestly 1993: 440–1)

---

[5] If we were to include the determining of pronouns as a test, then an illustration would be Fijian which, as we saw in §2.2.4 has singular, dual, paucal and plural. Number specification is obligatory if the referent of the pronoun (where number is marked) is human, otherwise it is optional (Dixon 1988: 53, 146; see also Schütz 1985: 252–5, 257–8). For the situation in Wayan, a local language within the Fijian subgroup, see Pawley and Sayaba (1990: 152, 156).

The point is that the dual is obligatory for pronouns but facultative for nouns.[6] This obligatory–facultative divide is within the dual number, and so the dual and the plural pattern differently. However, the divide is in accord with the Animacy Hierarchy. We need to capture this interesting interaction between facultative number and the Animacy Hierarchy. The minimal elaboration of our claims required to accommodate the Slovene data is the following:

> II   *Constraint on facultative divisions*
> If within a given number value there is an obligatory–facultative division, the nominals higher on the Animacy Hierarchy will mark the number obligatorily and those lower on the Hierarchy will mark it facultatively.

We represent this in figure 4.8, where □ indicates facultative number. That is, we

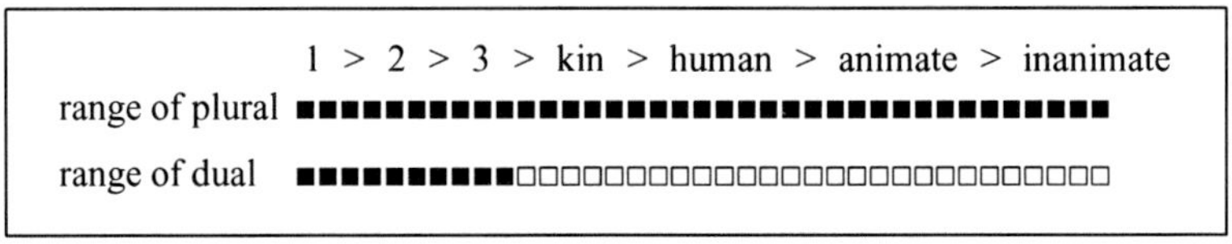

Figure 4.8 *Range of plural and dual in Slovene*

are claiming that there could not be a language similar to Slovene in all respects except that use of the dual was obligatory with nouns but facultative with pronouns. We also wish to rule out the possibility of a language like Slovene except that the lower part of the plural range was facultative and that of the dual obligatory (the converse of figure 4.8).

> III   *Relation between range and facultative use*
> If two number values have ranges of equal extent, but one includes a segment of facultative use and the other does not, the value with the facultative segment counts as having the smaller range.

With this addition our earlier constraint (I) will rule out the impossible version of Slovene, and similar cases.

The picture that emerges thus far is clear; each successive number value following the plural may have up to the same range as the previous choice. If it does not match the preceding one, it may have less extended range, or facultative use in place of obligatory use.

---

[6] It would be interesting to have more detailed data on when the dual is used with nouns. See §9.3.2 for some statistical information.

4.2 Minor numbers

We have seen how a language may have a number value in addition to singular and plural, say the dual, and have investigated the possible patterns which result. We now look at a class of cases outside those patterns, which I have termed 'minor numbers'.[7] These are additional values which involve a relatively small proportion of the nominals of a given language. We first consider three sets of data, and then discuss how they can be analysed.

4.2.1 The dual in Modern Hebrew

Smith-Stark largely restricted himself to the plural, but he specifically mentions the dual in Hebrew (1974: 669n6): 'Although I am not addressing that problem here, my first guess would be that the dual will also split along the same hierarchy as the plural. Bob Hoberman informs me however that such is not the case in Hebrew.' The Hebrew dual is indeed a problem.[8] In Modern Hebrew the number of nouns for which the dual is normally available is something under a dozen (David Gil, personal communication, compare Ritter 1995: 409–12).[9] There is a second restriction on the dual by comparison to the plural: it is found only in noun morphology, and not in the verb, as the following examples show:

(1) ha-yom   ʕavar   maher
    DEF-day   pass.PAST.3.SG.MASC   quickly
    'the day passed quickly'

(2) ha-yom-ayim   ʕavru   maher
    DEF-day-DUAL   pass.PAST.3.PL   quickly
    'the two days passed quickly'

(3) ha-yam-im   ʕavru   maher
    DEF-day-PL   pass.PAST.3.PL   quickly
    'the days passed quickly'

For agreement with a controller headed by a noun in the dual, the plural is used, as in (2); thus dual and plural pattern together (cf. §2.3.2). Nouns with the dual in Modern Hebrew are the mirror image of English nouns like *sheep*. Instead of

---

[7] The term was introduced in Corbett (1996); the account in this chapter supersedes that in the paper. Some of the cases treated as minor number there are better handled in other ways.

[8] The fact that the dual does not pattern like the plural in several languages was noted by Forchheimer (1953: 17–19) and considered further by Plank (1989: 296–312).

[9] Tobin (1988; 1990: 100–50) lists over 100 items and gives interesting textual examples; however, he does not distinguish the few nouns with a genuine dual (in opposition to a singular and a plural) from the larger number with a 'pseudo-dual', that is, a form which is historically a dual but which now functions as a plural (in opposition to a singular only). The term 'pseudo-dual' is from Blanc (1970), who surveys the status of the dual across the Arabic dialects.

having a missing form, these nouns have an additional form; they are irregular in terms of number marking but regular in terms of agreement.

If we return now to the type of noun involved, we find that those with genuine duals are primarily measures of time, for instance *ḥodšayim* 'two months'. Even within the category of measures of time, not all the nouns have a dual form. The nouns which have a dual denote inanimates, the type at the bottom of the Animacy Hierarchy. Moreover, the use of the dual in every case is facultative: there are no nouns which have a dual synchronically (in addition to a singular and plural) which is obligatory when referring to two entities. Clearly these instances do not form a top segment of the Animacy Hierarchy.

4.2.2   The dual in Maltese

Maltese too has the dual as a minor number value, and one which is on the verge of being lost. Fenech (1996) lists thirty-two nouns which have a dual (as distinct from the plural: other nouns preserve dual morphology but retain it in place of the plural). He groups them into expressions of time, number, old Maltese weights and measures (including coins), and some food items and miscellaneous familiar objects. Of these the dual is obligatory for eight nouns only, all of which denote time or number, for example, *jum* 'day', dual *jumejn* and *elf* 'thousand', dual *elfejn*. For the other nouns which have the dual, it is facultative. (It is therefore slightly healthier than the Modern Hebrew dual.)

Thus the Hebrew and Maltese duals fail to conform to the Animacy Hierarchy, and they are certainly unusual. Plank suggests (1989: 309) that 'If in any language some nouns are eligible for dual marking while others are not (or less readily), the criterion is whether or not they denote natural pairs'. However, since we find languages like Mansi (figure 4.2) in which the duality split is aligned with the plurality split, Plank adds the following condition (1989: 310): 'unless the criterion is the same as that determining the eligibility of nouns for other number differentiations'. Even this does not hold for Modern Hebrew or Maltese. For these the criterion is not the same for the dual as for other number values (and so the second part of the criterion cannot apply). But neither is it a matter of natural pairs since in neither language is it the case that the nouns which have a dual are equivalent to all and only the nouns denoting natural pairs. (Nor, of course, are the nouns which have a dual all nouns *except* those denoting natural pairs.) For further discussion on the unusual nature of the dual in Maltese and suggestive comparative statistics on some 200 languages with a dual see Plank (1996).

4.2.3   The paucal in Avar

The Nakh-Daghestanian language Avar has singular and plural. In addition, for a limited number of nouns, there is a paucal opposed to the plural. The paucal is used

Table 4.1 *Examples of the paucal in Avar*

singular	paucal	plural	gloss
nus	nús-al	nus-ábi	daughter-in-law
boróq	boróq-al	bórq-al	snake
t'ut'	t'út'-al	t'ut'-ál	fly
kután	kután-al	kútn-al	plough
bel	bél-al	búl-dul	spade
žul	žúl-al	žul-ál	brush

when the number of referents is restricted ('a few'), the plural for larger numbers ('many'). (Sulejmanov 1985, from whom the data are taken, calls them 'restricted plural' and 'unrestricted plural'.) Some examples are given in table 4.1. Sometimes, as in the last example in the table, the difference between paucal and plural is marked only by the position of the stress (cf. §5.3.3). Sulejmanov says only that this three-way opposition is available for a restricted group of nouns; he lists eighty-nine which have the contrast. Of these, only one is a kin term (*nus* 'daughter-in-law') and a further eight denote non-human animates. It appears that those nouns which have a distinct paucal form are not in general high on the Animacy Hierarchy. (Sulejmanov does not specify whether use of the additional form is obligatory or facultative overall, but he does say that with certain quantifiers the appropriate form is required, the paucal with 'a few' and the plural with 'many'.)[10]

4.2.4   Minor numbers: the problem

The ranges of the minor numbers we have looked at are given in figure 4.9 (p. 98). It is evident that these minor number values do not fit with our previous claims. On the other hand there is a pattern and we can base tentative claims upon it.

4.2.5   Constraints on minor numbers

Minor numbers appear not to be subject to the Animacy Hierarchy; in fact they appear in almost the worst places, since they are not close to forming top segments and may not even form a single segment. This is surprising, given the strength of the evidence we saw supporting the constraints of the Animacy Hierarchy (in chapter 3 and in §4.1). Though minor numbers require a relaxation of the typology of number, they do not vary without limit. We propose three constraints:[11]

[10] See Xalilov (1985) for data on the comparable system in Bezhta, another Nakh-Daghestanian language, and Xalilov (1995) for dictionary information on the nouns involved.

[11] These are an improvement on the accounts in Corbett (1996) and Corbett and Mithun (1996).

IV   *Size of minor numbers*

A minor number involves a proportion of the nominals of a given language which is relatively small by comparison to those involved in the major number(s), where being a major number for that language involves splitting the nominal inventory, taking some top segment of the Animacy Hierarchy.[12]

Why not claim simply that a minor number is one which involves a relatively small proportion of the nominals of the language (as we did at the beginning of §4.2)? The problem with that formulation is that a language with just a singular–plural opposition which involved relatively few nominals would fall under this definition as having a minor number: Central Pomo would be an example (§3.2.4.1). Yet Central Pomo and similar languages typically conform to the Animacy Hierarchy. Intuitively we want to say that there cannot be minor number without there first being major number (a plurality split). We therefore include this comparison in our constraint: the proportion of the nominals involved in a minor number is small by comparison to those involved in the major number(s).

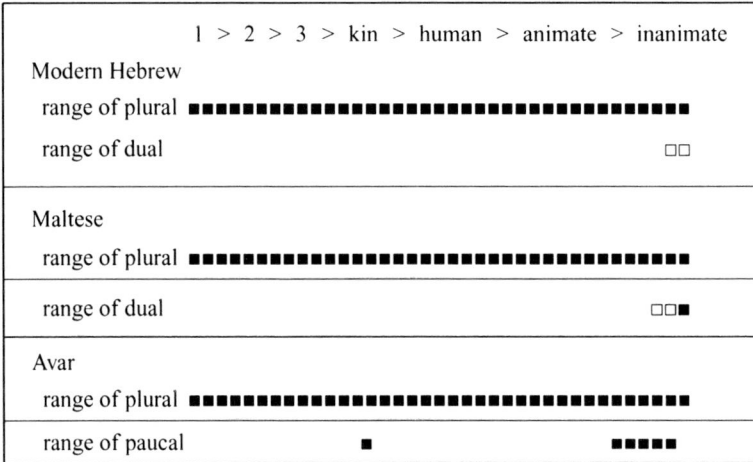

		1 > 2 > 3 > kin > human > animate > inanimate								
Modern Hebrew										
range of plural	■■■■■■■■■■■■■■■■■■■■■■■■■■■■■■■■■■■■■■■									
range of dual									□□	
Maltese										
range of plural	■■■■■■■■■■■■■■■■■■■■■■■■■■■■■■■■■■■■■■■									
range of dual								□□■		
Avar										
range of plural	■■■■■■■■■■■■■■■■■■■■■■■■■■■■■■■■■■■■■■■									
range of paucal			■					■■■■■		

Figure 4.9 *Range of minor numbers*

The first constraint (IV) concerns the number of nominals involved. The second concerns which they can be:

---

[12] The existence of such major numbers, taking a top segment of the hierarchy, was demonstrated in chapter 3 and in §4.1.

V   *Possible range of minor numbers*
     The nouns with the minor number will be within the range of those
     with the major number(s).

This pattern is clear from figure 4.9. The effect is that if we have, for instance, a language with singular and plural and minor dual, the nouns with the minor dual will be a subset of those which have the singular and plural. The type of language which is excluded is represented in figure 4.10. Though the nouns with the dual

> 1 > 2 > 3 > kin > human > animate > inanimate
>
> range of plural ■■■■■■■■■■■■■■■■■■■■■■■■
>
> range of dual   ■■■

Figure 4.10 *Impossible range for a minor number*

opposition in this hypothetical language form a relatively small proportion of the nominals involved in the major numbers they do not fall within the range of the major numbers and so, we claim, this system cannot exist.[13]

The final constraint concerns the values which may be involved:

VI   *Possible minor number values*
     Where a value is used as a minor number, this must be within a
     number system which would match an otherwise attested system of
     number values.

This means that all the possible systems in §2.3.2 are available. Thus, for instance, the system singular–dual–plural is possible, but not *singular–trial–plural. We will represent minor numbers in parentheses: the systems we have found are given in figure 4.11 (p. 100). We return to Avar in §4.5.5.

It can be seen that these systems do indeed match number systems discussed in §2.3.2. We return to the singular–paucal–plural system in §4.5.4. These constraints still leave a typology which is too permissive: a further constraint can be applied:

VII *Dispensability of minor numbers*
     Minor numbers are available only within systems which would match
     an otherwise attested system of number values were the minor
     number removed.

---

[13] Recall that we are talking of oppositions here. To have a dual number means having an opposition of dual versus some other number. A set of nouns which had the morphological form(s) of the dual and *no* other form would not be a counter-example because the dual would not be in opposition to any other number. Such nouns would be outside the number system, just as much as those with only forms identical to the singular or to the plural (see §5.8.1).

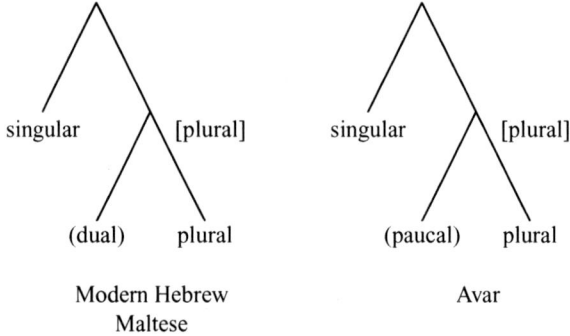

Figure 4.11 *Minor number systems*

The point of this constraint is that minor numbers are an 'extra', without which the number system would be normal. Thus if in the examples in figure 4.11 the minor number were removed, we would be left with a well-attested system. The effect of constraint (VII) is to rule out the possibility of a language having a system like: singular–(minor dual)–trial–plural. This would have been allowed by constraint (VI), since singular–dual–trial–plural is a possible system; the effect of constraint (VII) is to require that if there were a minor number in such a system it would have to be the trial. (A possible instance of a minor trial is found in Maṇarayi, a non-Pama-Nyungan language of the Roper River area of the Northern Territory of Australia, where the trial is found with the few subsection or social category terms, and with the first person pronoun, while other nominals have only singular–dual–plural, see Merlan 1982: 90, 100–2, 225; this system fits all the constraints given above.)

4.2.6 Minor numbers: review

Besides the three cases above, we have seen other likely instances of minor numbers earlier in the book. When we looked at greater plurals in §2.2.6, in languages like Fula, the data were rather sparse, but typically the examples suggested some group of nouns not forming a top segment of the hierarchy. We must be cautious, given the lack of data, but since we found greater plural as a major number in Mokilese (hence constraint (III) would be satisfied) we can tentatively treat languages like Fula as having a minor number (greater plural).

Though further examples are needed, we may speculate a little on the history of minor numbers. Of the examples we have just discussed, it is clear that in Modern Hebrew and in Maltese the minor number is a remnant of what was once a major number (the situation of Avar is not clear). However, it appears that a minor number can be an innovation too. In §2.2.7 we discussed the Breton dual and noted that it is a quite recent one. It is available for nouns denoting parts of the body and items of clothing that occur in pairs (Ternes 1992: 416–17). This is not a top segment of the Animacy Hierarchy; we are dealing here with a new minor number. This minor dual is obligatory with those nouns which have it.

Minor numbers are not straightforwardly subject to the Animacy Hierarchy; however, as we have seen, their distribution can be constrained. Since the same type of number value (such as dual) may be a major or a minor number, depending on the language, it is important that language descriptions make it clear which is intended: 'Modern Hebrew has the dual' is true, but potentially misleading. And more generally, it cannot be assumed that typological claims which are valid for major values will be similarly valid for corresponding minor values.

Similar oppositions between major and minor values may be found in other categories. The problem of minor genders (those which have few nouns in them) is discussed in Corbett (1991: 159–60, 170–5). As with number, there can be major genders which happen to have few members, and others where the nouns can be marked as lexical exceptions, for which the more restricted notion of 'inquorate gender' analogous to minor number is invoked. The comparison with number is clear: when only a small number of lexical items has a particular value, we are required to take the analysis further. There are instances when a number or gender has few members, but functions normally: thus if a language has few nouns which show singular and plural number, we have a (normal) major plural. Equally there can be idiosyncratic minor numbers and genders which are not subject to the normal constraints.[14]

4.3 Associatives[15]

Many languages have what have been called 'associative plurals', or 'group plurals' (Moravcsik 1994); earlier terms, more often used when applied to duals, are 'elliptic' and 'a potiori' (= 'from the stronger').[16] These forms consist of a nominal plus a marker, and denote a set comprised of the referent of the nominal (the main member) plus one or more associated members. The patterning of these forms appears to undermine the typology we have built around the Animacy Hierarchy, if we treat them as a third number. Either the associative plural or the ordinary plural

[14] In the category of case too we find comparable problems: thus Russian has six major cases, and two minor cases restricted to a small subset of nouns and available in restricted syntactic contexts. Unlike the other cases, these two are marked on nouns only (and a noun of the appropriate declensional type may have either or both of these minor cases).

[15] Section 4.3 draws heavily on Corbett and Mithun (1996). We are grateful to Mrs Frances Jack (Hopland Rancheria), Mrs Salome Alcantra and Mrs Florence Paoli (Yokaya Rancheria) and Mrs Winifred Leal and Mrs Eileen Oropeza (Point Arena Rancheria) for sharing their knowledge of Central Pomo, and to George Charles and Elizabeth Ali, both of Bethel, Alaska, for acting as consultants for Central Alaskan Yup'ik.

[16] 'Elliptic' is used for example by Edgerton (1910) writing mainly on Sanskrit and 'a potiori' by Grapow (1939) writing on Old Egyptian.

proves to be exceptional. We shall be concerned here with morphological marking of associatives; we deal with syntactic means (agreement) in §6.3.

4.3.1 Associatives: the problem

Consider first the Finno-Ugric language Hungarian (data from Edith Moravcsik, personal communication):

(4)   János
      'John'

(5)   János-ok
      'John-PL'
      'Johns' (more than one person called John)

(6)   János-ék
      John-ASSOC.PL
      'John and associates', 'John and his group', 'John 'n' them'

In Hungarian, the particular members of the group may vary according to circumstances (family, friends and so on), but they will be human and near-equals. The associative plural ending is added mostly to proper names and to nouns for kin terms, titles and occupations; examples formed with ordinary common nouns are strange.[17] The associative plural forms function as plurals for subject–verb agreement.

---

[17] Thus we find (Edith Moravcsik, personal communication):

(i) apa	cf. apá-ék		cf. apá-m-ék	
father	father-ASSOC.PL		father-1.SG.POSS-ASSOC.PL	
'father'	'father and his group'		'my father and his group'	

(ii) elnök	cf. az	elnök-ék	cf. az	elnök	úr-ék	
president	DEF	president-ASSOC.PL	DEF	president	Mr-ASSOC.PL	
'president'		'the president and his group'			'Mr President and group'	

The last form, including *úr* 'Mr', could be used as a form of address to the president (asking, for instance, when the president and associates will do something) but not as a form of address to the group. As mentioned above, nouns for professions can take the associative form:

(iii) tanító	cf. a	tanító-ék
teacher	DEF	teacher-ASSOC.PL
'teacher'		'the teacher and his group'

However, it is not available for other common nouns:

(iv) ember	cf. *az	ember-ék
man	DEF	man-ASSOC.PL
'man'		'the man and his group'

Table 4.2 *Personal pronouns in Hungarian*

	singular	plural
1st person	én	mi
2nd person	te	ti
3rd person	ő	ők

Since nouns for kin terms and some others denoting humans have two forms (associative plural and ordinary plural), we might expect to find the same with the personal pronouns. What we actually find is the situation in table 4.2. Each pronoun has only one plural form. The first and second person pronouns have suppletive plurals, while the third person pronoun uses the regular plural marker, as in *nő* 'woman' *nők* 'women'.[18] At first sight, we have a straightforward violation of the Animacy Hierarchy: the associative plural is available for a middle segment (nouns denoting kin and some other humans), rather than a top segment including the personal pronouns. This is illustrated in figure 4.12.

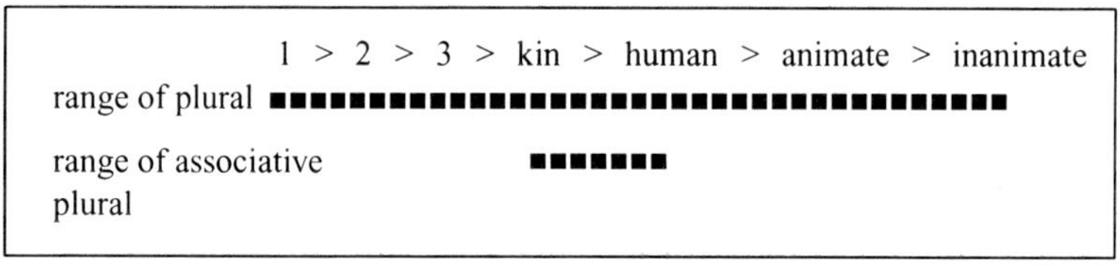

```
                    1  >  2  >  3  >  kin  >  human  >  animate  >  inanimate
range of plural   ■■■■■■■■■■■■■■■■■■■■■■■■■■■■■■■■■■■■■■■■■■■■

range of associative              ■■■■■■■
plural
```

Figure 4.12 *Associative plurals in Hungarian: first analysis*

A possible way out is suggested by Moravcsik (1994), who proposes that the first and second person plural pronouns universally have associative plural (group plural) meaning: '*We* and *you-PLU* are semantically group plurals in that *we* normally means "I and some others" (rather than "more than one speaker") and the normal meaning of *you* is also "you and some others" rather than "more than one listener".' The idea that these pronouns can have associative meaning goes back at least as far as Jespersen (1924: 192); recall, however, that we reached a rather different view in §3.7.1 above. Moravcsik links this interpretation specifically to the Animacy Hierarchy, and continues: 'It therefore makes sense that a special plural, such as the group plural, that applies to less than all nominals should apply

---

[18] Éva Csató points out (personal communication) that, in the oblique plural forms, pronouns of all three persons include a number marker; this is similar to the ordinary plural, not to the associative marker.

to personal pronouns and human nouns, and to proper names and kin terms in particular.' Thus if we treat the associative plural as a separate number, it is possible to claim that the top segment of the hierarchy is indeed involved. In some languages just the first and second person pronouns are involved, while in others, like Hungarian, kin terms and even other nouns denoting humans are involved.[19]

There are two problems. The first is the less serious. If the first and second person pronouns are associative plurals, why is this not clear in their form ? (For discussion of the forms of plural pronouns, including instances which have regular plural morphology, see Myrkin 1964 and §3.5 above.) A simple answer might be that the form need not be transparent, so long as there is some formal contrast, such as that between English *I* and *we*. The more serious problem concerns the ordinary plural. If the first and second person plural pronouns are associative plurals, then the ordinary plurals become exceptional, since they would typically involve some central segment of the hierarchy, but not the top. We would have to say that the claims of the Smith-Stark Hierarchy relate to associative plurals. The considerable data on the distribution of ordinary plurals, which have been partially understood by reference to the hierarchy, would now all be problematic; see figure 4.13. Figure 4.13 shows how by saving the associative plurals we make the ordinary plural exceptional.[20]

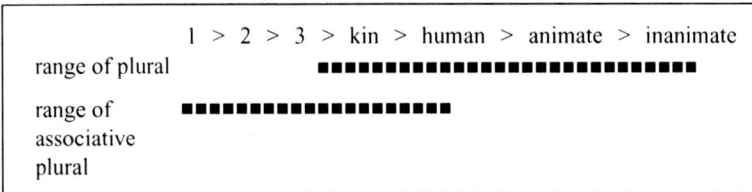

Figure 4.13 *Associative plurals in Hungarian: second analysis*

If we wish to continue claiming that the associative plural is a separate number, a last escape route would be to claim that it is a minor number (like the dual in Modern Hebrew, §4.2.1). Figure 4.12 makes this look attractive. But this is unsatisfactory, as

---

[19] This solution is more plausible in Smith-Stark's version of the hierarchy, for which it was intended, in which the third person pronoun is not given a separate position.

[20] It might be argued that we have been oversimplifying by viewing the pronouns as being either ordinary plurals or associative plurals. The first person plural may have ordinary plural meaning, if rarely, and the second person plural is often used as an ordinary plural. It could therefore be suggested that the associative plural is a part of the plural, and the personal pronouns cover the whole plural range. But if the associative plural is a part of the plural, why should we not treat the dual as part of the plural (since 'two' is included in 'more than one')? We do not do this because the dual (in the languages which have a dual) shows a regular form–meaning correspondence, which demonstrates that it forms a separate number. It is the lack of a formal contrast in the pronouns, as compared to formal contrasts like *Jánosok* (plural) versus *Jánosék* (associative), which makes the pronouns a clear problem with respect to the Animacy Hierarchy.

our data from Hungarian show. First, the associative plural meaning is available for the first and second person plural pronouns as well as for some 'higher' nouns: the problem is the lack of a form–meaning correspondence. And second, we would have created a minor number just to solve the problem, giving a system which does not correspond to an attested one. Unlike the case with the dual, we find no instance of an associative plural functioning as a major number parallel to an ordinary plural. Once again, either the associative plural or the ordinary plural would fail to fit the typology.

We will try two ways forward. First we look for straightforward morphological evidence on the relation between associative and plural. In Central Pomo we find suggestive diachronic evidence that they are, or rather were, separate. Second we look at a more complex number system, that of Central Alaskan Yup'ik, and here we are able to confirm the conclusion suggested by the Central Pomo data.

4.3.2   Central Pomo

Central Pomo belongs to the Pomoan family of Northern California and is spoken 100 miles north of San Francisco, with one dialect on the coast at Point Arena/Manchester and two dialects 50 miles inland, on the Russian River near Ukiah. Only a handful of speakers remain. Number is specified in Central Pomo in various ways and the distinctions found on nouns, pronouns, adjectives and verbs operate independently of each other (see Mithun 1988b, and §9.3.1 below). Only a few nouns have plural forms, most denoting human beings ('man', 'woman', 'child', 'old woman', most kinsmen). Several plural forms are simply irregular, but others are formed with a suffix -*(t̪)ay*. This takes the shape -*t̪ay* after vowels, but the initial *t̪* does not appear after consonants:

(7)   má·t̪a   má·t̪a-t̪ay   čá·č   čá·č-ay
       woman   woman-PL   person   person-PL
       'woman'   'women'   'person' 'persons'

The plural forms are generally used only when their referents are significantly individuated. Pronouns, by contrast, systematically show distinct singular and plural forms whenever they refer to humans (§3.2.4.1). Besides the relatively restricted plural marking for nouns, Central Pomo also has an associative marker -*t̪oya*, as in (8):

(8)   Norman Ball=t̪oya   lów-ač=ya   ʔe   mu·l.
       (name)=ASSOC   talk.PL-IMPRFV.PL=PERSE   be   that
       'Norman Ball and them were talking about that.'[21]

---

[21] Hyphens (-) are used here to indicate affix boundaries, and equals signs (=) for clitic boundaries. Central Pomo contains a rich inventory of evidential markers, among them the clitic =*ya* that marks information known from direct personal experience (PERSE).

The verbal morphology in (8) reflects the plurality of the subject. The verb root *lów-* 'talk' is inherently plural, denoting conversation in a group, and the suffix *-ač* is the plural form of the imperfective aspect. The associative phrase can fill other grammatical roles. In (9) it functions as the patient of the verb 'discuss'.

(9) Eileen=ṭoya-l=wa   ma   čanó-·d=a?
     (name)=ASSOC-PAT=Q   2.SG   talk.SG-IMPRFV.SG=IMMED
     'You're discussing Eileen and them?'

The associative enclitic appears with proper names, as in (8) and (9) above, and with kin terms as in (10):

(10) Ma-ṭhé-ṭo·ya   hínṭil   čanú   š?úduw-ay   ?i-n
      3.POSS-mother-ASSOC   Indian   word   not.know-PL   be-as
      'Because their parents don't speak the Indian language.'

The associative appears with indefinite pronouns, which are also used as interrogatives:

(11) Bá·=ṭoya=wa   mída   napʰó-w?
      who=ASSOC=Q   there   sit.PL-PRFV
      'Who [all] is living there now?'

The shape of the associative =ṭoya is distinct from that of the noun pluralizer -ṭay. If we look at the forms of the pronouns, however, we see evidence suggesting that the associative =ṭoya includes an original plural marker (table 4.3). The plural segment -ya appears clearly in the second person and in the last row of the table, the forms of the third person long-distance reflexive pronouns. The plural segment -ya is seen rather less clearly in the first and basic third person forms because of the erosion of certain unstressed initial syllables. The same plural segment -ya appears in the associative: =ṭo-ya.

Table 4.3 *Personal pronouns in Central Pomo*

	agent		patient		possessive	
	SG	PL	SG	PL	SG	PL
1	?a·	ya	ṭo·	yal	kʰe	yá·?kʰe
2	ma	máya	mṭo	máyal	mkʰe	máya·?kʰe
3	mu·l	mú·ṭuya	mú·ṭu	mú·ṭuyal	mú·kʰeị	mú·ṭuya·kʰeị
3.REFL	ṭi·	ṭíya	ṭí·ṭo	ṭíyal	ṭí·kʰeị	ṭíya·kʰeị

The situation in Central Pomo provides a valuable clue, suggesting that the present associative marker was formed from separate associative and plural segments. This leads us to ask whether number and associativity should be treated as separate categories. It is possible to analyse the Hungarian data in a similar way. The associative suffix -*ék* might be segmentable into two components, associative -*é*- plus a plural element -*k* also visible in the nominal plural suffix -*ok* and third person pronominal plural -*ők*. Moravcsik (§2.1.6 in forthcoming) discusses the advantages and disadvantages of this approach.

4.3.3   Central Alaskan Yup'ik

To progress further we shall look at a more complex system involving a third number value, the dual. This is often a good strategy with number problems. If we analyse a language with singular–dual–plural, and an associative, then theoretically we might find two outcomes:

Outcome A.   Four values: singular, dual, ordinary plural, associative plural

Outcome B.   Three number values: singular, dual, plural, plus an additional category, associativity, which we would expect to be available for dual and plural

A language with the properties we need is Central Alaskan Yup'ik, spoken in south-western Alaska in the Yukon-Kuskokwim Delta and Bristol Bay areas. According to Jacobson (1995: 1), in 1995 there were approximately 20,000 Central Alaskan Yup'iks, of whom some 10,500 spoke Yup'ik. Central Alaskan Yup'ik is one of the Yup'ik group of languages within the Eskimo branch of the Eskimo-Aleut family. Since this language is vital to the development of the argument, a brief sketch will be helpful.

Verbs contain pronominal suffixes referencing their core arguments. They distinguish singular, dual and plural number in all persons. The pronominal suffixes are preceded by one of a set of mood markers. Nouns also take inflectional suffixes, which mark an elaborate case system with a basic ergative–absolutive pattern. The absolutive form of the noun has no overt case marker, and the number forms are: singular *qayaq* 'kayak', dual *qayak* 'two kayaks' and plural *qayat* 'three or more kayaks'.

Inflectable words in Yup'ik, as in other Eskimoan languages, consist of an initial root (traditionally termed a 'base'), optionally followed by any number of derivational suffixes ('postbases'), then by inflectional suffixes ('endings'). There are hundreds of postbases, many with meanings corresponding to those of roots in other languages (for example, 'to buy an X'), many with meanings typical of derivation in other languages (nominalization), some with meanings typical of inflection elsewhere ('habitually'). There is a postbase in Central Alaskan Yup'ik that appears on proper names only, to give forms meaning 'N and family' or 'N and companion(s)':[22]

(12) cuna
'Chuna' (name, absolutive singular)

(13) cunankut   ayag-tu-t
Chuna.ASSOC.PL   go-INDIC-3.PL
'Chuna and his family/friends left'[23]

If it were just Chuna and one friend, the form would be:

(14) cunankuk   ayag-tu-k
Chuna.ASSOC.DU   go-INDIC-3.DU
'Chuna and his friend left'

The companion can be included overtly, by using the noun plus the enclitic =*llu*. Thus:

(15) cunankuk   arnaq=llu   ayag-tu-k
Chuna.ASSOC.DU   woman=too   go-INDIC-3.DU
'Chuna and the woman left'

What is specially relevant about these data is first that the associative meaning fits equally with dual and plural. It seems, therefore, that we do not need to recognize a new number value, namely associative plural, with the attendant problems for a typology of number. Instances of the use of duals in this way are known in the literature and while they make the 'extra number' solution (outcome A) less plausible, they do not eliminate it. It could be still claimed that Yup'ik has five number values: singular, ordinary dual, associative dual, ordinary plural, associative plural.

The second, and more important point about the Yup'ik data is that the associative morpheme -*nku*- and the number morphemes (-*k* dual, -*t* plural) are realized separately. This is made clear in table 4.4. Associatives can have separate morphology, and they should be treated as a different 'dimension' or category, not a part of the number category. Therefore the instances of special forms for associative plurals in other languages can reasonably be treated as portman-

---

[22] The associative is not available for kin terms. This may be because they would need to be followed by transitive pronominal suffixes to indicate possessor and possessed (N and N's kinsman), which would lead to considerable morphological complexity with the associative, especially if the whole had then to be inflected further for case. Data are from the dialect known as General Central Alaskan Yup'ik; for similar data on the Chevak dialect see Woodbury (1981).

[23] The absence of an overt tense marker indicates present and immediate past.

Table 4.4 *Associative and number morphology in Central Alaskan Yup'ik*

	dual	plural
associative	cuna-nku-k 'Chuna + one'	cuna-nku-t 'Chuna + associates'
ordinary	qaya-k 'two kayaks'	qaya-t 'three or more kayaks'

teaus.[24] To show this needs a combination of separate dual number AND a separable associative morpheme, which is exactly what Yup'ik has. Thus number and associativity represent different categories, which may interact in various ways.

From the point of view of the typology of number systems, this result means that associative forms no longer pose a problem, since they are not part of the number category. Looking ahead, since these two separate categories are established, an interesting project would be to investigate their interactions. For instance, a reasonable hypothesis is: 'if a language has a (major) dual and a plural, associative meanings if available will be equally available to both, whether or not there is special morphology for expressing associative meaning'.

Before moving on, we should observe the Yup'ik associative 'in real life': the speaker is Elena Charles, and analysis is by Marianne Mithun:

(16) Last fall-gguq   maaten-gguq
      last fall=gguq   maaten=gguq
      last.fall=HEARSAY   when=HEARSAY

      Franky-nguk   tekituk
      Franky-ngu-k   tekite-u-k
      Franky-ASSOC-DUAL   arrive-INDIC.INTRAN-3.DUAL

      camp-aput   yungqellruyaaqelliniuq
      campaq=aput   yuk-ngqerr-llru-yaaqe-llini-u-q
      camp-1.PL/3.SG   person-have-PAST-actually-apparently-
                                      INDIC.INTRAN-3.SG

      upallrulliniluteng
      upag-llru-llini-lu-teng
      change.residence-PAST-apparently-SUBORDINATIVE-3.PL

---

[24] It might be argued that it is impossible to separate associativity from number because associativity implies non-singular. However, as Martin Haspelmath points out (personal communication), the inclusive–exclusive distinction similarly implies non-singular; this distinction is not considered part of the category of number and, we would argue, associativity is a comparable case.

carayiim   piateng.
carayag-m   pi-a-ateng
bear-ERG   do-CONSEQUENTIAL-3.SG/REFL[25].PL

Franky-gguq   bother-enritellinilutek.
Franky=gguq   bother-nrite-llini-lu-tek
Franky=HEARSAY   bother-not-apparently-SUBORDINATIVE-
                                                    3.DUAL

Kiimek   Franky-nkuk   ayallruuk.
kii-mek   Franky-nku-k   ayag-llru-u-k
alone-ABL   Franky-ASSOC-DUAL   go-PAST-IND.INTR-
                                                    3.DUAL

'Last fall when Franky and his companion arrived they realized that there had been people at our camp. They had moved because a bear was bothering them. But Franky said that they (Franky and companion) were not bothered. Franky and his companion had gone up there by themselves.'

4.3.4 Associatives: summing up

We have seen how associatives seemed problematic for a typology of number. A possible solution was suggested by data from Central Pomo, but it was Central Alaskan Yup'ik, which has segmentable dual, plural and associative markers, which allowed us to demonstrate the dissociation of number and associativity. Thus associative meaning can be expressed in three ways: by special forms combining associative and number (as in Hungarian and Central Pomo), by a special associative, distinct from number (as in Central Alaskan Yup'ik) or by normal number forms. This latter method is very common; we illustrate it from Paumarí (an Arauan language of Brazil), which can use a normal plural possessive prefix, to show that the possessors are the named individual and associates (Chapman and Derbyshire 1991: 257):[26]

(17)   ida   Fatima   vakadi-vanami
       DEMONSTRATIVE.FEM   Fatima   3.PL.POSS-paddle.FEM
       'the paddle belonging to Fatima and others'

The combination of these three ways of expressing associativity shows that we are dealing with a category distinct from number, even though the two are frequently

---

[25] This is a fourth person or 'cofererential third person' pronoun, indicating that the people bothered are coreferent with the people who had moved.

[26] Further instances of the use of the plural to express associativity are given in §6.3; there it is plural agreement which is involved.

realized together. There is therefore no remaining problem in this regard for the typology of number systems.

4.4   Distributives and collectives

Descriptions of number systems, particularly those of the languages of North America, often include discussion of distributives and collectives.[27] As we shall see, the definitions can vary from author to author. The pervasiveness of distributives and collectives in North America was noted by Boas: 'It would seem that, on the whole, American languages are rather indifferent in regard to the clear expression of plurality, but that they tend to express much more rigidly the ideas of collectivity or distribution' (1911a: 37). Distributives and collectives are sometimes listed as additional values along the same dimension as singulars and plurals, as in Mathiot's description of Tohono O'odham (Papago): 'There are three nominal numbers: the nominal singular, the nominal plural and the nominal distributive' (1973: 36).

For our typology we need to establish whether distributive and collective should be considered as values on a par with singular, dual and plural, or as subvalues of plural, or as neither. We will concentrate on morphological markers, though both distributivity and collectivity can be expressed analytically or lexically as well. Distributive and collective meaning may be specified by independent words in analytic constructions, particularly determiners (equivalents of 'each', 'every'), and adverbials (distributive 'here and there', 'one at a time'; collective 'together', 'jointly'). There are many discussions of analytic and lexical distributives and collectives in the literature, including the collection edited by Bach et al. (1995). Distributives and collectives have a good deal in common. Sometimes they are defined as opposite values but as we shall see, the situation is more complex than that. Both can be a verbal or a nominal category. In this chapter we are concerned with nominal number, and so we shall concentrate on nominal distributives and nominal collectives (though comments in sources quoted may refer to both nominal and verbal markers). The general problem is that if they are number values, then they are problematic in terms of the Animacy Hierarchy.

4.4.1   Distributives

Distributives mark the separation of members of a group, whether entities, events, qualities or locations. Each is considered distinct in space, sort or time.[28]

---

[27] This section draws heavily on the much more extensive account in Mithun and Corbett (1995); I am grateful to Marianne Mithun for allowing me to use this unpublished work. See Mithun (1999: 79–94) for further discussion.

[28] For formal semantic accounts see among others Scha (1981), Choe (1987), C. Roberts (1987) and Link (1991). We might assume that 'distributive' is a notion borrowed from

Distributive marking on nouns has two primary functions: it may spread (distribute) entities over various locations or over various sorts (types). Boas described both in Kwak'wala (the language of the Kwakiutl), a Wakashan language of British Columbia:

> Thus the Kwakiutl, who are rather indifferent to the expression of plurality, are very particular in denoting whether the objects spoken of are distributed here or there. When this is the case, the distribution is carefully expressed. In the same way, when speaking of fish, they express by the same term a single fish and a quantity of fish. When, however, they desire to say that these fish belong to different species, a distributive form expressing this idea is made use of. (Boas 1911a: 37–8)

> Reduplication of a noun expresses rather the occurrence of an object here and there, or of different kinds of a particular, than plurality. (Boas 1911b: 444)

In some languages, nominal distributives show just the first function, the distribution of entities over space. Quileute, one of the two members of the Chimakuan family of Washington State, appears to be such a language (Andrade 1933–38: 187):

Footnote 28 (*cont.*)

> algebra and logic. It appears, however, that it has a long history as a grammatical term. The Shorter Oxford English Dictionary gives 'Expressing distribution; spec. in gram. Having reference to each individual of a number or class' and dates this use from 1520. Comparable uses in logic and mathematics are dated 1725 and 1855 respectively.
>
> The term 'distributive' is often used of expressions where there is no special marker of distributivity (§2.5). Thus Stone (1993a: 661), discussing Upper Sorbian, writes: 'In distributive expressions dual agreement is usual, notwithstanding arithmetic plurality' and he cites this example:

> (i) A   wón   přińdźe   zaso,   a   namaka   jich   spjacych;
>   and   he   came   again   and   found   3.PL.ACC   sleeping,
>
> přetož   jich   woči   běštej   wobćežen-ej
> for   3.PL.GEN   eye.DUAL/PL   be.PAST.DUAL   heavy-DUAL

> 'And he came again and found them sleeping, for their eyes were heavy.'
> (Matthew 26.43)

The point is that although twenty-two eyes in all were heavy, the agreement is dual since each disciple has two eyes (hence the construction is termed distributive). The fact that dual is available suggests that we are not dealing with some special use of number of the type to be discussed in chapter 7. It is the form of the verb which is significant in this example since *woči* 'eyes' is exceptionally both the dual and the plural form. For more examples see Jenč (1966).

(18) tukô·yo'   'snow'   tutkô·yo'   'snow here and there'
      t'súwi·tcił   'a boil' t'suwe·wítcił   'boils here and there'

In other languages, like Mohawk, an Iroquoian language of Quebec, Ontario and New York State, nominal distributives show only the second function, the distribution of entities over sorts (compare §3.7.2). The Mohawk nominal distributive appears with count nouns ('rocks'), mass nouns ('candy') and derived verbal nominals ('towel'; literally 'one wipes with it'). The Mohawk examples in this section are from Kaia'titáhkhe' Jacobs, analysed by Marianne Mithun:

(19) onén:ia'   onenia'shòn:'a
      o-nenia'   o-nenia'-shon'a
      NEUT-rock   NEUT-rock-DISTRIBUTIVE
      'rock(s)'   'various rocks'

      otsikhè:ta'   otsikhe'ta'shòn:'a
      o-tsikhe'ta'   o-tsikhe'ta'-shon'a
      NEUT-candy   NEUT-candy-DISTRIBUTIVE
      'candy'   'various candies'

      ierakewáhtha'   ierakewahtha'shòn:'a
      ie-rakew-aht-ha'   ie-rakew-aht-ha'-shon'a
      INDEF-wipe-INST-IMPF   INDEF-wipe-INST-IMPERFV-
                                                   DISTRIBUTIVE
      'one wipes with it'   'one wipes with it – various'
      = 'towel'   = 'paper products: towels, napkins . . .'

The term *onenia'shòn:'a* must refer to different sorts of rocks (say of different sizes or colours) but they need not be distributed in space. The term *otsikhe'ta'shòn:'a* may not refer to two or three pieces of one kind of candy, whether or not they are distributed spatially; it can refer only to different sorts of candies as say in a store. The term *ierakewahtha'shòn:'a* was coined when signs were put over aisles in a community grocery store. It refers to a full assortment of paper products: tissues, towels, paper napkins, and so on. It would not be used for a shelf filled with identical packages of paper towels, say, even if the packages were scattered on the shelf.[29]

---

[29] A likely reason why the Mohawk nominal distributive has only this second, 'sort' function is that Mohawk, like other Iroquoian languages, shows a high proportion of morphological verbs in natural speech (one count found a ratio of one noun to seventeen verbs). Many notions expressed by nouns, adjectives and adverbs in more familiar languages are typically expressed by morphological verbs in Mohawk. In particular, the location or position of entities is usually specified by verbs into which nouns referring to the entities are incorporated. Nouns referring to immovable objects seldom appear unincorporated. Thus since distribution over space is usually expressed by verbal distributives in Mohawk, the nominal distributive is restricted to distribution over sorts.

We now ask how, if at all, distributives fit into a typology of number. Our approach to additional number values given at the beginning of the chapter runs into potential problems. Where distributives are found in the nominal system they do not, in the examples found to date, involve a top segment of the hierarchy. The difficulty is the personal pronouns (often pronominal affixes in North America) which do not distinguish distributive forms. When nouns do have such forms, but the pronouns do not, this is a counter-example to constraints based on the Animacy Hierarchy.

An obvious move would be to treat distributives as a minor number, but this fails. First, there are languages where the distributive form is possible with a substantial number of nouns. Second, we have no clear examples of a distributive as a major number, while in the clear cases minor numbers are found as major numbers elsewhere (in other languages). Thus our typology becomes problematic if distributives are treated as part of the normal number system and we could not rescue it by attempting to treat them as minor numbers. The problem is analogous to that found with associative forms, which also do not affect a top segment of the hierarchy. In that case we showed that associatives are not a value of the number category but are a separate category (§4.3). A somewhat similar approach proves fruitful with regard to distributives. The evidence suggests that distributives should not be considered additional values comparable with the basic number values like singular, dual, and plural, nor as subdivisions of these.

The first type of evidence concerns cooccurrence patterns. In many languages, distributive markers may, but need not, cooccur with number markers. In Mohawk, nouns bear prefixes that specify the gender and, for humans, the number of the referent. The nominal distributive cooccurs both with plural prefixes, as in 'boys' below, and without plural prefixes, as in 'rocks'. (Neuter nouns in Mohawk are not generally marked for number.)

(20) raksà:'a   ratiksa'okòn:'a
      ra-ksa'-a   ra-ti-ksa'-okon-'a
      MASC-child-DIM   PL.MASC-child-DISTRIBUTIVE-
                                                        DIM

      'boy'   'boys'

      onén:ia'   onenia'shòn:'a
      o-neni-a'   o-neni-a'-shon'a
      NEUT-rock-NOUN.SUFFIX   NEUT-rock-NOUN.SUFFIX-
                                                DISTRIBUTIVE

      'rock(s)'   'various rocks'

Distributives and plurals may also cooccur on nouns in Eastern Huasteca Nahuatl (see §3.5; data from Kimball 1990: 203–5). Distributive meaning is indicated by a reduplicative prefix, while plurality is unmarked on inanimate nouns, but indicated on animate nouns by a suffix. (The possessive suffix also has a plural form -*wah* indicating plural possessors.)

(21) ke·mah   λa·lo·li·n-ki   we¢-keh   λah-λahpepečo·lli
      when   earthquake-PRET   fall-PRET.PL   REDUP-wall

      i·pan   λah-λaka·-meh
      on   REDUP-person-PL

      'when the earthquake took place, walls here and there fell on various people'

(22) yanopa   kim-po·wilia-h   nopa   na·na-meh
      thus   3.PL.OBJ-inform-PL   that   mother-PL

      ini·n-koh-kone·-wah   pa·pλeh   elto-keh   ne
      3.PL.POSS-REDUP-child-PL   why   be.PL   that (far)

      to·natih   i·wa·ya   me·¢λi
      sun   with   moon

      'Thus the mothers inform their various children why that sun and moon exist.'

The fact that the two kinds of markers, distributive and number, may but need not cooccur within a word suggests that they are not simply alternative number values.[30] Rather they are different categories. The argument is very similar to that for associatives. An additional point showing that distributive cannot be treated as a minor number (at least without weakening the typology) is that its range need not fall within that of the plural: in Mohawk, neuter nouns typically do not mark number but may take the distributive (19), while in Eastern Huasteca Nahuatl inanimate nouns do not take number marking but may take the distributive (21).

While we find distributives and plurals cooccurring, most distributives are not equally compatible with duals.[31] This fact may be due to our spatial sense; two

---

[30] An example from a quite different part of the world is found in Tolai (a Melanesian language of New Britain). Number is expressed by number words, especially *umana* 'plural (more than three)' and distributivity by reduplication. These can cooccur (Mosel 1982: 141). And in the Tungusic language Even, of north-east Siberia, distributivity can be marked on the verb, quite separately from nominal number, and in a position contrasting both with the collective and with the iterative (Maltshukov 1992).

[31] This should be borne in mind as a possible analysis when we find an additional marker besides a plural, as for a few nouns in Chemehuevi (Press 1979: 53); we should consider whether the addition may be a distributive (compatible with plural but not with dual). Since Chemehuevi is closely related to Southern Paiute, both belonging to the Numic branch of Uto-Aztecan, the account can be informed by Sapir's description of the latter (see, for instance, Sapir 1930–31: 213).

items are not normally said to be scattered 'here and there', whatever their relative positions. The incompatibility extends beyond the spatial configuration of objects. The Mohawk nominal distributive suffix cannot appear on dual nouns:

> (23) niksà:'a   not: *niksa'okòn:'a
> ni-ksa'-a   ni-ksa'-okon-'a
> DUAL.MASC-child-DIM   DUAL.MASC-child-
>   DISTRIBUTIVE-DIM
> '(two) boys'

Though nouns referring to inanimate entities like rocks show no overt number marking (*onén:ia* 'rock(s)'), such nouns are interpreted as referring to three or more entities when they contain the distributive suffix (*onenia'shòn:'a* 'various rocks'). A further type of evidence is that number markers are obligatory in many languages. By contrast, distributives on nouns are seldom if ever obligatory. Moreover, number is often an agreement category, which distributivity is not.

The separateness of distributives and plurals does not mean that they are unrelated. Distributives generally imply plurality: a single entity is not normally distributed over different locations nor over various sorts.[32] In languages without regular plural inflection for nouns, distributives may provide an important indicator of plurality, but by implication. The line between the two is not always clear, or stable over time. Nominal distributives can highlight the distinctness or individuality of entities. Nouns denoting humans are typically viewed as significantly individuated, so that in some languages, such nouns regularly carry distributive markers when there is reference to multiple humans. Such usage can lead to a reinterpretation of the marker as a plural; this has been noted several times, for instance in Quileute:

> At the present time, perhaps under the influence of English, the younger Quileute reduplicate their words to express plurality, without any connotation of distribution. Due to the nature of the occasion, it is difficult to determine in some instances whether distribution or plurality is denoted; but in by far the majority of the reduplicated nouns in the texts dictated by Séiχtis [an older speaker], distribution is clearly expressed, and in numerous occasions in which plurality was implied in the sentence, the nouns were not reduplicated. (Andrade 1933–38: 190)

---

[32] As Sapir said in his account of Southern Paiute: 'A distributively conceived noun is practically always logically plural at the same time, but need not be.' (1930–31: 257). See example (18) above for a non-plural distributive.

We conclude that though there are similarities between distributives and number values, distributives are not a part of the number system.[33] As with associatives, the fact that they can frequently cooccur with number shows that they are to be treated separately, and therefore do not constitute a counter-example to the constraints of the Animacy Hierarchy.

4.4.2 Collectives

As noted before, 'collective' is used in the literature in a variety of ways, as shown by Gil (1996: 66–70);[34] these uses are so different that the term has become almost useless. It has been used to cover what we have called general number (§2.1) and the examples we cover under corporate nouns (§6.2) among other things. Given this profusion of different senses, it is most important not to assume that what is described as a collective in one language is similar to that in another. In the use we discuss in this section, collectives have sometimes been understood as the natural opposite of distributives. One can see why this should be so (though in §4.4.3 we

---

[33] An interesting twist on the semantic interaction between distributives and plurals is the fact some languages show the opposite implication: plural markers may imply distributivity in contexts where they are otherwise excluded. Kibrik (forthcoming section IV.4.1) provides examples from Daghestanian languages of plural marking with non-count nouns. They are interpreted with a range of meanings comparable to nominal distributives in other languages: entities may be distributed over space, time or sorts. The following are from Chirag:

> (i) k'um-re
>   sour.cream-PL
>   'sour cream (in different vessels)'
>
> (ii) mag-ne
>   sweat-PL
>   'sweat (during several days)'
>
> (iii) XIal-e
>   fat-PL
>   'sorts of fat'

This use of plurals with non-count nouns with distributive effects is a type of recategorization, as discussed in §3.7.2.

[34] See also the discussion in Greenberg (1972: 19–25) and Kemmer (1993). Kuhn (1982) shows how in a single language (German) there can be a considerable variety of different phenomena labelled collective. At the extreme, 'collective' can be a purely morphological term. Thus in Breton (Stump 1989: 264) collectives denote more than one entity, behave like simple plurals and take plural agreement; however, they have no ending, but form the singular with a singulative suffix. They are defined then in terms of the distribution of affixes. If a noun has no ending in the plural, but has one in the singular, then it is a collective under this usage. (Following the discussion in §3.5, it is interesting to note that the nouns with collective and singulative are more heavily concentrated at the low end of the Animacy Hierarchy, Greg Stump, personal communication.) For the development of the Celtic singulative see Cuzzolin (1998).

117

shall see that things are not quite so simple). Each specifies a way of viewing members of a group. Distributives indicate that they should be individuated, considered separately, while collectives (in one use of the term) indicate that they should be considered together as a unit. It is this type of collective that we shall discuss here, as for instance in Montler's account of Saanich, North Straits Salish (1986: 101): 'This morpheme usually indicates a 'collective' idea, referring to a group of items considered together rather than a number of items considered individually. Translations usually are in the form of phrases such as "a bunch of . . ." or "lots of . . ."' While nominal distributives are often used of entities dispersed over space, nominal collectives typically refer to entities that are spatially contiguous, as in these examples from Sierra Popoluca, a Mixe-Zoquean language of Mexico (Elson 1960: 219):

(24) tʌg-áŋhoh   'many houses together, a village'
tó?·d-áŋhoh   'much paper in a pile'
ca-áŋhoh   'many rocks, a rocky place'

As with the distributive, the problem for the typology is that collectives are typically formed from nouns low on the hierarchy, and not with pronouns. (There are occasional claims for collective pronouns; however, the variation in the terminology is such that such claims are typically for instances which are not clearly recognizable as collectives of this type.) Evidence similar to that seen with distributives indicates that a distinction should be maintained between collectives and basic number. Like distributives, collectives may cooccur with number markers. For example, Yana contains a nominal collective suffix -*wi* (Sapir 1917: 22–3; Sapir and Swadesh 1960: 173):

(25) ʔi-   'tree, stick'   'i-wi   'firewood, wood'

Significantly, the suffix may cooccur with either the dual -*u:* or the plural -*ii*:

(26)	dal	'hand'	dal-u:-wi	'two hands'
	lal	'foot'	lal-u:-wi	'two feet'
	madjau-pa:	'chief'	mut'djau-ti-wi	'chiefs'
	si:win'i	'yellow pine'	sitin'i-wi	'yellow pines'

The collective noun 'firewood' in (25), without a number suffix, is a mass noun, while the nouns in (26), with number suffixes, are count nouns. Thus, as with distributives and with associatives we have clear evidence that collectives are a separate category, since they can cooccur with number markers.[35]

---

[35] Other examples of collectives occurring with the plural are found in the Salishan language Upper Chehalis (Kinkade 1995: 355–6) and in the Nakh-Daghestanian language Tsakhur (Kibrik 1999: 50–1).

Like distributives, collectives are related semantically to basic number, though their relationship is not precisely the same as that of distributives. The primary function of collectives is to specify the cohesion of a group, sometimes manifested in joint activity. Cohesion presupposes a multiplicity of group members. Thus a fleet of canoes (collective) must contain more than one canoe. Unlike distributives however, collectives are generally compatible with duals. Two objects can be viewed as a unit as easily as three or more. The occurrence of collective suffixes on Yana terms for body parts was seen in example (26). Similarly, two agents may act together jointly as easily as three or more.

Collectives, like distributives, contrast with basic number markers in never being obligatory (though of course they may become lexicalized).[36] Since collectives, like distributives, imply plurality this can pave the way for their reanalysis over time as number markers. For example, Greenberg (1972) notes the fact that Proto-Slavonic contained a collective suffix that derived collective noun stems. These derived stems have since been reanalysed to varying degrees in the different Slavonic languages as plural noun stems (Degtjarev 1982: 40–148).

4.4.3 Distributives and collectives: summing up

Distributives and collectives have often been considered opposites. Distributive markers indicate that entities are to be construed individually, as separate and distinct. Collectives indicate that they are to be construed together, as a unit. Their relations are more complex, however. First, their contexts of occurrence are not equivalent. As we saw, distributives are not normally compatible semantically with duals, but collectives are readily so. Collectives are often related to duals diachronically. Second, if the two were perfect opposites, one might expect that only one would be necessary in a language. Its absence would automatically imply the other.

---

[36] They may involve few nouns. For instance, in the Nakh-Daghestanian language Budugh, just five nouns distinguish a collective (Kibrik 1992:15) as in table i. For background information on plural formatives in Budugh and related languages see Ibragimov (1974), who claims that there was formerly a more general distinction of restricted plural or dual versus unrestricted plural.

Table i *Collectives in Budugh*

collective	plural
t'il-iber 'fingers (of one hand)'	t'il-imber 'fingers (of several hands)'
ʕül-über 'eyes (of one person)'	ʕül-ümber 'eyes (of several people)'
ibr-imer 'ears (of one person)'	ibr-imber 'ears (of several people)'
č'er-iber 'hair (of one person)'	č'er-imber 'hair (of several people)'
čärX-imer 'wheels (of one car)'	čärX-imber 'wheels (in general)'

Yet many languages have both distributives and collectives, often in addition to various number markers.

If we were to treat distributive and collective as basic number values, as has sometimes been proposed, then the typology of number as presented would be inadequate. Moreover, it could not be saved by treating these difficult cases as minor numbers because they are again exceptional. We examined the data more closely and established that the distributive and the collective are not basic number values. The strongest evidence for this conclusion is the fact that distributives and collectives can cooccur in some languages with the basic number values (usually with the plural for the distributive and with plural and dual for the collective). The observation that they do cooccur in some languages but need not is also in keeping with the fact that they imply plurality, but specify something more. Like associatives they are categories distinct from but related to number.

This section highlights a problem we have noticed before. The functions of markers identified as distributives or collectives in the literature vary so widely that a typologist reading that language X and language Y both have one of them might in fact be faced with two rather different phenomena. The same typologist might be even further misled by seeing no mention of the distributive in the grammar of language Z. Because of the relation between distributives and basic number marking, researchers have not always noted the distinction precisely. If a grammar is based solely on elicited translations of sentences, the difference may in fact never emerge; it may appear that the language has a plural, when in fact it has a distributive.

4.5   Top and second systems

There are furthers systems which require us to elaborate our typology. These have number value systems of different types at different points on the hierarchy. In a sense, that is nothing new. Consider again Yimas (as in figure 4.6 above). Earlier we concentrated on the range of the different values. Let us look again, this time considering the systems at different points (figure 4.14).

1 > 2 > 3 > kin > human > animate > inanimate			
range of plural	■■■■■■■■■■	■■■■■■■■■■■■■■■■■■■■■■■■■■■■	
range of dual	■■■■■■■■■■	■■■■■■■■■■■■■■■■■■■■■■■■■■■■	
range of paucal	■■■■■■■■■■		
system	top	second	bottom

Figure 4.14 *Number value systems of Yimas*

The first system, which we shall call the 'top system', covers the pronouns in Yimas and has the opposition singular–dual–paucal–plural (all the major number values of Yimas). The second system has singular–dual–plural, while the third is for those nouns which are not number-differentiable, that is, there are no distinct number values. The top system is fully normal; so is the second. And what we have labelled the 'bottom system' is for those nouns which are off the scale of number differentiability (a group which can be very large or vanishingly small, depending on the language; their form will be considered in §5.8.1). Let us concentrate on the second system: it is one which functions as the top system in many other languages. And in the languages which we focused on earlier in this chapter that was the case: the second system, found lower on the hierarchy, would be quite normal as a top system. However, there are languages which have a second system which can appear only as a second system and which is not found as a top system.[37] We discuss four types in turn, and then return briefly to minor numbers.

4.5.1 Conflated numbers

We find an interesting situation in Pame, an Otomanguean language with some 3,700 speakers in central Mexico; the data are from Gibson and Bartholomew (1979). For some nouns, the number system distinguishes one and two referents on the one hand from more than two on the other; thus singular and dual are combined versus plural, as in the examples in table 4.5. I propose the term 'conflated

Table 4.5 *Number distinctions of inanimate nouns in Pame*

singular	dual	plural	gloss
nacê		vacê	plum
macì		wacì	pitcher
cóndo		sóndo	egg shell

number' for the pattern of forms in the first column, since the system involves a conflation of number values as compared to a regular system (of the sort investigated in §2.3.2). This is the typical pattern in Pame for nouns denoting inanimates.

---

[37] It may be asked whether we should not treat for example associative as a value creating second systems. There are two problems: the main one is that this would miss the point about the interaction with the dual and the independent marking of number and associativity, as discussed above; a second problem is the fact that it would greatly weaken the typology, since lower down the hierarchy we would need a new 'third system', which would be the same as the first system for a given language, clearly missing the regularity by splitting between top and third system. This may be seen by consulting figure 4.12.

Table 4.6 *Number distinctions of animate nouns in Pame*

singular	dual	plural	gloss
kamá	kamái	kamát	murderer
pákkas	pákkaiš	pákkast	head of cattle
kopèc?	kopèič?	kopèst?	badger

The animates generally show a straightforward singular–dual–plural system, as table 4.6 shows. Thus the systems of Pame are as in figure 4.15.

top system	singular	dual	plural
second system	singular/dual		plural

Figure 4.15 *Top and second systems in Pame*

Allowing conflated numbers represents a weakening of the constraints on possible number systems. However, there is an important restriction, namely that these conflated systems are possible only in conjunction with a regular system (there will always be other nominals in the language which have a regular system). Moreover it will always be the nominals higher on the Animacy Hierarchy that exhibit a regular system. That is, there cannot be a language like Pame, but with the conflated system [singular/dual]–plural for animates and the singular–dual–plural system for inanimates.[38] We can add this constraint:

VIII   *Constraint on the position of conflated systems*
       A conflated system can occur only as a second system (i.e. it will occur together with a regular system and it will always be found lower on the Animacy Hierarchy than the regular system).

In Kala Lagaw Ya, an Australian language of the Western Torres Straits, in the Saibai dialect as described by Comrie (1981: 6–7), we find a comparable situation, with the same top and second systems as in Pame. However, in Kala Lagaw Ya the second system extends much higher, so that the split is between pronouns, which have singular–dual–plural, and nouns, which have [singular/dual]–plural. Thus *burum* is 'pig' or 'two pigs' while *burum-al* is 'three or more pigs'.

---

[38] We have been using forms with hyphens like 'singular–dual–plural' for a system of oppositions between values. 'Singular/dual' indicates a conflated value, applicable for one or two entities. Then [singular/dual]–plural describes an opposition between two values, singular/dual conflated on the one hand, and plural on the other.

In the case of Pame, the conflated system of the second system represents a conflation of the values of the top system (this can be readily seen in figure 4.15). The same is true in Kala Lagaw Ya. However, this is not always the case: the conflated system may be the conflation of the values of a system found elsewhere, but not in the same language. We find this situation in Tuyuca, a Tucanoan language (Eastern Tucanoan branch) with 800–1000 speakers in Colombia and Brazil, living along the Papurí and Tiquié Rivers and tributaries. The data are from Barnes (1990: 274, 285, 291). Tuyuca has a complex system of classifiers, which occur as suffixes. 'Inanimate classifiers occur in singular form when referring to one, two or three items, and in plural form when referring to four or more items' (Barnes 1990: 274). Here we have a conflation of three numbers. This is restricted to inanimates. Animates have an ordinary singular–plural system. Again then we have top and second systems, with the higher nouns having a regular system, and those lower on the Animacy Hierarchy having a conflated system. Here it is not the conflation of the system of the higher nouns, as was the case in Pame.

top system	singular	plural	
second system	singular/dual/trial		plural

Figure 4.16 *Top and second systems in Tuyuca*[39]

A final example is Larike, which as we saw in §2.2.3 has singular, dual, trial and plural. However, there are no free pronouns for use with non-human referents. Subject and object markers on the verb are available for non-human third persons, but there are only two forms here, not four (dual and trial forms are not available for non-humans): 'The 3rd person plural nonhuman affixes are generally used when referring to a large number. It is not uncommon for the singular nonhuman form to be used as limited plural' (Laidig and Laidig 1990: 95). This too is a case of conflation: the singular form is used to cover more values for non-human referents than it does for humans; it covers the dual and trial giving a number value which cannot be found as a major number.

These conflated systems are accommodated into the typology in that they occur only as second systems; they may be, but do not have to be, a conflation of the values of the top system of the same language. Conflation will be considered further in the discussion of inverse systems (§5.5). Before leaving conflated systems we should ask what possible values they can have. Given that few conflated systems have been described, there are two hypotheses open: first it may be that we can take the systems described in §2.3.2 and conflate values starting from the left (e.g. conflate singular

---

[39] This shows again clearly how 'plural' means different things in different systems.

and dual, conflate singular, dual and trial, and so on); or second, we may take any regular system and conflate all values except the plural. This is the more restrictive hypothesis and so, while waiting for further examples, we will adopt it here:

> IX *Possible systems of values for conflated systems*
> The systems of values for conflated systems are those of regular systems, with all values conflated except the plural.

This constraint allows for systems which have not yet been found; it remains to be seen whether they will be found or whether the constraint should be limited further.

4.5.2 Mass number (dialects of north-west Spain)

In various Spanish dialects, we find a distinct mass number. We take examples from the Lena dialect (spoken in the Asturias region of northwestern Spain), closely following Hualde (1992), who in turn makes extensive use of Neira (1955, 1982).[40] In Standard Spanish we find a straightforward singular–plural opposition of number; furthermore nouns are divided into two genders, masculine and feminine, which gives four distinct forms for agreeing elements such as adjectives. In the Lena dialect, by contrast, some nouns have three forms: in addition to *pílu* 'hair' (singular) and *pélos* 'hair' (plural) we also find *pélo* 'hair' (mass). Which nouns have this third form? There appear to be two restrictions. The first is semantic, the noun must have a possible mass interpretation. The second restriction is morphological: only masculine nouns ending in *-u* have a distinct mass form. Thus the masculine noun *kafé* 'coffee' can make no such distinction, nor can the feminine noun *boróna* 'cornbread'.

In terms of noun morphology, then, this is a strange distribution. However, the data from the Lena dialect are much more interesting than the purely morphological data suggest since the opposition between count and mass is indicated for other types of noun too, by agreement. Consider the following (Hualde 1992: 108):

(27) la   maéra tába sék-o
      DEF.SG.FEM wood   was   dry-MASS
      'the wood (mass) was dry'

(28) la   maéra tába sék-a
      DEF.SG.FEM wood   was   dry-SG.FEM
      'the (piece of) wood was dry'

---

[40] For further discussion and sources see Ojeda (1992b); see also Penny (1970), Hall (1968), who also considers comparable data from central-south Italian dialects, and Harris (1992: 82–4). Interesting data on additional dialects can be found in Klein (1980) and Klein-Andreu (1996).

Thus though a particular noun may not itself show a distinct form, the count–mass distinction may be indicated by agreement. Adjectives, for instance, may have a separate form. Besides *nígr-u* 'black (SG MASC)', and *négr-a* 'black (SG FEM)', there is a form *négr-o* 'black (MASS)' which can be used equally of masculine and feminine nouns:

(29) el   kafé   négr-o
      DEF.SG.MASC   coffee   black-MASS
      'the black coffee'

(30) la   boróna   négr-o
      DEF.SG.FEM   cornbread   black-MASS
      'the black cornbread'

In our discussion of the different tests for determining splits within number systems (§3.3) we determined that agreement gives clearer results than marking on the noun itself. That is the case here, as adjectival agreement shows. However, the definite article deserves further attention: in (29) and (30) we have masculine and feminine singular articles respectively, even though the adjective shows the mass form. Similarly in example (27) the article is feminine singular, despite the presence of an adjective in the mass form. The question then is where gender agreement is possible with mass nouns. According to Hualde (1992: 109) the mass feature 'will determine agreement with certain elements (adjectives outside the noun phrase or to the right of the noun in the noun phrase and clitics) and the gender feature will control the agreement of other elements (determiners and prenominal adjectives)'. It appears then that with these mass nouns gender agreement is found only within the noun phrase, otherwise we find mass agreement. This pattern is in accord with the Agreement Hierarchy, which we shall discuss in §6.2 (note that in §3.3 we claimed that the different positions of the Agreement Hierarchy give increasingly good results as tests for determining number splits and the Spanish dialect data are a case in point).

While many languages allow for the recategorization of count nouns as mass nouns (see §3.7.2), having a special additional form is rare. Again, given the limits of the data we should be cautious; however, the distinction is not limited along the lines of constraint (V); rather the lowest part of the nouns which differentiate number is involved. In other words, we appear to have another example of second system which is not found as a top system (see figure 4.17). The special second system, with a unique agreement form (and sometimes a noun marker in addition) for mass interpretation of count nouns, seems unsurprising, yet it is extremely rare. The count–mass distinction is typically coded in other ways, for example by means of determiner systems.[41]

[41] For examples of a special mass form in Scandinavian languages see Delsing (1993: 44–5).

top system	singular		plural
second system	mass	singular	plural

Figure 4.17 *Top and second systems in dialects of north-west Spain*

4.5.3 General number

We must now integrate into the picture the widespread systems with general number (discussed in §2.1 and §3.4). In their most common form, these have nouns for which the speaker need not make a distinction of number, but may distinguish singular and plural when required (we return to more complex variants in §4.5.4). They are relevant here because the system with general number is almost always the second system in a given language. It has been claimed, however, to operate as the top system in Asheninca (§2.1, note 9); we would expect that to be a possibility since, if a language can have no number (like Pirahã, §2.4), then a development to more common systems would most likely be through that recorded for Asheninca. However, since the overwhelming majority of languages with general number have it as a second system, we shall treat it in that way here.

Let us take for our example the Cushitic language Qafar. Here the personal pronouns are restricted to use for humans and there is a singular–plural opposition which is obligatory. For nouns denoting humans too, the plural is used for referring to more than one. But for other animates and nouns lower on the Animacy Hierarchy, the plural is not obligatory.[42] We saw in §2.3.3 how the initially attractive solution of treating the lower nouns as having an optional plural is unsatisfactory, since the pattern of overlapping of forms gives the wrong prediction. Recall too that while for many nouns the pattern is general/singular versus plural, for subsets of the lexicon as in many languages it will be singular versus general/plural (§2.1).[43] The distinguishing feature of this system, which we must not miss, is that for the relevant segment of the noun inventory there is a form which is non-specific as to number. This may be overwhelmingly the more frequent form, whether it has a secondary role as singular or as plural, and it is not restricted to nouns with mass interpretation.

The picture for Qafar, then, is that as a top system it has a straightforward singular–plural system, while as its second system it has general versus singular–plural.

---

[42] One view would be that it is derivational rather than inflectional, which fits with other facts: people have to think what the plurals are; there are competing forms, and speakers will disagree on whether a particular noun has a plural or not (Dick Hayward, personal communication; 1998: 627).

[43] In §2.1 we were concerned with the pattern for groups of nouns; here we are working at a somewhat more abstract level, characterizing the nominal inventories of languages in terms of a small number of systems. For the complex system of another Cushitic language, Somali, see Serzisko (1992).

top system	singular – plural
second system	general – [singular – plural]

Figure 4.18 *Top and second systems in Qafar*

At the bottom we find the non-number-differentiable nouns. The Qafar system, which in its essentials is like that of a substantial proportion of the world's languages, may be represented as in figure 4.18. Of course, languages vary as to how large a top segment of the Animacy Hierarchy is covered by the top system; in Qafar it extends down to the nouns denoting humans. Figure 4.18 shows the special status of general number. It is in opposition to a complete system. There is a division between treating number as not relevant or relevant, and if relevant then the choice is singular–plural. General number is special in that it typically occurs within a second system. It may very rarely occur within a top system, but it normally occurs within a second system, with a different top system above it.

In Qafar we find general opposed to a singular–plural system, which is common. We should ask what are the possible systems that general can be opposed to. Data are scarce on this question; the simplest answer at this stage is that any top system can in principle occur there (it remains to be seen if we can find motivated constraints to limit the possibilities). The most extended system parallel to general number found to date is that of Kaytetye (§2.3.3), shown in figure 4.19.

top system	singular – dual – plural
second system	general – [singular – dual – plural – greater plural]

Figure 4.19 *Top and second systems in Kaytetye*

Recall that the choice in the second system is not to mark number (general) or to mark it; if the latter choice is made, then it will be the appropriate number. Specifically, the plural is not used for two referents (Harold Koch, personal communication). The other respect in which systems including general number are special is that they frequently have no unique morphological form for general number (we saw too that it is rare for there to be a special form for mass). Some do, however, and it is to these that we now turn.

4.5.4 Bayso

We return to Bayso, one of the most fascinating languages for the study of number. Hayward's account (1979) is invaluable, but he had limited time to work on the language in the field, and there are tantalizing questions left open. We saw in §2.1 that

top system	singular – plural
second system	general – [singular – paucal – plural]

Figure 4.20 *Top and second systems in Bayso*

Bayso has a system for nouns with a morphologically distinct general number; if a number choice is made, however, then the choices are singular, paucal and plural. The different number values induce different agreements (in a complex system to be discussed in §6.1.1).[44] The pronouns have singular and plural. This is a very rare system, which we represent as in figure 4.20. In chapter 2, we were concerned with possible systems, and so we examined whichever nominals gave most distinctions. In Bayso, therefore, we took nouns with the system just described, the typical nouns which comprise the majority of nominals. Here we see a great difference between the top system and the second system, since the personal pronouns have a straightforward singular–plural opposition, and it is an obligatory system, while the number-differentiable nouns have an opposition between general and a three-member system.

We should consider the status of this singular–paucal–plural system.[45] There are few relevant languages on which to base generalizations and so we should be cautious. To the best of my knowledge, there is no extensively described case of a language with this system for the pronouns, that is, which has it as its top system. However, the Yuman language Walapai (Hualapai) is claimed to have singular–paucal–plural both for pronouns and for nouns (Redden 1966: 149–50, 159), which suggests that singular–paucal–plural is a possible top system. Bearing this in mind, we can re-evaluate the Bayso situation. Bayso shows that it is possible to have different systems operating at different points on the hierarchy (something we have now seen in several languages). The more complex system is found lower down the hierarchy in Bayso; that too we have seen before, for instance in Qafar. In Bayso the vast majority of the nominals have the more complex system; furthermore there is a distinctive marker for general number. (And Bayso has a further surprise in store, in §6.1.1.) What then of the singular–paucal–plural system? When discussing other languages with an opposition general versus other system, it seemed that the simplest claim, based on limited evidence, was that in principle these parallel systems

---

[44] It might be suggested that some or all of the number values of the nouns are derivational rather than inflectional, and that argument (one which we have tried to avoid) might be used to exclude them. Here there is no possibility of doing so since they determine different agreements.

[45] In earlier work I used 'major number' in a confusing way of the system of Bayso. The singular–paucal–plural system might be called the major system of Bayso in that most nouns have it, but it is not major in the sense of being used at the top of the hierarchy.

could consist of general versus any normal top system. That position would lead us to recognize singular–paucal–plural as a possible top system, which is supported by Redden's account of Walapai. (There are other ways forward here, but they would involve a complex account of possible second systems, in order to allow for conflated number systems and those with mass number, as well as the systems of Qafar and many similar languages, Kaytetye and Bayso and yet to exclude others.) Until further evidence becomes available the present typology appears simpler. Another advantage of accepting singular–paucal–plural as a potential top system is that Avar (§4.2.3) now fits neatly. It has singular, plural and a minor paucal, and so fulfils the constraints for having a minor number, notably constraint (VI).

4.5.5 Minor numbers revisited

Since we have returned to Avar, this is an appropriate point to revisit the question of minor numbers more generally. Major and minor numbers are to be distinguished clearly from top and second systems. Major and minor refer to particular number values of a given language: major number values are found for some top segment of the hierarchy; minor number values are not, and they are constrained in ways discussed earlier. Top and second refer to the systems in a particular language: the top system is that which combines all the major number values of the language; a second system in a given language is a different system operating from the point on the Animacy Hierarchy below which the top system ceases to operate.

Following the analysis of Bayso in the last section, we can now suggest the way in which two more difficult cases can fit. The first is Fula (Fouta Jalon dialect), which was discussed in §2.1. Pronouns and most nouns have a singular–plural system, but a sizeable minority of nouns have a general–[singular–plural] system, with the general number having a distinctive form. It is now plausible to analyse this general number value as a minor number. It adheres to the constraints in §4.2.5 above, since the proportion of the nominals involved is relatively small by comparison to those involved in the major numbers (constraint IV), the nouns with the minor number (general) are within the range of those with the major numbers (V), and finally the general used as a minor number is within a number system which would match an otherwise attested system of number values (VI). The latter constraint holds, provided we allow second systems to count for its purposes. Fula thus has two minor numbers under this analysis, a greater plural (§2.2.6 above) and a general.

The final type to consider here is that illustrated by Maltese (which is comparable to Syrian Arabic, discussed briefly in §2.1). In Maltese, a typical noun has singular and plural, as in the case of *raġel* 'man', *rġel* 'men'. As we have already seen, a very few nouns also have a dual. There is an additional number value to consider:

it is often called the collective.[46] As stressed in §4.4.2, the term is used variously. Clearly the collective in Maltese is very different from the types of collective plural discussed earlier; it is arguably the same as what we are calling the general (see Gil 1996, Mifsud 1996 for discussion). This additional form is available for a sizeable minority of nouns: nouns denoting fruits and vegetables are well represented; also included are some smaller animates, particularly insects (but never persons). The category still gains new members through borrowings. There is a further restriction in that the special form typically ends in a consonant, and its singular is formed by the affixation of *-a*. Thus we have 'collective' *dubbien* 'flies', singular *dubbiena* 'fly'.

How does such a case differ from a normal singular and plural pair? In Maltese the numerals 2–10 normally take a noun in the plural, while those from 11 upwards (like the numeral 1) take a singular. The singular *dubbiena* 'fly' occurs as expected with the numerals 11 and upwards, but the 'collective' may not appear with the numerals 2–10. Nouns which have a 'collective' have a third form, the 'determinate plural' (*dubbiniet*), which is used for this purpose, as in (32) below. The resulting morphological pattern of three forms is what distinguishes these nouns.[47]

A further distinguishing feature is that, depending on the 'number preference' of the noun (see Gil 1996), the 'collective' may have different interpretations. This strongly recalls earlier discussion of the general. In the case of *dubbien*, the natural interpretation is plural 'flies', but the use of the form can cover instances, if rarely, where only a single fly is involved.[48] Unusually for a minor number, this minor

---

[46] See Sutcliffe (1936: 30–1, 36–7), Aquilina (1965: 71–3), Borg (1981: 15–16, 106–9) and especially Mifsud (1996). Sutcliffe is perhaps best read in the light of the comments by Borg (1981: 106–9). For an account of the formal semantics of number in Arabic, which has various similarities, see Ojeda (1992a).

[47] There is an extremely small number of exceptions – nouns which have two plurals of which neither is a collective (see Sutcliffe 1936: 48–9; Fabri 1993: 24); the use of one of the plurals is typically restricted, often to idiomatic uses (Ray Fabri, personal communication). Then a small number of nouns have four forms. For instance, *ħajta* (singular) 'piece of thread', *ħajt* (collective), *ħajtiet* (plural – for use with numerals 2–10). So far this is like any other noun which has a collective and hence has three forms. The additional form is the plural of the collective *ħjut*, which for Fabri (personal communication) means 'sorts of thread' (compare Borg 1981: 107). This is an instance of recategorization (see §3.7.2).

[48] After some discussion, a group of native speakers agreed that if someone sued a restaurant alleging there had been *dubbien* in his soup, it would be no defence to say his accusation was untrue because there had been only one fly involved (see also the example in Mifsud 1996: 33). Equally, in a better restaurant, the following would be possible (Ray Fabri, personal communication):

> (i) Dik   is-soppa   x'fiha?   Basal   u   tadam.
>   That   the-soup   what.in.her?   Onion   and   tomato.
>   'What's in that soup?' 'Onion and tomato.'

Here there could be more or less than a whole onion and a whole tomato. Compare the discussion and quotations on the Arabic collective in Greenberg (1972: 24); see also Premper (1986). For the Tigre collective see Palmer (1962).

number value in Maltese has an effect on agreement; it does not have a unique agreement form, but it can induce variability. Collective nouns, including those whose number preference is plural (as with *dubbien* 'flies'), usually take singular agreement (according to Fabri 1993: 86–8) but especially colloquially they often take the plural (Mifsud 1996: 43–5). The following data and acceptability judgements are from Manwel Mifsud (personal communication, there appears to be wide variation).

singular

(31) Dik   id-dubbiena   l-kbira
      that.SG.FEM   the-fly   the-large.SG.FEM

      daħlet   mit-tieqa
      entered.SG.FEM   from.the-window

      'That large fly came in through the window'

determinate plural

(32) Dawk   il-ħames   dubbiniet   kbar[49]   daħlu
      those.PL   the-five   flies   large.PL   entered.PL

      mit-tieqa
      from.the-window

      'Those five large flies came in through the window'

'collective'

(33) Dak   id-dubbien   il-kbir
      that.SG.MASC   the-flies   the-large.SG.MASC

      daħal   mit-tieqa
      entered.SG.MASC   from.the-window

      'Those large flies came in through the window'

With singular nouns and with those in the determinate plural form (with a numeral 2–10) the agreements are just as expected. But with 'collective' nouns (33) we find masculine singular agreement both in attributive position and in the predicate. According to Manwel Mifsud, this is the normal agreement; however, some speakers would use the plural (*dawk id-dubbien il-kbar daħlu*) as a result of the influence of English. We also find variation in other syntactic positions (reported in Corbett 1996); these are in accord with the Agreement Hierarchy (§6.2). This is another system which deserves further study; it seems best to treat it as having a minor

---

[49] The article may optionally be included here: *il-kbar*.

number, the general. It is particularly interesting that there are a substantial number of nouns which have general number, and the group is gaining new members.

4.6 Conclusion

In this chapter we took the analyses of number values (chapter 2) and the Animacy Hierarchy (chapter 3) and integrated them. For many languages, that integration was quite straightforward: the additional number values (beyond the singular-plural systems considered in chapter 3) were added in, along fairly intuitive and obvious lines (§4.1). Then we found languages with small 'patches' of exceptions, groups of nouns with minor numbers, which were exceptional, but in strictly definable ways. Next we found categories which are clearly related to number, but which turned out not to be a part of number systems (associatives in §4.3 and distributives and collectives – one type of these – in §4.4). Finally we looked at various languages, some representing whole groups, others almost unique, which required us to extend the typology, primarily by introducing the notion of 'second system', which allowed for languages to have a type of number system operating for a lower part of the Animacy Hierarchy which would not normally be found as a top system.

At first it was relatively plain sailing: we had established the essentials clearly and with strong evidence, and so the natural move for building a complete typology was to put them together. By the end, progress was more difficult, because we needed to extend the typology to cover those languages which were less straightforward, and yet on the basis of less evidence. We gave a typology which includes the difficult cases, but we tried to make clear the options and the difficulties, so that others will be aware of the issues and may find new evidence and move the typology forward. Theory is about opening doors rather than closing them.

5

The expression of number

It is now time to look at the ways in which number is expressed. This rather basic issue is a surprisingly novel one. Of course, many grammars describe number marking in individual languages but little has been done towards a typology. We shall therefore give an initial typology, one which aims to list the possibilities (claiming that the listed types can exist and no more). The obvious candidates for number expression are all found: special words (§5.1), syntax (§5.2), morphology (§5.3) and lexical means (§5.4). We shall then examine three types of system which are distinctive and which belong here in a discussion of means because they do not give rise to new semantic distinctions. (This is why they were not treated in chapter 2.) These are inverse systems (§5.5), minimal-augmented systems (§5.6) and 'constructed' numbers (§5.7). Finally we take up the discussion of the reduced expression of number, considering the form of items which are not (or not fully) within the number system (§5.8).

The main typological point is the importance of comparing like with like. In previous chapters we examined number values and their ranges of availability and compared each of these across languages. Now we turn to the means of expression, and must continue to be clear about when our claims relate to meaning and when to the means of expression. Thus we have values such as dual or paucal (which are expressed in various ways), and we have systems of expression (such as inverse number); we cannot therefore treat inverse as a value to put alongside dual and paucal. Naturally, in this chapter we concentrate on the variety of means of expression, and on the patterns which are claimed to underlie this variety.

5.1   Number words

Some languages have special 'number words', just for the purpose of indicating number. Thus in Tagalog, virtually any constituent can be pluralized by the word *mga* [maŋa], perhaps best characterized as a clitic (David Gil, personal communication):

(1) mga   bahay
   PL   house
   'houses'

(2) mga   tubig
   PL   water
   'cups/units of water'

(3) mga   Marcos
   PL   Marcos
   'Marcoses'

(4) mga   ma-puti
   PL   STATIVE-white
   'white ones'

Another clear case is provided by Miskitu, a Misumalpan language of the Caribbean Coast of Nicaragua and Honduras (T. Green 1992):

(5) aras
   'horse'

(6) aras   kum
   horse   SG
   'a horse'

(7) aras   kumkum
   horse   several
   'several horses'

(8) aras   nani
   horse   PL
   'horses'

(9) yang   kauhw-ri
   1   fall-1.PAST.INDEF
   'I fell'

(10) yang   nani   kauhw-ri
    1   PL   fall-1.PAST.INDEF
    'We (exclusive) fell'

Note particularly that the pronoun in (10) takes the plural word in a regular way (recall §3.5).[1] There is interesting work to be done on the syntactic category of

---

[1] Other examples of this are Canela-Krahô, a Jê language of Brazil (Popjes and Popjes 1986: 175–6, 185–6, examples (309) and (368)), and Golin, a Chimbu language of Papua

number words, which varies considerably (Dryer 1989), and on their word-order properties (Dryer 1992: 104–5). In Dogon (a Voltaic language, within Niger-Kordofanian, spoken in Mali), the number word is a clitic found at the end of the phrase (Plungian 1995: 9–10):

(11) ɛnɛ   mbe
      goat   PL
      'goats'

(12) ɛnɛ   gɛ   mbe
      goat   DEF   PL
      'the goats'

(13) ɛnɛ   wo   mi   ŋ   ob-i-Ø   gɛ   mbe
      goat   3   1   OBJ   give-AOR-3.SG   DEF   PL
      'the goats which he gave me'

Number marking with *mbe* is not obligatory.[2] In Dogon the personal pronouns mark number (by suppletion) and a small number of nouns denoting humans have a plural marker (and this fits the pattern according to which different means of marking can follow the Animacy Hierarchy, see §3.5). With such nouns, the plural clitic is often used as well:

(14) nndɛ-m   mbe
      person-PL   PL
      'people'

Further examples of plural words can be found in Dryer (1989).[3] Diachronically, number words are a potential source of number morphology (§9.1.1). Of course, languages typically have quantifiers, with meanings such as 'many' or 'few', and various numerals (§6.7.1), but our interest here is in the purer number words, equivalent to plural.[4]

New Guinea (Bunn 1974: 55). For the complex interaction of number words with pronouns in Vietnamese, see Luong (1987).

[2] Our focus here is on the means of marking. As discussed elsewhere, these different means may have different uses. Thus the Dogon *mbe* can have a sort reading (§3.7.2), can be used with associative meaning (§4.3) and as an approximative plural (§7.3.3); here these uses are of secondary interest while we concentrate on means.

[3] See also E. Allan (1976: 380–3) on Dizi, where the plural word is phrase-final, Mosel (1982: 125; 1984) on Tolai, Macauley (1989) on Chalcatongo Mixtec, van den Berg (1989: 108–9) on Muna, Liclan and Marlett (1990) on Madija, and Frajzyngier (1997) on various Chadic languages. The third person plural pronoun may function as a number word, as in Angas (Newman 1990: 15), see also Westermann (1945–46). The rise of plural words in Creoles is discussed in Holm (1990).

[4] The remarkable phenomenon of 'promiscuous' number marking is found in languages of the northern north-west coast of North America, namely Haida, Eyak, Aleut and to a

5.2 Syntax

The way in which number is marked syntactically is through agreement. Often agreement is in addition to other morphological means of marking. For instance:

(15)   Those goats are eating the washing.

Here we find plurality marked on the head noun *goats*, the controller of the agreement, and by agreement on two agreement targets: the demonstrative *those* within the noun phrase, and the verb *are* outside the noun phrase. However, we may also find a comparable situation when the controller itself does not mark number:

(16)   Those sheep are doing nothing about it.

Here *sheep* is plural, though this is not indicated on the noun itself. We noted in §3.3 that where the morphological marking and control of agreement do not coincide, it is agreement which will be more regular in terms of the Animacy Hierarchy. It is important to note that the number marked on the verb is nominal number, indicating the number of sheep, rather than the number of eating events. We return to this distinction in chapter 8. Thus in a sense we have nominal number marked 'in the wrong place'; it is this displaced information which is the essential ingredient of agreement. Cross-linguistically, demonstratives and verbs are relatively frequent agreement targets, showing agreement in number either uniquely or combined with other categories, notably gender. Other targets can include articles, adjectives, pronouns, nouns (especially in possessive constructions), numerals, adverbs, adpositions and complementizers (see Corbett 1991: 106–15 for examples).

While agreement is often an additional means of marking number, as in (15) above, there are languages where the situation in (16) is prevalent. This particularly interesting situation is found in the Papuan language Amele (J. Roberts 1987: 162, 201, 203 and personal communication). Amele belongs to the Madang subgroup within the Trans New Guinea phylum. Here are some relevant examples:

Footnote 4 (*cont.*)
lesser extent Tlingit (Leer 1991). Here a clitic which marks number may be associated semantically with different pronominal forms.

> In Tlingit, for example, the number marker *has#* pluralizes animate third-person pronouns. Morphosyntactically, it is a proclitic; semantically, it associates with an animate third person in the word to which it is proclitic. If this word is a transitive verb, either subject or object (or both) may be animate third-person pronouns. In this case, the number marker is free to pluralize such a pronoun whether it is subject or object; and if both subject and object are animate third-person pronouns, the marker may pluralize either or both. (Leer 1991: 160).

(17) Dana   (uqa)   ho-i-a
      man   3.SG   come-3.SG-TODAY'S.PAST
      'The man came'

(18) Dana   (ale)   ho-si-a
      man   3.DU   come-3.DU-TODAY'S.PAST
      'The two men came'

(19) Dana   (age)   ho-ig-a
      man   3.PL   come-3.PL-TODAY'S.PAST
      'The men came'

In Amele the verb must agree in number with the subject, as shown in our examples by the formatives -i-, -si- and -ig-. (The formative -a indicates today's past tense; and the unmarked NP has a definite referent (J. Roberts 1987: 203).) The noun may show plural number by reduplication (*dana-dana* 'men'), but this is optional.[5] Number may also be indicated by pronominal copy, but this too is optional, as indicated by parentheses in our examples. Thus we have nominal number which must be indicated on the verb and which may optionally be indicated on the noun.

We have dealt with the cases of matching between the features of controller and target. There are rather different situations where mismatches between nominal and verb create a new number value, and these are discussed in §5.7. Problem cases of agreement which do not produce new number values are considered in chapter 6, where agreement is the central concern. The interplay of the syntactic and morphological expression of number is a recurring theme, and so we now turn to morphological expression.[6]

---

[5] William Foley (personal communication) suggests Arafundi as an even clearer example. Arafundi is spoken in Papua New Guinea and is an isolate or may be distantly related to the Piawi family. In six weeks of fieldwork Foley found no number marking of any kind on nouns, thus even more than in Amele the verb is the main locus of number marking. The pronoun does, however, mark number. Nichols (1992: 148–149) shows that in general number is 'highly prone to be drawn off the noun and marked by agreement, primarily on the verb'.

[6] A truly remarkable situation is found in Korean. According to Seok Choong Song (1975), plurality may or may not be marked on the noun by the marker -*tul*. The choice depends in part on definiteness (definite noun phrases are likely to have the head noun marked for number) and on the Animacy Hierarchy (§3.2): nouns denoting humans and other animates are much more likely to be marked for number than are inanimates. The plural marker may also occur in the predicate (Song calls it the 'ubiquitous plural marker'), and it is here that the special interest of Korean is to be found. Consider the following example (Lee 1991: 81):

   (i) ai-tul-i   Tom-eyke-[]   ppang-ul-[]   manhi-[]   cwuesseyo-[]
       child-PL-NOM   Tom-to   bread-ACC   a.lot   gave
       'the children gave Tom a lot of bread'

5.3 Morphology

We have seen many examples of the morphological expression of number in earlier chapters. It is widespread in the world's languages and very varied. Indeed one could describe a substantial part of the morphological resources of natural language while taking the examples exclusively from number. We shall consider the range of possibilities briefly. Given the necessary brevity an important distinction to bear in mind is that between the system of number marking in a particular language and that found with individual lexical items. In the book so far we have tried where possible to concentrate on whole systems: for instance, we have said that nouns in English distinguish singular and plural (and then discussed special cases like *sheep* and *friendliness*). In this section we shall instead concentrate on variety, even if small numbers of items are involved. We do this for two reasons. First, relatively little has been done on the distribution of morphological subsystems within languages. There are few languages for which we can state the proportion of nominals which mark number according to different methods. However, we did note the generalizations based on the Animacy Hierarchy in §3.5. The other reason for this approach is that the coexistence of different types of morphology is so common that it seemed more appropriate to emphasize this coexistence. Thus in §5.3.1 we are able to take almost all the different examples from a single language. The variety can become so extensive that in some languages number becomes almost a lexical matter (a possibility we return to in §5.4). We first consider the relation between stems and inflections in an abstract way (§5.3.1) and then look in turn at the range of variety within inflections (§5.3.2) and within stems (§5.3.3) and at zero

Footnote 6 (*cont.*)

The subject *ai-tul-i* is marked as plural. The plural marker *-tul* can also appear at any of the points indicated []. The *-tul* used in the predicate is not redundant. It indicates that the constituent to which it is attached represents new information (Lee 1991: 83). Furthermore it guarantees a distributive reading, as can be shown by the next two examples:

(ii) haksayng-tul-i   phwungsen   hana-lul   sasseyo
     student-PL-NOM   balloon   one-ACC   bought
     'the students bought a balloon'

(iii) haksayng-tul-i   phwungsen   hana-lul-tul   sasseyo
      student-PL-NOM   balloon   one-ACC-PL   bought
      'the students bought a balloon each'

In sentence (ii) the students may have bought just one balloon between them, or one each. Sentence (iii), with *-tul* marking the object constituent has only the second, distributive reading (see §2.5 and §4.4.1). The distributive role of *-tul* is stressed by Jae Jung Song (1997). For other research on this interesting construction and on number in Korean more generally see Kuh (1987), Unterbeck (1993), Kang (1994), Kim (1994), Prost (1992) and Kwak (1996).

expression (§5.3.4). Next we return to the issue of phrasal affixes as a type of clitic (§5.3.5) and finally look at multiple marking (§5.3.6).

5.3.1   Relations between stems and inflections

We start from the notion of 'base' (or 'basic inflectional stem'). The base of a lexical item is the form which cannot be further reduced as far as inflectional categories are concerned. The Russian noun *komnata* 'room' (nominative singular) has the plural *komnaty*. The base is *komnat-* and the inflections (endings in this instance) are -*a* (nominative singular) and -*y* (nominative plural). Why do we make the division there, rather than claiming, for instance, that the base is *komn-* and the inflections -*ata* and -*aty*? There are thousands of other nouns which can be analysed as taking the inflections -*a* and -*y* (such as *golov-a* 'head', plural *golov-y*, or *sten-a* 'wall' plural *sten-y*) but relatively few for which the other segmentation makes any sense. Let us consider a language which has at least two numbers, singular and plural. What are the possible relations between the number forms and the base for a given lexical item (or group of lexical items)? We first take a maximally general model, as in figure 5.1. How can the singular and plural forms differ from

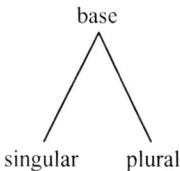

base

/\

singular   plural

Figure 5.1 *Potential distinctions for number marking*

the base? First they may differ in inflection. Or they can vary from the base through stem formation. These two devices, inflection and stem formation may occur separately or together. That gives three possibilities: difference just in terms of inflection, just in terms of stem, or in both. The fourth logical possibility is that neither inflection nor stem formation is employed. If this means that the singular form, plural form and basic stem are all identical, then clearly number is simply not marked morphologically for the items in question (as in the case of English *sheep* or Russian *kenguru* 'kangaroo(s)'). We therefore elaborate the model as in figure 5.2, allowing for different stems. Let us take examples of number marking, and consider in particular whether or not all the elements identified in the diagram are distinct in particular examples. Remember that different patterns often coexist within a single language; if an example is given from a particular language this does not mean that the pattern is the major one for that language.

If we start with the relations between the base and the stems, the first logical possibility is that all are distinct. This possibility can be illustrated by the irregular

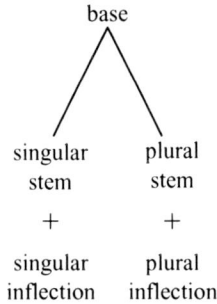

Figure 5.2 *Possible stems and inflections*

Russian noun, *xozjain* 'landlord'. The base is *xozja(j)-*,[7] the singular stem is *xozja-in-* and the plural stem is *xozja-ev-*. Both stems allow the addition of endings. Thus singular and plural are each indicated both by the stem and by the ending. The extreme type of difference is found in cases of suppletion, where there are different stems which are not related by any regular or irregular type of stem formation (though they show a regular grammatical opposition). An example is Russian *čelovek* 'person', plural *ljud-i* 'people'.[8] Note that we are indeed dealing with stems here: *čelovek-* 'person' takes normal singular inflections, and *ljud-* 'people' takes plural inflections. We return to suppletion in §5.4 and §9.2.2.

It is unusual for the base, the singular stem and the plural stem all to be distinct, in Russian and more generally. Often we find that the base and the singular stem are identical, as in figure 5.3 (there are interesting parallels with the systems of values in §2.1). A Russian illustration of this pattern is the noun *krylo* 'wing'. This has the base *kryl-*, to which the singular endings are added directly (*kryl-o*, *kryl-a*, *kryl-u* and so on). The plural stem is *kryl'j-* (the ´ marks palatalization of the preceding consonant), as in the nominative plural *kryl'j-a*. Why should we say that there is a distinct plural stem here, rather than that the nominative plural ending is palatalization plus *-ja* ? The point is that *-a* is a regular nominative plural ending, found on thousands of nouns which do not have a separate plural stem. (We return in §5.3.2 to the point about *-a* being a singular ending in *komnat-a* 'room' but a plural ending here.) The plural endings for the remaining cases of Russian are also found on other nouns (see table 5.2 below); we would be missing an obvious generalization if we claimed there were special endings right through the plural paradigm while in fact

[7] Since Russian orthography is largely morphophonemic, we use a transliterated form for simplicity here. The details of the use of *j*, being present in the root but not spelled in the stems, need not detain us.

[8] The Russian suppletion is matched by the natural English translations *person* and *people*, though of course *persons* does exist in English.

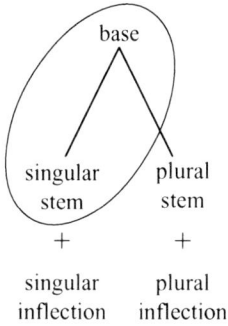

Figure 5.3 *Singular stem matches the base*

nouns like *krylo* 'wing' differ from other nouns only in having a different stem for the plural.

The next possibility is that the plural stem should be the same as the base as in figure 5.4. Again the pattern is found in Russian. The noun *bolgarin* 'a Bulgarian' has the base *bolgar-*, and the plural stem is identical, as in forms like the nominative plural *bolgar-y*. The singular stem differs, and is *bolgarin-*. Several nouns denoting nationalities and other social groupings behave in this way.

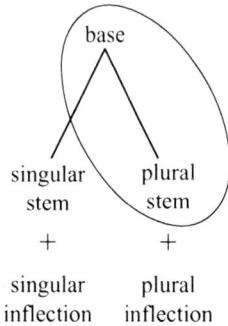

Figure 5.4 *Plural stem matches the base*

A final relation of base to stems is that all are identical, diagrammed as in figure 5.5 (p. 142). This situation is extremely common. Again in Russian we find many nouns like that for 'room', which has the basic stem *komnat-*. The (nominative) singular is *komnat-a* and the (nominative) plural is *komnat-y*. Here stem formation has no role, and the entire burden of signalling a difference in number is carried by the inflections.

We move on to look for identities elsewhere in the model. There is a further, initially rather surprising type of identity, shown in figure 5.6. This pattern suggests

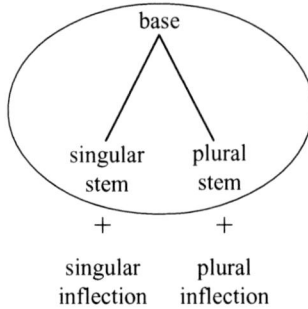

Figure 5.5 *Both stems match the base*

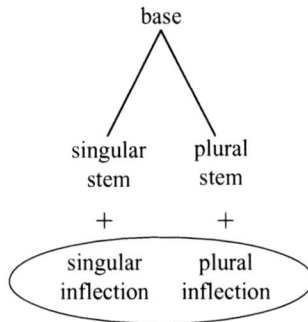

Figure 5.6 *Inflections not sensitive to number*

that the inflections used for singular and plural could be identical. This situation regularly occurs in Daghestanian languages for the majority of the large numbers of cases they distinguish (often just the absolutive is an exception). The Akhvakh noun *nido* 'forehead' shows a clear case of identical endings: we take absolutive and ergative cases to illustrate the point in table 5.1. In this example the base is *nido*, and the singular stem is identical to it. The plural stem is *nido-di-*. The absolutive case, in singular and plural, has no ending. In both numbers there is an oblique stem, distinct from the basic singular or plural stem; in the singular it is formed with *-la-*, and in the plural with *-le-*. The various oblique case endings are added to this stem; in our example the ergative case is given, and the appropriate ending is *-de*. As with the absolutive, the ending is the same for singular and plural. The point is that information about number is signalled by the differences in the stems: *-di-* indicates plurality for this noun, *-la-* shows singular oblique, and *-le-* plural oblique. Thus a form like *nido-di-le-de* indicates plurality twice. The endings have no role in the number system, their function is to mark the case of the noun. This identity of form of endings in the singular and plural is quite general in

Table 5.1 *Number marking in Akhvakh*
(Kibrik 1991: 260)

	singular	plural
absolutive	nido	nido-di
ergative	nido-la-de	nido-di-le-de

Daghestanian languages. It is to be distinguished from occasional syncretisms of form involving small numbers of nouns in languages where the coincidence of form is not systematic (we see an example from another language family in table 5.4 below).

There is a final pattern of identity we should mention again, that in which both stems are identical to the base, and where the stems are identical to the forms with endings (that is, there are no endings). Under these conditions the noun is indeclinable, hence number is not marked morphologically. There are numerous examples of this situation, both of languages where number is not marked morphologically on particular word classes (English adjectives, for example) or not marked morphologically at all. But more interestingly it may be found for a subset of a word class within a system where number is usually marked morphologically. Thus in Russian, the majority of nouns distinguish two numbers but some, especially foreign borrowings, do not. For example, *kenguru* may denote one or more kangaroos, and *taksi* may denote one or more taxis (the ambiguity will often be removed by elements showing agreement in number, see §5.2).

5.3.2 Inflections

In some languages a particular ending signals immediately what the number is. Thus in Central Alaskan Yup'ik, as we saw in §4.3.3, the ending *-t* indicates a noun in the plural. Compare this with the situation we met in Russian (§5.3.1), where *-a* signals the singular in *komnat-a* 'room', but plural in *kryl'j-a.* 'wings'. This is the first important typological distinction, between languages which have different inflectional classes (of nouns in this instance), like Russian, and those which do not, like Central Alaskan Yup'ik. In a language with distinct inflectional classes, we may know the significance of a particular ending only in respect of the particular stem it is attached to. Typically we find a restricted number of main inflectional classes, each with a sizeable number of nouns. Russian has arguably four inflectional classes for nouns (Corbett 1982; Corbett and Fraser 1993: 114–16),[9] shown in table 5.2.

---

[9] Establishing paradigms is not always straightforward; here we accept the traditional view for Russian of six cases and two numbers, hence twelve cells in all (see Comrie 1986, 1991 for discussion of the issues).

Table 5.2 *Major noun inflectional classes of Russian (transliterated)*

example	zakon 'law'	komnata 'room'	kost´ 'bone'	boloto 'marsh'
inflectional class	I	II	III	IV
singular				
NOM(inative)	zakon	komnata	kost´	boloto
ACC(usative)	zakon	komnatu	kost´	boloto
GEN(itive)	zakona	komnaty	kosti	bolota
DAT(ive)	zakonu	komnate	kosti	bolotu
INST(rumental)	zakonom	komnatoj	kost´ju	bolotom
LOC(ative)	zakone	komnate	kosti	bolote
plural				
NOM	zakony	komnaty	kosti	bolota
ACC	zakony	komnaty	kosti	bolota
GEN	zakonov	komnat	kostej	bolot
DAT	zakonam	komnatam	kostjam	bolotam
INST	zakonami	komnatami	kostjami	bolotami
LOC	zakonax	komnatax	kostjax	bolotax

This table shows clearly that inflections have a different significance for different nouns. There are several instances of the use of the bare stem, as in *zakon* 'law (nominative singular)' and *komnat* 'room (genitive plural)'. We shall return to the different inflectional cases shortly.

Most nouns, as in the examples in table 5.2, have a single stem, but some have stem modifications, as discussed in §5.3.1. These four inflectional classes cover the vast majority of Russian nouns, but there are some further variants and exceptions, for which see Timberlake (1993: 837–41), and several hundred indeclinable nouns;[10] the relation of exceptional number marking to frequency will be discussed in §9.3.3. We can get a picture of the distribution of the nouns over these four main classes by calculating the membership of around 44,000 nouns. Table 5.3 gives the number in each class, to the nearest fifty. Each class has a substantial number of nouns, but the dominance of class I is increasing over time.

We should return to the question of case, since this brings us to a second major type of difference. If we take a form like *zakon-a* 'law (genitive singular)' the information that it is singular is encoded in the inflection -*a*, but so is the fact that it is genitive. There is no way to pull apart the information about the two categories:

[10] Particular inflections can present great complexity of choice; a good instance is the Polish nominative plural for nouns denoting males, as shown by Dunaj (1993), also discussed by Wierzbicka (1988: 455–9).

Table 5.3 *Membership of the inflectional classes of Russian*[11]

Class	I	II	III	IV
Example	*zakon*	*komnata*	*kost´*	*boloto*
	'law'	'room'	'bone'	'marsh'
No. of nouns	20,700	13,600	3,950	5,750

this phenomenon is known as 'cumulation'. Number is often marked morphologically in this way, cumulated with case, or gender or person, depending on the word-class (see §9.2). On the other hand number can be expressed morphologically without cumulation, and in two different ways. In English, nouns such as *law* ~ *laws* mark number only, and so there is no cumulation. Alternatively, in languages like Uzbek (Mugdan 1994: 2550), number and case have separate markers, as in table 5.4.

Table 5.4 *Number and case in Uzbek*
(olma *'apple'*)

	singular	plural
NOM	olma	olma-lar
ACC	olma-ni	olma-lar-ni
GEN	olma-niŋ	olma-lar-niŋ
DAT	olma-ga	olma-lar-ga
ABL	olma-dan	olma-lar-dan
LOC	olma-da	olma-lar-da

In such languages, unlike in Russian, it is possible to identify the suffix *-lar* as the marker of plural number. The Uzbek type is said to have agglutinative morphology, and the Russian type fusional morphology. But agglutinative and fusional are poles of a continuum, with the great majority of systems lying somewhere between (Comrie 1989: 42–52). In this example, the case marker is outside the number marker, which is in accord with Greenberg's universal number 39 (1963):

---

[11] Brown et al. (1996: 57), calculated from Zaliznjak (1977). These statistics give a good first impression, but they do not take account of the effect of derivational morphology. Thus the majority of the nouns in class III have the suffix *-ost´* which forms abstract nouns from adjectives *(star-yj* 'old', *star-ost´* 'old age'). If the suffix is labelled as belonging to class III, then the number of distinct members of the class is substantially reduced. Similarly nominalizations in *-aniel-enie* (like *razrušenie* 'destruction', derived from *razrušit´* 'destroy') inflate the figure for IV (see Schupbach 1984 for discussion). Apart from via these suffixes, classes III and IV are barely productive.

Where morphemes of both number and case are present and both follow or precede the noun base, the expression of number almost always comes between the noun base and the expression of case.

The evidence we saw in Akhvakh (table 5.1) fitted even better. Recall the noun form *nido-di-le-de* 'forehead' (ergative plural), where the elements come in the order:

base   plural marker   [plural + oblique marker]   case marker

The marker which indicates number and case (oblique rather than direct) stands between the straightforward number marker and the straightforward case marker.

5.3.3   Stems

Stems can show changes from minor stress alternations to major restructuring. Cross-cutting this variation is the distinction between stem distinctions which alone signal number and those which occur in conjunction with inflections which distinguish number. We shall start from the smaller modification and progress to the larger; not surprisingly, the larger the modification the more likely it is to be the sole marker of number.

We start with **prosodic differences** in stems. Even these can be the only marker of number. Hence in Shilluk (discussed in more detail in §5.4) we find examples such as: *kîy* (with low-high tone) contrasted with *kíy* (high-low) 'plant(s) with edible roots'. The opposition of stress, on the stem as opposed to not on it (hence on the inflection) is found frequently. We can illustrate this from Russian, in order to fit with the inflectional information given earlier. Basically the stress can be on the stem or on the ending, and it can be the same in the singular and plural or different. This gives four main classes,[12] as shown in table 5.5. Clearly when singular and plural stems differ, this is only a secondary marker, since the inflection is normally a clear marker. Interestingly these are abstract patterns, which are available for different inflectional classes. Not all possibilities are found, but the majority are (given the four types of nominal stress and the four inflectional classes of table 5.2, we might expect sixteen combinations and in fact fifteen are found).[13] The distribution of these stress patterns is also of interest: a count of approximately 44,000 nouns shows that the vast majority (43,000) have fixed stress (40,300 in type A and 2,700 in type B); of the remainder, type C has under 450 nouns, type D under 350, and the subtypes together have around 250).[14]

---

[12] For details on the interesting but relatively small subtypes see Brown et al. (1996).

[13] The missing one is inflectional class III with stress pattern D. Note that the figure of fifteen is correct provided the small stress subtypes are counted with the main types. If only the main types are counted, then twelve combinations are found, out of the theoretically possible sixteen.   [14] Figures again from Brown et al. (1996: 57).

Table 5.5 *Basic types of nominal stress in Russian*

A		B	
singular	plural	singular	plural
stem	stem	ending	ending
kómnata	kómnaty	očkó	očkí
'room'	'rooms'	'point'	'points'

C		D	
singular	plural	singular	plural
stem (initial)	ending	ending	stem (predesinential)
véčer	večerá	vinó	vína
'evening'	'evenings'	'wine'	'wines'

A somewhat more substantial difference between stems is represented by **alternations**. For instance in the South Slavonic language Macedonian, there is a set of nouns where we normally find the bare stem in the singular and the stem plus -*i* in the plural, e.g. *koren* 'root', plural *koreni*. However, in nouns ending in -*k*, -*g* or -*x* we find an alternation to *c* (an unvoiced dental fricative), *z* or *s* respectively (Friedman 1993: 258), as table 5.6 illustrates. The point is that this alternation occurs in specific morphological environments. It is possible to find *ki*, *gi* and *xi* elsewhere. What was once a regular phonological alternation (the Slavonic second palatalization of velars) is retained as a morphological one.

Table 5.6 *Examples of stem alternations in Macedonian*

singular	plural	gloss
učenik	učenici	pupil (school)
parking	parkinzi	parking space
uspeh	uspesi	success

A more substantial modification is the addition of **augments** in the singular, or plural, or both. We saw several examples in §5.3.1, for instance Russian *bolgar-y* 'Bulgarians', singular *bolgar-in*, where the singular has the augment -*in*- before the regular endings. We also saw the case of Akhvakh. Nakh-Daghestanian languages are complex in this respect; there is a good deal of information available on the systems found, with data on how prevalent particular patterns are in particular languages: for an overview, see Kibrik (1991, forthcoming) and for more detail see

Kibrik and Kodzasov (1990: 251–310). We shall look briefly at another of them, namely Lak, whose nouns, like those of Akhvakh (table 5.1), may have up to four distinct stems as shown in table 5.7.

Table 5.7 *Lak* muIh *'sickle'*
(Kibrik and Kodzasov 1990: 137)

	singular	plural
absolutive	muIh	muIh-ru
genitive	muIh-li-l	muIh-a-l

In terms of our analyses earlier, the absolutive singular is the same as the base.[15] The absolutive plural is formed from the base with the formant *-ru*, and the absolutive has no ending, singular or plural. There is an oblique singular stem, formed from the base with *-li-*, and there is a plural oblique stem formed with *-a-*; then different case inflections are added, in this instance the genitive ending *-l*. This is not the only pattern in Lak. The important point here is to show the wealth of means available for stem formation. To form the oblique singular stem there are over thirty formatives available, and, though there are some recurring patterns, it has not proved possible to predict which one will be found with a particular noun. For forming the absolutive plural there are again more than thirty possibilities. Finally, to form the oblique plural there are over a dozen possibilities.

A rather different type of stem modification is known as **reduplication**. Instead of adding new material (as with augments) or modifying particular segments, reduplication primarily involves use of material from the specific lexical item. This may involve the whole as in Dyirbal (Dixon 1972: 242–3). Thus we find *ɲalŋga-ŋgu* 'girl-ERG', with the plural *ɲalŋgaɲalŋga-gu* 'girls-ERG'; note that the ergative inflection varies according to the number of syllables of the stem. Alternatively it may involve only a part (partial reduplication) as in these examples from Ilocano (table 5.8), an Austronesian language of the Philippines (Hayes and Abad 1989: 357–1; McCarthy and Prince 1995: 319). These and similar data have been extensively discussed, particularly within Prosodic Morphology. The central point is that reduplication does not specify a segment to be copied; rather it sets a template, to 'aim' at as it were: in the case of Ilocano this is a heavy syllable. The content of the reduplication is then dependent on the base. The last example *tra:-trák* suggests that copying the entire stem is excluded in Ilocano and so the vowel is lengthened in order to fit the heavy syllable tem-

---

[15] Kibrik and Kodzasov use 'nominative' rather than 'absolutive'.

Table 5.8 *Partial reduplication in Ilocano*

singular	plural	gloss
kaldíŋ	kal-kaldíŋ	goat(s)
púsa	pus-púsa	cat(s)
kláse	klas-kláse	class(es)
jyánitor	jyan-jyánitor	janitor(s)
yóyo	yoy-yóyo	yoyo(s)
trák	tra:-trák	truck(s)

plate. We have already seen several examples of reduplication. This morphological resource is used for a variety of purposes, of which signalling plurality is only one; it is particularly frequent in distributive use (§4.4.1) so cases must be analysed carefully.[16]

We now come to a dramatic type of difference, **internal modifications** to the stem. These are common in some of the Germanic languages (see table 5.9), where particularly for German the plural form is referred to as an 'umlaut' form.

Table 5.9 *Stem internal modification in Germanic languages*

	singular	plural	gloss
English	goose	geese	
	mouse	mice	
German	Apfel	Äpfel	apple
	Sohn	Söhne	son
Frisian	beam	bjemmen	tree
(Tiersma 1982)	stoel	stwollen	chair

[16] The literature on reduplication as a morphological and phonological problem is extensive: see McCarthy and Prince (1995: 332–3) and Spencer (1991: 150–6, 169–71) for references; for a typology see Moravcsik (1978). Discussions of reduplication which include reference to its use for marking plurality include Wilkins (1984) and Henderson (1990) on Arrernte, Kiyomi (1995) on Malayo-Polynesian languages, Gonda (1942) on the languages of Indonesia, El-Solami-Mewis (1988) who gives statistics on the use of reduplication as opposed to other means of plural marking in Somali, Haeberlin (1918) on Salish languages. In a survey of reduplication in the languages of Australia, Fabricius (1998: 14, 59) points out that it is used there for various sorts of plurality but not for reference to two. Recall that distributives typically are inappropriate for reference to two (§4.4.1), which serves as a reminder that we should be wary of suggested reduplicated plurals in case they are in fact distributives.

Note that sometimes the alternation is the only marker of number (as in the English examples and in German *Apfel ~ Äpfel*) but frequently there is a regular inflection too. (For the complexity of German see Köpcke 1988, 1993, 1994, 1998, and for Old High German see Salmons 1994.)

Table 5.10 *Examples of broken plurals in Arabic*

singular	plural	gloss
kalbun	kilaabun	dog
xaatamun	xawaatimu	seal (ring)
ḍamiirun	ḍamaaʔiru	pronoun
manzilun	manaazilu	residence

One of the systems that looks most complex at first sight is that found in various Semitic languages, where we find 'broken' plurals (which have stem-internal modification) as opposed to the 'sound' plurals which take a suffix. The different patterns of broken plurals are certainly complicated, as the Arabic examples in table 5.10 show (Ratcliffe 1998: 23). There are many subpatterns, and yet there is a good degree of predictability. This is also a case where there is statistical data on the distribution of the different types of plural marking (see Ratcliffe 1998).[17] We return to Arabic plurals in §6.6.

It is worth asking whether number could ever be marked by **subtractive** morphology, in other words whether number could be indicated by removing material. The examples we saw in §5.3.1, for instance Russian *bolgar-in* 'Bulgarian' with plural *bolgar-y* do not fit the bill. Here the singular is formed from the plural by the addition of the suffix *-in* , which can be attached to various plural stems in the same way. To find an example of number marking by subtractive morphology, one would need different phonological material to be removed, say the last segment, so that in imaginary English, the plural of *cat* would be *ca* and the plural of *dog* would be *do*. There is one instance which at first sight comes close to this, namely the Hessian dialect of German (see Golston and Wiese 1996 for sources). In Hessian German we do indeed find examples like the following: *hond* 'dog' plural *hon*, *viend* 'wind' plural *vien*, *bɛrk* 'mountain' plural *bɛr*, and *vɛk* 'way'

---

[17] Broken plurals have been important in the development of phonological theory; see for instance: McCarthy (1982, 1983), Hammond (1988), McCarthy and Prince (1990), McCarthy and Prince (1995: 345–6), and see Idrissi (1997) and Ratcliffe (1998) for discussion; for the development of the phenomenon, see Murtonen (1964) and Ratcliffe (1998); see also Wallace (1988) on Biblical Hebrew, Palmer (1955) on Tigrinya and Palmer (1962) on Tigre. For a connectionist model of the Arabic plurals see Plunkett and Nakisa (1997).

plural *vɛ*. This seems to be what we were looking for. However, it is always the same two consonants involved (underlying *d* or *g*), which suggests that we are dealing with phonological conditioning. Golston and Wiese (1996) argue that there is a constraint that Hessian plurals must end in a sonorant; this constraint is satisfied in various ways, including in some instances the loss of the final obstruent. Thus for some nouns (and which ones is phonologically determined) the plural is indeed a reduced form of the singular, but there is not a general rule 'subtracting' a segment to form the plural. Holsinger and Houseman (1999) offer an alternative analysis, again without the need for subtractive morphology. We conclude that while Hessian was the best candidate, it appears that number is not marked by means of subtractive morphology.

5.3.4 Zero expression

We saw in the last three sections how number may be marked by inflection or by the stem. However, the full range of possible differentiation is not normally found. We saw instances where one of the stems was identical to the base (in other terms it was the base plus zero); we also saw instances where number inflections were not maximally different (and again there were examples of stems with no inflection). These possibilities are not randomly distributed, but conform to certain patterns. Greenberg's universal number 35 (1963) states that: 'There is no language in which the plural does not have some nonzero allomorphs, whereas there are languages in which the singular is expressed only by zero. The dual and the trial are almost never expressed only by zero.' This universal conflates stems and inflections; it claims that whereas the singular may have zero expression (and the plural has additional material to form a plural stem, or a plural inflection, or both), the plural in a given language will not regularly have zero expression, though this may be the means for some nouns (see also §2.1). It is common for the singular to have zero expression; it is less usual for the plural to be marked in this way, even for a smaller group of lexical items.[18]

Finally we should note how odd English is in this respect. In the verb, the third singular (present) has a marker, while the plural does not: compare *she writes* with *they write*. But though unusual, English is not a counter-example to Greenberg's universal since elsewhere in the system the plural has non-zero allomorphs (on nouns: *writer* but *writer-s*).

---

[18] It is interesting to separate out stem and inflection in this regard. We noted the example of Russian *bolgarin* 'a Bulgarian' and similar nouns; here the base is *bolgar-* and the plural stem is identical, as in forms like the nominative plural *bolgar*-y. The singular stem is *bolgarin-*. In terms of stems the plural has zero expression for these nouns; there are relatively few which behave in this way. In terms of inflection, in the nominative singular there is zero expression (*bolgar-in* with no inflection); there are many nouns in Russian which mark the nominative singular by zero (see table 5.3).

5.3.5 Clitics revisited

Clitics should be mentioned again here, since the term covers a range of items which fall between being independent words and being inflections. Clitics are like independent words in that they are not bound to particular stems, but they are phonologically dependent on a host (for instance, they do not bear their own stress). One type of clitic attaches to a particular type of phrase, hence the more specific term for these, namely 'phrasal affixes'. We saw an example from Dogon in §5.1 above:

(20) ɛnɛ gɛ mbe
     goat DEF PL
     'the goats'

Here *mbe* is part of the phrase, but it is not required to attach to, say, a noun (as a Russian inflection might be), rather it simply appears last in the noun phrase and attaches to the preceding element. The diachronic development from independent plural word, to clitic, and finally to bound inflection may go through various intermediate stages, so that in a particular language the analysis can be difficult. Thus there are languages like Basque where various markers (including number) attach to the last element of the noun phrase, and there are several different items which that can be. But in a language where the noun phrase is noun-final, deciding whether a following item is a phrasal affix or an inflection on the noun is trickier, and in some instances probably undecidable.[19]

5.3.6 Multiple marking

Number is often marked in more than one way. It may be by two different means: by morphological means and by agreement, by morphological means and by a number word as in (14), or very commonly by two or more morphological means. We have seen numerous instances of stem changes together with inflection. Some languages show a profusion of means of marking number even on a single item.[20]

Within morphological marking there are also more systematic instances, where having two markers is the norm. One such is Breton, where the formation of diminutive plurals involves two plural markers, giving the structure: stem–PL–DIMINUTIVE–PL, as in the examples in table 5.11 (see Stump 1990: 104–5, 1991:

---

[19] A somewhat different type of complexity in the marking of number within noun phrases with different elements present is found in Dagaare (a Gur language spoken in parts of Ghana and Burkina Faso), for which see Bodomo (1997: 47–50).

[20] Turner (1976) shows how Seri and Chontal have between them eleven means of pluralization and some nouns show four of them at once (compare also Moser and Moser 1976 and Marlett 1990); for Ket see G. D. S. Anderson (1996) and for Breton see Trépos (1957); there are relevant points in Plank (1985: 61–5, 67–8, 77–80).

Table 5.11 *Formation of diminutive plurals in Breton*

singular	singular diminutive	plural	plural diminutive	gloss
bag	bagig	bagoù	bagoùigoù	boat
labous	labousig	laboused	labousedigoù	bird
bugel	bugelig	bugale	bugaligoù	child
kazh	kazhig	kizhier	kizhierigoù	cat

696–7, 1996 and references there; for comparable data on Yiddish diminutives see Perlmutter 1988). The diminutive plurals have two plural markers, whether the same one repeated as in *bagoùigoù* 'small boats' or two different ones, as in *labousedigoù* 'small birds' (*-ed* is the default for animates and *-où* for others; the remaining two nouns given have irregular plurals). It should be stressed that none of the instances in this section affect number values. The Russian *krýl'ja* 'wings', which has an augment, a plural inflection and a stress shift as compared to the singular is not 'more plural' than *komnaty* 'rooms', which has only a plural inflection. This multiple marking is therefore to be distinguished from the rare composed numbers (as in Breton, §2.2.7) where the additional markers have an additional semantic effect.

An interesting facet of multiple marking is usually known as 'double plurals', which are instances where an old plural gains a new plural marker 'on top of' the old one. For instance, the Middle English plural *childre*, gained a second marker of plurality, resulting in the modern form *children*. There are many examples of double plurals in a variety of languages.[21] Tiersma (1982) showed the particular interest of one type of double plural, for which we need the fruitful but not unproblematic notion of markedness. Originally developed in phonology, it was later applied to grammatical categories (see in particular Jakobson 1932, Greenberg 1966, Zwicky 1978, Tomić 1989, Battistella 1990, Croft 1990, Fradkin

---

[21] These are to be distinguished from the instances where particular nouns have two distinct plural forms, typically with an accompanying difference in meaning. For example, in Italian there is *l'osso* 'the bone' (masculine singular). There are two plurals: *le ossa* 'the bones' (feminine), sometimes called the 'collective plural', which would be used of bones which belong together, a particular person's bones, a skeleton, and a second plural *gli ossi* 'the bones' (masculine), sometimes called the 'distributive plural', for bones which do not belong together: it would be used, for instance, when buying bones for a dog. Few nouns are of this type in Italian; for examples and discussion see Rocchetti (1968), Brunet (1978: 30–76), Santangelo (1981), Vincent (1988: 289) and Ojeda (1995). Note that the difference in meaning between the plurals is somewhat separate from number, in contrast to the greater numbers discussed in §2.2.6.

1991 on Arabic and Janda 1991 on German). The idea is that many oppositions are not balanced: one member of a grammatical category is the normal or unmarked member, the other is marked. We see this in terms of semantics, form and frequency. If we take number, it is claimed that the singular is unmarked and the plural marked. In semantic terms, where number is irrelevant or unimportant it is the singular which is used (this is not fully clear, see McCawley 1968 and Ojeda 1992c for dissenting voices). In terms of form, we certainly see many instances where the singular has no marker but the plural has one, as discussed in §5.3.4. And in terms of frequency, the singular occurs considerably more frequently than the plural (§9.3.2).[22]

The notion of markedness is typically applied to categories as a whole, but it was known that there were interesting effects with particular items. Tiersma researched some of them and made the claim that: 'When the referent of a noun naturally occurs in pairs or groups, and/or when it is generally referred to collectively, such a noun is locally unmarked in the plural' (Tiersma 1982: 835). Several things follow, one being that nouns with double plurals are often those where the plural is the locally unmarked form. Table 5.12 provides examples from Dutch. Here we see clearly how the modern plural is formed with a suffix on the basis of what was formerly a plural in its own right.[23] (For further examples, from Lezgian, see §5.8.3.)

Table 5.12 *Double plurals in Dutch (Tiersma 1982: 438)*

singular	older plural	modern plural	gloss
blad	blader	bladeren	leaf
ei	eier	eieren	egg
kind	kinder	kinderen	child
lamm	lammer	lammeren	lamb

Borrowings also illustrate the local unmarkedness of the plural for certain types of noun. Thus the Russian for 'rail', borrowed in the context of railways, is *rel's*,

---

[22] Markedness proves harder to apply when there is more than one value, as we saw in the discussion of facultative values (§2.3.3). The problem can have a diachronic dimension, as demonstrated by Dench (1994), who shows how in languages of the Pilbara region of Australia, plural pronouns have been reformed on the basis of the dual, the opposite of what we would expect if the dual is the marked category as compared to the plural. The notion of default, which is related to markedness, has advantages (Fraser and Corbett 1997).

[23] A slightly different type of double plural can also be illustrated from Dutch. There are examples like *museum* 'museum' plural *musea* following the Latin original; there is also a regular native plural *museum-s*, and then the double plural *musea-s* (van Marle 1993), consisting of the original plural plus the native plural, this latter being frowned on by prescriptivists.

clearly borrowed from the plural form: rails come in twos after all. In Russian *rel's* is singular and has its own regular plural *rel's-y*. Tiersma gives examples from Karok, Cahuilla, Tetelcingo Aztec, Acoma, Yokuts, Chamorro and Czech. A particularly interesting example he gives concerns the Latin *folium* 'leaf'. Since leaves generally come in large numbers, the plural form *folia* was the unmarked one, and this developed into a new singular (with plural *foliae*). In Spanish, the descendant form was *hoja* (plural *hojas*). This was borrowed into Chamorro but the plural form was taken, and so *ohas* (singular) means 'leaf'.[24]

5.4 Lexical means

We now consider whether number can be a purely lexical matter, that is, whether there are languages where number forms would be specified for each nominal separately. In §5.3.1 we noted individual examples of this such as Russian *čelovek* 'person' ~ *ljudi* 'people', which is an example of **suppletion**. Suppletion is the relation between two stems when a regular grammatical opposition is expressed with maximum irregularity (see Mel'čuk 1994 and further discussion in §8.6). Within an inflectional system there may be larger or smaller numbers of items which are suppletive in respect of number, and these are instances of number being lexically marked. Suppletion is common with the pronominal system (as in *I* ~ *we*), but as we noted in §3.5 there are also languages in which the relations between singular and plural forms of personal pronouns are inflectionally regular.

It is interesting to ask how much of the nominal inventory can be specified lexically in a given language. In Obolo (a Niger-Congo language, Lower Cross sub-branch, spoken on islands in the Niger Delta; data from Faraclas 1984: 10–11, 34) most nouns do not change for number, thus *úwù* 'house(s)'. Only a few nouns, all denoting persons, mark number, such as *ògwú* 'person', plural *èbí* 'people', and *gwúñ* 'child', *bón* 'children'. It appears, then, that Obolo nouns mark number only lexically.

In many instances, however, although there is not full suppletion, different number forms are paired in ways which are not regular (this is sometimes called partial suppletion). An example is English *tooth* ~ *teeth*, where the forms are

---

[24] Unmarked forms are known to be more tolerant of irregularity than marked forms (Tiersma 1982: 841, following Greenberg 1966: 29). Locally unmarked noun plurals can therefore maintain irregularities which are regularized with marked plurals. When we consider the native irregular plurals of English, it is striking that they involve nouns for which a case can be made for local unmarkedness of the plural: *men, women, children, oxen, geese, mice, lice, feet* and *teeth*. It is interesting to note that in an analysis of the Cushitic language Bayso, which has a complex number system, the irregularities investigated by Corbett and Hayward (1987) involved several of the same items: the nouns for 'feet', 'oxen', 'teeth' and others.

clearly similar but are not related by any synchronically active rule (they show stem-internal modification §5.3.3). These must be lexically marked. They have a different status from ordinary singular–plural pairs, in that the plural is available for compounds, as in *teeth marks* whereas for ordinary plurals it is not **claws marks* (Kiparsky 1982: 137).[25] Once we consider forms which are phonologically similar but not related regularly, then we find languages where a substantial portion of the noun lexicon marks plurality in this way. They are unlike the English type of pattern, which has one dominant type of plural formation, and several irregular types with relatively few members. In some languages it is far from obvious whether there is one dominant type of plural.

Perhaps the extreme point in this regard is the particularly interesting patterns of number marking found in Nilotic languages.[26] We shall consider Shilluk, within the Luo group, as described by Gilley (1992). Shilluk is spoken by about a million people in Southern Sudan, along the Nile River in the vicinity of Malakal. Gilley quotes Kohnen, who in his Shilluk grammar published after thirty years of study states that 'A general rule for the formation of plurals in Shilluk cannot be given' (1933: 19). After detailed analysis Gilley confirms this and goes on to claim that each noun has two independent representations: singular and plural. These two forms are not totally dissimilar in most cases. For many nouns one form is the base to which a suffix is added (whether to form the singular or plural), while for some nouns both forms have a suffix.[27] Three patterns can be distinguished:

type A:		base *versus*	plural
type B:	singulative *versus*	base	
type C:	singulative	*versus*	plural

'Singulative' here indicates a singular which has a morphological marker, rather than being a base (where singular is indicated by the absence of a marker). The three patterns may be illustrated as follows:

type A:		ɲâŋ 'crocodile'	ɲáɲːī̱ 'crocodiles'
type B:	wàːrɔ̀ 'shoe'	wâr 'shoes'	
type C:	ácṵ̀ŋɔ̀ 'termite (type of)'		ácṵ̱ŋːì̱ 'termites'

[25] Booij (1996: 6–7) argues however that in Dutch and some other languages regular plural forms can feed compounding, as in Dutch *[student-en]team* 'students' team'.

[26] See Noonan (1992: 83–5, 166–8) on Lango, Welmers (1973: 28–9) on Dinka, and especially Dimmendaal (1983: 223–58) on Turkana. Dimmendaal suggests that within Eastern Nilotic number marking may not be as irregular as previous investigators have suggested.

[27] Note however that this morphologically basic form seems to have singular or plural meaning, depending on the form it is opposed to, rather than having 'general' meaning, from the information given by Gilley (1992: 63–5).

Since these patterns can be established, why should it be claimed that each noun has two representations? The problem is that the relations between the two forms are so varied and complex that, it is claimed, no plausible set of rules can be given. In terms of affixation, the situation is not too difficult: some nouns add a plural suffix (type A), some a singulative suffix (type B), some have both (type C), while some nouns have neither. But the difficulties arise within the stem: typically this is of the shape consonant–vowel–consonant. The initial segment may be consonant plus glide or just consonant. While the initial segment is usually the same in singular and plural, some nouns have consonant plus glide in the singular opposed to a single consonant in the plural, for example pyḕn ~ pé:nī 'sleeping skin(s)' (Gilley 1992: 84). The final consonant is generally the same; however, it may alternate: singular [l] or [r] may give [t], for example pāl ~ pât 'spoon(s)'. This does not hold for all nouns, as shown by acwị̄l ~ acwị̄:l 'brown cow(s)'. There are also other erratic alternations.

Most problems arise with the vowel in the consonant–vowel–consonant pattern of the stem. Here there are four sources of variation:

1 **vowel height**: the most common alternations in height involve two front vowels, as in rè:jɔ́~ ríc 'fish(es)', two back vowels, as in cúŋ ~ còŋ 'knee(s)', or two unrounded vowels, as in kwéy ~ kwà̰:y 'grand-father(s)'.

2 **vowel quality**: Shilluk has a set of 'breathy vowels', which may be described as bearing the feature [+expanded larynx]: these are: ị, ẹ, a̰, ɔ̰, ụ. Their [−expanded larynx] counterparts are i, e, a, ɔ, o. The vowel may or may not carry the feature [+expanded larynx] in both singular and plural, thus giving four possibilities:

    a. both [−expanded larynx]: kél ~ kè:l 'cheetah(s)'

    b. singular [−expanded larynx], plural [+expanded larynx]: ɲâŋ ~ ɲá̰ŋ:ị̄ 'crocodile(s)'

    c. singular [+expanded larynx], plural [−expanded larynx]: pyḕn ~ pén:ị 'sleeping skin(s)'

    d. both [+expanded larynx]: yẹ́p ~ yḛ̀:p 'tail(s)'

The types which have the same value of the feature in singular and plural are the more common; however, the quality of the vowel and the possibility of change in the plural are not predictable.

3 **tone**: there are three tones: high (´), mid (ˉ) and low (`); in addition sequences of tones can be found on a single vowel, such as high-low (^). While some tone patterns are restricted to the singular, and some to the plural, the majority of patterns are found on both. Some of the

157

many possibilities are illustrated on the examples already given. Others include kṳ̀l (low tone) ~ kṳ̌l (low-high) 'pig(s)', kǐy (low-high) ~ kîy (high-low) 'plant(s) with edible roots'. According to Gilley (1992: 90) 'It is a rare experience to find a singular/plural pair which has the same tone.' She claims that the tone cannot be predicted and so must be listed in the lexicon for both singular and plural forms.

4 **length**: Shilluk has short vowels, and long vowels (indicated by :). The data are complex, since the whole question of Shilluk syllable structure is involved. Suffice it to say that vowel length may vary between singular and plural: the vowel may be long in the singular and short in the plural: bṳ̀:r ~ bṳ̄r 'grave(s)', or the converse may be found: acwi̱l ~ acwi̱:l 'brown cow(s)'. (There may also be no variation between singular and plural, and this is commonly the case.)

Given the degree of variation according to these four factors, which cannot be predicted, Gilley concludes that singulars and plurals in Shilluk cannot be derived from a single underlying representation but that two forms must be stored for each noun. The claim is not that the two forms are totally unrelated: they are not fully suppletive (though Shilluk does have some fully suppletive singular–plural pairs, such as gin ~ já̱m:ī 'thing(s)'). Normally the initial and final consonants are shared. It is the vowel, and its attendant features, which accounts for the differences. It is as though the English plurals of the *foot ~ feet* and *mouse ~ mice* type made up a significant proportion of the lexicon (and with more possible types of variation). Shilluk therefore represents a language which marks number by means of a high degree of non-predictable stem variation. Of course, it is difficult to prove a negative, to prove that no set of rules can cover the data. But Gilley makes a plausible case that two forms of nouns must be remembered by the speaker rather than one being derivable from the other.

There are interesting implications for child language acquisition. Gilley (1992: 190–1) suggests that if Shilluk children must store two forms for nouns then, if children learn different languages at the same rate, this implies that 'children learning other languages *may* be memorizing more than had been thought'. However, though Shilluk is indeed near the extreme in its use of stem formation, it does not necessarily present a qualitatively different task for the language learner. Note first that Gilley reports a suggestion that Shilluk children generalize the use of the -*i* suffix for plural and then later learn the more complex forms, thus learning the most regular forms, overgeneralizing the rule, and later learning lesser regularities and exceptions. But there is a second important point about Shilluk: like other Nilotic languages, it appears to be moving towards becoming monosyllabic; thus the amount of phonological information which the child has to acquire for a single lexical entry – even if this involves two related forms for a noun rather than just one – may turn out to be no more than for many other languages which have considerable numbers of polysyllabic words. Of course, we do not know the relative load of storing information such as tone as compared to segmental phonemes, but it is likely that there is a trade-off of length as opposed to complexity; thus the Shilluk child, having to learn two complex one-syllable forms for many nouns may not face a harder task than the child learning a language in which plural formation is regular but in which many nouns are polysyllabic. Shilluk then represents almost the ultimate point in the lexical marking of number.

Outside Nilotic, there are other languages where there is a wide variety of plural forms. In a discussion of Hausa, Haspelmath (1989) argues that there are several competing patterns and none of them is the dominant one. He describes them using 'schemas', following work by Köpcke (1988) on plural formation in German (see these two references for other work on schemas).

5.5 Inverse number (and polarity)

In Shilluk we saw instances where the marking of singular number in one noun could be by the same formal means as are used for marking plural in another. We now look at languages where that is regularly the case. An unusual and very interesting system is found in Kiowa (a language of the Kiowa-Tanoan family, which in 1984 had 400 speakers in south-western Oklahoma). The main source is Watkins (1984: 78–100), following earlier work by Wonderly, Gibson and Kirk (1954), who introduced the term 'inverse', and Merrifield (1959). There is a marker -*gɔ́* (with various variants including -*dɔ́*) , which may be simply attached to nouns or may replace another suffix. It is termed an 'inverse' suffix, because it appears to change the basic number meaning of the stem to which it is attached. This switch can go in either direction, as shown in table 5.13.

Table 5.13 *Noun number markers in Kiowa*

singular	dual	plural	gloss
cę̂·	cę̂·	cę̂·gɔ́	horse
á·dɔ́	á·	á·	pole

The suffix -*gɔ́* ~ -*dɔ́* appears to have opposing effects, according to the type of noun.[28] We should first ask, however, why it is appropriate to label the columns

---

[28] The related language Jemez has a comparable but interestingly different system of number marking on nouns (Kenneth Hale 1956–57 and personal communication), as the table shows. In Jemez the inverse marker marks the dual, together with either plural or singular

'singular', 'dual' and 'plural'. There are two reasons: first, this matches the meanings of the forms, and second, the marking on the verb indicates number. For nouns like *cê·* 'horse', the verb shows a singular-dual-plural system, for example (Watkins 1984: 84):

(21) cê·   gyà-tʰɔ́n
     horse   1.SG.AGT/SG.OBJ-find.PERFV
     'I found a horse'

(22) cê·   nèn-tʰɔ́n
     horse   1.SG.AGT/DUAL.OBJ-find.PERFV
     'I found two horses'

(23) cê·-gɔ́   dé-tʰɔ́n
     horse.INV   1.SG.AGT/INV.OBJ-find.PERFV
     'I found some horses'

Note that the verbal prefixes mark subject and object, and it is the distinctions for objects that are of interest here, since they separate singular, dual and inverse. There are some complications, involving different inverse or plural markers, but typically the marking on the verb distinguishes three numbers. The two nouns in table 5.13 represent the main classes of Kiowa nouns. All animates behave broadly like *cê·* 'horse', in that the number marker, whether -gɔ́ or some alternative, is found only in the plural. Other examples include *tɔ́l* 'father'. (Interestingly, just one noun *t'áp* 'deer' does not decline, but it takes the same agreements as *cê·* 'horse': it is like English *sheep*.) There are also some inanimates which behave like *cê·* 'horse', such as *dén* 'tongue' and *p'ɔ́·* 'river, stream'. However, most nouns denoting inanimates behave like *á·* 'pole, stick'; it is not clear whether it can be predicted which inanimates behave like the animates.

There are smaller groups of inanimates with different behaviour, which are probably best viewed as irregulars. There are just four nouns ('orange', 'tomato', 'plum, apple', 'hair (on head)') which take the inverse marker -gɔ́ for singular and

Footnote 28 (*cont.*)
  (depending on the noun, in the main animates follow the first pattern and inanimates the second). For Taos see Trager (1961), for Tewa see Speirs (1972), and for comparisons across the family see Watkins (1995).

Table 5.i *Noun number markers in Jemez*

singular	dual	plural	gloss
ve·la	ve·læš	ve·læš	man
tʸetíbæš	tʸetíbæš	tʸetíba	box

plural but not for the dual. And then there are various other inanimates which do not mark number on the noun at all: some like *c'ó·* 'rock' are simple indeclinables for which the verb marking establishes number in a straightforward way. For a second group, the verb distinguishes only the dual. And the third group consists of those for which number is not distinguished; these include *kʰɔ́·dé* 'trousers' and *tó·* 'tepee'. These always take plural markers on the verb (they are *pluralia tantum*, as in §5.8.2 below).

If we concentrate on the main classes of nouns we see that each has a basic form, without *-gɔ́* and a 'less expected' form with it. Those denoting animates are singular/dual in their basic form, with *-gɔ́* signalling a shift from that number, while nouns in the main class for inanimates are treated as basically dual/plural, with *-gɔ́* and variants signalling a shift to singular. It looks as though we have a new number value, singular/dual (for nouns denoting one or two) in the case of those denoting animates. This would be a new number system, a possibility not allowed for in our typology of number values (§2.3.2). However, the verbal system resolves this apparent new value into the normal values singular and plural. As we saw in §4.5.1, such 'conflated numbers' can exist, but they occur lower on the Animacy Hierarchy with a regular system higher on the hierarchy. There could not be a language like Kiowa but in which the singular/dual conflation were not resolved by the verbal system and still occurred higher on the hierarchy than the dual/plural conflation (which is of course a normal plural). Conflated forms which give an irregular number value must occur lower on the hierarchy than a regular system of number values. Thus we are dealing with unusual noun morphology here: Kiowa does not give us new number values unknown elsewhere. The overall system is singular–dual–plural. Thus inverse systems are a matter of morphological arrangement and not of semantic values.

There are two interesting points of connection with the Animacy Hierarchy. First, the two main classes of noun in Kiowa, one with the inverse marker for plural and the other with inverse marking for singular, conform broadly with the Animacy Hierarchy, since the first contains all the animates. And second, we noted in §3.3 that there can be a mismatch between the evidence of marking on the noun and the evidence of nominal number marked on the verb. The latter is the more regular. We have a similar situation here, in that the marking of number on the animates gives an unexpected plural versus singular/dual system; however, the verb is quite regular in showing singular–dual–plural. The opposite cannot occur; we do not find the converse of Kiowa, with the nouns showing straightforward number values and the verb having an 'illegal' system (we are concerned with systems here and not with individual irregular items within a regular system). The marking of one number for some nouns and another for others also recalls the discussion of the marking of plural versus general and singular versus general in §2.1. What is remarkable about Kiowa is that the *same* marker is used for apparently opposing ends.

The notion of an inverse marker which indicates the less expected number gains some support from a quite different part of the world, from the Nilotic language Maa (Bernd Heine, personal communications). Various suffixes indicate singular or plural, depending on the noun; among them, the suffix -*ı* may be thought of as signalling the unexpected number. In the Maasai dialect, for instance, we have:

(24)　o-sínkirr-î　　ı-sínkır
　　　GN-fish-SG　GN-fish
　　　'a fish'　　　'fish' (plural)

There is a prefixed gender/number marker, and a number suffix. The Maasai have a taboo against eating fish. Thus their singling out one fish would be less expected, and the singular is marked with the suffix -*î*. However, the speakers of the Camus dialect, who live at Lake Baringo in Kenya, do eat fish. And for them, the forms are:

(25)　sínkır　sínkir-î
　　　fish　　fish-PL
　　　'a fish'　'fish' (plural)

The gender–number prefix vowel is lost in the Camus dialect. For these speakers the noun behaves as anticipated; the plural is the less expected number value, and has the special marker. This is a singular–plural system, not one with general number.

If we consider other means of marking number from the same point of view, then we find, elsewhere in the world, systems which are similarly surprising. Ross (1988: 293–305)[29] discusses the systems found in two groups of Oceanic languages. Nine are spoken in southern New Ireland: Lihir, Lamasong, Madak, Tangga, Bilur, Kandas, Ramoaainna (previously called Duke of York), Siar and Tomoip, and a further nine in northern Bougainville: Nehan, Solos, Petats, Halia, Taiof, Hahon, Tinputz, Teop and Papapana. These languages divide their nouns into two classes. The first class is readily identifiable as the class of nouns which head count noun phrases, as in this Ramoaaina example:

(26)　a　　　pap　　　a　　　kum　pap
　　　ART　dog　　　ART　PL　dog
　　　'a/the dog'　　'some/the dogs'

---

[29] I am grateful to Malcolm Ross for bringing this phenomenon to my attention and for generously supplying fieldnotes and references.

The second class, which we would expect to be those which head mass noun phrases, includes nouns denoting fish, fruit, birds and trees; we will here call them simply 'non-count'. The noun *pika*, which might be glossed 'bird' is a non-count noun (Ross glosses it 'poultry'). Together with the article, it denotes a portion or usual unit (§3.7.2):

(27) a   pika
      ART   poultry
      'a plate of poultry'

For reference to an individual bird, what Ross terms a 'quantity marker' (QM) is required, here functioning as a singulative:

(28) a   ina   pika
      ART   QM   poultry
      'a bird'

In this language, plurality is signalled as for the count nouns:

(29) a   kum   pika
      ART   PL   poultry
      'some/the birds'

The eighteen languages in question make a similar distinction of nouns into the two classes. However, the formal means used to make the distinction vary considerably, and there is some syntactic variation too. For our purposes, the languages of particular interest are those like Tangga, which shows the following pattern (Ross 1988: 295, 298):

(30) fel   am-fel   taŋa   fel
      house   QM-house   some   house
      'the house'   'the houses'   'some houses'

(31) man   an-man   taŋa   man
      bird   QM-bird   some   bird
      'poultry'   'the bird'   'some birds'

Here we see that the quantity marker *an/am/aŋ*, which indicates plural for count nouns, is also the singulative marker for non-count nouns. Hence we have a situation analogous to the Kiowa inverse system (though here only singular and plural values are involved).

Further examples are found in north Bougainville languages. In Nehan we find the following pattern (Ross 1988: 299, 301; this supersedes the account in Todd 1978):

(32) a um[a] o um[a]
  ART house ART house
  'a/the house' 'some/the houses'

(33) o dok[i] a dok[i]
  ART tree   ART tree
  'a tree, a stick' 'a collection of trees'

The bracketed final vowels are not realized in citation forms, nor phrase-finally. Some nouns can function as count and non-count, with related meanings, as is the case for *pos[o]*:

(34) a pos[o] o pos[o]
  ART banana ART banana
  'a/the banana' 'some/the bananas'

(35) o pos[o] a pos[o]
  ART banana ART banana
  'a banana tree' 'a collection of banana trees'

Thus both *a* and *o* signal singularity for some nouns and plurality for others. The other north Bougainville languages, apart from Hahon, share elements of inverse number systems, though with additional complications (Ross 1988: 299–301); for Halia see Allen (1987). An example of the type of complication which may arise is provided by Teop (Mosel and Spriggs 1993: 43–51). Here there are three classes of noun, which we may call the e-class, a-class and o-class, according to the article taken. The types of noun which typically belong in each class are summarized in table 5.14. Now consider the singular and plural forms of the articles taken by the

Table 5.14 *Classes of noun and their semantics in Teop*
(Mosel and Spriggs 1993)

	e-class	a-class	o-class
humans	+	+	−
animals	(+)	+	−
trees	−	−	+
fruit	−	+	−
manufactured items	−	+	+

nouns of these different types of noun in Teop (see table 5.15). Here two classes (the a-class and the o-class) exhibit inverse number, while the e-class does not. This means that we now have nouns which take different agreements and which can reasonably be said to belong to different genders (see Corbett 1991: 145–50 for defini-

Table 5.15 *Articles taken by different noun types in Teop*

	e-class	a-class	o-class
singular	e	a	o
plural	o	o	a

tions). A gender system has arisen in an unusual way and in an unexpected part of the world, as Mosel and Spriggs (2000) point out.

We might have expected that inverse systems would arise as mere accidents of phonological change. However Ross (1988: 301–5) gives some insight into the origins of these inverse systems which indicates that this may not be the case. He suggests that the *o* article which occurs with count nouns and that which occurs with non-count nouns have different origins; from comparative evidence he reconstructs an *u* form of the article, used to mark plurality with count nouns. However, there is no phonological reason for the falling together of the original *u* and *o* articles. Thus the limited evidence from Oceanic suggests that inverse systems are not merely the result of chance.

Once we are dealing with agreement (of the article and other targets) and with gender as well as number, then we come to the interesting phenomenon of **polarity**: the situation in which two markers are exponents of two features (gender and number) and when the value of one feature is changed the marker changes, but if both values are changed the form stays the same. The polar opposites are identical, hence the term 'polarity'. This phenomenon can be found in the Cushitic language Somali (data from Serzisko 1982: 184–6; see also Bell 1953: 12–13 and Saeed 1987: 114–16):

(36) inan-kii   baa   y-imid
     boy-the.SG.MASC   FOCUS.MARKER   SG.MASC-came
     'the boy (!) came'   (the (!) indicates that boy is focused)

(37) inán-tii   baa   t-imid
     girl-the.SG.FEM   FOCUS.MARKER   SG.FEM-came
     'the girl (!) came'

(38) inammá-dii   baa   y-imid
     boys-the.PL.MASC   FOCUS.MARKER   PL-came
     'the boys (!) came'

(39) ináma-hii   baa   y-imid
     girls-the.PL.FEM   FOCUS.MARKER   PL-came
     'the girls (!) came'

The postposed definite article has various morphophonologically determined variants: after any vowel except *i*, *kii* becomes *hii*, and after any vowel *tii* becomes *dii*. Given this, in the examples above the article used for the masculine plural might be considered the same as that for the feminine singular, while that for the feminine plural is the same as that for the masculine singular. The basic forms are as in table 5.16. Here masculine singular and feminine plural are the same (as are femi-

Table 5.16 *The definite article in Somali (basic forms)*

	singular	plural
masculine	kii	tii
feminine	tii	kii

nine singular and masculine plural); of course, the case would be more convincing if these basic forms were not subject to variation. While table 5.16 suggests a clear and surprising picture, things are actually more complicated. First, Somali has polarity only in noun-phrase-internal agreement. Examples (36)–(39) show that the verbal agreement forms are different: there the plural for both genders is the same as the masculine singular. And second, not all nouns fall into the pattern shown in (36)–(39). Some masculine nouns form their plural by partial reduplication and take the same article in the singular and the plural, for example *nin-kii* 'the man', *niman-kii* 'the men'. Thus not all targets show polarity, nor are all nouns included in the polarity system. (Conversely, a small number of nouns is exceptional in taking polarity type agreements for predicate agreement too: see Hetzron 1972, Zwicky and Pullum 1983.) The importance of polarity should not be overrated, as Speiser warned (1938).

Inverse number and the special case of polarity are surprising and interesting phenomena. However, they are interesting only as means of expression. They do not add to the semantic possibilities of number systems.

5.6 Minimal-augmented systems

In descriptions of certain languages of the Philippines, starting from Thomas (1955) on Ilocano, there was a perception that the data did not fit well into conventional accounts of person and number. Conklin (1962: 134–6) proposed a different analysis for Hanunóo, which also proved applicable to various languages of Arnhem Land in Australia. We shall follow the account of one of the latter, namely Rembarrnga, as described in McKay (1978, 1979). First consider the Rembarrnga forms given in table 5.17 (McKay 1978: 28). This analysis captures the facts, but it seems unsatisfactory: first the paradigm looks disjointed, and

Table 5.17 *Rembarrnga dative pronoun forms: traditional categories*

	singular	dual	trial	plural
1 inclusive	—	yʉkkʉ	ngakorr**bbarrah**	ngakorrʉ
1 exclusive	ngʉnʉ	yarr**bbarrah**	yarrʉ	
2	kʉ	nakor**bbarrah**	nakorrʉ	
3 masculine	nawʉ			
		barr**bbarrah**	barrʉ	
3 feminine	ngadʉ			

second there is a marker *-bbarrah*, marked in bold in table 5.17, which appears in an odd selection of cells. If we try to characterize *-bbarrah* in absolute terms, we find no solution: in one instance it is used of three individuals, in other instances it is for two. But if we treat it (and the entire system) in relative terms (Evans §7.1.1 in forthcoming) then a more elegant picture emerges. The form *-bbarrah* is used when there is one entity more than the logical minimum. For most cells that view makes no difference. However, for the first person inclusive, the logical minimum is two (otherwise it would not be inclusive). Thus *yʉkkʉ* is a minimal form (we can label it 1/2 to suggest it represents another person value) and *ngakorrbbarrah* is used where there is one more than that minimum, that is, three. We redraw the paradigm from this relative perspective (McKay 1978: 28) in table 5.18. This is a more satisfy-

Table 5.18 *Rembarrnga dative pronoun forms:*
minimal-augmented analysis

	minimal	unit augmented	augmented
1	ngʉnʉ	yarrbbarrah	yarrʉ
1/2	yʉkkʉ	ngakorrbbarrah	ngakorrʉ
2	kʉ	nakorrbbarrah	nakorrʉ
3 masc	nawʉ		
		barrbbarrah	barrʉ
3 fem	ngadʉ		

ing analysis. We have forms for the minimal number of the pronoun, for one more than that (the unit augmented form) and and for more than that again (aug-mented). The simplest system of this type would have just minimal and aug-mented. In such systems, with only two number values, the difference from conventional systems is in one form only. We see this clearly by comparing Ilocano

Table 5.19 *Traditional analysis of Ilocano pronominal forms*

	singular	dual	plural
1 exclusive	-ko		-mi
1 inclusive		-ta	-tayo
2	-mo		-yo
3	-na		-da

analysed in the two different ways. In the traditional analysis (table 5.19) there is just one dual form; from our discussion in §4.1, if there is an additional number value in one place only, the first person is exactly the place in which we would expect to find it.

Table 5.20 *Minimal-augmented analysis of Ilocano pronominal forms*

	minimal	augmented
1	-ko	-mi
1/2	-ta	-tayo
2	-mo	-yo
3	-na	-da

On the other hand, though the evidence is not as convincing as in Rembarrnga, there are grounds for favouring the minimal-augmented account for Ilocano given in table 5.20. The main difference is in the status accorded to *-ta*. The possible ambiguity of the first person inclusive dual or 1/2 minimal form in such cases is discussed in an interesting exchange (Greenberg 1988, McGregor 1989, Greenberg 1989, McKay 1990). Besides being found in Hanunóo as noted earlier, and other languages of the Philippines, minimal-augmented systems have been identified in various languages of Arnhem Land, starting with Burrara (Burera) (Glasgow 1964);[30] others are listed

---

[30] It is important to note how similarly these number systems behave to those we have seen before. Thus Gurr-goni is one of the four Manigrida group languages (the others are Burrara, as just mentioned, Nakkara and Ndjébbana), all of which have systems similar to that of Rembarrnga. In Gurr-goni the number distinctions are available only for reference to humans and higher animates (as in the systems discussed in chapter 2). Furthermore, in the third person the minimal form is unmarked even for reference to humans. However, if an augmented form is used, it must be the appropriate one. In other words, the minimal form acts rather like a general number form (partially similar to Kaytetye, §2.3.3); the choice is minimal/general or number-specific: if the latter is chosen it must be the appropriate form, that is, unit augmented versus augmented is not a facultative choice in Gurr-goni. The information on Gurr-goni is from Rebecca Green (personal communication).

in McKay (1978: 29). Following from these alternative analyses, the essential point is that minimal-augmented systems represent an alternative way of organizing the morphology of person and number. They do not give additional semantic distinctions in number. This is why we consider them here as an alternative means of expression, and not as a set of additional number values.[31]

5.7 'Constructed' numbers
Constructed numbers appear where there is a mismatch between number marking of different elements which produces additional number values. Consider the following data from the Uto-Aztecan language Hopi (Hale 1997: 74). The pronominal and verbal forms each make a two-way distinction:

(40) Pam   wari
      that.SG   run.PERFV.SG
      'He/she ran'

(41) Puma   yùutu
      that.PL   run.PERFV.PL
      'They (plural) ran'

However there is a third possibility:

(42) Puma   wari
      that.PL   run.PERFV.SG
      'They (two) ran'

The combination of plural pronoun and singular verb gives a dual ('they two ran'). This dual is 'constructed' from the number on the pronoun and that on the verb; we have a singular–dual–plural system, 'constructed' from the two parts. If we retain notional labels, then we could say that the pronoun distinguishes singular from dual/plural while the verb distinguishes singular/dual from plural. It must be stressed, however, that this is only a part of the system: animate nouns in Hopi have a straightforward singular–dual–plural system, indicated by three distinct markers.

Now consider Zuni, a language isolate with some 8,000 speakers in north-west New Mexico (data from Lynn Nichols, personal communications). No pronoun is found in the third person, and there is a dual marker available. The verb has a marker for the plural (as in (47) below), otherwise it takes no number marker.

---

[31] Similarly, the 'quasi-duals' of Bantu represent interesting combinations of person, but do not extend the semantic possibilities of number; for the complex system of Ngyembɔɔn-Bamileke, a Grassfield Bantu language of Cameroon, see S. C. Anderson (1985); for consideration of other complex systems using the 'augmented' notion see Noyer (1997: 148–54).

> (43) ʔaːči ʔaː-kya
> DUAL go-past
> 'they (two) went'

A pronoun is needed for first or second person:

> (44) hon ʔaːči ʔaː-kya
> 1.PL.NOM DUAL go-past
> 'we (two) went'

Here we have the dual marker, but the pronoun is plural, and the verb has no marker (hence is singular). Moreover, the dual marker may be dropped:

> (45) hon ʔaː-kya
> 1.PL.NOM go-past
> 'we (two) went'

This is an alternative to (44), and is similar to the Hopi equivalent form. It is not possible to reverse the markers:

> (46) *hoʔ ʔaːw-aː-kya
> 1.SG.NOM PL-go-past
> 'we (two) went'

This is ungrammatical in any interpretation. If both are plural, then not surprisingly the interpretation is plural:

> (47) hon ʔaːw-aː-kya
> 1.PL.NOM PL-go-past
> 'we went'

Where Zuni goes beyond Hopi is in using this system with nouns too. The plural prefix here is *ʔaː-* before consonant-initial stems, *ʔaːw-* before vowel-initial stems; the final *ʔi* of *ʔaːw-akcek(ʔi)* drops before *ʔa*:

> (48) ʔaːw-akcek(ʔi) ʔaː-kya
> PL-boy go-past
> 'two boys went'

> (49) ʔaːw-akcek(ʔi) ʔaːči ʔaː-kya
> PL-boy DUAL go-past
> 'two boys went'

Here again the dual *ʔaːči* can be included as in (49) or omitted as in (48). When it is omitted, we have a constructed dual, this time with nouns as well as with pronouns. Hopi and Zuni are both found in North America, as is Kawaiisu, a Uto-Aztecan language of the Numic branch, which also shows the phenomenon (see Zigmond, Booth and Munro 1991: 76). Elsewhere there is the complex case of Mele-Fila, as we saw in §2.2.6.

Before leaving constructed numbers there are several general points to make. The first is that while the phenomenon is surprising and interesting, it tends to be limited in terms of its extent within a number system. For instance in Hopi only the pronouns were affected: nouns had full marking. Second, and related to this: in all of the languages pronouns are involved; constructed number appears to affect the top of the Animacy Hierarchy, but we have rather few languages and so should be cautious about this claim. There are interesting differences between these systems and conflated numbers (§4.5.1) in that constructed numbers involve a top segment of the hierarchy, and the conflation (which is not in the nominal system) is resolved, in a way which gives an additional number value. And finally, the nature of the verbal forms requires careful scrutiny: at least in some cases we are dealing with verbal number, which we shall consider in chapter 8; see also the discussion of Chamorro in Durie (1986: 364–5). In such cases the number value is constructed from the value of nominal number of the pronoun or noun together with that which can be inferred from the participant number value of the verb.

Given what we have seen in Hopi, we might consider whether to treat British English as having a constructed number, shown in examples like:

(50)   This committee have decided . . .

Since the agreements are singular and plural, does this constitute a constructed number? There are differences which should make us suspicious: first the number value which arose in the constructed systems (typically the dual) was one found in regular systems. The English construction does not give rise to a normal number (from the inventory in §2.3.2). Nor does the construction affect a top segment of the Animacy Hierarchy. What we have rather is a set of nouns which vary in the number agreement they take (from target to target, from speaker to speaker, and most importantly from noun to noun). They are 'hybrids' in this respect, and will be discussed more fully in §6.2. Finally, note that these, like constructed number cases, are instances of a wider problem of mismatches in number: Kiowa (§5.5) showed a mismatch in the system found in the noun phrase and on the verb, there is also the Hebrew type (where the values on the verb are a subset of those on certain nouns, §4.2.1), and that type in turn can be seen in the context of differential marking on noun phrase and verb discussed in §6.1.1.

5.8   Reduced expression of number

We now turn to those nouns which for various reasons do not have the full range of number possibilities. Let us start with a basic singular–plural system as in English

Table 5.21 *Different indicators of number-differentiability*

	dog	sheep	scissors	friendliness
semantics	+	+	+	−
syntax	+	+	−	−
morphology	+	−	−	−

and consider the possible combinations for distinguishing number morphologically, syntactically and semantically.[32] Note that nouns can move from type to type, through intermediate stages. Let us begin at the right of table 5.21 with the non-number-differentiable noun *friendliness*. This noun cannot straightforwardly distinguish number in semantic terms. We can talk of *instances of friendliness*, *kinds of friendliness*, but nouns like *instances* and *kinds* indicate the semantic shifts or recategorizations (§3.7.2) involved. It shows no syntactic or morphological signs of number-differentiability (that is, no agreement or marking opposition). *Friendliness* then is simply off the scale of number-differentiability for English, being low on the Animacy Hierarchy. We might conclude that number is therefore irrelevant and no more need be said. But there is still the question of which number it is: its form and especially the agreements it takes show that it is singular, so it is called a *singulare tantum* (singular only) noun. Nouns which are non-number-differentiable are not always singular: even in English we have the contrast between *wheat* and *oats*. We will therefore ask how languages deal with nouns which are off the scale of number-differentiability (§5.8.1).

The noun *scissors* is rather different; it is exceptional in that it denotes a countable entity (there is no problem about counting pairs of scissors) but expressing the opposition in number typically requires a classifier, namely *pair*. The countability of *scissors* is not reflected in its syntax and morphology, since it has only plural forms (it is a *plurale tantum* noun). *Sheep* is number-differentiable as its syntax (agreement) shows, but lacks the appropriate morphology (a mismatch discussed in §3.3). It is defective just in terms of its morphology. We will consider various types of defectives in §5.8.2.

There is a second, cross-cutting distinction here. There are several nouns like *scissors*, which denote objects made of two similar parts (*trousers*, *goggles* and so on) and their defectiveness is motivated. *Sheep* on the other hand is an example of an individual defective noun, which does not represent a class of similar nouns (hence we have *goats*, *pigs* and *cows*). Surprisingly, *aircraft* behaves like *sheep*;

[32] Where by distinguishing number semantically we mean that we distinguish individuals and collections of individuals (as shown by the ability to enumerate them; see the discussion of Allan's work in §3.6 for a more delicate analysis).

these appear to be unmotivated exceptions. We discuss motivation further in §5.8.3.

Finally, *dog* is a typical noun of English; it may refer to an individual or to a set of individuals, and in the latter case the agreements it takes and the morphology are both plural (*the dogs are barking*). Thus *dog* is a fully number-differentiable noun, with all the possibilities (just two in English). Such nouns have been a main focus of attention, particularly in chapters 2 and 3. This section concerns those nouns not so favoured in terms of number.

5.8.1 Nouns which are not number-differentiable

Typically there is a set of nouns, very large in some languages, very small or non-existent at the other extreme (§3.7.2), which are off the end of the scale for number-differentiability, nouns like *friendliness* in English. As we noted in §3.6, the point at which the 'split' comes can vary slightly and in interesting ways between relatively closely related languages. *Friendliness* is a *singulare tantum* noun, but it is not defective. For a typical noun of its type in English, given where it stands on the Animacy Hierarchy, it has all the forms expected, namely one. Typically in English such nouns are singular. Their form usually suggests this and agreements show it clearly (*his friendliness was particularly appreciated that day*). Not all behave this way in English, thus we have *oats* in contrast to *wheat* (for discussion see Wierzbicka 1988: 459–60, 1991a, 1991b; Palmer 1990; Moravcsik 1991). There are many languages like English in this respect. Some with larger systems still work in the same way: in Mansi, which has a singular–dual–plural system, nouns which are not number-differentiable have just the singular (§4.1). However, this is not the only solution. In Manam (Lichtenberk 1983: 269) *all* mass nouns are plural, (as marking on the verb shows). In Turkana, some are singular and some are plural (Dimmendaal 1983: 224). In Bantu languages too, mass nouns are frequently split between singular and plural (Guthrie 1948: 851).

There may be other items which do not fully qualify as nouns: nominalizations of verbs in some languages come into this category. Such items usually remain outside the number system, and take default agreement (§6.1.2), usually singular, which makes them similar to *singularia tantum* nouns. Differences between such items and genuine *singularia tantum* nouns may be evident in conjoined structures; there is variation from language to language, but plural agreement is more likely, I suggest, with conjoined *singularia tantum* nouns than with conjoined nominalizations.[33]

---

[33] The reader may wish to investigate judgements on sentences such as:

> wheat and barley make/makes a good combination
> persistence and intelligence make/makes a good combination
> running and cycling make/makes a good combination

5.8.2 Defectives

Nouns like English *scissors* are defective, in that they have only one number form, and the other is missing, even though in semantic terms there would be no difficulty (for extensive examples see Wickens 1992). Since these instances involve twosomes, an obvious question is what would happen in a language with a dual. We turn to Central Alaskan Yup'ik (data here are from Marianne Mithun, personal communication, elicited from Elizabeth Ali). We saw in §3.7.2 that there are few mass nouns (which have just singular number); there are also relatively few nouns which are defective in terms of number in other ways. There are some examples, however: *uskurak* 'dog harness' is dual in form, appears with dual pronominal suffixes on the verb, and can be used for one dog harness or for two. Three or more dog harnesses would be *uskurat*. There is no singular form *uskuraq*. *Atasuak* 'summer trousers' functions similarly. (For comparative data on the dual in Eskimo languages see Hammerich 1959.) As so often, larger systems are valuable indicators. *Uskurak* is defective, in that it lacks a singular, but it is not *duale tantum*, it has two forms out of three. Consider this example, with *niicugnissuutet* 'radio':

(51) niicugni-ssuut-et   nipe-s-ki
     listen-INST.NOMINALIZER-PL   go.out-CAUS-
                                            OPTATIVE.2.SG/3.PL
     'Turn off the radio!'

This is the only number form available, so this noun is a *plurale tantum* (missing two forms out of three). Recalling the evidence from §3.7.2, we may summarize the noun types of Yup'ik as in table 5.22. The great majority of nouns are normal count nouns; of the mass nouns, most allow recategorization (§3.7.2); just a few like *meq* 'water' are not number-differentiable, and have just the singular. There are two sorts of defective nouns (within the *scissors*-type), those which have dual and plural, and those which have just the plural.

Table 5.22 *Main noun types in Central Alaskan Yup'ik*

		forms available		
description	example	singular	dual	plural
normal count noun	*qayaq* 'kayak'	+	+	+
mass noun (with recategorization)	*uquq* 'oil'	+	(+)	(+)
mass noun	*meq* 'water'	+	−	−
missing singular	*uskurak* 'dog harness'	−	+	+
pluralia tantum	*niicugnissuutet* 'radio'	−	−	+

Continuing with the different possible types of defective nouns, let us move on to the '*sheep*-type', those lacking morphological forms but being regular in terms of agreement. An interesting example is from the Nakh-Daghestanian language Tsez (Bernard Comrie, personal communication). It is *xex-bi* 'child(ren)'; this noun is plural in form (the *-bi* is a regular plural marker) and it has a full plural paradigm of case forms (thus the genitive is *xex-za-s*). It may denote one or more children, and takes the appropriate agreements, singular for one and plural for more than one. The noun *yˁana-bi* 'woman/women' behaves similarly.

There are still further possible types of defectiveness to be explored. Thus in Arbore, which has singular and plural (usually with one form also available for use as a general form; see §2.1) there are nouns with just one form, which depending on the noun may match the typical form of general number, singular or plural. And for the surprising defectives of Bayso, the adventurous reader should tackle Corbett and Hayward (1987), for which §6.1.1 is gentle preparation.

If we look at nouns which do not have the full range of values, whether because they are non-number-differentiable or because they are defective, then the data we have discussed suggest that the values line up broadly with the scheme of §2.3.2. Generally *singularia tantum* are the most common; we find instances with just the plural or with dual and plural but lacking the singular; *dualia tantum* are quite rare.

5.8.3 Motivation for defectives

The noun *scissors* is not a haphazard exception. It is an example of what Quirk et al. call 'summation plurals', which 'denote tools, instruments, and articles of dress consisting of two equal parts which are joined together' (1985: 300; see Wierzbicka 1988: 514–16 for discussion); Quirk et al. point out that the plural *-s* is often not found when such nouns are used attributively as in *a trouser leg*. Similarly the motivation for Yup'ik *atasuak* 'summer trousers' having dual and plural seems obvious, since we are used to *trousers* being defective. And this can be a persistent defectiveness: Russian has borrowed the word *jeans*, and created *džins-y*; the English *-s* is made part of the stem, and the Russian plural inflections are added, making the word *plurale tantum*.[34] The duality of *uskurak* 'dog harness' may not be so immediately obvious to us, but then most of us do not have regular experience of harnessing huskies. Sometimes the problem is the outsider's lack of knowledge; but for speakers too, of course, there may be no retrievable motivation. We noted *niicugnissuutet* 'radio', which is *plurale tantum* and a similar example is *allirtet* 'one-piece trousers with attached fur socks', also found only in the plural. Such nouns typically denote objects consisting of multiple parts. It does not follow that every noun

---

[34] This motivation carries over into *galife* 'riding breeches' which is indeclinable but also a *plurale tantum* noun in that it takes only plural agreements.

denoting objects of this type is *plurale tantum* in Yup'ik, any more than paired objects are of that type in English (for example, *bicycle* is quite regular). There are fascinating groups and oddities to be investigated. For instance, names of festivals and celebrations are often plural, as in Estonian, Finnish, Latvian and Lithuanian; examples include Estonian *kihlad* 'engagement', *varrud* 'christening party' (Tauli 1973: 79). Another common grouping is names of diseases, originally perhaps from the multiple signs on the body (for example, Estonian *sarlakid* 'scarlet fever'). The nouns in such groupings can motivate each other, even when the original motivation is lost.

There are other interesting cases, from small groups down to individual lexical items. In the Nakh-Daghestanian language Archi, *buwa* 'father' and *dija* 'mother' are both *singularia tantum* (Aleksandr Kibrik, personal communication). Even in English there are some surprising hidden cases. Quirk et al. (1985: 300–1) point out that there seem to be very few defectives in English, because generally the other form exists, though with slightly different meaning. For instance we have both *fund* and *funds*, but these do not match up completely as the singular and plural of a single lexical item (see earlier discussion of similar cases in §3.6 note 24). Conversely, suppletion (§5.4) may be viewed as two defectives functioning as a single lexical item.

Since defective nouns may be synchronically unmotivated, they can be reintegrated into the full number system. *Pluralia tantum* nouns are therefore a potential source for 'double plurals' (§5.3.6); if they are potentially countable, their plural form may be used as a singular, and a new plural suffix added; this appears to have happened for instance in the Nakh-Daghestanian language Lezgian (Haspelmath 1993: 81–2), where there are nouns like *gurar* 'stairs' and *purar* 'saddle', with the plural suffix *-ar*, but which now behave like normal count nouns and have the plurals *gurar-ar* 'staircases' and *purar-ar* 'saddles'. On the way to this point, nouns may take mixed agreements; the noun *sur* 'grave' gives the plural *surar*, which means 'cemetery', but this is itself countable. *Surar* 'cemetery' does not take a (double) plural suffix, but has alternative agreement possibilities:

(52) Či   šeher.di-n   surar   jeke-bur / jeke-di
     1.PL.GEN   town-GEN   cemetery   big-SBST.PL / big-SBST.SG

     ja.
     COP

     'Our town's cemetery is large.'

In terms of the types discussed earlier, *surar* 'cemetery' has moved beyond the *scissors* type in that it allows singular agreement, but does not yet belong to the *sheep* type in that it does not yet always take the number agreement matching the meaning.

5.9 Conclusion

We have examined the ways in which number is expressed, and found that they are many and varied, with morphological means providing the greatest variety. We also looked in detail at systems which are unusual in terms of the marking of number, yet which do not give new semantic distinctions. These were a useful reminder of the need to be clear whether claimed generalizations relate to number values or to the means of their expression, and more generally to be careful about comparing like with like. Having looked at the various means of expression, with morphology taking centre stage, in the next chapter we concentrate on syntactic questions.

6

The syntax of number

We saw in the last chapter that agreement is one of the ways of expressing number and this will be our main topic here. We first consider agreement and the types of mismatch which occur between the controlling noun phrase and the agreement target. Then we undertake a set of case studies leading to a typology of agreement options in number. There are three typological themes: once again we see the importance of being clear about terms, as we analyse systems where the number values of controller and target differ; we see the importance of hierarchies, this time in syntax; and there is a graphic illustration of how factors which can be identified as being at work in various languages interact in different ways to give very different results.

6.1 Controller versus target number

The first notion that we need is 'agreement', which is the covariance or matching of feature specifications between two separate elements, such as subject noun phrase and verb. We shall call the element which determines the agreement (say the subject noun phrase) the **controller**. The element whose form is determined by agreement is the **target**. The syntactic environment in which agreement occurs is the **domain** of agreement. And when we indicate in what respect there is agreement, we are referring to **agreement categories** or **agreement features**, as illustrated in figure 6.1. Of course, we are primarily interested in agreement in number.[1] The controller of agreement is a noun phrase. Cross-linguistically, the possible targets are more varied than many believe. Besides the obvious verbs and adjectives, we also find demonstratives, articles, possessives, participles, adpositions, adverbs and complementizers.[2] We will use the term 'agreement' in the

---

[1] The topic is becoming of increasing interest to psycholinguists; see for example Bock and Miller (1991), Vigliocco, Butterworth and Semenza (1995) and references there.

[2] Examples of these different targets are given in Corbett (1991: 106–15); while that source illustrates agreement in gender, in almost all the examples agreement in number is also involved.

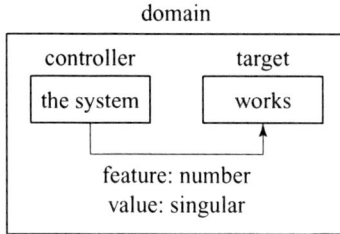

Figure 6.1 *Framework of terms*

wider sense to include the determination of the form of anaphoric pronouns, thus pronouns are possible targets.[3]

Though number marking appears on these different targets, it is still nominal number (as contrasted to verbal number, which we look at in chapter 8). What makes agreement so fascinating is that in domains where agreement in number takes place we can often find instances where the feature specifications on the controller and the target do not match, in other words, controller number marking and target number marking differ. First the system of controller numbers and that of target numbers may be different. We shall discuss the possibilities for this in §6.1.1. Or the controller may be outside the number system, giving rise to default number (§6.1.2). Or else the systems may be in harmony, but particular instances of controller and target may not coincide in number under certain circumstances. We shall see how this comes about in §6.1.3. Then our case studies will establish the factors which influence the choice between matching and failing to match.

6.1.1 Mismatches of system

At the simplest level the systems of controller and target number may differ in that one is absent or largely so. Not surprisingly, we find languages in which nominal number is expressed primarily on the noun phrase. In Lezgian (a Nakh-Daghestanian language), nouns mark number by suffixation, but finite verbs do not (Haspelmath 1993: 71–3, 127–36). And in French, as a result of attrition, number marking on verbs and on nouns is largely lost in the spoken language; the clearest marker of nominal number is the article (*le* and *la* singular, versus *les* plural). These languages are examples of type A in table 6.1. In Russian, which is typical of many Indo-European languages in this respect, nominal number is

---

[3] Most mainstream work on agreement uses the term in this sense, to include pronouns. Barlow (1991, 1992: 134–52) reviews the literature and finds no good grounds for distinguishing between agreement and antecedent–anaphora relations. See also the discussion in §3.2.4.1.

Table 6.1 *Place where nominal number
is primarily expressed*

type	main locus of marking	example
A	on noun phrase	Lezgian
B	on noun frase and verb	Russian
C	on verb	Amele

clearly signalled on the noun. It is marked elsewhere in the noun phrase by agreement and on the verb by agreement with the subject noun phrase (type B):

> (1) on   rasskazyva-et tebe   tak-ie   anekdot-y ?
>   3.SG.MASC tell-3.SG   2.SG.DAT such-PL.ACC joke-PL.ACC
>   'Does he tell you such jokes?'

The verb is singular, agreeing with the subject *on* 'he', and within the object noun
phrase *tak-ie* 'such' is plural agreeing with *anekdot-y* 'jokes'. The most surprising
type, type C, is exemplified by the Papuan language Amele, which we considered in
§5.2. We saw examples like:

> (2) dana (age) ho-ig-a
>   man   3.PL come-3.PL-TODAY'S.PAST
>   'the men came'

Here the verb must agree in number with the subject, while other markers are
optional. Thus we have nominal number which must be indicated on the verb and
which may optionally be indicated on the noun.

Returning to type B, there is a host of interesting questions concerning the relationship between the two types of marking in such languages: the number value
expressed on the noun and that expressed through agreement may differ. Where
number is marked on both controller and target, the values of the two systems may
not match. We discussed Modern Hebrew in §4.2.1, and saw that it has three controller numbers (for some nouns only), namely singular, dual and plural, but it distinguishes only two numbers (singular and plural) in the verb phrase. The same
agreement form of the target is used for both dual and plural subjects. The most
interesting case is with a dual subject:

> (3) ha-yom-ayim   ʕavru   maher
>   DEF-day-DUAL   pass.PAST.3.PL   quickly
>   'the two days passed quickly'

Here the feature specification of the controller includes [+dual] while the verb is [+plural]. Another type of mismatch occurs in Kiowa, where the nouns have an inverse system but the verbs have singular–dual–plural (§5.5).

Table 6.2 *Number forms of Bayso nouns*

general (unit reference)	singular (singulative reference)	paucal (paucal reference)	plural (multiple reference)
lúban a lion/lion(s)	lubántiti a/the particular lion	lubanjaa a few lions/some lions	lubanjool lions

There are more complex cases, as in the Cushitic language Bayso, which was introduced in §2.1. The account here is based on Hayward (1979 and personal communications) and Corbett and Hayward (1987). Nouns mark four categories of number which we may call general (used to denote either an individual member or the class of the referent), singular (a particular individual only), paucal (a small discrete number of individuals, from two to about six) and plural (for a plurality of individual members or units). In table 6.2 we give examples, with Hayward's terms in parentheses. Nouns also fall into two genders. We might then expect targets to have eight forms. In fact they have only three, as the agreeing verbal forms in the following examples show. (Recall from §2.1 the difficulty of translating general number forms.) The verbal forms in (4)–(11) are not given morphological glosses because that is precisely the point we are trying to work out.

(4) lúban   hudure
  lion.GENERAL slept
  'lion(s) slept'

(5) lubán-titi hudure
  lion-SG slept
  'a single/particular lion slept'

(6) luban-jaa hudureene
  lion-PAUCAL slept
  'a few lions slept'

(7) luban-jool hudure
  lion-PL slept
  'lions slept'

Surprisingly, three subject forms have the same verbal agreement. There are many nouns like *lúban* 'lion', which form the masculine gender in Bayso. The other gender, the feminine, may be represented by *kimbír* 'bird':

(8) kimbír   hudurte
    bird.GENERAL   slept
    'bird(s) slept'

(9) kimbír-titi   hudurte
    bird-SG   slept
    'a single/particular bird slept'

(10) kimbir-jaa   hudureene
     bird-PAUCAL   slept
     'a few birds slept'

(11) kimbir-jool   hudure
     bird-PL   slept
     'birds slept'

The distribution of verbal forms with a typical masculine noun like *lúban* 'lion' and a typical feminine noun like *kimbír* 'bird' is given in table 6.3 (where the rows and columns are labelled according to the controller). We see that for both types of

Table 6.3 *Forms of the predicate verb in Bayso*

	general	singular	paucal	plural
masculine	hudure	hudure	hudureene	hudure
feminine	hudurte	hudurte	hudureene	hudure

noun, the agreement forms for general and singular are identical: masculine nouns take *hudure* in both instances and feminines take *hudurte*. We need a way of referring to these target forms, since the distinctions are the same from target to target but the actual forms are different. So we might label *hudure* 'masculine' and *hudurte* 'feminine'. Next we see that nouns in the paucal, whether masculine or feminine, take *hudureene*. We return to an appropriate label for this shortly. Most nouns have a regular plural form and take 'masculine' agreement (there are various irregular patterns, restricted to small numbers of nouns, and a substantial proportion of these take masculine agreement too).[4] Thus nouns which have the controller number 'plural' take 'masculine' agreement. Of course, we could use other

---

[4] We leave them to one side here; details are in Hayward (1979: 104–5) and they are discussed in Corbett and Hayward (1987). These are the nouns referred to in §5.8.2.

labels, but the important point will remain, namely that the system for the controller is substantially different from that of the target. While the actual labels are not crucial ('X', 'Y' and 'Z' would serve the purpose), we should try to make them as helpful as possible. It may be a surprise, therefore, that for the forms like *hudureene*, which occur with paucal nouns, the proposed label is 'plural'. One motivation is that this is the traditional term for Cushiticists. More importantly the use of the term 'plural' is motivated by the behaviour of the personal pronouns. The subject/object forms of the third person pronoun are presented in table 6.4.

Table 6.4 *Third person pronouns in Bayso*

	singular	plural
masculine	úsu	iso
feminine	ése	

The important point is that the plural pronoun *iso* takes agreement forms like *hudureene*; hence the use of the term 'plural' for such forms. Thus the pronouns (the top of the Animacy Hierarchy discussed in chapter 3) have a straightforward matching system: masculine singular takes masculine agreement, feminine singular takes feminine agreement, and the plural (both genders) takes plural agreement. Returning then to nouns, the regular patterns of agreement are as in table 6.5; this time we give both the form of the verb and the label for it (and for other target forms).

Table 6.5 *Consistent agreement patterns in Bayso*

	general	singular	paucal	plural
masculine	hudure (masculine)	hudure (masculine)	hudureene (plural)	hudure (masculine)
feminine	hudurte (feminine)	hudurte (feminine)	hudureene (plural)	hudure (masculine)

The systems of controller number and target number are dramatically different for nouns in Bayso. There are four controller numbers, and three agreement forms, but they do not match up in an obvious way. We return to the question of why the plural agreement forms should be used with nouns in the paucal in §6.8 below.

A different but similarly surprising situation is found in other Cushitic languages. We will consider Qafar, an East Cushitic language, spoken by approximately 250,000 speakers in north-eastern Ethiopia and in Djibouti (Hayward and

Table 6.6 *Third person pronouns in Qafar*

	absolutive	nominative
masculine	kàa	ùsuk
feminine	tet	is
plural	ken	òson

Corbett 1988; the orthography and tone marking conventions there are followed here). The third person pronouns are given in table 6.6. These pronouns are typically used with antecedents denoting humans. The only other target which shows gender and number is the verbal predicate (which has no restriction to agreement with controllers denoting humans). There are two main conjugations of verbs, distinguished by the form and position of the subject agreement markers among other things; the non-emphatic perfect forms of *-emeet-* 'come' and *fak-* 'open' are as in table 6.7.

Table 6.7 *Perfect tense forms in Qafar*

	conjugation 1	conjugation 2
masculine	yemeete	fake
feminine	temeete	fakte
plural	yemeeten	faken

These verbal forms enable us to divide nouns into two classes: those which when singular take *yemeete, fake* and similar forms, and those which take *temeete, fakte* and similar forms. It makes good sense to give these two classes the traditional labels 'masculine gender' and 'feminine gender', since nouns denoting males are typically in the first group of nouns and those denoting females in the second. The surprising thing is that almost every simple noun phrase (that is, one that is neither conjoined nor quantified) in subject position controls either masculine singular or feminine singular agreement. The only simple noun phrases requiring third person plural agreement are *òson* 'they', *màra* 'people', *ùrru* 'children' and *agàbu* 'women'. The last three show distributional peculiarities and it is possible that they are moving towards becoming pronominal forms.

Nouns form their plurals in a variety of ways (Parker and Hayward 1985: 229–31), very often with the suffix *-itte*. The great majority of plural nouns have a phonological form which would be appropriate for feminine gender if singular, and in fact they actually do take feminine agreement. Thus the form labelled 'feminine' in table 6.6 can also mark plurality. Syncretism of this unexpected type is widespread in Cushitic (see Serzisko 1982). Again we have a problem of labelling, and we have two different systems at work. We start from the pronouns, the top of the Animacy Hierarchy, and label the forms on this basis; in particular we treat the forms *yemeeten* 'came' and *faken* 'opened' as plural. There is a different system in operation for noun phrases headed by nouns, and here plural nouns take feminine agreement (the converse of the Bayso situation). We shall see that Arabic has a comparable though interestingly different system in §6.6, and we return to Qafar, in particular to the complex question of agreement with conjoined noun phrases, in §6.5.4.

One final instance of controller and target number not matching is one we have already considered and so it deserves only a brief mention here. In the case of 'constructed' number (§5.7) there are two different systems: in Hopi we noted a singular versus dual/plural system on the pronoun and a singular/dual versus plural system on the verb, which between them construct a third number value, the dual.

6.1.2 Default number

A different type of mismatch arises when there is a problem with the agreement controller, which may be absent or it may lack a feature value. For instance, if instead of an ordinary noun phrase we have a whole clause as controller:

(12)   For Bill to make it to a 9 o'clock class is amazing.

Here the controller is not specified for number, yet the verb *be* has to have a number value. This is an exceptional case default (Fraser and Corbett 1997: 43–4). In English, as in language after language, the default number value is the singular. We might expect this to be universal. Before accepting this reasonable hypothesis, however, we should consider some remarkable counter-examples. One is the Kru language Godié, which has singular and plural; it also distinguishes human from non-human genders in both numbers, and in the singular non-human divides into three. The forms of the personal pronoun are given in table 6.8. Of these it is the plural pronoun ι which is used as the default form, the appropriate pronoun for nominalized verbs, whole phrases and longer discourse units. Marchese (1986: 239–40) gives examples, such as:[5]

(13)   mlʌlι   -í   wò   nʌʌ
       drink   -3.PL.NON-HUMAN.NEG   NEG   good
       'As for drinking, it's not good'

Kiowa, whose exotic number system was discussed in §5.5, also uses the plural as the default number value. If the object is unspecified or indeterminate, the plural

---

[5] Example (13) has been changed to match Marchese's 1988 transcription. It shows a topic–comment construction; *mlʌlι* 'drink' is a nominalized verb.

Table 6.8 *Personal pronouns in Godié*
(Marchese 1988: 325)

	singular	plural
human	ɔ	wa
non-human	ɛ a ʋ	ι

object prefix is used, thus in 'come and eat', 'eat' would have a plural object marker (Watkins 1984: 137–8; for instances of the dual see 145–6). A second example of this is with weather verbs (1984: 136):

(14) kʰí·dêl gyà-sál
      yesterday PL-hot
      'yesterday it was hot'

Godié and Kiowa are exceptions. The overwhelming majority use the singular as the default.[6]

Some languages also use the singular default in cases when it appears not to be needed, that is, when there is a fully specified noun phrase controller available. This widespread phenomenon is particularly strong in Norwegian and Swedish.[7] Here is a Norwegian example with the predicative adjective, which distinguishes singular from plural, standing in the singular (Faarlund 1977):

(15) pannekaker er   godt
      pancakes   COP   good.SG.NEUT
      roughly: 'Having pancakes is good'

The noun in (15) is plural but we find singular agreement. It seems that something is missing: with singular agreement, the sense is that eating pancakes is good, not any specific pancakes. Similar constructions have been identified elsewhere, often

---

[6] The default gender value shows much greater variation (Corbett 1991: 203–16). Having established the default number and default gender values, giving the 'neutral agreement form', we might expect that this would be the target equivalent of general number (§2.1) and they would match up (general forms would take neutral agreement). But this is not always the case. In Fula some nouns have a suffixless form which shows general meaning (§2.1). This form is not usually used in contexts where agreement is found, but when this does occur it is not the neutral agreement form (the *dum* gender form) which is used; instead there are various possibilities (Koval' 1979: 12–13).

[7] Examples in: Faarlund (1977), Hellan (1977: 102–8), Eriksson (1979), Nilsson (1979); for extensive discussion see Källström (1993: 188–246) and Hedlund (1992: 95–111).

they are characteristic of spoken language and not so well documented. Spoken Hebrew allows the following (Ruth Berman, personal communication):

(16) ha-samim   ze   bə'aya
      the drugs.PL.MASC   this.SG.MASC   problem
      'drugs is a problem'

This example may be analysed as a grammaticalized left-dislocation construction; the dummy pronoun *ze* occurs, just as it would with an infinitive phrase. And the interpretation is that the problem is drugs and what goes with them.

6.1.3 Mismatches for specific controller types

We now come to a range of interesting situations where controller and target have the same systems available, but where for given types of controller there need not be a match. Thus in English, subject noun phrases and predicate verbs (when in the present tense) have a singular–plural system, and normally they match by agreement. But we find a class of nouns like *committee*, which particularly in British English can take plural agreement when singular:

(17) the committee have decided

The noun *committee* has both number forms available, as does the verb *have*. But we find instances like that in (17) where the values do not match. Agreement rules are frequently formulated as though a controller's features were constant, that is, that all its agreements will be identical. In fact, we regularly find agreement choices: a given controller allows two (occasionally three) agreement possibilities, whether of the same target or for different targets. In either case simple-minded agreement rules would be inadequate. Feature mismatches and the associated agreement choices are therefore of great importance for an eventual overall theory of agreement, and we will consider them carefully here. The choices arise in turn from another type of mismatch, namely a mismatch between the semantic and formal properties of the controller. The controller may have the semantics expected of a particular number but a form which is normally associated with a different specification. Where we find agreement determined by the form we term it **syntactic agreement,** and when agreement is determined by the meaning it is **semantic agreement**. Controllers which allow agreement choices may be classified as in table 6.9. This classification is indicative but turns out to be too crude. There are indeed individual lexical items which induce agreement choices, like Serbo-Croat[8] *deca* 'children', which denotes a plurality but has the form of a singular

---

[8] Sadly I no longer know how best to refer to the largest of the South Slavonic languages, that used in different variants by many Bosnians, Croats, Montenegrins and Serbs. Since

Table 6.9 *Types of controllers which induce agreement mismatches*

controller type	example
lexical item(s)	Serbo-Croat *deca* 'children'
lexically restricted construction	nouns quantified by particular numerals
construction	conjoined noun phrases

noun. It is truly remarkable since it can take feminine singular, neuter plural and masculine plural agreements (Corbett 1983: 76–93). But there can also be large sets of lexical items which allow a choice, for instance British English nouns like *committee*. Then there are constructions which are lexically restricted, as in the case of quantified expressions involving particular numerals. Next we have constructions like the associative where the head noun may be any one from a large subset of those denoting humans, hence it is a lexically restricted construction, but the restrictions are quite loose. And there are construction types whose structure invokes agreement options, but which appear not to be lexically restricted, such as conjoined noun phrases. Thus table 6.9 is no more than indicative: the point is that controllers which allow agreement choices range all the way from unique lexical items to open-ended constructions; they are indeed pervasive. We shall investigate some of the most interesting in the following set of case studies.[9]

6.2 The Agreement Hierarchy and 'corporate' nouns in English

We are concerned with nouns which are singular morphologically and (typically) have a normal plural and yet, when singular, may take plural agreement, like *committee* as in (17) above. Such nouns are often called 'collectives' but, as we have seen (§4.4.2) this is an overused term, so for the class of nouns just described we will use the term 'corporate' (Nixon 1972).[10] Having an agreement choice here is

Footnote 8 (*cont.*)

the concern of this volume is linguistics, rather than socio-linguistics, it is natural to treat it as one language (the differences are comparable to those between different varieties of English). I considered taking out all the examples, to avoid the problem. Yet the language is a fascinating one, something to be treasured and advertised in a troubled area. Hence I have retained examples from the language of the Bosnians, Croatians, Montenegrins and Serbs, together with the traditional name I used in earlier work, namely Serbo-Croat.

[9] Agreement and mismatches were included in a questionnaire for which there are brief responses on nineteen languages in *Études linguistiques: Le problème du nombre* 1965. Some further sketches can be found in *Le Nombre* 1993.

[10] If we adopted a notional definition, just requiring the (singular) noun to denote a collection of individuals, then nouns like *forest* or *wood* (group of trees) would be included. Here, however, there is no possibility of agreement options. This is another instance of the

made possible by the semantics of the noun. However, the likelihood of examples like (17) being acceptable depends on the variety of English involved, and speakers from different parts of the world have very different judgements, as we shall see. Speakers of different varieties were asked to consider sentences apparently produced by non-native speakers of English and to correct them where necessary (data from Johansson 1979: 203; Bauer 1988: 254). The relevant test sentence is:

(18)   The audience were enjoying every minute of the show.

The results are shown in table 6.10. For each variety, N is the number of respondents, and the other figures are the percentage giving each response. There is substantial divergence between the varieties. Most speakers of British English were happy with the example as given, as were the majority of New Zealand English speakers. Very few speakers of American English concurred; they preferred *was enjoying*. Though there are no directly comparable data on Australian English, it appears to come between New Zealand and American English (see Watson 1979).

Table 6.10 *Judgements on agreement with 'corporate' nouns in three varieties of English*

		variety		
		GB (N = 92)	US (N = 93)	NZ (N = 102)
	no correction	77.2	5.4	72.5
response (%)	*was enjoying*	15.2	90.3	20.6
	other response	7.6	4.3	6.9

Another source of variation is the agreement target; while table 6.10 is concerned with the predicate, it is known that the relative frequency of plural agreement is different for other agreement targets such as the personal pronoun. So let us examine the different agreement targets. In attributive position there is no choice, only singular is possible:

(19)   this committee . . . / *these committee

Yet in the predicate, as we know, both numbers are possible in British English:

(20)   The committee has/have decided.

role of animacy (see §3.1); the agreement option is found primarily with collections of human individuals (*committee*), is excluded with inanimates (**the forest are* . . .) and is possible, though unusual in English, with non-human animates (*?the herd are restive*). See Allan (1986: 124–36) and Pollard and Sag (1994: 70–1) for discussion of corporate nouns, and Juul (1975: 85–114) for more examples. Formal semantic approaches can be found in Barker (1992) and references there.

The relative pronoun in English does not mark number but it controls number agreement in its clause and so its number can be inferred:[11]

> (21)　the committee, which has decided . . . / the committee, who have
> decided . . .

Both numbers are possible. This is also the case with the personal pronoun, and here speakers of American English admit the plural too:

> (22)　The committee . . . It . . . / They . . .

Thus with such nouns, for speakers of British English, syntactic or semantic agreement is possible for all agreement targets, except attributive modifiers, where only syntactic agreement is acceptable. Nixon (1972) counted examples of these agreements with nouns like *committee* in a corpus of British newspaper texts (100,000 words). In the predicate he found that plural agreement was used in 12.2 per cent of the cases (N = 181) while in the pronoun (he included possessive as well as personal pronouns) the plural was used in 27.4 per cent of the examples (N = 106). This type of controller then allows two different types of choice: for the attributive modifier the singular is required while for other targets there is an option; and within the targets where there is an option, the plural is more likely with the personal pronoun than with the predicate.

These data fit into a much more general pattern based on the Agreement Hierarchy (Corbett 1979), which consists of four target types, shown in figure 6.2.

> attributive < predicate < relative pronoun < personal pronoun

Figure 6.2　*The Agreement Hierarchy*

Possible agreement patterns are constrained as follows:

> For any controller that permits alternative agreement forms, as we
> move rightwards along the Agreement Hierarchy, the likelihood of
> agreement forms with greater semantic justification will increase
> monotonically (that is, with no intervening decrease).

The agreements with corporate nouns conform to this typological claim, and there is a good deal of further evidence, both from number, as we shall see again in §6.5.3 and §9.1.2, and from gender (Corbett 1991: 225–60; forthcoming b).

While agreement with corporate nouns is well known from English, it is found

---

[11] Not surprisingly, the choice of *who* rather than *which* is significant here.

more widely, for instance in Spanish (Nuessel 1984) and in Old Church Slavonic (Huntley 1989: 24–5), to take just two examples from Indo-European; and going further afield it is found, for instance, in Paumarí (an Aruan language of Brazil), where the nouns *ija'ari* 'people' and *jara* 'non-Indian' may be treated as singular or plural (Chapman and Derbyshire 1991: 287–8), and in Kabardian (a North-West Caucasian language, Kumaxov 1969: 70–1). Samoan has several such nouns, some morphologically simple, like *aiga* 'family' and some derived, like *'au-pua'a* 'group of pigs':

(23) Ua   momoe   uma   le   aiga.
        PERFV sleep.PL all   ART.SG family
        'The whole family were asleep.' (O lou igoa o Peko)

(24) 'A   tēte'i   le   'au-pua'a . . .
        but suddenly.awake.PL ART.SG COLL-pig
        'When the pigs suddenly awake . . .' (Moyle)

Note that the article is singular, but the verb is plural; the use of the verb in the plural is frequent but not obligatory (Mosel and Hovdhaugen 1992: 91, 443; and details of sources there).

The reason for the potential choice of agreement in these cases is clear. We have seen that the choice may be influenced by language variety but it is also constrained by linguistic factors, notably the Agreement Hierarchy.

6.3 Associatives (syntactic)

Associatives were discussed in §4.3; we noted forms consisting of a nominal plus a marker, which denote a set comprised of the referent of the nominal (the main member) plus one or more associated members: Hungarian *János-ék* (*János*-ASSOCIATIVE) 'John and his family/friends'. Some languages allow the use of the ordinary plural morphology with this same effect. A further possibility is to use syntactic means only. This is what we find in the Talitsk dialect of Russian, where a plural verb can be used with a singular noun phrase, to indicate reference to a person or persons besides the one indicated directly (Bogdanov 1968).

(25) Góša   pr'ijéxal'i!
        Gosha arrived.PAST.PL[12]
        'Gosha and his family have arrived!'

---

[12] Bogdanov's transcription has been transliterated in these examples. A similar construction is found in Maltese (Ray Fabri, personal communication; see also 1993: 276–8):

   (i) Brian ġie   Brian ġew
        Brian came.SG   Brian came.PL
        'Brian came'   'Brian and his family/friend(s) came'

This was used when the named person arrived with his wife and children; the fact that more than one person is involved is shown exclusively by the agreement. (These are not examples of honorific usage, and there is also a straightforward singular–plural opposition.) This plural agreement for associative meaning is not found in the noun phrase, and so conflicting agreements can occur:

(26) moj   brat   tam   tóža žýľi
     my.SG   brother.SG there also lived.PL
     'my brother and his family also lived there'

Here we find singular (syntactic) agreement of the attributive modifier and plural agreement in the predicate. No examples of relative pronouns are available but the personal pronoun in this construction is plural:

(27) Pra   Kuzʹmú my šýpka abʹisʹnʹitʹ tóža nʹe   móžym,
     About   Kuzʹma we much   explain   also NEG   can

     pašʹimú   onʹí nʹe   pʹišut vam.
     because   they NEG   write   you.DAT

     'We can't tell you much about Kuzʹma either, because they don't
     write to you.'

Again agreements in this construction adhere to the Agreement Hierarchy, with syntactic agreement in attributive position and semantic agreement in the predicate and personal pronoun.[13]

Footnote 12 (*cont.*)
And in Haruai, the construction is possible with a personal pronoun (Bernard Comrie, personal communication):

   (ii) n   dy-n-ŋ-a
       1.SG   go-FUT-1.PL-ASSERTIVE
       'I and some other(s) will go'

Here the verb form makes clear that some associate(s) must be involved.

[13] In §4.5.2 we considered Spanish dialects, particularly the Lena dialect (Hualde 1992), where some nouns can have a mass interpretation, and they then determine special mass agreement forms for targets outside the noun phrase, but they take masculine or feminine singular agreement of other targets within it (attributive agreement). This is fully in accord with the Agreement Hierarchy, since mass agreement represents semantic agreement and gender agreement (of mass nouns) is an instance of syntactic agreement. We should establish whether the distribution of the different agreements within the noun phrase is determined by the category of the target or by its position:

   (i) bwén-a   šénte
      good-SG.FEM   people
      'good people'

6.4 Honorifics (in Slavonic)

Number is frequently involved with forms of address, particularly polite address, a topic considered more fully in §7.1. Here we concentrate on the syntax of honorific pronouns.[14] When a plural pronoun is used for polite address it is the converse of corporate nouns of the last section like *committee*, in that we have a plural form being used for reference to a single individual. We might find plural agreement (syntactic agreement determined by the form) or singular agreement (semantic agreement determined by meaning), and indeed we find both, as shown in this Macedonian example (Koneski 1967: 332):

(28) Vie   ste   stanal-e   nervozen
      You   are.PL   become-PL   nervous.SG
      'You have become nervous'

Vie 'you (polite)', the honorific pronoun, has the form of a plural and the verb *ste* agrees with it as does the active participle. But the adjective, which also 'agrees', has the singular form, agreeing with the number of the person addressed. In a sense, all agree, but the targets do not all show the same feature values. The adjective may occur in the plural also (a less preferred variant according to Koneski):

(29) Vie   ste   mnogu   dobar / (dobri)
      You   are.PL   very   kind.SG / kind.PL
      'You are very kind'

The predicate noun is always singular in this construction in Macedonian:

(30) Vie   ste   mi   prijatel.
      You   are.PL   1.DAT   friend.SG
      'You are my friend.'

We need to home in on one part of the Agreement Hierarchy, namely the predicate,

---

(ii) šénte   bwén-o
      people   good-MASS
      'good people'

Where within the noun phrase the adjective precedes the noun, it takes the syntactic (gender) form (i); where it follows it takes the semantic (mass) form (ii). This too is in accord with a general pattern. Semantic agreement is more likely in targets which follow the controller than in those which precede. Where there is a split within a position on the Agreement Hierarchy (the attributive position in this instance) then the distribution of forms can be determined by word order (Corbett 1979: 218–20). We shall see further instances of the effect of word order (always with a preceding controller making semantic agreement more likely than if the target precedes) in §6.5.3 and §6.7.2.

[14] For discussion of the syntactic effects of nouns rather than pronouns being used as honorifics see Corbett (§2.1.1.5 in forthcoming b).

Table 6.11 *Agreement with honorific* vy *'you' in the Slavonic languages*

	finite verb	participle	adjective		noun
West Slavonic:					
Czech	pl	(pl)/SG	(pl)/SG		SG
Slovak	pl	pl/(SG)	SGSG		
Lower Sorbian	pl	pl	pl/SG		SG
Upper Sorbian	pl	(pl)/SG	(pl)/SG		SG
Polish dialects	pl	pl/SG	pl/SG		SG
South Slavonic:					
Bulgarian	pl	pl (96%) N = 167	SG (97%) N = 163		SG
Macedonian	pl	pl	(pl)/SG		SG
Serbo-Croat	pl	pl	pl/(SG)		SG
Slovene	pl	pl/(SG)	pl(SG)		SG
East Slavonic:					
Ukrainian	pl	pl/(SG)	(pl)/SG		SG
Belarusian	pl	pl	SGSG		
Russian	pl	pl	short form pl (97%) N = 145	long form SG (89%) N = 37	SG

Notes: Lower case indicates syntactic agreement, and upper case semantic agreement. The sources of the percentage figures are given in Corbett (1983). Other parentheses indicate less frequent or less preferred variants.

to see what the constraints on syntactic and semantic agreement are here. This was done by Comrie (1975), who showed how the considerable variation is constrained by what we shall call the 'Predicate Hierarchy'. Comrie drew data from a range of languages, but primarily from Slavonic; subsequently data on all the Slavonic languages were established (given in detail in Corbett 1983: 42–59) and they are shown in summary form in table 6.11. As indicated in the table, the Slavonic languages fall into three groups, West, South and East Slavonic (Macedonian is a South Slavonic language). Again there is great variation, but the overall pattern is clear. The predicate position on the Agreement Hierarchy may be split into the subhierarchy shown in figure 6.3.[15]

---

[15] Naturally we should consider how the two hierarchies combine. This is not straightforward: the Predicate Hierarchy forms a subhierarchy within the Agreement Hierarchy. For data and discussion see Corbett (1983: 76–93).

> verb < participle < adjective < noun

Figure 6.3 *The Predicate Hierarchy*

Reformulating Comrie's proposal we may claim that:

> For any controller that permits alternative agreement forms, as we
> move rightwards along the Predicate Hierarchy, the likelihood of
> agreement forms with greater semantic justification will increase
> monotonically (that is, with no intervening decrease).

6.5 Conjoined noun phrases

Suppose the agreement controller consists of conjoined noun phrases, such as *the owl and the pussycat*. We should ask first what the possibilities are (§6.5.1). In principle agreement may be with one noun phrase or with all of them. If agreement is with all of them, then we must ask what the agreement features will be (§6.5.2). The agreement features frequently make it clear whether agreement is with one noun phrase or with all of them, and so this construction is particularly fruitful for finding out which factors determine agreement choices (§6.5.3). We shall also look briefly at constructions which are related to conjoined noun phrases (§6.5.4).[16]

6.5.1 The options

Given a potential controller consisting of two or more conjoined noun phrases, we find instances where agreement is with just one of the conjuncts, as in this Russian sentence:

(31) Teper´ na nej byl sinij kostjum
     Now on her was.SG.MASC (dark) blue dress.SG.MASC

     i novaja belaja bluzka ... (Vojnovič; from Corbett 1983: 117)
     and new white blouse.SG.FEM

     'She was now wearing a blue dress and a new white blouse ...'

In this example the verb agrees just with the conjunct *sinij kostjum* 'blue dress', which is masculine singular. When we have agreement with just one noun phrase, we should ask which one it is. In (31) it is both the nearer noun phrase and the first. We can check which of those factors is more important by looking at examples

---

[16] For the formal semantics of conjoined noun phrase expressions see for example Hoeksema (1983), Lasersohn (1990).

where the controller precedes the target. (This affects the likelihood of agreement with one conjunct or with all conjuncts, as we shall see, but here we are concerned only with the possibilities.) This example is typical (from Cassubian, West Slavonic, Stone 1993b: 784):[17]

(32) Odraza   i   strach   czierowôł
      revulsion.SG.FEM   and   fear.SG.MASC   directed.SG.MASC

      jego   postępkama.
      his   actions

      'Revulsion and fear directed his actions.'

Here agreement is again with the nearer conjunct, but this time it is not also the first. This is the normal situation: agreement with one conjunct is generally agreement with the nearest conjunct[18] as shown in figure 6.4. It is worth stress-

      NP   NP   NP   TARGET

Figure 6.4 *Agreement with the nearest conjunct*

ing that this figure represents the normal situation when agreement is with one conjunct, since the data have been incorrectly cited on more than one occasion. Moreover, its theoretical significance needs to be drawn out. Agreement with the nearest conjunct, which may be first or last in the set of conjuncts, suggests that linear order rather than syntactic structure is involved. In that case more general cognitive processes are involved, and we should be looking for explanations to psychologists, who have demonstrated the importance of first and last positions in lists in other domains (see for instance Brown, Preece and Hulme 2000).

There is, however, a further rare possibility. It is *distant* agreement, that is to say agreement with the first conjunct, which, with subject–verb word order, is not the nearest. Examples occur in Slovene (a South Slavonic language, Lenček 1972: 59):

---

[17] Cassubian is treated by some as a highly distinctive dialect of Polish while others consider it a separate language.

[18] For interesting instances of agreement with the nearest conjunct see the Albanian data discussed in Morgan (1984) and Pullum (1984). Data from Old Danish can be found in Bjerrum (1949). Here is an example from English:

  (i) 'The conditions and everything else was in their favour,' Dalglish said with a straight face, 'so it's credit to the lads that they dug in so well and got a result.'
      (*The Guardian* (Sport) 26.1.98 , p. 1)

(33) knjige   in   peresa   so   se
     book.PL.FEM   and   pen.PL.NEUT   AUX.PL   REFL

     podražil-e
     got.dear-PL.FEM

     'books and pens have become more expensive'

This must be an instance of agreement with the first conjunct; agreement with all would require the masculine plural. Agreement with the more distant conjunct has also been found in Serbo-Croat (see Megaard 1976) and Latin (Kühner and Stegmann 1955: 53, 55, 58–9). This general situation of distant agreement may be represented as in figure 6.5.

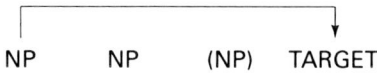

NP   NP   (NP)   TARGET

Figure 6.5   *Agreement with the first, most distant conjunct (rare)*

Thus agreement can be with just one conjunct, normally the nearest; occasionally agreement with the first (most distant) conjunct is available. The possibility which is excluded here is agreement with the last (most distant) conjunct. In the languages for which I have substantial information, when agreement with the first (most distant) conjunct is available, it occurs as a less frequent alternative to agreement with the nearest conjunct.

The last possibility is that there is agreement with all conjuncts. This is clear in example (34) from Slovene (Lenček 1972: 60):

(34) Tonček   in   Marina   sta
     Tonček.SG.MASC   and   Marina.SG.FEM   be.DU

     prizadevn-a
     assiduous-DU.MASC

     'Tonček and Marina are assiduous'

The predicate, being in the dual, clearly cannot agree with one of the conjuncts. It must agree with both conjuncts, or more generally with all conjuncts. This is represented in figure 6.6. The use of the masculine in such instances is interesting; for

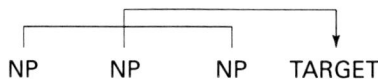

NP   NP   NP   TARGET

Figure 6.6   *Agreement with all conjuncts (resolution)*

the complexity of gender resolution see Corbett (1991: 269–306). Thus the normal possibilities are agreement with the nearest conjunct (syntactic agreement) or with both/all the conjuncts (semantic agreement).

6.5.2 Number resolution

When the target agrees with two or more conjoined noun phrases this means there must be some computation of what the values will be. This computation is what Givón (1970) termed a **resolution rule**. This is now the usual term, but it must be borne in mind that resolution rules can apply even if there is no clash of features.[19] If we have a string of singular noun phrases there is no feature clash, but if we find plural agreement that is the result of number resolution. Number resolution like person resolution is relatively straightforward when compared with gender resolution.[20] The number resolution rules for languages with a dual, like Slovene, are as follows:

1 if there are two conjuncts only, both in the singular, then dual agreement forms will be used;
2 in all other cases plural agreement forms will be used.[21]

When we have two singular conjuncts, the resolved form is the dual in Slovene, according to our first rule (Priestly 1993: 433):

(35) Milka   in   njeno tele   sta
     Milka.SG.FEM and   her   calf.SG.NEUT AUX.DU

     bil-a   zunaj
     been-DU.MASC   outside

     'Milka and her calf were outside'

---

[19] For further discussion see Pullum and Zwicky (1986). In the interests of clarity I believe we should maintain the distinction between resolution on the one hand and agreement with a single conjunct on the other (though both of these are treated as instances of resolution by Pullum and Zwicky). Their notion of resolution is based on the type of problem it addresses (how to cope with multiple conjuncts). I reserve the term resolution for a particular solution to that problem: specifically the one which requires access to the features of all conjuncts (as opposed to other solutions which, for instance, use the features of one conjunct and 'ignore' the others).

[20] Nevertheless it is quite difficult to handle adequately in a formal syntactic theory; for analysis within the framework of Generalized Phrase Structure Grammar see Farkas and Ojeda (1983), Morgan (1984), Warner (1988) and Sag et al. (1985: 152–5); an account in Lexical Functional Grammar is given by Dalrymple and Kaplan (forthcoming).

[21] An additional complication arising from the interaction with gender resolution (for which see Corbett forthcoming a) need not detain us here.

With dual and singular conjoined we find the plural, by the second rule:

(36) dve teleti in eno žrebe so
two calf.DU.NEUT and one foal.SG.NEUT AUX.PL

bil-i zunaj
been-PL.MASC outside

'Two calves and a foal were outside'

Similarly with more than two singulars (Lenček 1972: 61):

(37) Marina, Marta in Marjanca
Marina.SG.FEM Marta.SG.FEM and Marjanca.SG.FEM

so prizadevn-e
be.PL assiduous-PL.FEM

'Marina, Marta and Marjanca are assiduous'

Of course, in languages where there is no dual, the first rule is not required.

6.5.3 Resolution or agreement with the nearest conjunct

A situation found in many languages is that resolution is possible, and so is agreement with the nearer conjunct. Agreement with all conjuncts (resolution) is a case of semantic agreement, and so the choice is constrained by the Agreement Hierarchy (§6.2). Taking modern literary Russian as an example, we find the picture shown in table 6.12 (from data in Corbett 1983: 158); in each case we give the total number of examples (N) in a corpus and the percentage in which number resolution was found.

Table 6.12 *Agreement with conjoined noun phrases in Russian (target factors)*

attributive		predicate		relative pronoun		personal pronoun	
N	% PL	N	% PL	N	% PL	N	% PL
34	12	230	70	10	100	26	100

Here we see that resolved forms show a monotonic increase, as predicted by the Agreement Hierarchy. The fit is actually better than figures from this corpus indicate, for singular relative pronouns do occur, if infrequently. There is also a surprise here, in that plural agreement (resolution) is possible in attributive position. While English allows only agreement with the nearer or nearest conjunct (*this man and woman*), Russian allows the plural:

(38) Marija zadumalas´ ob ostavlenn-yx
Maria thought about left.behind-PL.LOC

muž-e i dočer-i: kak oni
husband-SG.LOC and daughter-SG.LOC how they

tam, čto s nimi?
there what with them

'Maria thought about the husband and daughter she had left behind, and wondered how they were and what was happening to them.'

(Maksimov, *Karantin*)[22]

The singular is more common, however:

(39) Èt-a vzyskatel´nost´, samokritičnost´ tože
This-SG.FEM exactingness self-criticalness also

raspolagal-i k nemu.
disposed-PL to him

'This exactingness and self-criticalness also disposed me favourably towards him.' (Černov, Introduction to Smol´janinov, *Sredi morennyx xolmov*)

The very possibility of resolution here is interesting, though it is the less favoured option.[23]

Note that (39) also shows plural predicate agreement (*raspolagali* 'disposed'), the more common choice in the predicate. Let us now home in on this position of the Agreement Hierarchy. If we keep the target 'still', that is, consider only examples with predicate agreement, we can isolate the controller factors involved. The main target factors which favour resolution rather than agreement with one conjunct are precedence and animacy: if the agreement controller precedes the target this favours resolution, and if the controller is animate this also favours resolution. This is demonstrated by the data in table 6.13.[24] The table shows, for instance, that

---

[22] There is an interaction of controller factors here; as we shall see, the fact that the controller is animate is a factor in favour of semantic agreement.

[23] For careful discussion of a comparable construction in Hausa see Schwartz, Newman and Sani (1988).

[24] Spanish data (thirteenth to fifteenth centuries) come from England (1976: 813–20); statistics on German are calculated from Findreng (1976: 145, 165–6, 197); the Russian and

Table 6.13 *Agreement with conjoined noun phrases*
(controller factors)

	animate		inanimate	
	N	% PL	N	% PL
subject–predicate				
Medieval Spanish	288	96	243	31
German	1,095	96	1,702	67
Russian	115	100	67	85
Serbo-Croat	21	100	35	91
predicate–subject				
Medieval Spanish	318	69	239	6
German	379	93	925	40
Russian	89	84	114	28
Serbo-Croat	23	70	62	26

in the Medieval Spanish texts there were 288 examples of conjoined noun phrases which denoted animates and which preceded the predicate; of these 96 per cent had a plural predicate (thus number resolution occurred in 96 per cent of the cases).

It is evident from table 6.13 that if the controller stands before the target, and if it denotes animates, these conditions indeed favour resolution. When both factors are present, all four languages give overwhelming preference to the resolved form. When either one is present, the resolved form is found in a significantly higher proportion of the cases than when neither is present. In Medieval Spanish and in German the animacy of the subject exerts a stronger influence than its position, while in Russian the two factors are of about equal weight, and in Serbo-Croat the more important factor appears to be precedence. (In Spanish and German there is also evidence showing that 'concrete' subjects take plural predicates more often than 'abstract' subjects do.) Note that the two factors combined may produce such pressure that the choice is removed and only the resolved form is possible; this happens in Russian and Serbo-Croat, where the combination of animate conjuncts and subject–predicate word order makes the plural obligatory in the genre investigated.

Serbo-Croat data are taken from modern literary texts (Corbett 1983: 105–35; 139–40). For comparison of English and German see Berg (1998: 52); for discussion of English see Quirk et al. (1985: 759–63). For the argument for treating precedence as a controller factor see Nichols, Rappaport and Timberlake (1980) and commentary in Corbett (1983: 137, 154, 175).

In these cases the factors have to 'collaborate' to force one outcome, but there are languages where one of the factors alone is sufficient. In Hungarian (Edith Moravcsik, personal communication) if the subject consists of conjoined animate singulars, the verb may be in the singular or in the plural, with the plural preferred.

(40) John és   Jill   megérkezt-ek/megérkezett.
      John and   Jill   arrived-PL/arrived.SG
      'John and Jill arrived.'

However, if the conjoined singulars are inanimate, the singular must be used:

(41) A   könyv és   a   kommentár
      ART   book   and ART   commentary

      megérkezett/*megérkezt-ek.
      arrived.SG/arrived.PL

      'The book and the commentary arrived.'

Thus without animate conjuncts resolution is not possible. We can find a similar example for precedence; according to Aoun, Benmamoun and Sportiche (1994: 207–8) in Moroccan Arabic agreement with the nearer conjunct is possible only when the target verb precedes the controller:

(42) Mša   ʕumar w   ʕali
      left.SG.MASC   Omar   and   Ali
      'Omar and Ali left'

Here the singular is possible (as is a plural verb). With the controller preceding, however, only agreement with all conjuncts is possible:

(43) ʕumar w   ʕali   mšaw/*mša
      Omar   and   Ali   left.PL/left.SG.MASC
      'Omar and Ali left'

The examples do not yet prove the point, since we know that animacy of the subject also favours resolution. However, Elabbas Benmamoun confirms (personal communication) that with inanimates too, in his judgement resolution is required:

(44) l-kas   w   z-zlafa
      DEF-glass.MASC   and   DEF-bowl.FEM

      thərrəsu/*thərrsat
      broke.PL/broke.SG.FEM

      'the glass and the bowl broke'

Thus the factors which we saw having varying effects in different Indo-European languages (table 6.13) can have an absolute effect: animacy in the case of Hungarian and precedence in Moroccan Arabic.

6.5.4 Conjoined noun phrases and comitative constructions
There is a scale of related constructions, from genuine coordination at one end to noun phrases with adjuncts which are irrelevant for agreement at the other. So far we have concentrated on noun phrases conjoined with *and* and equivalents. There is work on agreement when other coordinating conjunctions are involved, for instance Peterson (1986) on disjunction in English, and Parker (1983) particularly on *neither . . . nor . . . .* Then there are instances where the coordination is not quite so balanced. The situation in the Cushitic language Qafar (see §6.1.1 above) is at first bewildering. We need to consider the form used for number resolution, and the factors which influence whether or not resolution applies. Here is an example in which singular pronouns are conjoined (the conjunction *kee* 'and' cliticizes on to the first conjunct, lengthening any final vowel):

(45)   kàa-kee   tèt   temeete/yemeeten
      he-and   she   came.SG.FEM/came.PL
      'he and she came'

(46)   tèt-kee   kàa   temeete/yemeeten
      she-and   he   came.SG.FEM/came.PL
      'she and he came'

Two agreement forms are possible: *temeete* (feminine singular but also used with plural subjects, as discussed in §6.1.1 above) and *yemeeten* (plural, as found in agreement with *òson* 'they'). The form *yemeeten* must result from number resolution and represents semantic agreement. But the question remains as to the source of the form *temeete*, since it is found both when there is a feminine conjunct nearest (45) and when there is not (46). The various possible analyses are evaluated in Hayward and Corbett (1988). Here we shall take the conclusion from that article, namely that *temeete* in (45), (46) and similar examples is a default form, used when agreement fails to operate. The feminine singular does indeed function as the default (§6.1.2), as shown by nominalizations (Parker and Hayward 1985: 287ff.):

(47)   kàa   catnam   nèl   tingiddibeh
      him   help.1.PL.NOMINALIZER   us.on   force.3.SG.FEM
      'we are obliged to help him'

Why should the default form be used in sentences involving conjoined noun phrases? By comparing the forms of the pronouns in (45) and (46) with table 6.6

above, we see that the absolutive forms are used. And this is normally true of the heads of conjoined noun phrases in Qafar. Besides pronouns, those masculine nouns which are vowel-final have a distinct nominative case form, used when they occur in subject position. However, this is replaced by the absolutive if they occur in conjoined structures:

(48) woò   baacoytaa-kee   kày   toobokoyta   temeete/yemeeten
     that poor.man-and   his   brother   came.SG.FEM/came.PL
     'that poor man and his brother came'

Both nouns are in the absolutive form; the nominatives would be *baacoyti* and *too-bokoyti*. The key point is that only noun phrases headed by a nominative case form can control predicate agreement. Otherwise the default form, the feminine singular, will be used. Thus the forms like *temeete* are feminine singular, representing default agreement. There are two plausible ways in which to account for the appearance of this default agreement. The first is to claim that the structure as a whole lacks the required agreement features, not being headed by nominatives, and so the default form results. The alternative is to claim that it arises from failed agreement with the nearer conjunct which, being in the absolutive, does not have the features required to determine an agreement form, and so the default form results. The second alternative (failure of agreement with the nearer conjunct) is the preferred analysis, since it represents a lesser claim; it suggests that Qafar is basically similar to the other languages where agreement with conjoined noun phrases has been analysed in detail. In other words in Qafar, as in the languages discussed earlier, agreement may be with all conjuncts (in which case the plural results) or just the nearest (feminine singular). What is unusual is that the nearest conjunct, rather than controlling ordinary agreement, may fail to determine the agreement form so that a default form results.

Let us move on to the factors which favour one or other agreement form, that is to say, the factors which make the operation of number resolution more likely. Qafar has subject–object–verb as its basic order, though object–subject–verb is also a possible order. Thus the verb is normally final and so there is no question of the position of the subject relative to the predicate playing a role. We therefore concentrate on the influence of animacy. When all conjuncts denote humans, both feminine singular (default) and plural agreements are normally possible, as also in (48) above:

(49) woò   baacoytaa-kee   kày   barra
     that poor.man.SG.MASC-and   his   wife.SG.FEM

     temeete/yemeeten
     came.SG.FEM/came.PL

     'that poor man and his wife came'

Qafar readily accepts the failure of number resolution to apply when noun phrases denote humans (and precede the predicate as in normal Qafar word-order). This is strikingly different from the situation in the Indo-European languages for which data were given in table 6.13. The likely explanation is that *kee* 'and' takes a rising intonation, which is tantamount to a pause break (see Parker and Hayward 1985: 224, 291). This separation of the conjuncts makes agreement just with the nearest conjunct more likely in Qafar than in the other languages investigated. Thus the conjuncts are not as balanced as in the languages discussed above; the construction is less prototypically one of conjoining than in English or Russian.

With noun phrases headed by non-human animates there is a degree of uncertainty about the acceptability of plural agreement:

(50) wàkrii-kee   yangùla
      jackal.SG.MASC-and   hyena.SG.MASC

      kudde/?kuden
      ran.away.SG.FEM/ran.away.PL

      'the jackal and the hyena ran away'

Thus non-human animates in Qafar are treated as 'less animate' than humans, and number resolution is less likely. With inanimates, feminine singular (default) agreement is the norm:

(51) daroò-kee   cadò
      grain.SG.FEM-and   meat.SG.FEM

      tummurruqe/*yummurruqen
      have.finished.SG.FEM/have.finished.PL

      'the grain and meat have run out'

In some examples the plural, though still the less favoured alternative, was not completely excluded. When all conjuncts denote inanimates then resolution is the less likely option; it can, however, be made possible by secondary factors linked to animacy, namely the separateness (individuation) of the entities and agentivity.

We have concentrated on predicate agreement, since the greatest number of possibilities is found here. The other agreement target which shows number distinctions is the personal pronoun. *Òson* 'they' is used primarily for reference to persons. In reference to conjoined noun phrases denoting humans only *òson* is possible. Thus number resolution is obligatory in the personal pronoun, unlike the situation found in the predicate. This is in accord with the constraint of the Agreement Hierarchy (§6.2) that semantic agreement must be at least as likely in the personal pronoun as in the predicate. For non-human antecedents, demonstratives (which do not differentiate singular and plural) are more natural. But if a personal pronoun is used, then it will be plural if its antecedent consists of conjoined noun phrases. No singular form could be elicited. Thus though the number of agreeing targets is restricted in Qafar, the distribution of syntactic and semantic agreement is one which is sanctioned by the Agreement Hierarchy.

Finally we come to comitative constructions, which are on the extreme edge of conjoining. They have a head noun phrase and a dependent (marked with an oblique case and/or an adposition).[25] The question is then whether the dependent has a role in agreement. Agreement may be just with the head (syntactic agreement), or the fact that reference is to more than one individual may produce plural (semantic) agreement. Often both are possible, as in the Slavonic language Belarusian (Bukatevič et al. 1958: 292):

(52) dzed   z   unukam   laviŭ
      grandfather with grandson.SG.INST catch.PAST.SG.MASC
      rybu
      fish

      'grandfather and grandson were fishing'

(53) brat   z   sjastroju   pajšl-i   u   tèatr
      brother   with sister.SG.INST   go.PAST.PL to   theatre
      'brother and sister went to the theatre'

We have data from the corresponding construction in the closely related Russian, in comparison with conjoined noun phrases (two separate corpora, one literary and one from the language of the press; see table 6.14). As we might expect, semantic agreement is less likely with comitative phrases than with conjoined noun phrases, since comitative phrases are less balanced than coordinated phrases. We cannot investigate the effect of animacy here, since almost all examples of comitatives in Russian involve human referents. Since animacy favours semantic agreement, this shows that the difference between the two constructions is more marked than the figures suggest. If the comparison were with conjoined noun phrases with animate referents, the difference would be even more marked.[26] We return to a related construction in §7.2.2.

---

[25] The adposition may turn into a conjunction, giving transitional constructions on the way; this happens, for instance, in Bantu languages (see for example the account of Chichewa in Corbett and Mtenje 1987).

[26] For the comparable construction in Polish, see Dyła (1988: 386), Szupryczyńska (1991). For a small amount of Slovene data see Lenček (1972: 61–2); for a discussion of the semantics of these constructions in Russian and Polish see McNally (1993); the discussion of Russian is taken further in Dalrymple, Hayrapetian and King (1998). For Hungarian see Hetzron (1973).

Table 6.14 *Agreement with conjoined and comitative phrases in Russian*[27]

	conjoined noun phrases		comitative phrases	
	N	% PL	N	% PL
literature	85	67	9	44
press	753	96	30	50

6.6 Arabic (agreement with plural noun phrases)

The agreements found with plural noun phrases in Arabic are initially surprising. However, we have already met similar phenomena, which will contribute parts to the jigsaw, and there are valuable data from the work of Kirk Belnap. In talking of 'Arabic' we must be more specific, since Arabic covers a considerable time period from the pre-Islamic works of the sixth century, through Classical Arabic to the several modern varieties of Modern Arabic; there are substantial differences between these varieties and Modern Standard Arabic, the shared conservative standard. Classical Arabic had three numbers: singular, dual and plural, and two genders: masculine and feminine. The dual was an obligatory category. It is greatly reduced in the modern varieties. Where the true dual is preserved, it is restricted to a subset of the nouns, and it is typically facultative.[28] Although the dual agreement forms are lost, in the relevant dialects noun phrases headed by nouns in the dual still differ from plural noun phrases with respect to agreement. There is variation, but duals take plural agreement (the form used with plural pronouns), while plurals take the feminine singular or the plural (Ferguson 1959: 620–1). The situation in such varieties (Cairene Arabic for example, Belnap 1993: 111) is as in table 6.15; as before, the rows and columns are labelled according to the controller. Cairene Arabic, like many other dialects, has lost gender distinctions in the plural, and so there are only three agreeing forms. Once again we have a mismatch between the controller system (which distinguishes three numbers, and two genders, as shown by the labels on the rows and the columns in table 6.15) and the

---

[27] From Corbett (1983: 154–5). The literary corpus consists of Panova's *Sputniki* (1946) and Nekrasov's *Kira Georgievna* (1961); the figures for the language of the press come from Graudina, Ickovič and Katlinskaja (1976: 31, 346). There is an unfortunate transposition of headings in my original table: the data are correct above.

[28] See Blanc (1970: 43–4). There are numerous examples of 'pseudo-duals', that is forms with the old dual morphology preserved, but functioning as plural; this happens frequently with paired body parts for example (Blanc 1970).

Table 6.15 *Consistent agreement patterns in
Cairene Arabic*

	singular	dual	plural
masculine	masculine	plural	feminine OR plural
feminine	feminine	plural	feminine OR plural

target system (which has three forms, given in the cells). This type of system should now be partly familiar. It is somewhat reminiscent of that of Bayso (§6.1.1 above), another Afro-Asiatic language and therefore distantly related. We shall return below (§6.8) to the question of why plural agreement should be used with dual controllers but not necessarily with plural controllers.

What is new for us in Cairene Arabic is that there is a choice of forms for agreement with plural noun phrases (feminine or plural agreement),[29] and data on their distribution. As we investigate the distribution of the feminine singular (syntactic agreement) and the plural (semantic agreement),[30] we shall find ourselves on partly familiar ground. While Modern Standard Arabic has standardized rules of agreement, other modern varieties (as well as the earliest texts) show more variability. We will concentrate on Cairene Arabic. Here, as in many other vernacular varieties, when we have a plural noun denoting humans, plural agreement is expected, but feminine singular agreement is possible too (examples from Belnap 1999: 171):

(54) riggaala   kuwayyis-iin/(kuwayyis-a)
      men.PL   nice-PL/nice-SG.FEM
      'nice men'

Conversely, if the plural head noun does not denote a human then feminine singular agreement is usual, but plural agreement is also found:

(55) biyuut   kabiir-a/(kubaar)
      houses.PL   large-SG.FEM/large.PL
      'large houses'

This is a variation on a familiar theme: controllers with higher animacy are more likely to take semantic agreement (plural here) than those with lower animacy. With Cairene Arabic we can go further, since Belnap (1991: 57–61, 157–65; 1999) gives data from twenty-six sociolinguistic interviews collected in Cairo in 1990. In table

[29] Interestingly the feminine is not the default form, but the masculine, used for instance where there is a clausal subject (see Cowell 1964: 421 on Syrian Arabic).

[30] Arabists sometimes use the terms 'deflected' (our 'syntactic') and 'strict' (our 'semantic'); see Ferguson (1989), Belnap (1993: 98n1).

Table 6.16 *Agreement with plural noun phrases in Cairene Arabic (Belnap 1999: 174)*

head	plural (semantic) agreement %	N
human sound plurals	94	34
human broken plurals	90	140
(non-human) animate broken plurals	35	20
inanimate sound plurals	4	144
inanimate broken plurals	3	191

6.16 the different types of target (adjective, verb, pronoun) are treated together, but the different types of controller are distinguished. Disregarding for a moment the distinction between 'sound' and 'broken' plurals we can see that when the subject is headed by a noun denoting a human, plural agreement is likely, and with inanimates, feminine is likely. Interestingly those with nouns denoting animals come in between. There is also some evidence (see Belnap 1999 for more detailed analysis of the data) that the type of the plural matters. As discussed in §5.3.3, Arabic is known for its 'broken' plurals, those where plurality is shown by stem alternation, for example *beet* 'house', *biyuut* 'houses'. 'Sound' plurals are those where plurality is indicated by affixation, for example *ḥaaga* 'thing', *ḥagaat* 'things'.[31] When other factors are allowed for, there is some evidence that for a given controller type (human or inanimate – there are no comparable data for the non-human animates) sound plurals are more likely to take plural agreement than broken plurals. At first this is rather surprising: we do not expect morphological type to affect agreement. However, Belnap quotes Wright (on Classical Arabic) where he says that broken plurals denote 'individuals viewed *collectively*' whereas sound plurals refer to '*distinct* individuals' (1967: 233). If this distinction survives at least partially, then the agreements are understandable: the sort of noun which has a sound plural is that where the referent is likely to be individuated. Hence it is not the morphological form which is directly determining the agreement, rather the morphological form is an indicator of the type of noun we are dealing with. While we have concentrated here on animacy, word order is also significant in Cairene Arabic: controllers preceding the target are more likely to control plural agreement than those following.

Belnap goes on to discuss target factors: the effect of the Agreement Hierarchy, and of 'real distance' (the degree of separation of controller and target). For preceding targets the data here are insufficient to make further claims (few targets

---

[31] Only stressed vowels may be long, so instead of *ḥaagaat* the form is *ḥagaat.*

occur preceding their controller by more than a couple of words) but for following targets the data are impressive. 'Real distance' can be seen in the next example (Belnap 1999: 176):

(56) šiwayyit ḥag-aat . . . miš bi-tartiib
few   thing-PL   not   by-rank

Ɂahammiyyit-ha . . .   wi-baʕdeen   ni-šuuf Ɂiza
importance-their.SG.FEM (6)   and-afterward   we-see   if

kun-na   ni-rattib-hum
were-we   we-order-them.PL (11)

'a few things . . . not in order of their importance . . . and afterward we'll see if we were ordering them'   (Riham, female, 21, student)

In (56), the head is *ḥag-aat* 'things': the feminine pronoun *-ha* is six words from its head (including those omitted) while the plural pronoun *-hum* is eleven words from the head, as indicated in parentheses in the example. The picture from the corpus is given in table 6.17 (based on Belnap 1999: 176). Here the picture is very clear. The greater the distance by which the target follows the controller, the greater the likelihood of semantic agreement.

Table 6.17 *Effect of distance of target from controller in Cairene Arabic*

distance from head (in words)	plural (semantic) agreement %	N
1	21	276
2	36	115
3–5	43	141
6–8	47	57
9–45	91	64

For data on Classical Arabic and Modern Standard Arabic see Belnap and Shabaneh (1992), where it is suggested that the prevalence of feminine singular (syntactic) agreement is a later development in Arabic; its expansion is considered in more detail in Belnap and Gee (1994). For Cairene Arabic see Belnap (1993, 1999) and for Syrian Arabic see Cowell (1964: 420–8). The change in agreement pattern is used as evidence relevant to the wider question about the history of Arabic and the status of Classical Arabic in Ferguson (1989) and Belnap (1999).

6.7 Agreement with quantified expressions (mainly in Slavonic)

Our main interest is in the agreement possibilities, but we should first look briefly at the number of the noun within quantified noun phrases.

6.7.1 Number of noun in quantified noun phrases

Given a language with a basic singular–plural opposition, what would we expect to find in constructions with noun phrases with numerals above '1'? One obvious answer is that the noun would be in the plural and that the phrase would control plural agreement (both for semantic reasons). Thus in English:

(57) The first five applicants deserve to succeed.

A second answer would be that, since the number of entities is made clear by the numeral, no further marking is required and the default (singular) forms would be used. This is what we find in Hungarian:

(58) két   lány   beszélget
      two   girl.SG   chat.SG
      'two girls are chatting'

(The plural of *lány* 'girl' is *lányok*, and the plural of *beszélget* 'chat' is *beszélgetnek*; neither would be used in (58).) Moravcsik (1998) makes the interesting claim that 'there is no language where plural-referent nouns are plural-marked when occurring with numerals but not plural-marked in other contexts'. In other words, the numeral phrase is the most likely place for plural number marking not to be required.

The third possibility is that both singular and plural would be used. This is the situation in Slavonic. This is true of agreement, as we shall see in §6.7.2. And within the noun phrase, singulars and plurals are found, but typically in a given set of circumstances one of the two is required, according to strict and quite complex rules (see, for instance, §4.10 of the different language descriptions in Comrie and Corbett 1993 and §9.1.2 below). Thus in Russian, with the numeral *odin* 'one' we find a singular (except for *pluralia tantum*), but with *dva* 'two', *tri* 'three' and *četyre* 'four', in the direct cases, the noun is in the genitive singular:

(59) dva   žurnal-a   tri   sosn-y
      two   magazine-SG.GEN   three   pine.tree-SG.GEN
      'two magazines'   'three pine trees'

An attributive adjective will be in the plural, with a choice of case (particularly with feminine nouns):

(60) dve   interesn-ye/interesn-yx   knig-i
      two   interesting-PL.NOM/interesting-PL.GEN   book-SG.GEN
      'two interesting books'

211

This complicated situation (and there are different complexities in other members of the family) comes about as a result of the loss of the dual (lost in most of the Slavonic languages, but not in Sorbian or in Slovene, as we saw above), with the more adjectival numerals '3' and '4' behaving like '2'. With '5' and similar numerals the plural is used:[32]

(61) pjat´ interesn-yx   knig
      five   interesting-PL.GEN book.PL.GEN
      'five interesting books'

There is a slightly similar situation in certain Celtic languages, which have also largely lost the dual (though it is re-emerging in Breton, as we saw in §2.2.7). In Scottish Gaelic we find the following surprising situation: with numerals above three the plural is used. With *dà* 'two', for masculine nouns we find the same singular form as with *aon* 'one', while for feminines the dative/prepositional singular is used:

(62) aon   taigh   aon   làmh
      one   house.MASC   one   hand.FEM
      'one house'   'one hand'

(63) dà   thaigh   dà   làimh
      two   house.MASC   two   hand.SG.FEM.DAT
      'two houses'   'two hands'

These unexpected forms are remnants of the dual (MacAulay 1992: 197); note the initial mutation on *thaigh*. In Irish, the morphological loss has gone further, and the plural is used with numerals 'three' and above, and the normal singular with 'one' and 'two', according to Dochartaigh (1992: 62, 77), leaving no morphological sign of the origin of this behaviour in the former dual. Similarly in Manx (Thomson 1992: 113, 118) the singular was used after *un* 'one' and *daa* 'two' (also after *feed* 'twenty' and *keead* 'hundred'). Thus the synchronic situation arising from the loss of the dual is rather odd; it can survive because the number marking of the noun in these numeral phrases is redundant.

We find interesting parallels in the synchronic situation in the Micronesian language Mokilese (see §2.2.6; the data are from Harrison 1976: 75, 78–9, 93–5). In Mokilese, nouns do not mark number, except by a change in the suffixal determiner. With no numeral, then, as would be expected, a plural determiner is used for two or more, and the singular for one:

---

[32] For more on the complexities of these numerals see Corbett (1993) and references there. In compound numerals the last element determines the form of the nouns, hence after *sto odin* '101' the singular is used, and after *sto dva* '102' the genitive singular. (Similarly in Manx the numerals which require the singular do so for compounds ending in that numeral.) For the loss of the dual in Slavonic see references in §9.1.2 note 7.

(64) lih-e   lih-kai
      woman-DEM.SG   woman-DEM.PL
      'this woman'   'these women' (two or more)

If a numeral is present, with those from three upwards the demonstrative may be singular or plural:

(65) kipar   jil-pass-o
      pandanus.tree   three-CLASSIFIER-DEM.SG
      'those three pandanus trees'

(66) kipar   jil-pass-ok
      pandanus.tree   three-CLASSIFIER-DEM.PL
      'those three pandanus trees'

Pas (*pass* before the suffix here) is the numeral classifier for long objects. If the numeral is one or two, then the singular must be used:

(67) kipar   rah-pass-o
      pandanus.tree   two-CLASSIFIER-DEM.SG
      'those two pandanus trees'

Here, however, there is no evidence of an earlier dual demonstrative to provide a historical explanation for this surprising synchronic situation (Sheldon Harrison, personal communication).

Within the noun phrase then, the numeral may determine number in surprising ways. Besides the expected plural (for semantic reasons) and singular (the default form, used since number is redundant) we also find languages which require both singular and plural according to the numeral. Most Slavonic languages are of that type. They are also interesting in terms of predicate agreement.

6.7.2 Factors determining the choice in predicate agreement

Predicate agreement with numeral phrases in Slavonic shows considerable variation, both within languages and when we compare across the family. Often more than one form is possible. The following Russian examples are both acceptable:

(68) vošl-o   pjat´   devušek
      came.in-SG.NEUT   five.NOM   girl.PL.GEN
      'five girls came in'

(69) vošl-i   pjat´   devušek
      came.in-PL   five.NOM   girl.PL.GEN
      'five girls came in'

The choice is affected by the controller factors which are now familiar: animacy of the subject (animate subjects favour semantically justified agreement), and precedence (semantically justified agreement is more likely in subject–predicate order). Since these two controller factors are independent, we can cross-classify for them. Table 6.18 records examples of agreement with a set of quantifiers in a selection of Russian literary texts of the last two centuries.[33] It is clear that both animacy and

Table 6.18 *Predicate agreement with quantified expressions in Russian*

	animate			inanimate		
	SG	PL	% PL	SG	PL	% PL
subject–predicate	11	48	81	21	20	49
predicate–subject	24	23	49	70	18	20

precedence exert a major influence on the agreement form selected. The plural, the form with greater semantic justification, is more likely if the subject is animate and if it precedes the predicate. With both factors exerting an influence, the likelihood of semantic agreement is greatest, with neither factor it is lowest, and with one but not both it falls in the middle (as in (68) and (69)). There is an interesting comparison with the Russian data in table 6.13. The basic pattern is the same but semantic agreement is overall more likely with conjoined noun phrases than with quantified expressions.

In addition to these two factors, the quantifier itself also has a substantial influence, and the data available suggest that this influence is independent of animacy and precedence (Corbett 1988: 48). Let us concentrate on the effect of the numeral: table 6.19 gives data on the different Slavonic languages. In the table DUAL (where available) and PL(URAL) represent semantic agreement. When a cell has a single entry (e.g. 'PL'), this indicates that the form is used in the majority of instances, though not necessarily all. Thus in Slovene, the plural is normal with '3' and '4', but the singular may be used in expressions of time. Where we do not have more precise data, these few exceptions are ignored (time expressions also account for some of the singular forms with '2', '3' and '4' in other languages). A gap indicates a lack of data.[34]

---

[33] Details in Corbett (1983: 150–3).

[34] The data were discussed in Corbett (1983: 220–4). The judgements and statistics presented are taken from Suprun (1969: 175–87) unless otherwise stated. In Slovak, with the numerals '5–10' the plural is used with masculine personal forms and otherwise the singular; exceptions amount to less than 1 per cent of the examples, according to Suprun. *Sto* 'hundred' takes the singular (Ján Bosák and Ľubomir Ďurovič, personal communications). Sorbian preserves the dual number; otherwise agreements are broadly similar to those of Slovak

Table 6.19 *Predicate agreement with numeral phrases in Slavonic*

	2	3	4	5–10	100
West Slavonic					
Czech	PL	PL	PL	sg	sg
Slovak	PL	PL	PL	PL/sg	sg
Sorbian	DUAL	PL	PL	PL/sg	sg
Polish	99% PL	91% PL	‖100% PL	7% PL	
	(N = 123)[35]	(N = 43)	(N = 15)	(N = 68)	
South Slavonic					
Old Church Slavonic	DUAL	PL	PL	(PL)/sg	
Bulgarian	PL	PL	PL	PL	PL
Macedonian	PL	PL	PL	PL	PL
Serbo-Croat	97% PL	89% PL	83% PL	7% PL	
	(N = 735)	(N = 249)	(N = 133)	(N = 1,161)	
Slovene	DUAL	PL	PL	sg	sg
East Slavonic					
Ukrainian	83% PL	79% PL	74% PL	38% PL	21% PL
	(N = 208)	(N = 150)	(N = 34)	(N = 45)	(N = 14)
Belarusian	92% PL	78% PL	63% PL	39% PL	‖50% PL
	(N = 219)	(N = 67)	(N = 16)	(N = 49)	(N = 2)
Russian	86% PL	77% PL	76% PL	50% PL	
	(N = 541)	(N = 247)	(N = 68)	(N = 220)	

(Suprun 1963a). Old Church Slavonic data are given in Suprun (1961: 81–6); for the '5–10' entry, he has ten examples of singular predicates, six of plural predicates and two where one source has singular agreement and another has plural. However, Večerka (1960: 197) states that in the Gospels the singular is used in the overwhelming majority of instances, hence the plural entry is bracketed. Suprun also gives an example with *sъto* 'hundred', one with *tysęšta* 'thousand' and one with *tьma* 'ten thousand', all three with singular agreement. The Polish figures are calculated on the basis of examples given in Suprun (1963b); instances where the numeral itself is in the genitive are excluded. The final Polish entry is for numerals of all types from '5' up to '999'. There are also seven examples of agreement with *tysiąc* 'thousand', all of them singular. The Serbo-Croat statistics are taken from Sand (1971: 51–2, 73); the figure for *dva* 'two' includes examples with *oba* 'both'; '2–4' include compound numerals ending in '2–4' and the remaining figure is for all other numerals above '4'. Judgements on Slovene are from Vincenot (1975: 196) as well as from Suprun (1969: 176). The final entry for Ukrainian includes examples with *sorok* 'forty' as well as *sto* 'hundred'.

[35] Thus in the Polish texts scanned there were 123 examples of phrases with the numeral '2' controlling predicate agreement, of which 99 per cent (rounded to the nearest whole number) showed plural agreement.

The South Slavonic languages Bulgarian and Macedonian differ from the others in using the plural with all numerals above '1' in almost all instances. They are somewhat like English in this respect, while other Slavonic languages use both singular and plural. The remaining South Slavonic languages (Old Church Slavonic, Serbo-Croat and Slovene) use the dual (when available) with phrases with the numeral '2'; otherwise they show a strong preference for plural agreement for quantified phrases with the numerals '2–4', and for singular agreement (though with varying degrees of tolerance towards the plural) with numerals from '5' upwards. In several languages the distinction between '2–4' on the one hand, and '5' upwards on the other, is fairly sharp. However, the statistics for Serbo-Croat and Polish show that here the division is not absolute. It is in these languages, together with those of the East Slavonic group, where the situation is more fluid, that we find the most interesting data. The overall picture is clear: the higher the numeral the more likely is singular agreement. The form which is semantically justified becomes more likely the lower the numeral. This is clearly true in the straightforward cases like Slovak. The statistical data too support this claim, apart from two minor inconsistencies (indicated in the table with ‖). These two cases need not concern us as the sample size for both numerals is small. Even apart from these, it is not the case that there is a statistically significant difference between every pair of successive numerals in each language. However, statistical advice is that the pattern is so overwhelming that statistical tests of significance are superfluous. What is important is that, apart from the two exceptions mentioned, the rank order of the numerals according to the frequency with which they take plural agreement is the same in the different languages and that this order is inversely related to numerical value. There is strong evidence that the lower the numeral is, the more likely it is to take semantically justified agreement. In the next section we ask why that should be.

We have concentrated on the complexities of Slavonic but there are other challenging cases too: for agreement with numeral phrases in Armenian see Sigler 1992, for Finnish see Karlsson (1959a), for Qafar see Hayward and Corbett (1988: 268–70).

6.8   Constraints on agreement systems

Consider first non-matching systems and how the values correspond in them. In Bayso, paucal controllers take plural targets (while plural controllers take masculine targets); we saw that Cairene Arabic dual controllers take plural targets, while plural controllers may take a plural target but may also take a feminine one. This seems strange: if anything, should not the plural controller take the plural target (the target which we would find with plural pronouns)? There is a strong hint as to what is going on in the previous section, where we saw – also surprisingly – that in Slavonic languages, the larger the numeral in a subject numeral phrase, the smaller the chance of it taking a plural predicate. The groups which we quantify with larger numbers are the groups which are less individuated and conversely are more likely to be viewed as a unit. For this reason they are more likely to be encoded grammatically as nouns (Corbett 1978). And as a result, when there is a choice of agreement, the higher numerals are more likely to be treated somewhat more like nouns and control singular agreement. In Bayso, paucal forms are for smaller groups (two up to around six), which are therefore more individuated than those for which plural forms of the noun are used. The paucal forms take the semantically justified plural. Similarly in Cairene Arabic, how can it be that controllers in the dual would take the plural but that those in the plural would have an alternative? Two individuals are easiest to individuate, and so the plural will be used here. Thus the Bayso and Arabic situation parallels that found in Slavonic; the more individuated the subject the more likely plural agreement becomes.

Agreement choices require first that the controller be of an appropriate type (and these range from individual lexical items to free constructions, as we saw in table 6.1). Given such a controller, the next level of constraint is provided by the Agreement Hierarchy, which determines the possible types of target which may be involved in a particular agreement choice. Thus with corporate nouns in English, semantic agreement is possible in all positions except in attributive position (which is of course a possibility sanctioned by the hierarchy). Other evidence came from associatives and from conjoined noun phrases. The predicate position can be subdivided into the Predicate Hierarchy, and we saw good evidence for this from honorifics. Within positions on the Agreement Hierarchy, 'real distance' can have an effect; a target following its controller by, say, ten words is more likely to take semantic agreement than is one only five words distant (evidence from Cairene Arabic was provided in §6.6 and there is comparable data for agreement with corporate nouns in English in Nixon 1972).

Given that a choice is possible (the controller is of the right type and the target is at an appropriate position on the Agreement Hierarchy), then there are other controller factors which favour semantic agreement. The first is precedence: controllers preceding their targets are more likely to control semantic agreement than those following. For this we saw evidence from conjoined noun phrases in various languages and from Russian numerals. And second, those denoting animates are more likely to take semantic agreement than those denoting inanimates: again we saw evidence from conjoined noun phrases and from numerals. Then in Cairene Arabic and in Qafar we found evidence that instead of a simple animate–inanimate distinction we should rather distinguish between human, other animate and inanimate.

This last factor ties up of course with the Animacy Hierarchy – it is another reflection of the same tendency. But it also ties up with the first factor discussed in this section, namely individuation: we are more likely to individuate humans than inanimates. Thus in the myriad unlikely agreements we have seen, the same underlying determining factors are at work.

6.9   Conclusion

In this chapter we have seen how being clear about the use of terms can pay off handsomely; when we analysed systems where the number values of controller and target differ we were able to make sense of the apparently wayward systems of Bayso, Qafar and similar languages. We saw again the importance of hierarchies, in allowing us to understand variation both across languages and, at the level of fine detail, within small sections of the syntax of particular languages. Finally we saw how we could isolate particular factors in different languages and then observe how they can combine in other languages to give rather different outcomes. This approach is a hallmark of syntactic typology: we first identify factors in languages which provide the most favourable setting and then use them in the analysis of languages which present a more complex picture.

7
Other uses of number

We have considered the meanings regularly associated with the different values (plural, dual, paucal and so on). We now come to other uses of number, that is, instances where the regular expression of number is taken over for purposes other than its normal meaning. For instance, in honorific usage, plural forms are often used of a single addressee to indicate respect. The semantic and pragmatic effects of number in such uses cannot be derived in the normal way from the usual meanings of the number values. Given that number is often cited as a straightforward grammatical category, apparently reflecting semantics in a regular way, these other uses are found surprisingly frequently. They occur even in familiar languages: we shall see cases where a particular use identified in some distant language turns out to be rather frequent closer to home.

There are three broad groups of these other uses: first there are honorific uses (§7.1), as just mentioned; second there are unexpected uses in the general area of conjoining (§7.2); and finally there are various special uses, affective ones in the main (§7.3). In analysing these uses, there are three questions which will recur. The first is whether all number values are available for the particular use; often there are restrictions, and for affective use it is never the case that all values are available. The second is why these uses can be available, particularly since number frequently is a relatively clear reflection of semantics. Often we shall see that the real-world number of the referent is available from another source. And third, we should ask whether these uses are unique to number or whether the same effect is available through other means.

These other uses, especially affective uses, are more challenging than 'straightforward' cognitive meanings; it is difficult to be sure whether the types proposed are all distinct, or indeed how many of them are properly affective. Since the form–meaning correlations are less obvious, there has been a curious discontinuity in the tradition. Recent grammars give relatively little space to the problem, yet earlier, Indo-Europeanists examined the problem carefully (we refer below to work by Löfstedt and Edgerton, and they provide references giving an entry into the nineteenth century discussions). The typological point then is that once the broad correlations are established, for a construction or for a category, there is still plenty to be done, and the level of detail necessary typically requires careful sifting through substantial amounts of data, from speech or writing.

7.1 Honorifics and related uses

It is well known that in the languages of Europe, the plural pronoun is used to a single addressee as a mark of respect or politeness. In Russian, for instance, when addressing an adult with whom one is not on familiar terms, one uses *vy* 'you', the same form as for addressing more than one person. The singular form *ty* is reserved for familiar use, for addressing children and so on.

We can extend the picture in four ways. First, it is not just a European phenomenon. In Mparntwe Arrernte the second person plural is used for 'kin avoidance and respect' with a single addressee. Mparntwe Arrernte is spoken in the area around Alice Springs in Australia: it is one of the Arandic group, which is a subfamily within Pama-Nyungan. In a discussion of avoidance behaviour, Wilkins (1989: 46–7, 123) discusses the case of a woman and her eldest brother. The brother has been through initiation, and so he and his younger sisters have to practice avoidance behaviour (for instance, they may not pass things directly to each other). In terms of language, they may speak to each other, provided they maintain a certain linguistic distance, they use the plural form of verbs 'when talking to one's avoided sibling about an action that s/he is performing or should perform. Similarly, the members of this pair address each other using 2nd person plural pronoun forms'. This can be seen in a woman's description of an interaction with her eldest brother (David Wilkins 1989: 47 and personal communication):

(1) Apmwerrke,   merne-rlke-kerte,   kere-rlke-kerte
    yesterday   bread-too-PROP,   meat-too-PROP

    irrpe-nhe-ke   pmere   kake-kenhe-ke.
    go.into-DO.PAST-PCOMP   home   elder.brother-POSS-DAT.

    Re   ne-tyeme   chair-le   T.V.   are-rle.ne-me-le.
    3.SG.S   sit-PPROG   chair-LOC   T.V.   see-CONT-NPPROG-SS.

    Kele   ayenge   angke-ke   ikwere: 'Kere-rlke,
    OK   1.SG.S   speak-PCOMP   3.SG.DAT   meat-too,

    merne-rlke   nhenhe   the   knge-tyenhe   arrekantherre',
    bread-too   this   1.SG.A   carry-NPCOMP   2.PL.DAT

    kenhe   re   atyenge   angke-rlenge: 'Table
    but   3.SG.S   1.SG.DAT   speak-DS: Table

yanhe-ke   arrerne-warr-Ø-aye,   the   fridge-ke

that(mid)-DAT   put-PL.S/A-IMP-EMPH,   1.SG.A   fridge-DAT

arrerne-tyenhenge?'   Kele   ayenge   lhe-me-ng-ewe.

put-SUBSEQUENT   OK   1.SG.S   go-NPPROG -ABL-EMPH +

'Yesterday I went through into my elder brother's house with some bread and some meat. He was sitting in a chair watching T.V. So I said: "I'll carry this bread and meat in for you" [plural form but a single addressee], but he said to me: "Put it on the table [plural verb form, but again only a single addressee], I'll put it in the refrigerator later." So then I left.' (It is important that the food was left on the table and that no actual contact or act of 'face to face' giving was performed.)

Note that glosses and their abbreviations have been modified slightly; abbreviations used only here are: PROP proprietive case, DO.PAST doing an action while moving through or past a place, PCOMP past completive, NPCOMP non-past completive, PPROG past progressive, NPPROG non-past progressive. A is for the transitive subject and S for the intransitive subject, A/S indicates a subject marker in either configuration, SS is the marker for same subject and DS for different subject. EMPH emphatic, EMPH+ strong emphatic.

Arrernte has a dual, but it is the plural which is involved here and not the dual. A similar use for avoidance language (and also to mark hostility) is reported in Djaru (Tsunoda 1981: 215–20). The plural pronoun is taking the place of the singular for address in Khasi (War 1992); and there are further examples from many parts of the world, as in Usan (Adelbert Range, Papua New Guinea, see Reesink 1987: 57) and in Kannada (Bean 1975).[1] Thus the use of number for honorific purposes is clearly not an exclusively European phenomenon.

We can improve on our original statement further, since the plural is not just a marker of respect; it may be used to indicate modesty: 'Very common both in Greek and Latin is the Plural of Modesty, e.g. the use by an orator of *nos* for *ego* in speaking of himself and his acts . . . In the primary use of this figure the speaker sinks his individual personality, and identifies himself with the people, class, or craft to which he belongs; whence the name' (Bell 1923: 74). Examples are found in

---

[1] For more examples see Head (1978) and Brown and Levinson (1987: 198–203); for an instance of second and third person plural forms being used to show respect in a Cushitic language see Amborn, Minker and Sasse (1980: 45–9, 97) where it is reported that in Dullay these forms are used for the priest-chief and his main wife. And in the Oceanic language Tigak the plural is used for women who are mothers (Beaumont 1979: 74). The possible motivation for the honorific use of number is discussed by Malsch (1987).

the usage of Russian peasants, as in this instance from Chekhov;[2] the questioner is
an investigator, the respondent a peasant:

(2) - Čem   zanimaeš´-sja?
      what   occupy.2.SG-REFL

- My   pastux-i . . .   Mirskoj   skot   pas-em . . .
  1.PL   herdsman-PL   village.ADJ   livestock   pasture-1.PL

'What is your occupation ?'
'I am a herdsman . . . I look after the village livestock . . .'

Though it is only the respondent's occupation in question he uses *my* 'we' rather
than *ja* 'I', so as not to set himself apart as it were. A similar use is found in this
example from the same source:

(3) - Nužno   govorit´   *vy* . . .   Nel´zja   tykat´!   Esli   ja
       necessary say   2.PL   Must.not   use.thou   if   1.SG

  govorju   tebe . . .   vam   *vy,*   to   vy   i
  say   2.SG.DAT   2.PL.DAT   2.PL   then   2.PL   EMPH

  podavno   dolžny   byt´   vežlivym!
  the.more   must   be   polite

  - Ono   konečno,   vašeskorodie!   Nešto   my   ne
    that   of.course   your.worship   really   1.PL   NEG

  ponimaem?   No   ty   slušaj,   čto   dal´še . . .
  understand?   but   2.SG   listen-IMP   what   further

'It is necessary to say "you" (polite). It is not permitted to say "thou". If
I say "thou" . . . "you" to you, then you all the more so must be polite!'

'Yes of course, your Worship! Do you really think I [1st plural] don't
understand? But thou listen to what happened next. . .'

Here, the confusion and the humour are created by the two interlocutors – investigator and herdsman – having different address systems. The latter responds with
my 'we' to a direct question about whether he understands.

The third respect in which our initial summary statement needs extension is that
this use of the plural does not involve only pronouns (and verbal forms agreeing

---

[2] The example is taken from Chekhov's *Ty i Vy* (you.SG and you.PL) published in 1886. The
humour is built entirely round problems of incompatible systems of address. A similar
scene is found in Vladimir Vojnovič's *Žizn´ i neobyčajnye priključenija soldata Ivana
Čonkina: roman-anekdot v pjati častjax*, Paris: YMCA, 1976.

with them). The plural morphology of the verb may be the only indicator, as in this example of a maid talking of her master and mistress, also from Russian (from Turgenev's novel *Nakanune*, 1860):

(4) 'Mamen´ka   plačut,   - šepnula   ona   vsled   uxodivšej
     Mother   cry.3.PL   whispered   3.SG.FEM   after   leaving

     Elene,   a   papen´ka   gnevajutsja . . .'
     Elena   and   father   be.angry.3.PL

     '"Your mother is crying", she whispered after Elena, who was
     leaving, "and your father is angry . . ."'

Here the plural verbs, even though the subjects are singular, indicate the speaker's respect for the people referred to.

The form of different agreement targets in such honorific constructions, with pronouns and nouns, has been considered by Comrie (1975) and Corbett (1983: 42–59), and was discussed in part in §6.4. Though this is rare, even the number value of predicate nominals may be affected, as in the Bantu language Chichewa (and also in example (3) above). In Chichewa, to show respect, all agreements with a noun like *bambo* 'father' will be plural:

(5) bambo   anga
     father   PL.my
     'my father'

The singular *wanga* 'my' would be inappropriate. And, as mentioned, the plural would be usual for the nominal predicate too (Corbett and Mtenje 1987: 9–10n3):

(6) bambo   ndi   aphunzitsi
     father   be   PL.teacher
     'father is a teacher'

Note that *ndi* does not inflect for number.

The fourth respect in which our initial statement was too narrow is that this usage is not restricted to the use of the plural for the singular. The use of singular for plural is found in Russian forms of address. Military orders addressed to several, when a morphological imperative is used, are in the singular:

(7) stanovis´
     stand.IMP.2.SG
     'fall in'

(8) razojdis´
     disperse.IMP.2.SG
     'fall out'

It might be thought these are just curious lexicalized expressions. However, the use is productive, as suggested by this example from Pasternak's *Doktor Zhivago*, where a crowd at a railway station is trying to get on a train:

(9) Ej, rebjata, navalis´, nažm-i!
hey lads push.IMP.2.SG press-IMP.2.SG
'Hey, lads, push, shove!'

The plural *rebjata* 'lads' shows that the imperative is addressed to more than one; one interpretation is that they are being treated as a crowd rather than as individuals (further examples can be found in Švedova 1980: 640).

Examples (7)–(9) raise two issues frequently ignored in discussions of the use of number in address, namely the use of other number values like the dual and the ways of addressing more than one person.

Consider first the use of other numbers. Kobon (Davies 1981: 153–4) has singular, dual and plural. For addressing and referring to certain types of relative (one person or more than one) the plural must be used. The categories are: '(i) a female relative through marriage of a male ego (except wife of ego); (ii) the wife of a male cross-cousin of a male ego; (iii) husband's brother; and (iv) the husband of a female cross-cousin of a female ego.' The dual is used to address or refer to 'certain mail affines of a male ego':

(10) Bama kale au-ab-il
wife's.father 3.DUAL come-PRES-3.DUAL
'My father-in-law is coming'

Here both the pronoun *kale* and the verb stand in the dual. A related though slightly different use is found in Limbu, a Tibeto-Burman language of Nepal (van Driem 1987: 221–2); here first person inclusive forms are used as polite forms (for addressees unknown to the speaker, or requiring respect). The dual is used for a single addressee, and the plural for two or more.

Another interesting use of the dual is found in Paamese. Here the dual inclusive forms may be used for addressing a large crowd, particularly if the speaker wants to win over the audience: 'The speaker is effectively speaking to each addressee individually, and the use of the dual in such circumstances is more directly appealing to the individual in the large group' (Crowley 1982: 80). According to Michael Cooke (personal communication), in Djambarrpuyngu (which has around 3,000 speakers in north-east Arnhem Land), there is singular, dual and plural, and when speaking to a crowd, the dual inclusive may be used for a more personal effect. This is clearly comparable to Paamese. Recall too the discussion of Sursurunga (§2.2.5) in which the dual is used for the singular when the referent is in a taboo relationship to the speaker and the greater paucal is used in hortatory discourse, bringing the addressees into a group as it were. We noted too that in Marshallese the paucal is used rhetorically to give an illusion of intimacy.

In Ndjébbana (a non-Pama-Nyungan language spoken on the central north coast of Arnhem Land, Australia), generalizations about a normal sequence of events can be expressed in the singular even though a large group of people is involved (McKay 1984: 146–8). McKay gives examples from the account of a fish poisoning ceremony. But more surprisingly, it is also possible to use unit augmented forms (normally for referring to two; see §5.6) in these circumstances:

(11) Marlémarla   njirri-ngódja   djawalárra
      poison.berries 1.UNIT.AUG/3.MINIMAL-call   lily
      'We (two) call the poison berries "lilies"' (to fool the spirits)

Here the unit augmented form is used, even though this is a general statement of the practice of several people.

Table 7.1 *Forms of address in Boumaa Fijian*

addressee	appropriate form
actual or potential mother-in-law, father-in-law, son-in-law, daughter-in-law	2 dual
brother or sister (of opposite sex) (also possible to show special respect for elder sibling of same sex)	2 paucal
village chief (also possible for any old person)	2 plural (for respectful *reference* 3 plural may be used)

Consider now a complex number system, which is used to particularly good effect for purposes of address. It is that of Boumaa Fijian, where there is a four-way number system in the pronouns: singular–dual–paucal–plural. According to Dixon (1988: 53): 'All three non-singular second person forms can be used for addressing just one person, according to the Boumaa conventions of social inter-action.' For some addressees, avoidance behaviour is required, as shown in table 7.1. For full details of pronoun use in Boumaa Fijian see Schmidt (1988), and for the conventions in Standard Fijian see Milner (1956: 41). In Oroha, another Oceanic language, this time of the Solomon Islands, the dual or paucal is used for 'a chief or a person of importance' and 'a mother, either by herself or with her child, is addressed in the dual' (Ivens 1927: 594).[3]

---

[3] Sources for other languages where the dual is used for address to an individual are listed in Guðmundsson (1972: 44 n11).

Let us move to the matter of addressing more than one person. We might expect that if the plural can be used for polite address to one person (where otherwise the singular would have been expected), it would also be available for polite address to two persons (where the dual would have been expected). This is what we find in Sanskrit; MacDonell (1927: 180) states that the plural is sometimes used in address 'as a mark of great respect' in place of singular or dual; moreover the plural may be used for self reference by the speaker in place of singular or dual. And coming to the present, Stone, describing the West Slavonic languages Upper and Lower Sorbian (1993a: 623, 635), says that the plural pronoun *wy* 'you' can be used as an honorific 'to address one person (or two)'. This is as we would have expected. But now consider Slovene, a South Slavonic language, and so a relative of Sorbian. According to Priestly (1993: 414) in Slovene for polite address, the second person plural replaces the second person singular, but it does not replace the second person dual.[4] One of his consultants suggested the following contrast, when offering seats in a bus (the pronoun would normally be omitted):

(12) Ali se boste (Vi) used-l-i?
     Q REFL AUX.FUT.2.PL (you.PL) sit-PARTIC-PL.MASC
     'Would you like to sit down?' (Polite, to one person.)

(13) Ali se bosta (Vidva)
     Q REFL AUX.FUT.2.DUAL (you.DUAL)
     used-l-a?
     sit-PARTIC-DUAL.MASC
     'Would you like to sit down?' (To two persons; no change here.)

Thus the plural is used for polite address for one addressee but not for two. Moreover, in Slovene there is dialectal and archaic use of the third person plural in place of the second singular, again for polite address (1993: 415), and as with the second person this is used in place of the singular but not in place of the dual. The claim that the honorific usage may differ for two addressees as compared to one is supported by data from Old Icelandic; here too there was a singular–dual–plural system and the plural for honorific usage was less used for two speakers/addressees than for one (Guðmundsson 1972: 34–58).[5] Thus the restriction is on the form to

---

[4] I am grateful to Tom Priestly for reconfirming this interesting finding with several speakers of Slovene and to Janez Orešnik for his intuitions. While most agree with Priestly, there is not complete unanimity for all situations; further investigation is required. In the written language the dual pronoun *vidva* 'you two' is written with an initial capital to show honorific use.

[5] And after the loss of the dual, in Modern Icelandic there is still a difference between individual and group: 'It is clear that there is some difference in the honorific usage between the singular and the plural, as a group of individuals who would each be addressed in the honorific singular is as a rule addressed in the ordinary plural' Guðmundsson (1972: 68).

be replaced (or indeed on the number of persons to be addressed politely) rather than on the form which can be used.

Interestingly the dual may be used in place of the singular in Slovene when the first person is used for the addressee ('How are we today?') as in this nice example from Janez Orešnik (personal communication). At the end of an acupuncture session the doctor might say to the patient:

(14) Gospod Orešnik, zdaj bova   pobral-a
     Mr   Orešnik, now   AUX.FUT.1.DUAL take.out-DUAL

iglic-e
needle-PL

'Mr Orešnik, we'll take the needles out now'

Of course, just the doctor will take out the needles.

Let us now consider the three questions posed at the beginning. The first was whether all number values are available for the particular use. That is a more interesting question than it first seems. We wish to compare with 'normal' use of number where, for a given pronoun or noun, all number values are available and they have equivalent effects (that is, cat-SG is the same as cat-PL and cat-DUAL, except for the quantity of cats). With honorific use there are generally restrictions as compared to this situation. In many languages just the plural is available for this other, non-normal use (the singular can, of course, be used for addressing a single addressee, but there is no honorific effect and that usage is as predicted from the normal number value). In those instances where we found that other values (singular, dual and paucal) had honorific effects these were generally specific uses for that number. For instance, the use of the singular for addressing a group in Russian, where there is arguably a grouping effect, is quite different from the honorific plural: they are not values along the same scale. Hence although different values can be used for honorific purposes there are usually restrictions on these uses.

Our second question was why these uses can be available. Usually the number of addressees is evident from the context of speaking, hence the semantic value of number can be satisfied. This can still lead to problems, as the quote from Chekhov illustrates; in writing too, the potential confusion caused by honorific plurals is mitigated in several languages by the use of initial capitals for honorific pronouns.

And third, we asked whether this use is unique to number or whether the same effect is available through other means. Politeness can be marked at the same time as number and separately from it, as shown by the Austronesian language Muna. The sentence 'you go' might be translated as in table 7.2 (van den Berg 1989: 51,

Table 7.2 *Number and politeness markers in Muna*

	singular	plural
neutral	ihintu o-kala	ihintu-umu o-kala-amu
polite	intaidi to-kala	intaidi-imu to-kala-amu

82); *ihintu* is a free pronoun whose inclusion would be emphatic. Here *to-* marks polite address, irrespective of number. Though we are used to number being used for marking honorific use, there are other means for doing so, as in Muna, and in the extensive systems of lexical honorifics.

7.2 Unexpected feature values in coordination
In §6.5.1 we analysed coordination structures and found the two normal possibilities of agreement with the nearest conjunct or with all the conjuncts. Here we examine two types of construction in which the feature values used are higher on the scale than would be justified by semantic considerations.

7.2.1 The relational (dual and plural)
A particularly unusual use of number is found in the Finno-Ugric language Mansi, which has something under 4,000 speakers on the left bank of the River Ob´ in western Siberia. In this language, according to the account in Rombandeeva (1973: 42), noun phrases referring to two separate single but closely related items are found in the dual.

(15) ēkwa-ɣ   ōjka-ɣ   ōl-ēɣ
   woman-DUAL man-DUAL live-PRES.3.DUAL
   'a wife and husband live'

Each noun is in the dual, though there is one woman and one man; in this sentence we can see from the form of the verb that there are only two and not four people involved. The next example is comparable: (the difference in the dual forms results from the form of the stem: the dual marker is *-ɣ* for stems in *-a* and *-e*, and *-aɣ* otherwise (Rombandeeva 1973: 58)):

(16) taw mis-aɣ-e   luw-aɣ-e   iŋ
   he cow-DUAL-3.SG.POSS horse-DUAL-3.SG.POSS still

   ōn's'-ij-aɣ-e
   keeps-PRES-DUAL.OBJ-3.SG

   'he still keeps his cow and horse'

Here the morphology on the nouns suggests that four animals are involved, whereas in fact there are only two, as the dual object marker on the verb indicates.[6]

An analogous construction to that of Mansi was found in Sanskrit, particularly in Vedic Sanskrit; it is a specific type of the 'dvandva' compounds (MacDonell 1916: 268–70; 1927: 169–70). The terminology is a little confusing. Ordinary dvandva compounds consist of nouns (sometimes adjectives or adverbs) in a coordinative relation. There is one inflection for the noun compound, which will be dual if two entities are denoted and plural if more. But Vedic dvandvas, of which a few survive into Classical Sanskrit, are the ones of direct interest here; they are sometimes called 'double-dual dvandvas'. The usually quoted Vedic example is this (MacDonell 1916: 269):

(17) mitrā́-váruṇā
      Mitra.DUAL Varuna.DUAL
      'Mitra and Varuna'

Mitra and Varuna are the names of gods, closely associated and commonly mentioned together (the conditions which nearly always apply when this construction is used).[7] Each noun stands in the dual,[8] but again both have singular referents. Here the hearer's knowledge of the world would have been sufficient to ensure understanding (there was only one Mitra). The type with inflections on both nouns appears to be restricted to duals.

There was some debate among Indo-Europeanists as to the origin of this construction, with the dominant view being that of Delbrück, which was developed by Edgerton (1910). According to this view, the starting point is the 'elliptic' dual (which we have called the 'associative'), as in examples like *mitrā́* where Mitra in the dual number is used for Mitra and the other one normally associated, i.e. Varuna. Edgerton points to the analogy of personal pronouns, where the first person dual typically indicates the speaker and an associated person. The next stage is illustrated by instances where the dual noun is explained, as it were, by the inclusion of the other member, in the singular, 'Mitra (DUAL) and Varuna (SINGULAR) too'. The following stage is the surprising one: the second member takes the dual, assimilating to the first. Edgerton (1910: 115) suggests 'a desire to keep alive the pair-notion', and cites in support the fact that the parallel construction

---

[6] Further examples, from Mansi, and from the related Khanty (Ostyak) can be found in Ravila (1941: 14); see also Nikolaeva (1995: 170–1 for Khanty); for the construction in Nenets (a Samoyedic language) see Tereščenko (1973: 19).

[7] For the religious significance of these pairings see Gonda (1974).

[8] In cases other than the nominative, vocative and accusative, only the second member declines. Jamison (1988) includes relevant points in a discussion of a related construction.

with plurals is extremely rare. The similarities between Indo-European and Finno-Ugric in this regard are stressed by Gauthiot (1912). However, while the account of the origin of this construction in Indo-European may be adequate, Ravila (1941: 14) suggests that there are problems with it for Finno-Ugric, claiming that the elliptic dual is not normal in Ob´-Ugric (i.e. Mansi and Khanty). He discusses special cases (1941: 23); for instance, when the pair have been mentioned already. So it may be that the dual–dual construction has not arisen in Ob´-Ugric from an elliptic dual (see Honti 1997: 46–8 for further discussion).

As emerges from the account so far, in languages with singular, dual and plural, this construction is either predominant with the dual or restricted to the dual. At first sight this is an odd restriction. I believe the reasons for this are external rather than an essential part of the number system. First, it has been established that conjoined structures typically have two conjuncts; for example, Findreng (1976: 196) gives separate figures for the conjoining of two abstract nouns or more than two in German: 87 per cent of the cases (total 2,277) involved conjoining two elements only. We also know that the singular is the most common number. Hence the typical conjoined construction consists of two singular noun phrases. Second, and clearly related to this, in the real world there are plenty of items that come as linked pairs, there are relatively few that come as threesomes. Hence factors of typical construction and typical situation militate against this construction for anything but conjoined singular noun phrases, which will occur with the dual in languages which have this number value. Note that the construction is not limited to languages which have a dual. Mordvin, another Finno-Ugric language, has lost the dual, but has the construction and uses the plural: 'old.man-PL old.woman-PL' for 'the old man and woman' (Honti 1997: 47, 62–3). It appears that the motivation is to highlight specially tight connections, of which the most common type is the pair: this then is the natural preserve of the dual, when available, and otherwise the plural can serve the purpose.

Why is such a construction possible, when it appears to come into direct conflict with the normal feature values? In examples (15) and (16) from Mansi there is a marker on the verb showing the number of referents. However, there is not always a grammatical indicator of this type. In the Vedic Sanskrit example (17) the hearer's knowledge of the referents would mean there was no ambiguity.

In response to our third question, it is possible for a language to have a separate marker to fulfil this unusual function of number marking. Dyirbal (Dixon 1972: 230–1: see also 51, 62) has a marker *-gara* 'one of a pair' and another *-mangan* 'one of many':

    (18)   burbula-gara   baniɲu
           burbula-GARA   come
           'Burbula and another person are coming'

(19) burbula-gara   badibadi-gara   baniɲu
      burbula-GARA   badibadi-GARA   come
      'Burbula, being one of a pair, and Badibadi, being the other of the
      pair, are coming'

These markers in Dyirbal may be seen as associative markers (§4.3).

7.2.2 Pronominal coordination

There are interesting effects with pronouns. Take this Russian example:

(20) my   s   Alešej   napekl-i   pečen´e   uže
      1.PL   with   Alesha.INST   bake.PAST-PL   cake   already
      'Alesha and I have already baked the cake'

From the setting of this utterance (it is from a conversation transcribed in
Zemskaja and Kapanadze 1978: 244) it is clear that the speaker has two people in
mind, herself and her grandson Alesha. This is fully normal in Russian, and indeed
the form in (20) is the natural translation of 'Alesha and I'. In this construction *my*
'we' is plural when the other participant is included: it is not 'we plus Alesha' but
'we once Alesha is included'. (In other circumstances the same form could be used
for 'we (plural) plus Alesha' but that is less common.) Thus the plural value
appears not to have its usual semantics.[9] Similarly, in (21):

(21) my   s   toboj
      1.PL   with   2.SG.INST
      'you and I'

This typically means 'you and I' (unlike English, Russian has no constraint about
putting the first person after others). Example (21) could mean 'we and you'. We
may also use the second person plural in the secondary element:

(22) my   s   vami
      1.PL   with   2.PL.INST
      'you (PL or honorific) and I'

Here another theoretical ambiguity is introduced because the second person could
be a plural or a polite form (§7.1). An example of the construction in the third
person is given by Timberlake (1993: 866):

---

[9] William Ladusaw (reported in Aissen 1989: 524) suggests that in such constructions the
pronoun should be taken as the head, and the prepositional phrase (or equivalent) as an
adjunct which modifies the head. The modifier does not, under this interpretation, introduce additional referents but merely introduces further reference conditions on the head
(thus *my* 'we' requires that its reference should be a set consisting of the speaker and at least
one other individual, while the adjunct requires further that the set must contain Alesha).

> (23) oni   s   Parnok   živ-ut   v   èto   vremja   na   dače
>   3.PL   with   Parnok   live-3.PL   in   this   time   at   dacha
>   'she and Parnok are living at the dacha then'

Constructions broadly comparable to these examples are very widespread, though as we shall see they vary somewhat in detail. They are what Schwartz (1988b) calls the 'plural pronoun construction'. They are always subject to person resolution (compare number resolution in §6.5.2), that is, first person takes precedence over second, and second over third. Thus we may find the equivalent of first person with other: 'we with-you', 'we with-him/her'; or second person with third: 'you (plural) with-him/her'; or third person with third: 'they with-him/her'. (We do not find, for instance, 'they with-you' meaning 'he/she and you'.)

These constructions may extend into pronominal possessive adjectives (Isačenko 1962: 481):

> (24) naš-i   s   toboj   vospominanija
>   1.PL.POSS-PL   with   2.SG.INST   memory.PL
>   'our memories' (yours and mine)

Here the pronominal possessive adjective is in the first person plural when we might have expected the first person singular.[10]

When we compare across languages we find three main types of variation, concerning the obligatoriness of the construction, the balance between the elements, and the presence or absence of the pronoun.

In the Russian examples, Timberlake suggests that the construction with a plural pronoun is normal for first and second persons and preferred for third persons (1993: 866); this seems right, for while alternatives occur in corpora they are a small minority. In other languages the plural pronoun construction is not favoured to the same degree; in Slovene, Priestly suggests that ordinary coordination is equally acceptable (1993: 434).

In the examples examined so far, the secondary element in the construction has been clearly subordinate, governed by a preposition, which makes the whole construction like the comitative in form (§6.5.4). Most of the examples reported from different languages are of this type. However, there are also instances which are more

---

[10] A remarkable variant on this construction is found in Mansi. A normal start to a story is of this form (Elena Skribnik, personal communication):

> (i) ēkwa-piɣriś   ākw-ēn-tǝl   ōl-ēɣ
>   Ekwa-Pigrish   aunt-POSS.DUAL-INST   live-PRES.3.DUAL
>   'Ekwa-Pigrish (folklore hero) lives with his aunt'

Within the comitative phrase 'Ekwa-Pigrish with his aunt' the possessive is actually dual 'counting in' the aunt as it were.

like balanced coordination, where the secondary element has no subordinating marker. Edgerton (1910: 112) cites Old English *wit Scilling song ahōfon* literally 'we-two Scilling . . .', which means 'Scilling and I raised a song'. This usage is sometimes called the 'sylleptic dual'.[11] Aissen (1989: 519) gives Yapese as a further example.

The last main type of variation concerns the presence or absence of the pronoun. If a language drops personal pronouns, whether generally or to a restricted extent, then it will typically do so in this construction too, as for instance in Lower Sorbian (Stone 1993a: 663 citing Janaš 1984: 171–2):

(25) Som   nježelu   doma   był-a.
     AUX.1.SG Sunday   at.home be.PAST-SG.FEM

     Smej   z   nan-om   šach   grał-ej
     AUX.DUAL   with   father.SG.INST   chess play.PAST-DUAL

     'On Sunday I was at home. Father and I played chess.'

In both sentences in (25) the subject pronoun is dropped. In the second sentence, if it were included the form would be *mej z nanom* 'we (dual) with father, i.e. father and I'). With no pronoun present it is the verb form which makes clear the person and number of the subject, hence Schwartz (1988a) calls this construction the 'verb coded construction'. It too is widespread. For further examples and discussion see Schwartz (1988a, 1988b) and Aissen (1989).

Finally, let us consider these pronoun problems in terms of the three general questions about other uses. The forms available, depending on the language, are dual and plural (in those instances where the singular is used that is merely the normal use of the singular). Second, this other use can work because it is frequently evident from other sources (the participants of the discourse and the wider context) what the number of referents is. However, it must be admitted that the construction makes this harder rather than easier to establish. (It would be an interesting study to establish how many of the theoretical ambiguities are ever problematic; it may well be that in languages which have the plural pronoun construction the ordinary reading, where, say, the pronoun would be plural for normal reasons, is handled in a different way.) And third, are there other means available? Here, of course, many languages use the straightforward coordination *you and I*, or more usually *I and you.*

---

[11] 'Pronouns in the sylleptic dual refer to a pair, and are accompanied by a noun denoting the subordinate member of the pair and already included in the pronominal reference' (Plank 1989: 327n22); Tesnière (1951) uses the term in a similar way. The construction is not restricted to the dual; in languages with a dual, however, the sylleptic dual will tend to be frequent because conjoining most often involves just two conjuncts, and these more usually denote singulars rather than other values (see §7.2.1), hence the sylleptic plural is less often noticed.

7.3 Special uses

At various points in the book we have noted instances where number is used for other purposes, for instance for distributive use (§4.4.1 note 28) and for associative use (§6.3). The special uses to be discussed here are more limited in their distribution, they are almost all affective in nature, and they are almost all restricted to the plural.

7.3.1 The exaggerative plural

According to Whitney's description of Finnish (1956: 202) 'In popular speech of an exaggerating, strongly affirmative or boasting nature, especially when two or more objects are listed, each singular, they are sometimes put in the plural . . .' He gives two examples. The first was accepted by my consultants (Jouko Lindstedt, Arto Mustajoki and Hannu Tommola), though it struck them as dated:

(26) Hän   on   lukenut kreik-at   ja   latina-t
      3.SG   AUX   studied Greek-PL   and   Latin-PL
      'he/she has studied Greek and Latin'

This emphasizes that the person in question knows a lot. The second example given by Whitney was found less good. However, the following were proposed instead as fully acceptable (as spoken forms):

(27) Tässä on   mies, joka on   kiertä-nyt
      here   is   man   REL   AUX   circle-PST.PARTIC

      Saksa-t   ja   Espanja-t.
      Germany-PL   and   Spain-PL

      'here is a man who has been (around) in Germany and in Spain'

(28) Häne-llä   on   auto-t   ja   kesämöki-t
      he/she-ADESSIVE   is   car-PL   and   summer.cottage-PL

      'he/she has cars and summer cottages'

Example (28) implies that the person is rich. While there are Finns with more than one car, it would be very unusual to have more than one summer cottage. However, a response suggesting the hearer knows that the person being discussed really has, for instance, only one car would be ridiculous (or at best a rather bad joke). If there were really plural referents then the partitive plural would be used (*auto-ja ja kesämökke-jä*).

Most examples of this pattern involve two conjuncts (see also Mey 1960: 72 on this, and for more examples Yli-Vakkuri 1986: 62–6). Adding a third conjunct is just possible; this is made better if there are two instances of *ja* 'and'; moreover a special slower intonation is required. But even a single noun phrase may be involved, as Hannu Tommola points out (example from the writer Unto Seppänen, quoted from Hakulinen 1968: 421):

(29) Vielä   tässä   venäjä-t-kin   pitä-isi   osa-ta!
      as.well   here   Russian-PL-also   must-COND.3.SG   can-INF
      '(so you suppose) one should know (also) Russian (language), too!'
      = 'So you expect me to know Russian too!'

This might be used when the speaker thinks he or she knows a lot, has done all that is wanted, and is annoyed at a suggestion that in addition to everything else a knowledge of Russian is expected too. According to Hakulinen (1961: 328) this usage is found in Vepsian and Lapp too.

Consider also this example from *Alice in Wonderland*, chapter 4:

(30) 'It was much pleasanter at home,' thought poor Alice, 'when one
      wasn't always growing larger and smaller, and being ordered about by
      mice and rabbits.'

At this point she has come across one mouse ('the Mouse') and one rabbit ('the White Rabbit'). In this example we find conjoined noun phrases, though this is not required in English. The 'exotic' use of Finnish is available in English too.

This special use is restricted to the plural. It functions because normally the real world number is available (particularly in cases like (29)), and there is no obvious comparable unique morphological marker, since there is the curious requirement that normally two noun phrases should be involved.

7.3.2 The intensificative

Intensificative usage comes under various names: it is sometimes called 'augmentative' (as in Sten 1949),[12] 'emphatic' (as in Löfstedt 1928: 36–8, who gives Latin examples), or 'hyperbolic'. It appears to be related to the exaggerative, but there is no preference that there should be conjoined noun phrases. Given this difference, and the fact that the typical effect produced is also different, it is appropriate to retain the two as separate uses. In Russian this usage is known as the 'hyperbolic' plural.[13] Often intensificatives show dissatisfaction, as in two Russian examples from speech (Krasil'nikova 1990: 85):

(31) Kto   èto   košel'k-i   raskidyva-et
      who   this   purse-ACC.PL   scatter-3.SG
      'Who's been leaving purses lying around?'

---

[12] Also in Kraus (1977: 78–81), where English examples are given.
[13] See Arbatskij (1972); for further examples and several references see Brusenskaja (1992: 44–5), Krasil'nikova (1990: 85–7) and Panov (1968: 167–57).

This was said in the context of one purse being visible. The plural is therefore known to be 'inaccurate' (here from the situation, in other instances it might be from general knowledge). And note too that the English translation works similarly.[14]

(32) Vy   tam   piš-ete   na   nemeck-ix
    2.PL   there   write-2.PL   on   German-PL.PREP

    jazyk-ax
    language-PL.PREP

    'You're there writing in German'

Here the affective usage is even more obvious, since the plural has no straightforward interpretation. The plural is also used for effect in newspaper headlines; Klobukov (1998: 128–31) calls it the 'sensational plural', and gives interesting Russian examples, including this one:

(33) Bandit-y   napadajut   na   inkassator-ov,   daže   ne
    robber-PL   attack   on   collector-PL.ACC   even   not

    udostoverivšis´,   est´   li   u   nix   den´gi
                                   (*Moskovskij komsomolec* 20.9.97)
    making.sure   is   Q   at   them   money

    'Robbers attack collectors without even checking if they have any
    money'

From the article it becomes clear that one robber tried to rob one guard. Here a single bad event is made to seem typical, by being pluralized, and so the effect is that the situation is made to appear worse than the bald facts would suggest. Examples of intensificative plurals are also found in Romance languages (Sten 1949: 57–9),[15] including their use for polite effect, as in French *mes respects à Madame* 'my regards to Madame', where the plural of the abstract noun again is not a normal plural; again the English translation has a plural, and English uses further instances, such as *congratulations*.

Consider now data from Dench (1995: 95–6) on Martuthunira (Pilbara Region of Western Australia). He claims that in the following two examples 'the plural suffix is used to group together a set of separate actions which are distributed through time, yet involve the same participants. The plural marks a body-part which undergoes an action a number of times.'

---

[14] A comparable use of what he calls a distributive suffix in the verb is given for Usan (Adelbert Range, Papua New Guinea) by Reesink (1987: 112).

[15] See also Furukawa (1977: 161–71) on French.

(34)　Ngayu　　　　kalya-rnu　　　　ngulu　　　yiriny-tu,
　　　1.SG.NOM　bite-PASS.PRFV　that.EFF　mosquito-EFF

　　　ngayu　　　　kalya-rnu　　　　　nyina-nguru　marnta-ngara-a
　　　1.SG.NOM　bite-PASS.PRFV　sit-PRES　　　arm-PL-ACC

　　　wii,　　　kartara　wii,　　　jal.yu　wii
　　　maybe　cheek　　maybe　neck　　maybe

　　　panga-ngara-rri-nguru-rru.
　　　itch-PL-INVOLUNTARY-PRES-NOW

　　　'I've been bitten by a mosquito. My arms (in a number of places)
　　　perhaps, maybe my cheek, maybe my neck etc. will be getting lots of
　　　itches.'

(35)　Ngayu　　　　parna-thurti　warrpurri-layi　nguu-ngara-thurti
　　　1.SG.NOM　head-CONJ　　bathe-FUT　　face-PL-CONJ

　　　jirli-thurti　thala-ngara-rru　puntha-layi.
　　　arm-CONJ　chest-PL-NOW　wash-FUT

　　　'I'll wash my head and all, my face (i.e. splash it a number of times)
　　　and arms, and then wash my chest (i.e. splash it a number of times).'

Dench makes the important observation that the dual cannot be used like this. We have 'arm', 'face' and 'chest' marked with the plural. At first sight we might seem to have verbal number marked on the noun (see §8.3). I suggest that a better interpretation is that we here have exaggerative use, and the effect of the exaggeration is to imply several bites and several splashes. However, Nicholas Evans suggested (personal communication) rather that the plural indicates 'parts of arm'; this would be a special use, restricted to body-parts. I emailed Alan Dench to ask, but sadly the last speaker died in 1995 before Dench was able to check these possibilities. I believe that one or other of these suggestions is correct and that we are dealing with a special use of nominal number, not the expression of verbal number on the noun.

The question that is not normally asked here is which values are available. When we consider a language with a dual, we find that this is not used in the intensificative. In Slovene one may say (Janez Orešnik, personal communication):

(36)　Kdo　krade　denarnic-e?
　　　who　steals　purse-PL
　　　'Who keeps stealing purses?'

This would be appropriate as an intensificative for one or for two purses. However, it is not possible to use the dual *denarici* '(two) purses' as an intensificative (to show a less strong feeling than that conveyed by the plural). The dual would have the literal meaning. Typically the construction has its effect because the real-world number of the referent is known, and the effect results from the discrepancy between the speaker's presentation of the situation and the hearer's knowledge or supposition of it. Here the corresponding separate morphological marker would be the augmentative in various languages.[16]

There is a related special use which we should consider here. We saw in §2.2.6 that occasionally there are special morphological forms indicating an excessive number, sometimes called 'plurals of abundance'. Ordinary plurals may also be found in this use; when there is no special morphological form we may call it the 'plural of excess', which is a type of intensificative. Note that in Syrian Arabic, where there is a special plural of abundance there is no dual of abundance (Cowell 1964: 368). Similarly, in languages where ordinary plurals can be used in this way, duals cannot. The obvious instance in which ordinary plurals are so used is when their normal use is not required, typically with nouns which usually do not head countable noun phrases. Thus in Lezgian, such plurals may be used for a great quantity (Haspelmath 1993: 81):

(37) Nek'-er bul   x̂u-raj
     milk-PL   abundant   be-OPTATIVE
     'May the milk be abundant'

In Koryak (Žukova 1972: 131) the plural of nouns for 'meat', 'sugar' and so on indicates a larger quantity than the singular, and a similar use is found in Fula (Koval' 1997: 135). We find the converse in Manam, where nouns denoting mass concepts all take plural marking on the verb: here the singular may be used for a small quantity (thus 'water' takes the plural, but 'a little water' the singular; Lichtenberk 1983: 269). Before leaving the intensificative, we should consider whether it could apply to a noun phrase which is 'already' plural. It appears that it can; consider this example from Anindilyakwa, which has about 1,000 speakers on Groote Eylandt (the large island in the Gulf of Carpentaria, Northern Territory, Australia):

(38) yirrimwirntamwirntakalhalhikaniwa
      yirra-mwirnta(ka)-mwirntak(a)-akalhalhik(a)-ani-wa
      1.EXCL.NON_SG-REDUP-PL_SUBJ-REDUP.go-TENSE-
                                                    ALLATIVE
      'a very large number of us kept on going towards (it)'

---

[16] There is also overlap here and in some other cases with the use of reduplication; thus Moravcsik (1978: 324) notes its use for 'the meanings of increased quantity, intensity, diminution and attenuation'.

To make the structure clearer, a segmented form is given on the second line, with assimilations and deletions disregarded. The relevant part is the plural subject marker *mwirntaka*, which is reduplicated, to suggest something more than a normal plural. The data are from Leeding (1989: 118, 227, 425), who writes that reduplication of the plural marker 'intensifies or increases the number' (1989: 425).[17]

For the intensificative then, in its various guises, only the plural is available; the construction works because the hearer can usually infer the real-world number from other information; and it has parallels in augmentatives (for which reduplication is a possible means of expression).

7.3.3 The approximative

Karlsson (1959b) gives examples of the use of the plural in Finnish, when there is a single referent, to express approximation. It is used particularly in relation to expressions of place, time, numerical quantity and state. Some of his examples are dated, but the approximative use of the plural is still current. Imagine, for instance, that A says he is afraid of flying. A possible response from B is:

(39) e-n   ymmärrä   (noita)   pelko-j-a-si
       NEG-1.SG   understand   (those)   fear-PL-PARTITIVE-your
       'I don't understand your fear'

Here the plural is natural (according to Jouko Lindstedt, Arto Mustajoki and Hannu Tommola), even though one fear has been expressed. The plural is vaguer, and so more polite. According to Cruse (1994: 2861, following Lewis 1967: 247) a similar use is found in Turkish. For instance, compare *burada* 'here' (literally 'in this place'), with *buralarda* 'hereabouts' (literally 'in these places'). For a comparable use in Mayali see Evans (§7.5.5 in forthcoming). A related use may be seen in English *walkies*, *drinkies* and so on; this attenuative use is almost exclusively used in speaking to children.

One further related use which deserves mention is illustrated in this example from Dogon (Plungian 1995: 11, citing Tembiné 1986: 75):

(40) ibɛ   ya-ɛ-w   yo,   isu   mbe   nie   mbe
       market   go-AOR-2.SG   if   fish   PL   oil   PL

       bawiɛ
       buy.IMP.2.SG

       'if you go to the market, buy fish, oil and similar things'

---

[17] Another language where pluralizing a noun that is already plural gives a plural of abundance is Miya (Schuh 1998: 199); in Miya this is restricted to plural nouns which do not take the canonical plural morphology but show some sort of irregularity.

Here the number word *mbe* (§5.1) occurs after the two nouns and the force of it is not that of the normal plural, nor that of the sort plural (§3.7.2) but suggests other things approximately like those listed. See Genetti (1994: 45) for a similar use in the Tibeto-Burman language Newari.

The approximative requires more research. There is evidence only for the use of the plural; when languages with the approximative and additional number values are found it seems a safe prediction that the other values will not be available for approximative use. The construction functions again because in many instances the real-world number is available from elsewhere. A comparable morphological indicator might be the diminutive in certain languages.

7.3.4 The evasive

In languages with gender systems, problems can arise when the speaker wishes to refer to a person without reference to sex. This may be because *they* do not know the sex, or because no specific person is intended. One of the appropriate genders may be selected as a default; alternatively a different gender (such as the fourth gender in Archi) may be selected as an 'evasive' device (see Corbett 1991: 222–3). A different evasive device is to use the plural, if gender is not distinguished there. Thus Alamblak (a Sepik Hill language of Papua New Guinea) distinguishes masculine and feminine in the singular, but not in the dual or plural. If 'the speaker is either unable or unwilling to indicate the gender of an object' (Bruce 1984: 98) then the third plural is used:

(41) yën-m   heawrahtm   indom   yamtn
     child-3.PL she.will.bear.them another   month.in
     'She will bear a child in another month'

Note that it is indeed the plural which is used, not the dual (though the dual similarly does not distinguish gender). This is a technique available in English (examples in Newman 1992). We can evade the problem of *he* or *she* by using the plural *they*:

(42) If a student wishes to change options they should see their tutor immediately.

Thus from the restricted evidence available it appears that only the plural is used as an evasive form; the construction works because typically specific number information is not available or not necessary: thus in (42) we do not know how many may wish to change. I have not found a language with a separate morphological possibility for evasive usage. There is an instance of a separate lexical item, the pronoun *ni* of Zande, which is used if no specific individual is intended or if the individual is unknown (Claudi 1985: 95–6).

7.3.5 The anti-associative

An unusual possibility is found in West Greenlandic (Fortescue 1984: 247). In the case of words for boats and ships, like *umiarsuaq* 'ship', it is possible to use the plural for the vessel and its crew, for instance:

(43) umiarsuit
      ship.PL
      'a ship plus its crew'

It is significant that this language has a dedicated nominal affix used specifically for the normal associative, namely *-kkut* 'and family/companions' (as in *palasi-kkut* 'the priest and his family'). Some other languages use the plural for that purpose. Clearly then the special form with ships is not an extension of the associative plural. According to Michael Fortescue (personal communication) this special usage is found in all Eskimo languages. For those with just a singular–plural opposition, the plural form of any noun denoting a means of transport can be used for the vehicle together with its rider(s) or passenger(s). A nice example is the West Greenlandic *siikilit* (plural) 'bicycle plus rider', a borrowing of the Danish *cykel* 'bicycle'. Fortescue suggests the origin for this use is to be found with the words for sledge. These are plural (dual in the Eskimo languages which preserve the dual) since they consist essentially of two runners.

I propose to call such constructions the 'anti-associative' for the following reasons. We have seen from West Greenlandic that it is not merely an extended associative. Moreover whereas in the associative the main member and the associated members (§4.3) typically all denote humans, in the anti-associative the main member denotes a non-human, while the associated members denote humans. Danièl' (1999: 369) suggests that plurals of place names used to denote inhabitants could be viewed similarly. This is found in Mari (Cheremis), a Finno-Ugric language with over half a million speakers around the middle Volga and to the east of it; it has a special associative form, but the ordinary plural can also be used as an associative. If the plural suffix is added to a place name, this denotes the people who are at the place or who live there (Alhoniemi 1993: 70):

(44) Morko-βlakə̂n
      Morki-PL
      'the inhabitants of Morki'

More surprisingly, the associative suffix can be used in the same way in Mari (Alhoniemi 1993: 70):

(45) Pujal-mə̂t
      Pujal-ASSOCIATIVE
      'the inhabitants of Pujal'

Here then we see the converse of the normal associative, in that the main member (the place in this instance) seems not necessarily to be included. Another language which uses the plural as in (44) is Comanche (Charney 1993: 51).

The number values available in the anti-associative are the dual and the plural, depending on the number of associated members. The way this construction works is relatively straightforward for the 'inhabitants type' (44): speakers know there are not numerous places with the same name, and so will look for a different reading. But the 'transport type' anti-associatives of West Greenlandic are more problematic: it seems reasonable to expect that the plural of 'boat' and 'bicycle' might have its ordinary reading. And, not surprisingly, there is no obvious separate morphological marker corresponding to this remarkable usage.

7.4 Conclusion

Once these other uses are pointed out, then it is often possible to find examples in very familiar languages (as with the intensificative in English); it is curious, therefore, that number has gained the reputation of being a largely semantic category, while these surprising uses have gone largely unnoticed. For some of them, there is a good deal of research still to be done.

We noted several uses where only the plural is available: for affective uses that seems to be always the case. For the remainder too, there were generally restrictions, and we noted the different situation in conjoining structures (which arises because of the preponderance of conjoining involving two singular conjuncts). At first we might say that these uses are available precisely in situations where, by various means, the real-world number of the referent can be otherwise established. It remains to be seen whether this suspiciously neat solution will hold for the full range of data. It seems that there are cases where the use of a plural pronoun politely to a singular addressee can cause confusion. Perhaps it will be possible to maintain the weaker claim that the different other uses will always centre on situations where the real-world number of the referent will be establishable. Typically these other uses are paralleled in other languages by a dedicated morphological marker, or by some other device.

The chapter has shown that though we have established the broad typology of number, there are several interesting uses which are not understandable as straightforward uses of the relevant number value. Pinning them down requires detailed and careful work. The typological point then is that once the broad correlations are established, for a construction or for a category, there is still much more to be found out, and the sort of detail required typically requires careful work with substantial amounts of data.

8
Verbal number

In the introduction we drew attention to the distinction between the more familiar nominal number, which relates to entities, and the less well known verbal number, which relates to events. In this chapter we take a closer look at the latter[1] and draw comparisons with nominal number. The general typological point will be the need to be careful about terms, and to distinguish carefully between phenomena before attempting a typology. Recall that by verbal number we mean number related to the semantics of the verb, and not merely marked on it; this is clear in the example from Rapanui (§1.2):

(1a) ruku   (1b) ruku ruku
      dive   dive dive
      'dive'   'go diving'

The form in (1b) suggests more than one dive, but not necessarily more than one diver: the event is in a sense plural.[2] Contrast this situation with the English sentence:

(2) the sheep jump

Even though the verb *jump* shows number (plural), while the noun does not, this is still nominal number – it is the number of sheep which is indicated. Even if number is marked on the verb and there is no noun phrase present (as frequently occurs in pro-drop languages), this does not necessarily indicate verbal number. Serbo-Croat regularly drops subject pronouns unless stressed:

(3) došl-i   su
     came-MASC.PL be.3.PL
     'they came'

---

[1] A major analysis of the subject is that of Durie (1986); Frajzyngier (1985) was a forerunner, as was Dressler (1968) and Mithun (1988a) gives a diachronic perspective. Nor should the work of Jensen (1952: 17–20) be forgotten; he noted the distinctiveness of verbal number and gathered data from different language families. For a survey of how quantification differs for verbs and nouns see Gil (1993).

[2] Newman (1980: 13n23) suggested the term 'pluractional', but use of this term is largely limited to Africanists.

Verbal number

The participle marks gender and number, and the auxiliary marks number and person. The plurality marked by both elements is nevertheless an instance of nominal number: it simply indicates the number of those who came. It marks just the same distinctions as those of the pronoun (which can be present):

(4) on-i   su   došl-i
     3–MASC.PL   be.3.PL   came-MASC.PL
     'they came'

The change in word order is because *su* is a clitic and must occupy the second position.

With these potential false trails averted, let us now consider verbal number in more detail. A good starting point is the following examples from Central Pomo, a Pomoan language of Northern California (Marianne Mithun, personal communication).[3] The suffix -*ṭ* indicates multiple occurrences of an action. Thus *ščéw* 'tie' is opposed to *ščéṭ'* 'tie (plurally)' (final obstruents are automatically glottalized):

(5a) háyu   š-čé-w   (5b) háyu   š-čé-ṭ'
      dog   hooking-catch-PRFV   dog   hooking-catch-PL.PRFV
      'he tied up the dog'   'he tied up the dogs'

Since there were several 'dog-tying events' in (5b), we may reasonably infer that there were multiple dogs, though this is not stated (the form of the noun does not change). Conversely, in the English translation, the nominal plurality of *dogs* suggests that there was more than one dog-tying event, though this is not stated. The English versions in (5a) and (5b) are the most likely translation equivalents of the Central Pomo sentences, but the number systems of the two languages are rather different. For typology we must recognize differences of this type, which demands more careful analysis than simply working from translation equivalents.

We first establish the regions of the world where verbal number is found (§8.1). We then look at the types of meaning expressed (§8.2) and where verbal number is expressed, contrasting it with nominal number (§8.3). This leads to the question of possible tests for distinguishing it from nominal number (§8.4), to the items which may be involved (§8.5), and to the means of expression (§8.6). Next we look at other uses of verbal number (§8.7). Several of these sections (those on meaning, items involved, means of expression and other uses) are parallel to full chapters in the account of nominal number. The comparisons all point to nominal number having greater possibilities than verbal number. We ask why this should be so in (§8.8).

---

[3] The data are from Frances Jack, speaker. For a description of the different strategies for marking number in Central Pomo see Mithun (1988b), and for the degree to which they survive during language obsolescence see Mithun (1990).

8.1 The geographical extent of verbal number

Verbal number is relatively little known, and yet it has been claimed to exist in many languages from different parts of the world. It is widespread in North America, where 'verbal number markers are generally more pervasive, productive, and elaborate than nominal number markers' (Mithun 1988a: 231). The phenomenon is found in each of the four major families of Africa (Brooks 1991): the Chadic group is particularly well documented (Newman 1990: 53–87), while for Semitic see Greenberg (1991), and for the Khoisan language ǂHòan see Gruber (1975) and Collins (1998). It is also found in certain Paleoasiatic languages (see papers in Xrakovskij 1997), various languages of the Caucasus (Georgian will be illustrated below), in the South Central Dravidian group of languages of southern India (Steever 1987), in some Austronesian languages, for instance in Tokelauan (Myksvoll 1995), and in Papuan languages (Foley 1986: 128–30).[4]

8.2 The meaning of verbal number

This area of verbal number is perhaps the least well researched; and the difficulty is compounded by the fact that the terminology is not standardized. For example, Eulenberg (1971: 73), discussing a reduplicated verb in Hausa, says that it is representative of:

> a derivational category widespread among Nilo-Saharan and
> Afro-Asiatic languages, though rather marginal in Niger-Congo.
> This category is variously known as the *intensive, habitative,*
> *frequentative, repetitive,* or *plural* verb . . . it has the general meaning
> of a repeated action, an action simultaneously performed by several
> agents, an action performed on more than one object, or various
> combinations of these 'plural' meanings.

We will consider possible meanings first in a rather speculative way, looking at English sentences, and then examine how these possible meanings are reflected in verbal number. Consider this sentence:

(6)   Margot sang a song

This could mean that she sang it once, or several times. We could express the latter meaning with *over and over.* Note that this possible difference is retained independently of nominal number; it remains when the subject noun phrase is plural:

(7)   the girls sang a song

---

[4] Verbal number in the language isolate Burushaski is discussed by Tiffou and Patry (1995).

Again, one rendition of the song may be intended, or several. In other words, the singing might be thought of as singular or plural; many languages mark this distinction by verbal number. It might also be said that there is a difference between one singer singing a song (once or several times) and several singers singing it: singing in a choir is different from singing a solo. Such differences resulting from the number of participants in an action may also be encoded in a language as a different type of verbal number. Thus we distinguish two main types of verbal number: **event number** and **participant number**. We will consider them in turn.

8.2.1 Event number

Event number can be illustrated from Hausa, a Chadic language (Eulenberg 1971: 73–4):

(8a)	naa	aikee	su[5]	(8b)	naa	a"aikee	su
	I	send	them		I	send.PL	them

Note that both have a singular subject and a plural object. Example (8a) has a simple verb, but (8b) has a verb with partial reduplication, which marks it as 'intensive' or 'plural'. Example (8a) can be used with the meaning 'I sent them at the same time to the same place' and (8b) would not be appropriate there. Both examples could be used with the following meanings:

(9) I sent them at the same time to different places

(10) I sent them at different times to the same place

(11) I sent them at different times to different places

Thus the 'plural' verb *a"aikee* indicates that the sending was not simple; rather it involved more than one time or more than one place, that is, more than one 'sending-event'. Its use is not obligatory, however. The important thing is that the use of the 'plural' verb here indicates the number of sending events; it is an instance of verbal number of the event type.[6]

What distinctions can be made within verbal number of this type? The most common is single event versus multiple event, but larger inventories can be found. Thus Southern Paiute has markers for possibilities including 'continuous repetitive action ("patter") or durative iteration ("gnaw")' (Mithun 1988a: 217, following Sapir 1930–31). But such instances should put us on our guard. Given a language which, in terms of number, had only the verbal opposition in the Hausa

---

[5] *naa* 'I' is in a form marking completive aspect; the verb is *aikaa* 'to send' but the *-aa* ending changes to *-ee* because of the presence of a pronominal object.

[6] Even in this clear case the potential link to nominal number is evident, since multiple sendings are likely to involve a plural object.

examples above, would we say it had the category of number? Many would say rather that it had aspect: repeated versus non-repeated action is a classic aspectual distinction.

Why then should event number be considered here at all if it may be a type of verbal aspect? First because it is worth noting the parallelism between number for the noun (number of entities) and aspect for the verb (number of events).[7] Second, because the way in which number of this type is marked on the verb may also serve other purposes, which may be harder to distinguish from other types of number, in particular it may mark verbal number of the participant type (see §8.2.2 below). And third, because for certain language families there is a tradition of using the term 'plural verb' in such instances and so this usage should be discussed. However, 'event number' may reasonably be taken as a type of verbal aspect.

8.2.2 Participant number

We can see this in Huichol (a Uto-Aztecan language of west-central Mexico, data in Comrie 1982: 113):

(12) nee   waakana   ne-mec-umiʔii-ri   eeki
     1.SG   chicken.SG 1.SG.SUBJ-2.SG.OBJ-kill.SG-BENEF   2.SG
     'I killed the chicken for you'

(13) nee   waakana-ari ne-mec-uqiʔii-ri   eeki
     1.SG   chicken-PL 1.SG.SUBJ.-2.SG.OBJ-kill.PL-BENEF   2.SG
     'I killed the chickens for you'

The verb form varies (*umiʔii* versus *uqiʔii*) according to the number of the participants (chickens). We shall see below (§8.4.1) that this is indeed an instance of verbal number.

Ainu, one of the languages of Japan, is particularly interesting in this respect (Shibatani 1990: 48–55). It has ordinary plural verbs: thus from *kor* 'have' there is the form *kor-pa* 'have many things'. Ainu also has causatives; from *kor* 'have' there is a causative *kor-e* 'give' (cause to have). The singular causative suffix is -*(r)e*-*te*. This causative suffix can be added to a plural verb: *kor-pa-re* 'cause someone to have many things'. However, the causative may also be plural, in which case it takes the form -*(y)ar*, as in pairs like *sitoma* 'be afraid', *sitoma-yar* 'cause people to become afraid'. This too can be added to a plural verb: *kor-pa-yar* 'cause people to have many things'.

---

[7] A good instance of the aspect–number link is seen in Holisky's (1985) analysis of the Nakh language Tsova-Tush. See Cusic (1981) for a discussion of the relations between verbal number, tense and aspect, and recall §3.6 note 19 for further references.

Given just the examples so far, we might ask whether we are dealing with anything more than agreement in number. The phenomenon is rather different; the primary function of such forms 'is not to enumerate entities, but to quantify the effect of actions, states, and events' (Mithun 1988a: 214). These examples of alternative forms for singular and plural are rather more like classificatory verbs. These latter are verbs which are semantically compatible with a restricted set of noun phrases: for example, in Klamath (a language of Oregon) the appropriate verb for 'give' depends on the type of object given (Mithun 1988a: 214–15, following Barker 1964: 176):

(14) lʸoy   'to give a round object'
      nᵉoy   'to give a flat object'
      ksʸoy 'to give a live object'

These may be compared to the English verbs *eat* and *drink*, which share the meaning 'ingest' and are used according to the type of item ingested. But the actions are sufficiently distinct to be classified as different activities. Similarly in Klamath, giving a round object is different from giving a flat one. Most interestingly, giving several objects is different again:

(15) sʔewan? 'to give several objects'

This verb is used for giving several objects whether live or not, round or flat. This illustrates clearly that some verbs require objects of particular types, and that being numerous is just one of these possible types. Thus it can be argued that we are not dealing with grammatical number any more than the other verbs require us to deal with 'grammatical roundness', it is simply a matter of the lexical meaning of the verb. Nevertheless, we need to be careful to distinguish such instances of verbal participant number from nominal number, and this is more difficult than with event number. We shall draw the contrasts in detail in §8.4 below.

What distinctions can be made within participant number? According to Durie (1986: 356) the opposition is usually singular versus plural, or one and two versus three or more. (This latter opposition, illustrated in table 8.1 below, is one that is found with nominal number in restricted circumstances, see §4.5.1.) But often sources are not clear on this point, rather they refer to 'multiple participants' or some such phrase. This is understandable when we think of English verbs like *scatter*: in the intransitive use, one person cannot scatter, and two or three can hardly do so. Ten clearly can. Equally in the transitive use, one cannot scatter two seeds, nor perhaps three, but it is hard to say what the lower limit would be. Thus so-called plural verbs often require 'multiple participants', and do not show a strict singular–plural contrast as may be found with nominal number.

There are occasional examples of a three-way opposition, however; they are restricted both in the number of languages in which they are found and in the number of items involved. Karok distinguishes singular, dual and plural, as do Mikasuki and other Muskogean languages (Booker 1978, 1982: 15–16).[8] Cook (1974) reports that in Sarcee, an Athabaskan language of Canada, there is a contrast singular, dual and plural for 'walk' (and he also quotes comparable Navajo,[9] Tahltan, Kaska and Chipewyan examples). But other verbs in Sarcee with verbal number distinguish only one/two from more than two; this is not a clear boundary, in that speakers hesitate between the forms when two participants are involved (Cook 1974: 114n5). A singular–paucal–plural contrast is reported in Mojave but only for a single verb (Durie 1986: 360 following Munro 1976; see Langdon 1988 for more on the Yuman family). Slave, an Athabaskan language of northern Canada, has a few cases where there are different verb forms for number (Rice 1989: 790–2; those listed there are close to an exhaustive list, Keren Rice, personal communication). The different types are as in table 8.1 (there is dialect variation). There may be three different verb forms, or two, or

Table 8.1 *Verbal number in Slave*

'singular'	'dual'	'plural'	gloss
-da	-kee	-kw'i	be seated
	-tį	-yeh	eat
-we	-dé		die

indeed the normal case which is for there to be no distinction of this type based on number. The traditional labels are again slightly misleading, in that the dual is not strictly for two but may be used for a small number (Keren Rice, personal communication).

8.2.3 Mixed event and participant number

Some languages have both types of verbal number, and may signal both using the same formal device. For example, in Shokleng, a Gê language of southern Brazil, verbal number is usually of the participant type, but it can occasionally encode event number (Urban 1985: 177n4):

(16) tã wũ   kil   lãŋlãŋ   katẽ
      he 3.NOM cry.out jump.PL   come.SG.ACTIVE
      'he came shouting and jumping'

---

[8] There is a good deal on Koasati; for the formation of dual verbs see Kimball (1991: 322–4) and for an analysis of their use in an interesting text see Kimball (1993).

[9] For an original and not uncontroversial account of Navajo classificatory verbs and number see Witherspoon (1971).

Here there is a single participant, but the verb *lāŋlāŋ* 'jump' is 'plural' showing repeated action (plural event). The opposite situation is reported for (partial) reduplication in Tonkawa, an American Indian language formerly spoken in Texas. Here verbal number primarily signals repeated action, but it may also be used to indicate that 'many persons are engaged in a particular action' (Hoijer 1933–38: 27, 61). And in Ngan'gityemerri (Daly family), reduplication of the verb root may give an iterative interpretation or a multiple participants interpretation (Reid 1990: 185–9).

8.2.4 Values

Let us compare possible values with those found in nominal number. Nominal number shows several values: besides the basic singular–plural distinction, we find duals, paucals and trials. The largest systems have five values in all, as we saw in §2.2.5. In contrast, verbal number is almost always restricted to a 'singular–plural' distinction; as we saw in §8.2.2, instances of the 'dual' are reported sporadically (for instance in the Athabaskan and Muskogean families), but these typically involve extremely few verbs. It is not clear, however, that 'singular' and 'plural' are the appropriate terms. When glossing 'plural' verbs, Foley (1986: 128–9), quoting from different sources on Papuan languages, uses 'one ~ some' or 'one ~ many', as shown in table 8.2.

Table 8.2 *Examples of verbal number in three Papuan languages*

language	'singular'	gloss	'plural'	gloss
Kiwai	agome	one drowns	iagome	some drown
	agiwai	give one	iagiwai	give some
Fasu	pari	one stays	popari	many stay
	mara	get one	mora	get many
Barai	fi	one sits	kari	many sit
	abe	take one	ke	take many

Similarly Mithun (1988a: 213), giving North American data, again from a variety of sources, uses 'one ~ group' or 'one ~ several'. Such glosses are more accurate and helpful than the 'singular ~ plural' shorthand which is often employed, hence the scare quotes in table 8.2 and elsewhere in this chapter. It seems likely that many of the instances glossed as 'plural' in the literature would be more accurately glossed as 'several'. We noted earlier the analogy to English verbs like *scatter*. Thus so-called 'plural' verbs may require multiple participants, and do not show a strict singular–plural contrast as may be found with nominal number. In some cases it is claimed that there is a distinction between a form for one or two versus a form for more than two, a distinction which is restricted in nominal number (see §8.2.2; the analysis of Chamorro in Durie 1986: 364–5; Anderson 1992: 127–8; and the discussion of constructed number in §5.7).

The indeterminacy of the verbal number values is another helpful hint as to the nature of verbal number. It makes good sense that the number of participants appropriate for using the 'plural' form would differ from verb to verb. This suggests it is part of the lexical meaning of the verb. Thus the relation of the verb to its subject or object with respect to verbal number is one of semantic compatibility (and not agreement), as noted in §8.2.2. Hence asking which values of verbal number there are is not a straightforward question; we are really asking which number-like properties can be relevant to the semantics of verbs, and we see that sometimes quantifiers such as 'many' provide a better comparison than the values of nominal number. Though the distinctions of verbal number do not closely match those of nominal number, there is a clear asymmetry; we find more distinctions made in nominal number systems than in verbal number systems.

8.3 Locus

We should ask where nominal and verbal number are expressed. We might reasonably expect that nominal number would be expressed on an element of the noun phrase, typically the noun, while verbal number would be expressed on the verb. Thus in English we have *cat* ~ *cats* (nominal number expressed on the noun) and in Rapanui we noted *ruku* ~ *ruku ruku* 'dive' ~ 'go diving' (verbal number expressed on the verb by reduplication). However, this is not the only possibility. We saw in §6.1.1 that nominal number may indeed be marked on the noun phrase, but that it may also be marked on the noun phrase and on the verb by agreement (in languages like Russian) or it may be marked primarily on the verb (as in Amele). This gives us the range of possibilities for expressing number shown in table 8.3.

Table 8.3 *Place where number is primarily expressed*

		nominal number	verbal number
A	on noun phrase	Lezgian	NOT FOUND
B	on both	Russian	NOT FOUND
C	on verb	Amele	Georgian

When we turn to verbal number, in all the examples we have considered, verbal number is expressed on the verb: I have been unable to find examples of verbal number being expressed on the noun phrase (a claim made independently by Gil 1993: 281). An example would be a language in which one could say something like: *the children sneezed* meaning 'one child sneezed several times'. It is not immediately obvious, however, that the claim is correct. Dench (1995: 95–6) gave data from Martuthunira and claimed that a plural marker on a noun could be used to indicate that it underwent an action a number of times. However, this was discussed in §7.3.2, where it was argued that the examples involve intensificative use, and are not counterexamples to the regularity shown in table 8.3.

We should ask why there should be this asymmetry in the locus of nominal and verbal number marking. I suggest that number marking is found originally 'where it belongs'; that is, nominal number is marked on the noun phrase and verbal number on the verb. As is well known, a possible route for the development of verb agreement is from pronouns, which, being nominal, frequently mark nominal number. When these become attached to the verb, and develop into agreement markers, we find nominal number marked on the verb. Thus for nominal number there is a progression from type A in table 8.3 to type B. There are two plausible ways for type C marking of nominal number to develop. Either directly from type A, in languages where number is marked on pronouns but not on nouns and the number of noun phrases can be indicated by a 'pronominal copy'.[10] The pronominal copy could become affixed to the verb and give rise to an agreement system. Or else C might arise from B by attrition of number marking on the noun. However, there is no corresponding route for verbal number to become marked on the noun phrase. Verbal number starts as type C and has no means to move to any other type.

8.4 Diagnostics for verbal number

Since both nominal number and verbal number can appear on the verb, it may not be obvious which type of number is involved. This is particularly the case when verbal number is of the participant number type. There are some helpful diagnostics, which we shall discuss in turn (see Durie 1986: 357–62). While in many instances the difficulty is one that can be resolved by more careful analysis, sometimes the situation may be genuinely unclear, and verbal number may be able to develop towards nominal number (see §8.4.4). There is a further difficult distinction which need not detain us, namely that nominal number may in turn appear as agreement or as pronominal affixes; here our main purpose is to distinguish verbal number from nominal number of whatever sort.

8.4.1 Ergativity

Agreement in number may be controlled by the subject, or by subject and object, or it may operate on an ergative basis, that is, it may be controlled by the absolutive

---

[10] Such languages distinguish *man he came* (the man came) from *man they came* (the men came).

noun phrase (equivalent to the subject of an intransitive and the object of a transitive). Verbal number operates on an ergative basis: if the number of participants is relevant it will be that of the most directly affected argument of the verb (the absolutive). Thus in English the difference between the intransitives *run* and *stampede* involves among other things the number of subject participants, while that between the transitives *kill* and *massacre* concerns the number of object participants.[11]

We regularly find verbal number operating on an ergative basis, while in the same language nominal number marked on the verb operates on a different basis. A clear example is Huichol, from which we took an earlier example (Comrie 1982: 99):

(17) (nee) ne-nua
      1.SG 1.SG-arrive.SG
      'I arrived'

(18) tiiri   yihuuta-ti   me-niuʔaziani
      children two-SUBJ   3.PL-arrive.PL
      'two children arrived'

In these examples there is a prefix marking nominal number (*ne-/me-*) but the verb stem is also different. Just from this evidence we could not tell whether this latter change was an instance of verbal number or not. However, according to Comrie (1982: 114): 'Verb stem alternation in Huichol is controlled by the number of the entity most directly affected by the situation described by the verb. With transitive verbs, this is the patient; with intransitive verbs, this is the single argument thereof, irrespective of the extent to which this has agent or patient properties.' This is demonstrated by the following examples (1982: 112):

(19) wan   maria maa-ti   me-neci-mieni
      Juan Maria and-SUBJ 3.PL.SUBJ-1.SG.OBJ-kill.SG
      'Juan and Maria are killing me'

(20) nee   wan   maria maa-me
      1.SG Juan Maria and-NON.SUBJ

      ne-wa-qiini
      1.SG.SUBJ-3.PL.OBJ-kill.PL

      'I am killing Juan and Maria'

---

[11] One exception is Ainu, where verbal number may be sensitive not only to the number of a plural object but also to that of a plural subject (Shibatani 1990: 50–4).

Here it is clear that the pronominal affixes on the verb are according to subject and object, but the stem of the verb depends on participant number, that of the object of the transitive verb. (Another example is Kiwai, Foley 1986: 128–31.) Thus verbal number of the participant type depends on the entity most directly affected (the absolutive), which may contrast with other marking on the verb.

8.4.2 Marking of different values

A particularly graphic illustration is provided by the South Caucasian language Georgian (Aronson 1982: 243, 406–7, quoted in Durie 1986):

(21) ivane še-mo-vid-a   da   da-ǰd-a
      John   PRV-PRV-enter-AOR.3.SG   and   PRV-sit.SG-AOR.3.SG
      'John entered and sat down'

(22) čem-i   mšobl-eb-i   še-mo-vid-nen
      my-AG[12] parent-PL-NOM   PRV-PRV-enter-AOR.3.PL

      da   da-sxd-nen
      and   PRV-sit.PL-AOR.3.PL
      'my parents entered and sat down'

The verb 'sit' has different forms according to whether one person sits (*da-ǰd-*) as in (21), or more than one (*da-sxd-*) as in (22), unlike the verb 'enter'. But it also agrees in number with the subject (as does 'enter'). So are there any grounds for claiming that we have a case of verbal number? Could we not simply say that this is a complex type of agreement? We can isolate the difference by taking an example with a numeral phrase:

(23) čem-i   sam-i   megobar-i   še-mo-vid-a
      my-AG   three-AG   friend.SG-NOM   PRV-PRV-enter-AOR.3.SG

      da   da-sxd-a
      and   PRV-sit.PL-AOR.3.SG

      'My three friends entered and sat down'

Numerals require a singular noun (*megobari*) and numeral phrases control singular agreement (a phenomenon noted for other languages in §6.7.1). This singular agreement is found on both verbs. The second, which takes its form according to the number of participants, shows the plural verbal form *dasxd-*, since there is more than one participant in the action. Thus the same verb marks both verbal

---

[12] This agreement marker (AG) -*i* is syncretic, covering nominative singular and plural, and genitive singular and plural.

and nominal number but they have different values: a 'plural' verb occurs with singular agreement.[13]

A contrast in nominal and verbal number can also be found in Huichol (Comrie 1982: 112); nominal number is not distinguished on the verb for inanimates (only for animates is there a singular–plural distinction); however, for those verbs that have verbal number, if the main participant is plural, even if inanimate, the plural form of the verb can be used. Finally in the Salish language Moses-Columbian there are twenty or so verbs which exist in pairs to mark verbal number; these also allow the other regular forms of pluralization: 'A pluralized "singular" form refers to more than one entity acting or existing independently, not as a group; a pluralized "plural" form refers to more than one group' (Kinkade 1981: 263).

8.4.3 Differences in availability

We have already noted the differences in the values available for nominal and verbal number (§8.2.4). Different inventories of values for nominal and verbal number may be available in one and the same language, though as yet few examples have been identified. Durie (1986: 360) suggests that in Karok several verbs have singular–dual–plural for verbal number, while the nominal number system has only singular–plural. Another possible example, this time with more values in the nominal number system, as we would expect, is Kiwai, where verbal number distinguishes two forms, but the nominal number system (expressed on the verb) has singular, dual, trial, plural (Foley 1986: 129–30). Durie discusses two further differences in availability, which we will note here. There may be syntactic environments in which there is no agreement, for instance infinitives and imperatives; in the absence of agreement the verbal number distinction will be preserved. And similarly there may be morphological environments where derivation will not respect inflectional differences, but will maintain the difference of verbal number.

8.4.4 Possible development towards nominal number

Sometimes it is difficult to distinguish verbal number of the participant type from agreement in number, because information is scarce or a description may be poor

---

[13] Aronson (1982: 406–7) also gives examples of plural verbs, which are transitive, whose form depends on the number of the referent of the object (contrasting, for instance, 'breaking one thing' and 'breaking several things'. According to Aronson, notionally plural objects (even if grammatically singular because of the presence of a numeral) cooccur with these plural verbs. It is worth noting that ordinary ('nominal number') object agreement in Georgian is restricted to first and second person objects (1982: 169), which again shows that verbal number is distinct. Furthermore, plural verbal number may be found for plural indirect objects; Aronson (1982: 407) gives the example of 'send something to people' rather than 'to someone'. For further discussion, and for the history of verbal number in Kartvelian languages, see Tuite (1992).

(when eliciting examples it is easy to confuse the two). There are also instances where there is better data and where it is still difficult to decide. Such instances appear to be close to the boundary. It might therefore be possible for verbal number to develop into nominal number. There are at least three factors which would make the change more likely: having many verbs which show verbal number, having ergative syntax (so that the argument with which the verb was semantically compatible in terms of number was also a possible agreement controller) and having obligatory use of the 'plural' form under some circumstances. There are languages which have some or all of these characteristics, and which may be moving towards having agreement.

A possible candidate is Gitksan, a Tsimshianic language closely related to Nisgha (earlier called Nass). It has under 500 speakers, in northern British Columbia, and most fluent speakers are over forty. The data are from Rigsby (1996 and personal communication). The first point is that a great majority of the verbs have singular and plural forms (distinguished by prefixation or reduplication), though some have only one form. Sometimes reduplication (but not prefixation) may mark plurality of events. The plural of event is restricted to transitive verbs and is probably not available for all of them. Usually, according to Rigsby, plural marking signals participant number. Gitksan has VSO word order and ergative syntax. Where there is a plural object Rigsby considers the use of the plural verb to be obligatory and regular, to the extent that he treats it as absolutive verb agreement. This would put Gitksan at an extreme of the typological space. The number forms are highly irregular in verbs (as in nouns) and give the appearance of a derivational category. On the other hand, if the verb regularly matches the number of the absolutive noun phrase this would suggest that number is an inflectional category. Gitksan has all three of the properties mentioned and so might be moving from verbal number to agreement in number.[14]

Situations which are similar at least in part can be found elsewhere. An interesting example is described by Langdon (1992): languages of the Yuman family of California and Arizona have verbal number, but in one group, the Pai group, verbal number must be marked when appropriate (rather than being optional as elsewhere in the family). In one member of this group, Hualapai (Walapai), there has been a further development: most nouns have plural forms (unlike in the other languages). Thus the verb and its argument may both mark matching number. However, most sentences do not contain a noun phrase, rather just a verb. Nevertheless, this is closer to agreement than in the other members of the Yuman family, although there is some way to go. Finally, Newman (1990: 56) gives data on

---

[14] For a proposed analysis of an individual marker moving from marking verbal number to nominal number in the development of Georgian see Tuite (1992).

Kanakuru; this language belongs to the Chadic family where there are many instances of verbal number. Kanakuru has only about seven verbs with singular/plural pairs; however, these verbs obligatorily match the patient in number, and to that extent the phenomenon looks like agreement. It will be interesting to see whether someone can find a secure case of the development of agreement from verbal number of the participant type, and document the stages of the development.

8.5 Items involved in the verbal number system

Of course, the main items involved in verbal number are verbs, as we have seen in our examples.[15] Verbal number can also be marked by lexical means, typically by adverbial expressions of the type *twice, many times, on several occasions*. We should also ask which particular verbs are involved, and contrast this with the range of nominals affected by number. The latter varies greatly, as we saw in chapter 3. At one extreme are languages in which nouns typically do not mark number, like Warrgamay, and at the other end of the scale we have those like Central Alaskan Yup'ik in which almost all nouns can mark number. We saw that the patterning of nominals which distinguish number is to be understood in terms of the Animacy Hierarchy.

Verbal number differs in two main ways. First, we typically find that relatively few verbs show verbal number distinctions. A helpful view of the range of verbal number can be gained from Oron and Ibibio, both belonging to the Central Branch of the Cross River languages (within Niger-Congo) and spoken in Calabar Province, Nigeria. For Oron, Simmons (1956: 251) recorded 544 verbal roots, and of them just 10 show verbal number (the verbs for 'buy', 'cut', 'die', 'fill', 'hatch', 'hide', 'put on', 'shoot', 'take' and 'take out'). In most cases the two forms share an initial consonant. In the case of Ibibio, Simmons (1957: 2) identified 577 verb roots, of which 24 differentiate singular and plural forms. Kinkade (1981) investigated Salish languages and found twenty or so in Moses-Columbian, a few more in Coeur d'Alene, rather fewer in other Salish languages. Hale, Jeanne and Pranka (1991: 270) give slightly more for Hopi. Occasionally, however, a higher proportion is found: for the Nakh-Daghestanian language Hunzib, van den Berg (1995: 81–3) states that some 40 per cent of verbs can mark plurality, by suffix or infix: it

---

[15] It may be that clear instances of verbal number can be found on adjectives; first it must be shown that the 'adjectives' are distinct from verbs in the particular language, and then that they do indeed show verbal number. Possible cases are found in Cushitic languages, for which see Banti (1988: 212–13, 230, 235–6) and references there. Banti notes several examples of plurality being marked by reduplication in 'adjectival words' (a wider class than prototypical adjectives), and suggests that: 'reduplication in adjectival words, as a marker of the plural, but often also of the elative or other functions, always implies similar kinds of reduplication in true verbs' (1988: 240).

appears that usually it is for participant number, but sometimes also for event number.

Second, the question of the specific verbs involved is much less clear than for nominal number. Some generalizations may be made: the verbs typically denote situations where the nature of the event or state is substantially affected by the number of participants immediately involved. Many are intransitive verbs of position such as 'sit', 'stand' or 'lie', or of motion such as 'go', 'walk', 'run' or 'fly', or transitives that indicate causation of motion, such as 'take', 'pick up', 'carry', and 'throw'. (See Booker 1982 and Mithun 1988a on North America, Newman 1990 on Chadic, Durie 1986 generally.) Booker's (1982) analysis of languages of North America suggests that if any verbs show verbal number they will be verbs of motion and position/location, and that it will not be found with transitives unless it is also found with intransitives.[16]

There is an additional, less obvious difference, which concerns further distinctions beyond the initial number distinction. In nominal number, if there is, say, a dual as well as a singular–plural distinction, then in many languages the split follows that of the plural. That is, nouns which have a plural also have a dual. (There are several types of possible exception, however, as discussed in §4.1 and §4.2.) Verbal number is rather different. According to Booker (1982: 24–5), in North America there is never a three-way distinction without an accompanying two-way distinction; if some verbs show a three-way distinction, there will always be others which have a two-way distinction. In this respect nominal and verbal number are quite different.

8.6 Expression of verbal number

The morphological means used to mark nominal number are extensive indeed, as we saw in chapter 5. Nominal number may be marked by inflection, by stem alternation and by inflectional marking together, or by stem alternation without inflection for number. Within stem alternation there are various means from stress placement, through various segmental relations to the end point of suppletion. Turning to the means for marking verbal number cross-linguistically, we find stem modification (frequently reduplication) used commonly, sometimes with a high degree of complexity, as for instance, in Yuman languages (Langdon 1992), and also numerous instances of quite separate verbs being used. In the latter case the relation between the forms is often said to be one of suppletion (as though the opposition were similar to English *go* ~ *went*), but this usage is misleading. We are not dealing with suppletion here.[17] Rather we have two different verbs. An English

---

[16] Booker considered only cases where the two verb forms were not phonologically related.

[17] See Mel'čuk (1994: 383–7, 403–4); informally, suppletion is the equivalent of job-sharing: there is a defined job to be done, usually it is done by an individual, sometimes it is shared,

analogy would be *kill* versus *massacre*. The problem is that since nominal number is widespread as an inflectional category (often in languages which also have verbal number) and we are used to paradigms constructed on that basis, then sometimes this view is imposed on verbal number forms, which are not inflectionally related.[18]

Table 8.4 *Examples of verbal number in Tonkawa*

'singular'	gloss	'plural'	gloss
ha-idjona-	one person goes up	da-idjona-	several persons go up
ha-glana-	one person goes down	da-glana-	several persons go down
ha-ixena-	one person goes across	da-ixena-	several persons go across

When the two verbal number forms are related in form, then we have a derivational relationship. There can be varying degrees of productivity. Thus in Tonkawa (Hoijer 1933–38: 56–7) there are several 'plural' verbs of the type in table 8.4. Hoijer notes that these verbs are formed with the elements *ha-* and *da-*, which originated in the verbs *ha·na-* 'one person goes off' and *dana-* 'two or more persons go off'. While here there is a marker for both forms, often there is an additional marker just for the plural (see the Kiwai examples in table 8.2). But sometimes, as with nominal number, the 'singular' in verbal number may contain more phonological material than the 'plural' (cf. §5.3.3). For instance, in Alabama, we find *batat-li* 'hit once'; but *bat-li* 'hit repeatedly'; this is cited by Anderson (1992: 65–6), along with examples from other Muskogean languages: Choctaw and Koasati.[19]

The comparison between nominal and verbal number is again partly misleading: for nominal number we may find all the inflectional means for building paradigms (though also we may find limited means in given languages); for verbal number we find the possibility of quite separate lexical items being used, and the morphological resources of derivational morphology. Once that important distinction is

---

in which latter case we have suppletion. So an English verb has to occur in present and past contexts (*help* ~ *helped, laugh* ~ *laughed* and so on) and the verb *go* does so with unrelated forms (*go* ~ *went*). But either way, the same job is done. The nature of the 'job' here is defined in terms of the many regular verbs. With verbal number we have 'additional staff' available, who do more than the usual job. Thus the relation of *kill* and *massacre* (where *massacre* requires multiple objects) is one where there is an additional semantic distinction, not available for other verbs (typically the majority).

[18] As an analogy, Hungarian has nouns for 'cow', 'bull', 'man', 'woman' and so on, but this does not mean that they are grammatically opposed and that Hungarian has the category of gender.

[19] For the importance of these examples see Martin (1988). Other examples are found in Cushitic, for instance in Dullay (Amborn, Minker and Sasse 1980: 117); see also their note 4 for the term 'singularitive', due to Paul Black, for a 'singular' verbal number form with additional morphological material (similar to the 'singulative' in nominal number).

259

made, then the basic point still holds, namely that there are more extensive means available for expressing nominal number than verbal number.

8.7 Other uses

In chapter 7 we saw frequent use of nominal number for other purposes. This seems to be rare for verbal number. It may just be that since verbal number itself has had less attention the other uses have not been reported. More likely, perhaps, is that because the number of verbs involved in verbal number is typically rather limited, the use of such forms for other purposes is not a promising strategy. There is one good example, however. In Ainu the forms showing verbal plurality may be used as honorifics (Shibatani 1990: 54–5). This example is from Refsing (1986: 151):

(24) Iarmoysam   un   nispa   sinewpa kusu   arki...
      next.village from   gentleman   visit.PL in.order.to come.PL
      'the gentleman from the next village has come to visit...'

Both verbs show verbal number; the singulars would be *sinewe* 'visit' and *ek* 'come', and the use of the plural (verbal number) form indicates respect for the gentleman.[20]

There is a second other use for verbal number, which is related to classification. We looked briefly at classificatory verbs above (§8.2.2); certain languages of North America have classificatory verbs, which distinguish the way in which flexible objects and liquids move, and how people handle them. The language which interests us here, however, namely Creek (formerly called Muskogee), uses verbal number in a similar way. In this language, when cloth-like objects are involved, we find the 'dual' form of verbal number (for those few cases where there are three verbal forms, otherwise the 'plural' is found), and with liquids the plural is normal (Haas 1948: 246):

(25) islá·fkan   awéykeys
      knife   1.SG.threw.away.SG
      'I threw away the knife'

(26) islá·fkan   akáhyeys
      knife   1.SG.threw.away.DUAL
      'I threw away (two) knives'

(27) nú·ckan   akáhyeys
      handkerchief   1.SG.threw.away.DUAL
      'I threw away the handkerchief'

---

[20] Another language which uses verbal number for honorific purposes is Central Pomo (Marianne Mithun, personal communication).

Since handkerchief is cloth-like, the verb is of the type to appear with dual objects.

(28) islá·fkan   apaláhteys
     knife   1.SG.threw.away.PL
     'I threw away (three or more) knives

(29) wa·kapisí·n   apaláhteys
     milk   1.SG.threw.away.PL
     'I poured out the milk'

With liquids (29) the verb form is as for plural objects (28). For comparable phenomena see Watkins (1976: 23–4) on Choctaw, Kimball (1991: 450–60) on Koasati, and Kimball (1991: 460n4) for sources on the situation in other Muskogean languages.

8.8   Motivation for the asymmetries

We have noted four main types of asymmetry between verbal and nominal number: in values (§8.2.4), locus (§8.3), range of items involved (§8.5) and means of expression (§8.6). In each case nominal number has more extensive possibilities than verbal number. How are we to account for these asymmetries?

Let us start with values; as we saw in §8.2.4 nominal number systems may have up to five values, while verbal number rarely exceeds two. We might look to paths of grammaticalization as the motivation here. There is a way for numerals to attach to pronouns, giving rise to the multi-valued number systems found in Austronesian languages (§2.2.5). If there were no potential route which could give rise to multiple values for verbal number we would have explained this asymmetry. Consider, however, the situation in Mayali (a Gunwinjguan language of Western Arnhem Land, Australia). Evans (1995: 227) quotes examples like the following:

(30) bamurru   ga-mirnde-rri
     magpie.goose   3.NON.PAST-many-stand
     'there are many magpie geese, there are magpie geese all over the
     place'

Mirnde- 'many' is an optional prefix which stands after the obligatory prefixes and before the root. Here it suggests geese stretching out in all directions; if instead *djangged-* 'bunch' were used, this would suggest a flock tightly bunched together, while *gaberrk-* 'mob' would imply they were together, but not necessarily crowded. Note that these prefixes imply the number of geese: there is nothing in the noun morphology to do so. Interestingly too, these quantifiers typically have absolute

261

scope, that is they quantify the subject of intransitive verbs and the object of transitives, just as is normal with verbal number. These prefixes provide a type of verbal number; however, they are not straightforward quantifiers. The three quoted all give information about spatial disposition as well as about quantity. Nevertheless, we are very close to verbal number. It is particularly interesting, then, that Evans (1995: 259–63) gives suggestions as to the origins of various quantificational prefixes. While necessarily tentative, they are that these prefixes originate from noun incorporation, adverb incorporation and gerundive incorporation. Incorporation is widespread (it is also very productive in Mayali) and so it seems a specially plausible source for verbal number forms. This origin would allow several values for verbal number. It seems, therefore, that the fact that we rarely find more than a binary division is not a restriction imposed by the paths of grammaticalization.

Before leaving grammaticalization as a potential motivation, we should consider whether this would be an explanation for the asymmetry in the range of items involved (§8.5). Here we should consider a detailed hypothesis about the rise of verbal number in the South-Central Dravidian languages, due to Steever (1987). He sees its origin in echo compounds, that is, compounds formed by reduplication with one syllable replaced by a specific echo syllable (like Yiddish English *fancy schmancy*). These forms are found elsewhere in Dravidian, thus Tamil *viyāparam* 'business', *viyāparam kiyāparam* 'business and the like' (where the echo syllable is *ki-*). Compound verbs could be created by the same means, and Steever claims that such forms were subsequently reduced in the development of verbal number. Thus he suggests that modern Kūi *ṛūs-k-a* 'stroke repeatedly' (the ordinary verb base is /ṛūsi-/ 'stroke') is derived historically from the postulated echo compound /ṛūsi kī-si-pa/ (where *kī* is again the echo syllable, *-si-* is the unaltered part of the reduplication and *-pa* is the infinitive suffix). With this type of development, there is no structural reason why verbal number should not be widespread within the verbal lexicon. Given Steever's study, it appears that where we find that verbal number is restricted in the range of verbs for which it is available, we should not attribute that to a restriction imposed by possible grammaticalization paths.

There is, however, an asymmetry where the paths of grammaticalization provide a plausible motivation. When we discussed the asymmetry of locus (nominal number may be expressed on nouns and verbs, but verbal number is expressed on verbs but not nouns; §8.3), we noted that nominal categories can come to be expressed on verbs by agreement, but there is no similar route for verbal number to attach to nouns. Thus grammaticalization may well be the motivation here.

For the remaining problems, it is tempting to suggest that the explanation for the asymmetries we have observed is that nominal number is inflectional and verbal number derivational (cf. §3.4 note 14). That would be insufficient: first, as is well known, the inflectional–derivational boundary is problematic; second, nominal number can arguably be derivational; and third, we would still need a reason for the proposed division between the two types of number. We therefore propose two related reasons for the remaining asymmetries.

The first can be traced to Bybee, who introduces the notion of 'relevance', which will be helpful here: 'A meaning element is *relevant* to another meaning element *if the semantic content of the first directly affects or modifies the semantic content of the second*' (Bybee 1985b: 13). She points out (1985b: 23) that the number of participants in a situation can have a profound effect on that situation, as in situations where *stampede* is appropriate rather than the simple verb *run*. The number of participants is relevant for such examples. However, this is not generally the case with verbs. For many verbs, the number of participants has only a marginal effect on their meaning: we would not expect to find a 'plural' verb for *breathe* or *compute*; hence verbal number is restricted to being expressed in just part of the verb inventory, and does not achieve 'lexical generality' (see also Bybee 1985a: 34–9; 1985b: 16–17, 102–5; and Mithun 1988a: 231–2). While number may be equally applicable to a substantial proportion of the entities denoted by the noun inventory, its relevance to events varies greatly from one type to another, as we have just seen, and so it tends to be limited to relatively small parts of the verb inventory. This is a potential explanation for the asymmetry in terms of range of items involved (§8.5).

The second reason follows from the first. If there are many nouns with number oppositions, this provides system pressure against lexicalization of the number opposition. Nouns whose plural and singular are not straightforward pairs can be maintained as lexical items by the pressure of the majority of regular pairings. This pressure helps to explain the variety of expression of nominal marking as compared to verbal number, the asymmetry of means of expression (§8.6).

How then are we to account for the asymmetry in values (§8.2.4)? Again the explanation is more likely to be relevance: as suggested earlier, there are few verbs for which the number of participants directly affects the semantics of the verb. We should not, however, be fully satisfied with 'relevance' as an explanation. It is still rather vague, and runs the risk of being circular; we may say that particular verbs in a given language come in pairs, according to verbal number, because number is 'relevant'. The problem is to demonstrate the relevance, apart from the existence of verbal number.

The evidence we have considered suggests four asymmetries pointing in the same direction, with nominal number showing greater possibilities in terms of values, locus, range of items involved and means of morphological expression. Three explanations were offered, namely, paths of grammaticalization, relevance and system pressure, which are separate factors pushing in the same direction rather than a single motivation.

8.9 Conclusion

Verbal number is a widespread phenomenon. Unfortunately the lack of agreed terms has led some to consider it as being geographically restricted, whereas similar systems are found widely distributed, though referred to by different names. Sometimes it is hard to distinguish it from nominal number, particularly when verbal number of the participant type is well developed in a language; here careful analysis and careful use of terms are both important. And this is also a general methodological conclusion, namely that care over the use of terms, through careful selection and consistent use, is more necessary than ever. For instance, the misuse of the term 'suppletion' has led to verbal number being treated as nominal number in some instances. For typologists, it is equally important to compare like with like and to separate unlike from unlike.

9

Conclusion and new challenges

We will review briefly the route we have taken, and then draw out some threads which have run through the book, mainly in order to consider future prospects. We started by identifying all the number values we could find, whichever type of nominal showed them (chapter 2). Then we kept the values still and looked at the different types of nominal involved in the simplest singular–plural systems. We established that their distributions were constrained by the Animacy Hierarchy (chapter 3). Next we put the possible systems of number values together with the hierarchy and found that this typology covered a great deal of the data and the variation, but had to be elaborated to account for phenomena such as conflated number (chapter 4). Then we turned to the means of expression of number, and again found great diversity (chapter 5). The initially daunting difficulties of agreement in number were made manageable, once we drew a clear distinction between controller and target number (chapter 6). In chapter 7 we examined the 'other' uses of number, which are many and varied, and found that they too begin to fit into a typology. And then in chapter 8 we turned to verbal number, showing how different it is from nominal number and examining why.

While we have been able to make considerable progress, it is clear that there are many aspects still to be better understood. In this concluding chapter we consider how number systems change over time (§9.1), a topic we have already referred to several times. Then we look at the interactions of number with other categories (§9.2), which has also surfaced at intervals. Next we turn from the systems and patterns of number to the way in which they are used (§9.3), in particular to the statistical distribution of number values. A logical next question is how speakers acquire the system (§9.4). And then we review some of the ways in which psycholinguists are attempting to understand number (§9.5).

9.1 Diachrony

We have noted several instances of the historical development of number systems, though the main emphasis of the book has been on synchrony. That was for good reason, since previously there was a good deal of material on number, but little which systematically investigated the range of possible systems. Here we consider work on diachrony: first the ways in which number systems develop and grow (§9.1.1) and then the ways in which they decline, often leaving considerable 'fall-out' as a result of their partial loss (§9.1.2).

9.1.1 The rise of number

Our typology suggests a coherent picture of how number systems may arise. However, though there are some significant studies, relatively little detailed work has been done on the rise of number systems, and there are no doubt some surprises in store. For most current number systems we have no sure information on their source. In chapter 5 we saw the wealth of means by which languages mark number, from number words to inflectional affixes and stem alternations. The prediction from work on grammaticalization is that the earlier stage is the one where we find independent words, which over time are likely to be reduced phonetically and semantically. Thus number words are the expected source of number systems; as an example, the rise of the number word *ol* in Tok Pisin (from English *all*) is described in Aitchison (1990); see Mühlhäusler (1981) for more detail. We can push the question back further, and ask where number words come from. Here we find a variety of sources, including nouns denoting collectives (Bisang 1996: 547–8, Luutonen 1999), pronouns (Dryer 1989: 875–6), and demonstratives (for various sources of number markers see Frajzyngier 1997: 193–4 and references there).[1] And within an already existing number system, as we saw in §4.4.1, distributives may develop into plurals, as may collectives (§4.4.2). Once there is a number word or set of number words, this may develop into bound morphology; and eventually into systems of great complexity, as we saw in chapter 5. And number-differentiating pronouns may become attached to verbs, giving number-differentiated affixes: for examples of this development in various languages of North America see Mithun (1991).

Suppose a language develops several number markers. A possible scenario is for them to be differentiated according to animacy (distinguishing 'a number of humans' from 'a number of animals' for instance); their use in such instances is

---

[1] The development of number as an instance of grammaticalization is discussed by Lehmann (1995: 56–9). The development of number marking in Uralic has been investigated by Ravila (1941) and Honti (1997), and in part of the family by Luutonen (1999). In particular, Luutonen (1997) investigates Mari, where the development of number marking has led to remarkable possibilities of alternative ordering of markers (number–possessive and possessive–number), such that both the following may be found (Luutonen 1997: 13):

(i) joltaš-em-βlak	(ii) joltaš-βlak-em
friend-1.SG.POSS-PL	friend-PL-1.SG.POSS
'my friends'	'my friends'

The development of a plural marker from a marker for unidentified participants in various languages of North America is traced by Mithun (1993).

determined by the Animacy Hierarchy, and can in time give rise to inflections similarly distributed in accord with the hierarchy, as we find in several languages (§3.5).[2] In any case, the pattern of systems in existing languages gives a clear prediction as to which nominals will be involved: number systems will develop at the top of the Animacy Hierarchy, and spread down to varying degrees (§3.2);[3] see Shields (1991–92) for discussion of Indo-European in this regard. The patterns of number which we investigated in chapter 2 also provide predictions for diachrony. We saw that it is common for languages to have an opposition between general/singular and plural (§2.1). That is, the plural is used to indicate 'more than one', but the general/singular form (typically with no marker of number) is not specific as to number. We would predict that systems could develop from this optional use of number to the obligatory use, as in the English type of singular–plural opposition.[4] This is not to claim that all languages will end up with the same system; rather that the development in terms of the systems in §2.1 is likely to be from the 'general/singular versus plural' type to the 'singular versus plural' type.[5] The latter system may decline owing to the attrition of markers, which could lead back to the beginning of the cycle.

So far we have considered the basic singular–plural opposition. Where do further number values come from? The clearest evidence here comes from Austronesian languages. In §2.2.4 we saw clear evidence that the dual, trial and paucal of various Austronesian languages can be traced back to the numbers for 'two', 'three', and either 'three' or 'four' for the paucal, depending on the system in which it is found (see particularly table 2.3). We see something similar in the use of the numeral 'two' to renew the dual in Slovene, and in Breton (§2.2.7). Breton has a

---

[2] As a first stage in this development, the Arauan language Madija of Peru and Brazil has a number word *deni*, which occurs only in noun phrases denoting humans (Liclan and Marlett 1990: 107–9).

[3] In the case of verbal number, the verbs likely to be affected are in part predictable too (§8.5). The rise of verbal number was discussed in §8.8. For a surprising instance of the development of a plural auxiliary in Javanese, see Katrina Hayward (1998). The possible development from verbal number towards nominal number was considered in §8.4.4.

[4] Smirnova (1981: 83) suggests that in some Iranian languages an unmarked vs. plural system (in terms of number marking) may develop singular markers, to give a singular–unmarked–plural system (in which the unmarked form is used for general number). She states that Kurdish has almost reached this point.

[5] Various complicating factors may intervene. There has been a good deal of research on the complex development of number marking in African-American Vernacular English and on a range of creoles: see for instance Poplack and Tagliamonte (1989, 1994) and Bailey, Maynor and Cukor-Avila (1989); Tagliamonte, Poplack and Eze (1997) discuss Nigerian Pidgin English, while Singler (1991) is an investigation into Liberian English; on Sea Island Creole (Gullah) see Rickford (1986, 1990) and Mufwene (1986); for Papiamentu see DeBose (1974) and Dijkhoff (1983). A good entry point into this literature is Poplack, Tagliamonte and Eze (1999).

new dual, based on the numeral *daou* 'two'. It is still a minor dual but is obligatory with the few nouns which have it; when emphasis on two referents is required the numeral is used in addition (Ternes 1992: 416–17).

9.1.2 The decline of number

We have seen various pieces of evidence showing the decline of number systems in various languages, and again our typology helps understand what is going on. Change will be from one possible system of number values to another, as defined in §2.3.2. A language with singular–dual–trial–plural may lose the trial (since singular–dual–plural is a possible system) but it may not lose the dual, unless it first loses the trial. Once again Austronesian languages provide helpful evidence. We noted in §2.2.3, §2.2.4 and §2.2.5 that forms based on the numeral 'three' or 'four' frequently have a paucal meaning; we also saw how the paucal can come to be used for fairly large numbers, when a group is contrasted with an even larger one (§2.2.4). Then there was the puzzle of the plural form in various languages being a development of a form with a 'three' or 'four' in it (Capell 1971: 260–2; Lynch 1977, 1986; Ross 1988: 101; Laidig and Laidig 1990). The picture becomes clear if we look again at Mokilese (§2.2.6). Mokilese has a greater plural in the personal pronouns (Harrison 1976 calls it the 'remote plural') (see table 9.1).

Table 9.1 *Mokilese personal pronouns (Harrison 1976: 88)*

	singular	dual	plural	greater plural (remote plural)
1st person: exclusive	ngoah, ngoahi	kama	kamai	kimi
inclusive	—	kisa	kisai	kihs
2nd person	koah, koawoa	kamwa	kamwai	kimwi
3rd person	ih	ara, ira	arai, irai	ih

The plural was once a trial, and the old plural survives as the greater ('remote') plural (Sheldon Harrison, personal communication). The remote plural forms are little used, being reserved for large groups of people, typically not present at the conversation. One can see the likely development. The original trial develops into a paucal, as has happened in numerous related languages. The drift from trial to paucal is easy to understand, since they occur in similar configurations (§2.3.2). The paucal is used for small numbers, but then for larger ones when there is some sort of comparison (those in our village versus those outside, for instance). As the quantity it may refer to increases, so it is used more frequently, gradually squeezing out the old plural. Mokilese is particularly significant, because the old plural is hanging on, with a greatly reduced role. In related languages where we see only a plural based historically on a form with a numeral in it, the development has gone a stage further, so that the original plural is lost.[6]

Another development, which is comparable in some respects, is found in Icelandic. The plural pronouns took on honorific use, and the old dual pronouns became plural (Guðmundsson 1972). Here again the original plural pronouns move out of the number system as it were, and the system of number values is reduced. A similar change occurred in Cassubian (Stone 1993b: 775–6).

There is a substantial body of work on instances of the loss of the dual.[7] We have noted some of the possible consequences. In varieties of Arabic, some nouns preserve the old dual form and lose the plural form (those nouns which were more often used in the dual). This is no longer a true dual, opposed to singular and plural, and so it is sometimes called the 'pseudo-dual' (§4.2.1 note 9). In some languages the dual is almost lost, but just a few lexical items retain a three-way opposition, giving a minor dual (as with Hebrew §4.2.1 and Maltese §4.2.2).

The loss of a number value may leave complications in morphology, as just discussed, and in syntax, as we noted in §6.7.1, where we discussed examples from Celtic and Slavonic. Let us consider Slavonic a little further. The majority of Slavonic languages have lost the dual number, but it has left curious traces. Typically the effect is found in constructions involving the numerals 'two', 'three' and 'four' (also the word for 'both'). In such constructions, there are morphological effects with a few nouns in some languages, and more extensive syntactic effects in several languages. However, the special forms have lost their semantic significance; they occur only with the numerals which determine them. We are therefore not dealing with a minor number. For the morphological effects let us consider Russian. Here phrases consisting of a numeral 'two', 'three' or 'four' plus a noun (when the phrase occupies a position demanding the nominative case) require the noun to stand in the genitive singular. The link to the loss of the dual is that for some types of noun the dual and the genitive singular were identical, hence the apparent genitive forms trace back to duals. Just a few nouns have a special form, differentiated by stress from the ordinary genitive singular. For instance, we find

---

[6] More straightforward simplification of an original singular–dual–paucal–plural is seen in some Lower Sepik languages (Foley 1986: 219–29).

[7] The dual and its loss in Semitic is detailed in Fontinoy (1969), its situation and decline in Greek is discussed in Cuny (1906), Bolling (1933) and Sobolevskij (1960); its loss in Iranian languages is documented in Molčanova (1975). There is a substantial literature on the Slavonic dual and its loss: Belić (1932), Isačenko (1941/1976), Dostál (1954), Iordanskij (1960), Moszyński (1985), Remneva and Kijanova (1991), Janda (1996: 175–202; 1998) and Žolobov (1998). Though lost in almost all the contemporary languages (leaving traces in morphology and syntax, see §6.7.1 and Naylor 1972), the dual is preserved in Slovene and Sorbian; see discussion in Tesnière (1925a, 1925b), Lötzsch (1965), Ermakova (1966), Jenč (1966), Lenček (1982), Derganc (1988, 1994); the current situation in Sorbian is summarized in Stone (1993a: 614).

dva časá 'two hours, two o'clock', while the normal genitive singular of *čás* is *čása*. The only other nouns involved are *rjad* 'row', *šar* 'sphere', *šag* 'step'. The important point is that the special forms like *časá* can only be used with the numeral: they have no independent semantic value.

There are also some interesting agreement effects. For these we will consider the Serbo-Croat and concentrate on masculine nouns, the most interesting in this regard. As in Russian, in phrases with the numerals 'two', 'three' and 'four', masculine nouns require a special form, a survival of the dual number which is synchronically a genitive singular. It is variously called the 'count form', 'dual' and 'paucal'; we shall use the term 'count form' to make clear that it is not an additional number value. Moreover, attributive modifiers must take the ending -*a*; for some (such as *ovaj* 'this', in (2) below) this form is not the same as the genitive (which would be *ovog*), and it has been argued that it should be analysed synchronically as a neuter plural (Corbett 1983: 13–14, 89–92):

(1) dva   dobr-a   čovek-a
     two   good-COUNT   man-GEN.SG (= COUNT)
     'two good men'

No matter how this form *dobr-a* is analysed, it is an unexpected one, resulting from the presence of the numeral. This time the unusual effect is a syntactic one, and the number of nouns involved (all the masculine nouns) is substantial. In the predicate the count form is found, but so too is the masculine plural form:

(2) ov-a   dva   čovek-a   su
     this-COUNT   two   man-GEN.SG   be.3.PL

     dobra / dobri
     good.COUNT / good.MASC.PL

     'these two men are good'

The count form *dobr-a* represents syntactic agreement. The masculine plural *dobr-i* (which is the same as would be found with an ordinary masculine plural noun with no overt quantifier) represents semantic agreement. The relative pronoun is also found in both forms:

(3) dva   čovek-a   koj-a / koj-i . . .
     two   man-GEN.SG   who-COUNT / who-MASC.PL
     'two men who . . .'

The personal pronoun must take the masculine plural form *oni* (*ona is unacceptable). Thus we have syntactic agreement in attributive position, both types of agreement of the predicate and relative pronoun and only semantic agreement of the personal pronoun. This unexpected agreement form, in competition with the masculine plural, is thus distributed in accordance with the constraint of the Agreement Hierarchy (§6.2). We can go further, in that there are figures for the relative frequency of the two forms in the positions where there is an option. These are derived from Sand (1971: 55–6, 63) and presented in table 9.2. The table shows a monotonic increase in the likelihood of agreement forms with greater semantic justification. Thus the agreements found with this remnant 'count' form are fully in line with the constraints of the Agreement Hierarchy.

Table 9.2 *Percentage distribution of count and plural forms in Serbo-Croat*

	attributive	predicate	relative pronoun	personal pronoun
percentage showing plural (semantic) agreement	0	18 (N = 376)	62 (N = 32)	100

We have considered the particular types of decline of number systems. Over and above these there is the general process of attrition of morphological systems. Even as markers are being lost, however, number distinctions may be maintained through an interplay of different factors, as Poplack shows in her study of Puerto Rican Spanish (1980, 1981). The outlines of how number systems rise and decline are clear, but the details leave much to be found out.

9.2 Interactions

As we gain a clearer understanding of the grammatical categories, like number and case, and of the ways in which they rise and decline, it is natural to investigate the interactions between these categories. There is an interesting tradition of such work: Greenberg (1963) includes important observations, and Aikhenvald and Dixon (1998) is a recent contribution. When looking at interactions, there are several points to bear in mind. First there is the directionality of the relation: number typically determines gender but may be determined by case. Second, while investigators who look at number normally consider the singular–plural opposition, we should of course look at more extended systems. Third, it is important too to keep apart systematic correspondences running right through the system in a particular language from, for example, minor syncretisms affecting only a small part of it. And finally, when discussing interactions involving number we should be clear whether we are referring to controller number or target number (§6.1).

9.2.1   Gender

The category with which number has closest relations is gender,[8] and it is typically gender which is dependent on number. Greenberg (1963) suggests the following universal (number 37): 'A language never has more gender categories in nonsingular numbers than in the singular.' To see what Greenberg is claiming, consider the Russian data in table 9.3. Russian verbs in the past tense and all adjectives distin-

Table 9.3   *Forms of Russian* byl '*was*'

	singular	plural
masculine	byl	
feminine	byl-a	byl-i
neuter	byl-o	

guish three genders in the singular, but do not distinguish gender in the plural. We do not expect to find a language which is the opposite, with no genders in the singular and three in the plural. There are languages with three genders in singular and plural (like Slovene), and with three in the singular and two in the plural (like Tamil). These are the relations covered by the universal. Note that we are dealing with target genders and numbers, that is, the gender and number distinctions of agreeing elements (Corbett 1991: 154–7). This is one of Greenberg's universals which has best stood the test of time. Even so, there are languages which appear to be counter-examples, in particular the Northern Khoisan language Ju|'hoan, with three genders distinguished by singular pronouns but four in the plural (Güldemann 1999, following Dickens 1992). Certainly Greenberg's claim holds true in the overwhelming majority of cases (provided it is seen as relating to language systems as a whole, rather than to individual lexical items, cf. Plank and Schellinger 1997).

We should consider how Greenberg's claim might be extended to larger systems. If there is a difference between plural and other non-singular values, then in those other number values we would not expect to find more gender distinctions than in the plural. Consider the Slovene forms in table 9.4 in this respect. Here we find three genders distinguished in the singular, and in the plural, but only two in the dual, where feminine and neuter share a form. However, here Yimas shows a contrary picture (Foley 1991: 167–8).

---

[8] Corbett (1991: 132, 147–58, 170–6, 189–203), see also Carstairs-McCarthy (1994: 771–2).

Table 9.4 *Forms of Slovene* bil *'was'*

	singular	dual	plural
masculine	bil	bil-a	bil-i
feminine	bil-a	bil-i	bil-e
neuter	bil-o		bil-a

A more complex type of interaction, but involving only singular–plural, is found in the demonstratives of Taiap (Kulick and Stroud 1992: 208), as shown in table 9.5.

Table 9.5 *Taiap demonstratives*

	singular			plural
	close to speaker	farther away	far from speaker	
feminine	aŋgɔdɛ	aŋgidɛ	aŋgudɛ	aŋge
masculine	aindɛ	anindɛ		

Here we find more distinctions within the demonstratives for feminine than for masculine, but these distinctions, together with gender, are all neutralized in the plural.

Another interesting interaction is found in Jarawara, a dialect of the Madi language of the Arawá family. Jarawara has around 150 speakers living near the Purús river in southern Amazonia (Dixon 1995: 265, 290). Agreement targets distinguish two genders, masculine and feminine:

(4) jomee tafa-ka
    dog   eat-DECLARATIVE.MASC
    'the dog is eating'

(5) banehe   tafa-ke
    tamandua eat-DECLARATIVE.FEM
    'the tamandua (giant anteater) is eating'

Now consider a plural subject:

(6) jomee mee   tafa-ke
    dog   3.PL eat-DECLARATIVE.FEM
    'the dogs are eating'

The plural for animates is indicated by the third plural pronoun. But all pronouns take feminine agreements, irrespective of the sex of the referent(s), as in:

(7) ee   tafa-ke
     1.INCL   eat-DECLARATIVE.FEM
     'we (inclusive) are eating'

So the distribution of the two agreement forms is as follows:

1 the masculine is controlled by a noun phrase headed by an animate singular masculine noun, or by an inanimate masculine noun (since inanimates are not specified for number);
2 the feminine is controlled by everything else.

The point is that again number determines the agreement in gender. We noted other surprising interactions in §6.1.1 and §6.6.

9.2.2 Case

Number frequently interacts with case (and grammatical relations). Let us look first at interaction in terms of the values available. In Barbareño Chumash all verbs contain a pronominal prefix marking the subject (Marianne Mithun, personal communication). The prefixes are regular, as we saw in table 3.9, and they distinguish singular–dual–plural. Verbs also have object markers, but here the distinction is just between singular and plural. Thus how many values there are for number depends on the grammatical relation involved. Where there is a difference, we expect to find more number values for subject than for object, more for direct cases than for oblique.[9]

Turning from the availability of number values to their use, we find a similar effect. The same values may in principle be available for different cases, but be used to different extents. For example, in Nivkh nouns have general/singular versus plural forms, in other words the plural is not required even when more than one entity is referred to. However, the plural marker is more likely to be omitted in oblique cases than in the nominative (Panfilov 1976: 22); see the discussion of Koryak in §9.2.4 for a comparable case. In the Papuan language Arafundi, subject agreement in number is obligatory, while object agreement is optional but usual (William Foley, personal communication). Now consider the situation with three number values, of which one is facultative. This is what we find in Ancient Greek, where singular and plural are obligatory but the dual is facultative. Diver (1987: 107–8) gives statistics on use of the dual in Homer, and shows that, as we would

---

[9] In agent–patient systems too we may find a similar interaction. Thus in Mohawk, verbs show singular–dual–plural distinctions in first and second persons for both agent and patient, but in third persons, the agent forms distinguish singular–dual–plural distinctions, but patient forms distinguish only singular and plural (Marianne Mithun, personal communication). Here the interaction is with person as well as case.

have expected, the use of the dual is greater in the nominative than in the oblique cases.

In all the instances so far, case determines number (number is better differentiated in direct cases, where the noun phrase is more prominent). However, the dependency does not always go in this direction. Consider the forms of a typical Slovene noun in table 9.6. There are different inflectional classes in Slovene and the

Table 9.6 *Paradigm of Slovene* kǫt *'corner'*
(Priestly 1993: 399–402)

	singular	dual	plural
NOM(inative)	kǫt	kǫta	kǫti
ACC(usative)	kǫt	kǫta	kǫte
GEN(itive)	kǫta	**kǫtov**	**kǫtov**
DAT(ive)	kǫtu	**kǫtoma**	kǫtom
INST(rumental)	kǫtom	**kǫtoma**	kǫti
LOC(ative)	kǫtu	kǫtih	kǫtih

syncretisms (identities of form) vary somewhat from class to class. In considering this paradigm we will concentrate on syncretisms which hold generally for nouns in Slovene. The dual dative and dual instrumental (given in bold in table 9.6) are syncretic, and this is true of any Slovene noun (similarly for the dual nominative and accusative). Hence number determines case. The syncretism of genitive dual and plural is also marked in bold. This syncretism holds for any Slovene noun too (as does the syncretism of locative dual and plural). Hence case determines number. We find both dependencies in a single language, which is something that Aikhenvald and Dixon said they had not found (1998: 63n20); they suggest that such a situation if found would be transitory, but this remains to be demonstrated.

There is a further layer of interaction between case and number here. Some Slovene nouns have stem alternates, determined by number. As we would expect, given the discussion in §2.3.2, there is typically one stem for the singular and another for dual and plural, as in *grâd* 'castle', dual *gradôv-a*, plural *gradôv-i*. However, one noun has one stem for singular and dual, and a suppletive stem (§5.3.1) for the plural (see table 9.7). Here, remarkably, we see that the syncretism of number leads to an alternation of stems within the dual, according to case. (It shows that syncretism can be directional: the genitive dual depends on the genitive plural, they are not simply the same.)

We have seen several examples of case determining number, and the Slovene pattern where both case determines number and number determines case. Other instances where number determines case include Kala Lagaw Ya, where Comrie

Table 9.7 *Slovene* člóvek *'man, person'*
(Priestly 1993: 401)

	singular	dual	plural
NOM	člóvek	človéka	ljudjệ
ACC	človéka	človéka	ljudî
GEN	človéka	**ljudí**	**ljudí**
DAT	človéku	človékoma	ljudệm
INST	človékom	človékoma	ljudmí
LOC	človéku	**ljudệh**	**ljudệh**

(1981: 9) shows that there are no case distinctions in the plural. Consider also these examples from the Baltic language Latvian (Veksler and Jurik 1978: 87):

(8) Grūti   dzīvot   bez   draug-a
     hard   to.live without friend-GEN.SG
     'It's hard to live without a friend'

(9) Grūti   dzīvot   bez   draug-iem
     hard   to.live without friend-DAT.PL
     'It's hard to live without friends'

(10) Skolotāji runā   par   grāmat-u
     teachers   talk   about book-ACC.SG
     'The teachers are talking about a book'

(11) Skolotāji runā   par   grāmat-ām
     teachers   talk   about book-DAT.PL
     'The teachers are talking about books'

We see that the prepositions in these examples take different cases in the singular and plural. While prepositions vary according to the case they take in the singular, they all take the dative case in the plural.[10] Thus the case used with a preposition depends on number. This is the converse of earlier examples in the section, which shows again that number may depend on case, and case may depend on number.

---

[10] A couple of qualifications are required. There are *post*positions which require the genitive in the singular and plural (Veksler and Jurik 1978: 87; Fennell and Gelsen 1980: 297). Some dialects preserve prepositions which take the genitive in both singular and plural (Axel Holvoet, personal communication). We need not enter here the question of the number of cases to be recognized, for which see Fennell and Gelsen (1980: 61, 148).

9.2.3 Person

We dealt with the interaction between person and number in large part in chapter 3. We found that if number is not available for all persons, then it will be found first of all in the first person, then in the second, and in the third only if in both first and second also (§3.2.4). Thus person determines number. Then in chapter 4 we saw how this carried over into more complex systems, so that in Arapesh the plural is found in all persons but the dual in the first person only (§4.1).

Table 9.8 *Forms of Cree* sīsīp *'duck'*

	singular	plural
proximate	sīsīp	sīsīp-ak
obviative	sīsīp-a	sīsīp-a

Some languages have an additional distinction in the person system, further dividing the third person into proximate and obviative; the proximate is for the entity closer to the centre of attention, while the obviative is more backgrounded. This distinction is found in various Algonquian languages of the northern United States and Canada; the forms here are from Plains Cree (Wolfart and Carroll 1981: 37), though comparable patterns can be found in some other Algonquian languages. Consider first the forms of *sīsīp* 'duck' in table 9.8. For this noun, and similar ones, number depends on person (obviation); there is a distinction in the proximate but not in the obviative. But when we look at *mīnis* 'berry', in table 9.9, we find a different distribution of similar inflections. Here we find number marked but not obviation. This in turn depends on animacy: *sīsīp* 'duck' is animate, and other animate nouns behave similarly, while inanimates behave like *mīnis* 'berry'. Thus the determining feature is animacy: animate nouns distinguish proximate from obviative while inanimates do not (the verb will however reflect this difference). For animate nouns, those in the proximate distinguish number, those in the obviative do not (number depends on obviation), for inanimates number is distinguished but not obviation.

Table 9.9 *Forms of Cree* mīnis *'berry'*

	singular	plural
proximate	mīnis	mīnis-a
obviative	mīnis	mīnis-a

Sometimes syncretisms go in the unexpected direction (unexpected against the background of §3.2.4). Hua is a member of the Gorokan family of Papua New Guinea. Table 9.10 gives the forms of the free pronouns (Haiman 1980: 215). Here

Table 9.10 *Free pronouns in Hua*

	singular	dual	plural
1st person	dgai	ra'agai	rgai
2nd person	kgai	**pa'agai**	**pgai**
3rd person	kai	**pa'agai**	**pgai**

we see that person depends on number (the second and third persons are distinguished only in the singular). Thus number usually depends on person, but person may depend on number.[11]

9.2.4 Definiteness

Aari is an Omotic language, spoken in the Gemu-Gofa highlands of south-west Ethiopia. Nouns may inflect for case and number, but only when marked as definite (Hayward 1990: 442–5); here then the availability of number depends on definiteness. Aari nouns have five forms, the indefinite (which does not mark case or number) and four case/number forms. An example is given in table 9.11. For a noun in Aari to be differentiated for number, it must first be a count noun (non-count nouns have three forms, indefinite and two case forms when definite). If it is a count noun and is definite, then there are two number forms available, singulative and non-singulative (which can be interpreted as plural).[12] Personal pronouns have singular and plural. And in another Omotic language, Gamo, any noun phrase marked as plural must be definite (Dick Hayward, personal communication).

Table 9.11 *Noun forms in Aari (*tiilé *'water pot')*

indefinite		definite	
		singulative	non-singulative
tiilé	nominative	tiilesín	tiilená
	accusative	tiilesinám	tiilenám

---

[11] There are several other examples in Highland New Guinea languages; for instance. Haruai distinguishes singular and plural, and has a single form for second and third persons plural (Bernard Comrie, personal communication); see also Scott's account of Fore (1978: 57) for a pattern like that of Hua. For the interesting relation of person to number in some Eskimoan languages see Smith (1979), and for a reconstruction of the earlier situation see Fortescue, Jacobson and Kaplan (1994: 443–8).

[12] While this system with a singulative marker is surprising, it is not a contrast of singular versus general/plural (cf. §2.1) since Aari has the indefinite with no marker at all, which we might treat as a general form.

A somewhat similar situation is found in a different part of the world. In Kambera, an Austronesian (Central Malayo-Polynesian) language with approximately 150,000 speakers on the island of Sumba in Eastern Indonesia, there are three articles: one is singular and definite, one is plural and definite and one is for proper names (Klamer 1998: 92, 141). This means that an indefinite noun phrase is not specified for number. The possibilities for noun phrases headed by ordinary nouns are: *na uma* 'the house' *da uma* 'the houses' and *uma* 'house or houses (indefinite)'. In Basque (Larry Trask, personal communication; Lafitte 1962: 55) markers attach to noun phrases. If a noun phrase has a definite determiner it must be marked for number, while if it has an indefinite determiner, it cannot be marked for number. (For more on this interaction see Plank 1987: 181–2; and Krámský 1972: 74–89.)

The situation in Koryak (a Chukotko-Kamchatkan language of northern Kamchatka) is of particular interest (Žukova 1972: 95–102). First there is an interaction between number and case. Koryak nouns have nine to twelve cases depending on type, and three numbers (singular, dual and plural). However, these three numbers are distinguished only in the absolutive case. There is a further, more intricate interaction. Nouns decline in two different ways, with one of the paradigms including a definiteness marker before the case ending. Nouns which do not denote humans may not take the definiteness marker. Nouns denoting humans are of two types: some always take the definiteness marker (nouns like *appa* 'Daddy') while the others may take the marker (when definite). The definiteness marker comes in two forms, one singular, the other according to Žukova for a combination of people. Thus whereas in the absolutive there are three numbers, in other cases, even for the favoured nouns (definite and human), there are only two.[13] Clearly we have an interaction between number, case and definiteness.[14]

---

[13] A male personal name plus this second marker could mean 'X and wife', 'X and family', 'X and work group', in other words it can function as an 'associative' (§4.3). However, with a noun like 'child', the meaning would be 'the children', so clearly the type of noun has an effect on the interpretation of this article. It should be pointed out too that with a noun like 'grandmother' in the absolutive (where the ordinary singular, dual and plural are found), when it is definite and dual the more natural interpretation is an associative one, such as 'grandmother and granddaughter'. Thus the ordinary numbers can have associative interpretations, and the second article can have an ordinary number interpretation (with the type of noun and the context favouring one or other interpretation).

[14] There are further interactions possible. In the case of logophoricity, if the plural triggers the use of the logophoric pronoun, then so will the singular (Hyman and Comrie 1981: 33). For the interaction of number with switch reference see Reesink (1987: 201–2) for Usan and Kewa, Comrie (1998) for Haruai, and Roberts (1997) for Papuan languages more generally; the question here is whether subjects which vary only in number will take same subject or different subject markers. Interaction with possessives is discussed in Corbett (1987: 301–2); various Slavonic languages have possessive adjectives which are available provided the possessor is singular; if plural then the genitive must be used.

There is much more to be done in documenting possible interactions and finding explanations for the patterns observed.

9.3 Use of number

We have looked at the component parts of number systems, comparing them across languages. We now ask how they are integrated in particular languages. We contrast languages where the different components have dramatically different roles (§9.3.1). Next we look at the way in which the different number values may be distributed in texts (§9.3.2), and then, staying with morphology, we examine the relation between frequency and regularity (§9.3.3).

9.3.1 Integrated systems

If we take an overall view of the way number is expressed in different languages we find great differences. There are relatively simple systems, like that of Lezgian, discussed in §6.1.1. Number is expressed on the noun, and there is no verbal agreement. On the other hand there are languages where things appear simple if we look at just one part of the system, but which turn out to be quite complex. Thus in Central Pomo (§4.3.2), relatively few nouns mark number. However, information about number is diffused through the sentence:

> The number distinctions found on pronouns, nouns, adjectives and verbs operate independently of each other, and differ in important ways.
>
> Pronouns distinguish number only for referents that speakers choose to classify as human. Sometimes pronominal number does not even indicate the number of referents at all, but respect. Nouns distinguish number only for some human referents, and only when their distribution is pertinent. Adjectives distinguish number whether the entities modified are human or not, but only when the individuation of the qualities they express is significant. Verbs indicate number through a multiplicity of devices, but in all cases, the primary function of these devices is to quantify various aspects of events or states, rather than to count entities. They may specify multiple effects, collective agency, multiple events, internal repetition, or multiple ongoing activities, but they do not quantify participants directly. Each number marker in Central Pomo is determined separately, and serves a subtly different function, directly related to its location within the grammar. (Mithun 1988b: 536)

A comparable variety of means is found in Mayali (Evans, chapter 5 of forthcoming). Here number may be expressed on the head noun (by full or partial reduplication), or by words such as plural demonstratives, numerals or the plural adjective -*wern* 'many', or on the verb at various places, by the pronominal prefix slots, numero-spatial prefixes, and by means of the reflexive/reciprocal.

There is much more to be done in understanding how such apparently diffuse systems are used. We noted earlier (§2.1) how in systems where number is in principle optional, there may be combinations of circumstances in which plural number marking, if appropriate, would be expected, and hence its lack is a clear indicator of singular number. Here it is the interaction of the number system with other factors which gives the hearer the information about number. This is an area where there is particularly challenging research to be undertaken.

9.3.2 Statistical distribution and markedness

Consider again the forms of a typical Slovene noun, as in table 9.6 above. The forms are presented in eighteen cells, which can be justified on distributional grounds (Comrie 1986, 1991). As already discussed, there are several interesting instances of syncretism. In this mode of presentation each cell is of equal status, and from a morphological point of view, that is appropriate. If however we look at the way in which the forms are used, in Slovene and more generally, then they are of differing status. Let us look for evidence as to how the different number values compare in language use. Greenberg (1966: 31–2) gives data based on counts of running text in four languages, French, Latin, Russian and Sanskrit. In each instance in table 9.12, a figure for the number of nouns is given, followed by the relative frequencies of the use of the number values. For comparison with Greenberg's data on Russian, taken from Josselson ('Russian (Jos.)' in table 9.12),

Table 9.12 *Frequency of different number values (of nouns) in texts*

language	number of examples	singular	plural	dual
French	1,000	74.3%	25.7%	—
Latin	8,342	85.2%	14.8%	—
Russian (Jos.)	8,194	77.7%	22.3%	—
Russian (Štejn.)	102,173	71.5%	28.3%[15]	—
Sanskrit	93,277	70.3%	25.1%	4.6%
Slovene (Oz.)	11,711	72.5%	26.9%	0.6%
Slovene (New.)	2,182	75.3%	24.2%	0.5%
Upper Sorbian	not given	64%	30%	6%

[15] The remaining 0.2 per cent of instances were indeclinable nouns; Štejnfel'dt counted according to morphology not agreement, which would have disambiguated some of the instances here.

I have added data from Štejnfel´dt (1963: 31, 52), ('Russian (Štejn.)' in table 9.12).[16] Of the languages for which Greenberg had data, only Sanskrit has the dual number. Fortunately, these data can be supplemented by information on the two modern Slavonic languages which have the dual. For Slovene there are data from Ozbalt (1973),[17] based on a corpus consisting of prose fiction, non-fiction, newspapers and correspondence ('Slovene (Oz.)' in table 9.12) and from Neweklowsky (1988), a corpus of literary prose ('Slovene (New.)'). And for Upper Sorbian there are data on the standard written language from Faßke (1981: 420).

It is evident from table 9.12 that the forms for the different number values are not used equally in these languages. The singular occurs much more frequently than the plural. Where there is a dual this is much less commonly used than the plural. This ordering is in harmony with what we found in §2.3.1: the dual was ranked below the plural there since languages may have a plural and no dual, but not the reverse. The frequency data may be thought of in terms of markedness (§5.3.6, this was Greenberg's point in citing the frequency data). The very low frequency for the dual in Slovene as compared to Sanskrit is at first surprising; recall, however, that the Slovene dual is facultative (§2.3.3), so there will be instances where two are referred to but the dual is not used.[18]

Table 9.13 *Frequency of different number values in Slovene prose texts*

part of speech	number of examples	singular	plural	dual
noun	2,182	75.3%	24.2%	0.5%
adjective	693	73.3%	25.7%	1.0%
pronoun	1,079	82.2%	15.9%	1.9%
verb	1,902	82.0%	15.6%	2.4%

It would be good to look more closely at the use of the forms in a single language, one with the dual, and there are indeed additional data available on Slovene. In table 9.13, we give the use of number for those parts of speech which mark it in

[16] In a very different type of study, Padučeva (1967: 1477) investigated a Russian text, and found that subjects could establish the appropriate number value of a noun phrase, in examples in the text where the crucial morphology was removed by the experimenter, in around 95 per cent of the instances. The experiment is not fully clear, but it deserves following up, given the surprisingly high figure of redundancy suggested.

[17] I am grateful to Tom Priestly for bringing this source to my attention. There are calculation errors on page 278 of that source which have been corrected here.

[18] It would be helpful to have better data about Upper Sorbian: the high figure for the dual in comparison to Slovene is surprising. Unfortunately Faßke does not give the size of his sample, and it is not certain that in this instance only nouns are involved. For other statistics on the use of the dual in Upper Sorbian see Jenč (1966).

Slovene, again from the corpus of literary prose (extracts from 15 modern writers) analysed by Neweklowsky (1988). We see that the overall ranking of singular, plural and dual is the same, but that there are differences between the parts of speech. The differences make sense in view of what we know about the facultative nature of the Slovene dual (see §2.3.3 and §4.1). Neweklowsky also investigated a corpus of similar size taken from newspapers (1984) and here the plural was found substantially more frequently than in the literary texts (though still much less frequently than the singular). And in an investigation of a single work by Rudi Šeligo, Eri-Birk (1976) found a somewhat higher use of the dual (3.9 per cent for nouns, pronouns and adjectives taken together, 6,613 examples). The relative frequency of the use of the number values can thus vary from genre to genre and from writer to writer but the ranking is the same for Slovene.

Table 9.14 *Alternations between singular and plural in Frisian*

alternation	singular	plural	gloss
/iə ~ jɪ/	stien	stjinnen	stone
/iə ~ jɛ/	beam	bjemmen	tree
/uə ~ wo/	stoel	stwollen	chair
/oə ~ wa/	doar	dwarren	door

Though we have looked in more detail at the use of number values in the last table, we can still 'turn up the magnification' as it were. We could look at the different cases, and investigate whether the number values were used differently there.[19] Or we could look not at large groups of lexical items, as we have done so far, but at individual ones. If the singular is used in the majority of the instances, that does not necessarily mean that we shall find that picture for every item. Tiersma (1982) showed that there is indeed considerable variation. When investigating dialects of Frisian spoken in the Netherlands, he noted nouns which show an alternation of diphthong between the singular and plural stems; examples are given in table 9.14. The nouns in the table, when plural, have the plural inflection -*en* in addition to the modified stem. The number of nouns with a stem alternation is decreasing. Since the singular is considered to be the unmarked number (§5.3.6), we would expect the singular stem to be preserved, and for its use to be generalized to include the plural too. This is in indeed what happens in most instances as we see in the alternatives in table 9.15, where the old form is maintained by conservative speakers, and the newer form is used by innovative speakers. For the innovative

---

[19] For this the interested reader is referred to Ozbalt (1973) and Eri-Birk (1976).

Table 9.15 *Regularization of Frisian nouns with stem alternations (normal case)*

CONSERVATIVE		INNOVATIVE		
singular	plural	singular	plural	gloss
koal	kwallen	koal	koalen	coal
miel	mjillen	miel	mielen	meal
poel	pwollen	poel	poelen	pool

speakers the singular stem has become the stem for singular and plural, and plurality is marked for these nouns simply by the productive plural inflection -*en*. There are a few nouns, however, for which the change has operated in the opposite direction (for some innovative speakers in certain dialect areas), as seen in table 9.16.

Table 9.16 *Regularization of Frisian nouns with stem alternations (special case)*

CONSERVATIVE		INNOVATIVE		
singular	plural	singular	plural	gloss
earm	jermen	jerm	jermen	arm
goes	gwozzen	gwos	gwozzen	goose
hoarn	hwarnen	hwarne	hwarnen	(animal) horn
hoas	vjazzen	vjazze	vjazzen	stocking
kies	kjizzen	kjizze	kjizzen	tooth
spoen	spwonnen	spwonne	spwonnen	shaving, splinter
toarn	twarnen	twarne	twarnen	thorn
trien	trjinnen	trjin	trjinnen	tear

The question is why precisely these nouns should be involved. Tiersma (1982: 835) proposes the following principle (as discussed in §5.3.6):

> When the referent of a noun naturally occurs in pairs or groups, and/or when it is generally referred to collectively, such a noun is locally unmarked in the plural.

If indeed the noun meaning 'arm' is locally unmarked in the plural, then it is understandable that its plural stem resists levelling, and the singular stem is lost in favour of the plural.[20] To support the claim about this and the other nouns which

---

[20] Comparable data on various Italian dialects are cited in Maiden (1990: 198–9, 209–10).

Table 9.17 *Use of number values with nouns locally unmarked in the plural*

	Dutch		English		German		Spanish	
	plural	N	plural	N	plural	N	plural	N
'arm'	53.8%	93	56.3%	215	—		61.7%	115
'goose'	50.0%	2	42.9%	7	47.4%	38	55.6%	27
'horn'	—		—		56.1%	132	81.8%	11
'stocking'	68.8%	16	83.3%	6	83.9%	62	—	
'tooth'	76.0%	25	83.7%	123	80.4%	341	65.0%	20
'shaving'	—		—		67.7%	31	—	
'thorn'	50.0%	2	—		65.7%	105	0%	6
'tear'	96.4%	28	75.6%	45	79.8%	178	85.2%	27

have generalized the plural stem, Tiersma gives data, from a variety of sources, on the relative frequency of singular and plural with these nouns, as in table 9.17 (for each the percentage of plural instances has been calculated, and the total number (N) of instances is given).

The evidence is indirect, since it relates to languages other than Frisian. Nevertheless it is convincing, particularly when we recall the data given earlier showing that in a sample of Indo-European languages the singular occurs considerably more frequently than the plural, roughly in three instances out of four.[21] For the nouns in question here, where data on comparable lexical items are available, the plural is generally found more frequently than the singular. Thus these nouns are quite different in their distribution of number values from the general picture obtained by averaging over large numbers of items. (We shall examine parts of the noun inventory of a language looking for links with irregularity in §9.3.3.)

An extension to the notion of local markedness which Tiersma did not consider is that when larger numbers of oppositions are involved it may be a relative notion. We saw above that the plural is normally more frequent than the singular and the dual is more frequent than the plural. For certain nouns, those which typically occur in pairs, the dual may be locally unmarked as compared to the plural. Evidence for this may remain even if the dual is lost. This has happened in most of the Slavonic languages, as we noted in §9.1.2, yet these languages retain traces of the dual in irregular plurals. For example, Russian *uxo* 'ear' has the plural *uši* in place of the regular **uxa*, and *plečo* 'shoulder' has *pleči* instead of **pleča*. These

---

[21] For discussion of English irregular plurals like *teeth*, and their frequencies see Anshen and Aronoff (1988: 650–1).

irregular plurals go back to dual forms: it is more common and natural to talk of two ears or shoulders rather than, say, seven. The dual was more frequent than the plural for these nouns and it is the dual forms which survived as irregular plurals.[22] With the loss of the dual, the plural *uši* can denote two or more ears (usually just two), and so the previous dual form survives as a plural.

As shown by statistical data, and by certain types of irregularity, particular nouns stand out from the rest in terms of their use of number values. This is of great importance for psycholinguists; in experiments where quite small differences are crucial for the results, it is vital that the items selected do not unbalance the task. In any experiment involving number, it is standard either to avoid or deliberately to select (depending on the experimental design) those items which like *tooth* and *tear* are 'plural dominant'.

9.3.3 Frequency and irregularity

We have seen how the frequency of the number values varies from noun to noun. We now turn to the relation between frequency and irregularity. It is accepted that there is such a connection (see, for example, Greenberg 1966, Bybee 1995). But there is the question of whether the frequency envisaged is based on the lexeme and all its forms, or just on the irregular form(s). To investigate this we consider a detailed study of a single language (Russian). Various analytical choices had to be made, and these are justified at length in the paper on which this section is based (Corbett et al. forthcoming); here we shall take them as given; the statistical method too will be accepted without argument here. The essential information on Russian morphology can be found in §5.3.1, §5.3.2 and §5.3.3.

The general claim that there is a relationship between frequency and irregularity is one with which almost any linguist would agree. Clarifying what the claim means leads to an interesting range of possibilities. For instance, we looked initially for a straightforward linear correlation between regularity and frequency; however, the data suggested that it was more appropriate to search for a more complex relationship and an investigation based precisely on number distinctions turned out to be fruitful.

Let us start with irregularity and consider its *extent*. Within a given lexeme (lexical item) it might be that every form could be irregular independently; or else it might be that forms come in groups which are regular or irregular together. A second question concerns the *degree* of irregularity. The singular ~ plural stems of Russian *čelovek ~ ljud-i* 'person ~ people' form an irregular relation, that of suppletion (§5.3.1, §5.4); also irregular are *sosn-á ~ sósn-y* 'pine ~ pines', where there is

---

[22] See Priestly (forthcoming) for another relevant case (from the Slovene dialect of Sele in Carinthia, Austria). The Arabic pseudo-duals, mentioned in §9.1.2, similarly survive in nouns which were more commonly used in the dual.

an alternation of stress (§5.3.3). Intuitively, the first type of irregularity is more severe than the second. If there is a relationship between frequency and irregularity, then we might claim that it will be sensitive to degrees of irregularity. To test this claim we set up a scale of irregularity, devised of course without reference to frequency (§9.3.3.3).

Frequency can be viewed in two ways. Given a noun whose plural is irregular, with what precisely do we expect to find a relationship? It is easiest to see the alternatives if we consider a corpus and look at the tests we might apply. We might compare lexemes one with another or we could compare regular and irregular forms within lexemes. For the first approach, we could count up how many times each lexeme occurs in the plural. Since we are counting only plurals (without respect to other forms, i.e. the singular) we call this the *absolute frequency* of a lexeme's plural. We can then compare the absolute frequency of plural of different lexemes, regular and irregular, to see if there is a relationship between irregular plurals and their absolute frequency. There is, however, a quite different way to look at the plural. That is to compare it, within the lexeme, with the other available forms. For a given lexeme, we can count how often it occurs in the plural as compared with the number of times in the singular. This is the *relative frequency* of the plural. We can then compare the relative frequency of the plural in lexemes where it is irregular with that in lexemes where it is regular, as we consider further in the next section.

9.3.3.1   Terms and hypotheses

To test the relationship between irregularity and frequency we look for a particular kind of anomaly in the corpus. An anomaly in the plurals of the corpus could be of two types. The first is in terms of an anomalous count of plurals for a lexeme compared to the amount one would expect for a typical lexeme of the corpus; this is *absolute plural anomaly.* What is compared is an absolute number of plurals for a lexeme with the distribution of the absolute number of plurals in the corpus. (The number of occurrences of, say, *mice* is compared with the number of occurrences of *cats, dogs* and so on.) The second type of anomaly is a relative one. Here it is the proportion of instances of the lexeme that are plural which is examined. The distribution of plural proportions can be calculated for the lexemes of the corpus, and if the given lexeme's proportion of plurals is extreme compared to this distribution, we would have identified a *relative plural anomaly.* (Here we look at the number of instances of *mice* as opposed to *mouse*, and compare this proportion with that of *cats* versus *cat* and so on.)

We should also allow for the possibility of the anomaly being due to a single cell of the paradigm. (This requires a language with larger paradigms than those of English.) If one specific cell had an extreme proportion compared to the distribution of the proportion of that cell throughout the corpus, then we would have an instance of *cell anomaly*. The anomaly is that a given lexeme has a significantly higher (or lower) than average proportion of word forms for a given cell (for instance, more instances of the genitive plural, in proportion to the other cells, than the average). We define cell anomaly in relative terms only, because formulating it in absolute terms might lead us to observe plural (or singular) anomaly in disguise. (The cell might be above or below the average simply as a consequence of its singular or plural being above or below the average.)

We therefore investigated three hypotheses:

> *Hypothesis 1a:* There is a relation between absolute plural anomaly and irregularity.

If Hypothesis 1a were confirmed, we would have shown that there is a relation between irregularity and frequency. In order to state the relationship more precisely, we would need to go further. If we observed absolute plural anomaly in certain groups of lexemes this might still be because the lexeme as a whole was anomalously frequent. We need a test which will tell us whether the frequency relationship is with the lexeme as a whole, or whether it is specifically with the lexeme's irregular forms. This test is provided by Hypothesis 1b.

> *Hypothesis 1b:* There is a relation between relative plural anomaly and irregularity.

We also needed to test whether there was a stronger relationship with irregularity when we combined plural anomaly (either absolute or relative) with the more specific cell anomaly. In other words, if a lexeme's plural forms occurred more frequently than average, and a particular cell in the plural was proportionally more frequent than average, would we be right in expecting the noun in question to be even more irregular? This test is provided by Hypothesis 2, which allows us to look for a stronger (and more fine grained) relationship with irregularity.

> *Hypothesis 2:* Given Hypothesis 1a or Hypothesis 1b is true, there is a stronger relationship between irregularity and the combination of plural anomaly and cell anomaly.

A particular case and number combination might occur more frequently than average either due to the lexeme occurring frequently or to the fact that the cell occurs unusually frequently in comparison with all word forms in the corpus (absolute frequency of the cell).

9.3.3.2 The data

Russian was a good choice for this investigation for two reasons. First, noun paradigms have sufficient cells for us to tease apart the irregularity of the lexeme in a subparadigm (the plural), and that of one of its word-forms (table 5.2). Second, irregularity in Russian is highly varied, ranging from suppletion to shift in stress (§5.3.1 and §5.3.3). We tested the hypotheses on the nouns in the Uppsala corpus of Russian (see Lönngren 1993 for details).[23] Since we were interested in estimating proportions in different categories, we recorded only those lexemes which occur at least five times. Our dataset contains around 5,440 lexemes, accounting for some 243,000 word forms from the entire one-million-word corpus.

9.3.3.3 The Irregularity Scale
We specifically wished to tease apart the irregularity of a lexeme and that of one of its inflectional forms. Since we intended to investigate the relationship with frequency, we needed to exclude any frequency consideration when determining regularity. In other words, we required a measure of *structural irregularity*, as determined by comparing forms according to a set of principles. We started from the expectation that a regular noun should have a single (unchanging) stem, a fixed stress, and a consistent set of endings; we treated each irregularity type as a step away from this view of regularity. On this basis we proposed the following scale, justified in Corbett et al. (forthcoming).

(12) Irregularity Scale
       suppletion (8) >
           pluralia tantum >
               stem augments (5–7) >
                   segmental stem irregularity (4) >
                       stress stem irregularity (3) >
                           segmental inflectional irregularity >
                               stress inflectional irregularity (1–2) >
                                   full regularity (0)

Each noun in our dataset was assessed according to this scale. The numbers in parentheses indicate the parts of the scale addressed as groups in table 9.18.[24]

---

[23] The basic dataset created can be found at: http://surrey.ac.uk/LIS/SMG, along with a readme file.

[24] Most of the terms arose in chapter 5. We distinguish segmental irregularities from prosodic ones (related to stress). A 'stress stem irregularity' involves movement of stress within the stem while 'stress inflectional irregularity' implies movement of stress onto or from the stem. Naturally we could not investigate *pluralia tantum* nouns in terms of relative plural anomaly. Segmental inflectional irregularities largely affect single cells in Russian, so these were investigated for Cell Anomaly. As reported at the end of §9.3.3.4 we found little evidence here for Cell Anomaly.

9.3.3.4 Discussion of results

Our results proved extremely interesting. We found relations between frequency and irregularity and a certain degree of correspondence with the Irregularity Scale. We also found evidence that prosodic and non-prosodic morphology are affected differently by frequency.

Absolute Plural Anomaly: Our first hypothesis (1a) was confirmed. There is a relation between absolute plural anomaly and irregularity. Below we give eight groups of nouns from the corpus divided up to match sections of our Irregularity Scale; we made a further distinction between two stress patterns which divide the singular and plural. Group 1 nouns have stem stress throughout the singular but ending stress throughout the plural (pattern C in table 5.5); group 2 nouns have the reverse, namely ending stress throughout the singular, and stem stress throughout the plural (pattern D). The eight groups are given in table 9.18. For each of the

Table 9.18 *Absolute Plural Anomaly in eight groups of nouns*

Group	Type of irregularity	Median plural count	Observed number of types	p-value
1	end stress plural	9	64	<0.001
2	end stress singular	5	80	<0.05
3	stem stress alternation	22	2	0.25
4	stem alternation	96	3	<0.001
5	stem augment in plural	10	24	<0.001
6	stem augment in singular	15	10	<0.05
7	stem augment in both	14	14	<0.05
8	suppletion	935.5	3	<0.001

irregularity groups in the table the median value for plural occurrences was significantly higher, as the p-values show, than for the corpus as a whole, with the single exception of Group 3. (The p-value represents the probability that a median value more extreme than that observed could have occurred purely by chance. A value <0.05 is reasonable evidence that there is a relationship between anomaly and irregularity. A value <0.01 is strong evidence that there is a relationship.) Thus seven out of eight groups confirm hypothesis 1a.

If we order the groups according to the median value, we get the following: Group 2, Group 1, Group 5, Group 7, Group 6, Group 3, Group 4, Group 8. The data do not support irrefutably the ordering given in table 9.18 because, despite the fact that the anomalies for seven of the groups are significant, the differences between the groups are in some cases insignificant. This also means that the ordering in (12) has not been disproved: the data here could still be consistent with the principled ordering of the Irregularity Scale, which is an interesting result. Groups 3 and 4 have small sample sizes which means that their place in the ordering suggested by table 9.18 should be treated with some scepticism.

What was shown definitely is that both singular augments and plural augments (§5.3.3) are related to absolute plural anomaly. We might have argued that singular augments, that is, additional stem material in the singular, with nouns showing plural anomaly, are there to mark the unexpected number (for that noun). However, this argument could not apply to nouns showing plural anomaly and having plural augments, since here the augment marks what is the expected number. In other words, it appears that having an augment throughout a particular number (irrespective of whether it is singular or plural) is related to a lexeme having a high plural anomaly. While we might have expected an augment in the plural to be associated with higher occurrence of singulars than the average for the corpus, the opposite is the case. Thus there is a relationship between frequency and irregularity in absolute terms. We now test our Hypothesis 1b in order to see if this is also true in relative terms.

Relative Plural Anomaly: The groups 1–8 were tested for the next of our hypotheses. Evidence for Hypothesis 1b turned out to be not as strong as that for Hypothesis 1a, and involved irregularity groups of a specific type. We found evidence for Hypothesis 1b for two groups, and arguably for a third. The stronger evidence is for Group 6 (where there is a stem augment in the singular), and Group 5 (where there is a stem augment in the plural), and the weaker evidence is for Group 4 (where there is a stem alternation). In each case the irregularity is segmental rather than prosodic. The results are given in table 9.19. Thus we find some evi-

Table 9.19 *Relative Plural Anomaly in eight groups of nouns*

Group	Type of irregularity	Median plural proportion	p-value
1	end stress plural	0.2	0.1
2	end stress singular	0.15	0.54
3	stem stress alternation	0.18	0.54
4	stem alternation	0.68	0.06
5	stem augment in plural	0.36	0.03
6	stem augment in singular	0.82	<0.001
7	stem augment in both	0.32	0.4
8	suppletion	0.62	0.16

dence that the frequency of occurrence of the irregular forms, and not just frequency of occurrence of the lexeme as a whole, does relate to irregularity of the forms in question. However, if the irregularity affecting an entire subparadigm is a

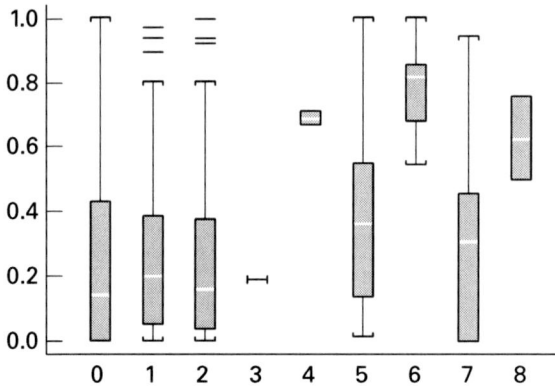

Figure 9.1 *Irregularity type and plural anomaly*
y axis = proportion of plurals; x axis = irregularity type (cf. table 9.19):
0 = regular, 1 = stress C, 2 = stress D, 3 = stem stress alternation, 4 = stem
segment alternation, 5 = stem augment in plural, 6 = stem augment in
singular, 7 = different stem augment in singular and plural, 8 = suppletion

prosodic one, there is no evidence for a relationship between this irregularity and a
high relative frequency. In the box plot in figure 9.1 the prosodic groups (Groups 1,
2 and 3) have much lower medians than the others.[25] The median is represented by
the white line in the middle of the box; the box itself represents a range of proportions covering the middle 50 per cent of the lexemes in the category; the whiskers at
the ends of the lines cover the remaining 50 per cent, except outliers which are indicated separately with horizontal bars (Daley et al. 1995).

It is an interesting and significant result to find that relative frequency of occurrence in the plural appears to be important where non-prosodic irregularity is concerned, but not where prosodic irregularity is concerned. Thus the degree of
irregularity matters. Prosodic irregularities involve a high absolute plural anomaly
but no relative plural anomaly. This means that there is a high number of plurals
(absolute plural anomaly) and also a high number of singulars to match the plurals
(no relative plural anomaly). Thus the prosodic irregularity may relate to the frequency of occurrence of the lexeme as a whole (the lexeme's plural must be frequent
to give the absolute anomaly, and its singular must also be frequent otherwise it
would show relative anomaly). In contrast, the fact that certain non-prosodic irregularities have significant relative plural anomalies indicates that these may be
related to the frequency of occurrence of a subparadigm, namely the plural.

---

[25] Recall that for Hypothesis 1a this does not exclude a relationship between absolute frequency and irregularity for these prosodic irregularities.

Hence we have identified an effect which applies to the lexeme as a whole, and one which applies to the plural subparadigm. Having found effects applying to the highest level (the lexeme) and a middle level (the subparadigm), we looked to see whether we could find any effect relating to the lowest level, that of the single cell.

Cell Anomaly: Delving deeper into the paradigm, we examined the frequency of occurrence of individual case and number cells to establish whether this could be related to their irregularity. We looked at the absolute frequency of occurrences for all cells of given lexemes with one individual irregular cell.[26] This was in order to address Hypothesis 2, which was looking for a stronger relationship based on cell irregularity and cell anomaly. Since we were looking for an effect not caused by Hypotheses 1a and 1b, we had to concentrate on cells which do not have a significantly high lexeme frequency. Having investigated this (the nominative plural proved the best candidate) we found little evidence for Hypothesis 2.

9.3.3.5   Frequency and irregularity: conclusions

Our Hypothesis 1a, that there is a relation between absolute plural anomaly and irregularity, is strongly confirmed. Nouns which have an irregularity involving a split between singular and plural will tend to be nouns which occur frequently in the plural. There is a less dramatic but still significant effect when only stress is involved. There are some indications of a relation between the degree of irregularity and the degree of plural anomaly.

Hypothesis 1b, that there is a relation between relative plural anomaly and irregularity, was less strongly confirmed. Where we did observe an effect, that is to say, where the plural was used in proportion to the singular significantly more frequently than found generally through the corpus, the irregularity was always a segmental one. Furthermore whether the irregularity concerned the singular or the plural, we still found a high relative plural frequency (nouns with an augment in the singular still have a high plural relative anomaly).

When we moved down to examine single cells (Hypothesis 2), we found no evidence that irregularity is related to a high relative frequency of a specific cell in the paradigm, once the effects discussed under Hypothesis 1a and 1b were factored out. This is an interesting result, since it implies a structuring of lexical items. It suggests that an individual irregular cell does not stand out from its subparadigm (singular or plural) in terms of frequency.

There are three morphological levels which might be relevant for frequency effects. The first is the level of the lexeme as a whole; the second is the level of the subparadigm of the lexeme; and the third is the level of the individual cell. We

---

[26] This includes lexemes for which the cell in question is the only irregularity, as well as lexemes for which the cell irregularity is accompanied by a singular–plural irregularity defined independently of that cell irregularity.

found no evidence for an effect relating to the third of these levels. We did find evidence for a relation with the other two. This relation may be sensitive to the type of the irregularity. For the relation with the first level, the lexeme as whole, the clearer evidence comes from prosodic irregularities. For the second of these levels, the number subparadigm, there is evidence from non-prosodic types of irregularity (figure 9.1). This shows the importance of looking at a language like Russian with substantial paradigms (whereas in English we cannot distinguish between the plural as a cell and the plural as a subparadigm). Thus number has been a key in investigating the relation of frequency and irregularity.

9.4   The acquisition of number

There has been rather little work done on the acquisition of number, by children and by second language learners: perhaps researchers have imagined it to be straightforward. However, the research that there is includes some significant work. There is a famous and still impressive study by Berko (1958), who presented children with drawings of new entities, the most celebrated being a bird-like creature called a 'wug', and asked them what two such creatures would be called. She worked with two groups of children (one group aged four to five, and the other aged five and a half to seven). She found that there was a difference between the groups in their ability to produce the expected plurals in that the older group did significantly better overall. There were also considerable differences according to the phonological type of the noun given (children did much better when /-s/ or /-z/ was required than when /-əz/ would give the appropriate plural form). The careful methodology means the paper is still well worth reading. Anisfield and Tucker (1967) followed Berko but included recognition tasks as well as production tasks. In production, they found that at age six, English children who were asked to give the plural of nonsense words appeared to use the generalization that plurals are longer than singulars.[27] Alongside this experimental work, observational research grew in importance, with a strong impetus provided by Brown and his group (Brown 1973: 330–1). It became evident that the acquisition of number morphology is not a simple matter: there is a considerable time between the first appearance of the plural and its regular use in obligatory contexts (Brown 1973: 256–8). Observational studies extended to other languages: as one example, Kunene (1986), who observed a child learning siSwati, found that nominal stems were acquired before the affixes that mark number and that number was first expressed

---

[27] Solomon (1972) followed Berko's method. Further research is reported in Derwing and Baker (1979: 210–14). Derwing (1980) showed how English pluralization can be described in a variety of ways, and Derwing and Baker (1980) evaluated these approaches using an acquisition experiment. For a unique rule for signalling number in acquisition by a language-impaired child see Camarata and Gandour (1985).

by other means, such as possessive pronouns. When nominal morphology was acquired, for some nouns the singular was acquired first and for some the plural.[28]

A language which has been particularly well studied is German, whose number morphology is complex (§5.3.3). Not surprisingly Park (1978) found that the task of learning number is harder for the German child than for the English child. It also emerged that children not only used singulars in plural contexts, but also when they had acquired plural forms they used them in singular contexts too. There were numerous examples of double plurals (§5.3.6), such as *Kind-er-n* 'children', where in adult speech *Kind* is singular and *Kind-er* plural. These findings were confirmed by Koehn (1994) and Müller (1994) in work on bilingual German–French children. Clahsen et al. (1992) compare the acquisition of number by language impaired and unimpaired children, and suggest that for both groups the distinction between regular and irregular morphology is vital.[29] Köpcke (1998) reviews research on the acquisition of German together with earlier results from English. There is also some work on the acquisition of number in German by second language learners (Phillips and Bouma 1980, Wegener 1995, Parodi, Schwartz and Clahsen 1997).

A lot has been learned, and yet the languages studied have been predominantly of one type, that with a two-value number system, with obligatory use of number, expressed by inflectional morphology. We can hope for new developments as results from child language acquisition inform our accounts of number systems and conversely as the range of possible systems encourages research on the acquisition of many more different types of number system. A similar point applies to psycholinguistic work, to which we now turn.

9.5 The psycholinguistics of number

Number has featured often in psycholinguistic work; we shall see that this is for good reason, and that there are further experiments which could prove fruitful were a wider range of languages investigated. Number has several attractions for psycholinguists: the semantics are, apparently, fairly straightforward and as a result it is not difficult to devise experimental situations which involve manipulating number.[30] Furthermore, in many languages the majority of nouns have plurals,

---

[28] See also Levy (1983) on Hebrew. There are considerable differences in the age at which children acquire the plural in different languages, as Giancarli (1999) points out; child learners of Arabic acquire the system late, as might be expected in the light of the examples in §5.3.3 (Omar 1973: 144–65).

[29] See also Clahsen et al. (1996), who compared German and English children; this research links to work by Kiparsky on level ordering noted in §5.4 and to research on English children by Gordon (1985b). The role of frequency in the acquisition of number is evaluated by Bartke, Marcus and Clahsen (1995).

[30] Its use for investigating linguistic relativity was mentioned in §3.4 note 11 and the interest for psycholinguists of agreement in number was pointed out in §6.1 note 1.

and so stimuli can be chosen from a sufficient pool to control for a variety of factors. It is the morphology of number which has been of particular interest. In an experiment in which subjects were asked to recall a short list of words, which might include a plural noun, van der Molen and Morton (1979) found interesting errors. Sometimes the plural would be transferred as it were to a different noun, which suggested that the plural marker was stored separately from the stem. And more generally, after a review of various evidence, Hawkins and Cutler (1988: 304–5) conclude that 'at some level it is necessary to process stems and affixes separately'. This view coincided with linguists' expectations. However, it has been challenged by connectionist approaches, in which linguistic knowledge is represented in associative networks. Broadly speaking, connectionist approaches treat inflected forms through a single mechanism, as contrasted with approaches where there is storage of stems (and irregularities) and some processing operation for regular morphology (for connectionist approaches to number morphology see Plunkett and Nakisa 1997). The debate continues (see for instance Baayen, Dijkstra and Schreuder 1997 on Dutch, and Baayen, Burani and Schreuder 1997 on Italian). A promising line is to address a particular problem (such as number), using a variety of procedures. These can include: asking subjects to form the plural of nonce (non-existent) nouns and of unusual nouns (Köpcke 1993: 183–203) or to judge different plurals offered for nonce nouns (Marcus et al. 1995); lexical decision tasks, in which subjects are asked to indicate whether a word is an existing one or not, and their response is timed (Clahsen, Eisenbeiss and Sonnenstuhl-Henning 1997); priming experiments, in which subjects are presented with two stimuli, in different relations to each other (including, for instance, items which are inflectionally related), and again responses are timed (Sonnenstuhl, Eisenbeiss and Clahsen 1999); neuro-imaging techniques, in which activation in the brain is investigated as subjects process or produce inflected forms, and investigation of subjects with various neurological problems, who may have access to part but not all of the number system (see for instance Kehayia, Jarema and Kądziela 1990). Interesting discussion of these issues and references can be found in Clahsen (1999), published with a debate which gives an idea of the divergence of views in this area.

In this sort of work, it is vital to control for the frequency of the words tested (§9.3.2), since it is known that subjects can react more quickly to frequent than to less frequent forms, as well as for word-length, and so on. But we should also think about the properties of the particular language used for the experiments. A large proportion of psycholinguistic research is based on English, which is often not the ideal language for the particular purpose. Clahsen (1999) makes this point strongly: if we wish to investigate possible differences between regular and irregular number morphology, English would not be a good language to choose, because regular nouns have segmentable suffixes in the plural but not the singular (*cat ~ cats*) while irregulars typically do not (*woman ~ women*). Whatever we discovered about regular plurals in English might be a result of the presence versus absence of a suffix. Furthermore the default plural suffix (-*s*) is also overwhelmingly the most frequent. It is safer to investigate German, where there are irregular as well as regular nouns with suffixes, and where the default suffix (also -*s* according to Clahsen) is not the most frequent. There is also more choice in the stimuli to use: while English has relatively few irregular plurals, German has many irregular nouns, of various types.

Given the variety we have seen earlier in the book, we should take this argument further; German and English are closely related, and by comparison several other languages offer promising configurations of the relevant factors, and yet others present new challenges. Most psycholinguists working on number have been restricted to the binary oppositions singular–plural, yet as we saw in §2.2 many languages have three or more number values. The largest systems are found with pronouns rather than nouns, but duals on nouns are common. Given a singular–dual–plural system, the question of regularity becomes more complex than in English or German, in that a lexical item may be regular in respect of one number opposition but irregular in respect of another (see, for example, Priestly 1993: 401 on Slovene). These larger systems also bring with them interesting frequency effects: singulars are normally more frequent than plurals, but the reverse holds for certain lexical items, such as *teeth* (§9.3.2); when a dual is available, it is typically the least frequent value, though for some lexical items it is the most frequent. The existence of dual-dominant nouns is of relevance for the work on singular- and plural-dominant nouns, by Baayen, Levelt and Haveman, reported in Levelt, Roelofs and Meyer (1999: 13–14); they asked subjects to name pictures of one or two identical objects. Not surprisingly, it took speakers longer to produce *noses* than *nose*. But with nouns where the plural is dominant (more frequent), as in *eye ~ eyes*, both the singular and the plural were significantly slower than for comparably frequent singular-dominant nouns.

German and English are also similar in that number is an obligatory category. But in many languages, like Japanese (§2.1 and §3.4), the plural would be used if the speaker wanted to draw special attention to the quantity, but is not obligatory. This difference has implications for the frequency of use of the different number values, for the input for language acquisition, and in some languages for the degree of agreement among speakers of the form of the plural. German clearly outdoes English in terms of the degrees of irregularity, and this is important for the debate, as we noted above. From a broader perspective, however, German nouns fall into a moderate number of (relatively) neat classes, when compared with Nilotic languages, such as Shilluk (§5.4). Given the high degree of irregularity, much greater than that of German, Shilluk suggests tantalizing questions as to how far the balance can be tipped towards irregularity.

Clahsen has shown the benefits of seeing English not as if it were Language, but rather as just one (typologically rather odd) language. By moving the focus to German, he clarifies the issues he wishes to address. There are many similar moves to be made; and psycholinguistic work based on languages which are radically different from English and German can lead us to ask questions which these languages would not provoke. But time may be short: as we noted in §1.1, of the world's 6,000 languages only around 250 are 'safe', in the sense that they are likely to survive for at least another 100 years.

9.6   The final note

We have looked in detail at a fascinating grammatical category. On the way we have employed the main typological techniques. We recognized the need to begin by casting our nets widely (chapter 2), which showed how remarkably varied number can be. We saw the importance of hierarchies (chapters 3 and 6). And then in chapter 4 we noted the powerful analyses which result from combining our two complementary analyses, that of number values and that of the hierarchy of nominal elements involved. More than once we saw the importance of comparing like with like, as in chapter 5 where we moved from comparing number values and their ranges across languages to comparing the means of expression of number across languages. In chapter 6 we saw how factors which can be isolated as being at work individually in various languages may in combination allow us to understand the workings of apparently much more complex systems. One effect of chapter 7 (on special uses of number) was to remind us that even when the broad correlations are established, for a construction or a category, there is much more to do, once we check the broad findings against the rich data of usage. And in the chapter on verbal number (chapter 8) we were reminded of the need to be careful about terms, and to draw distinctions carefully between phenomena when attempting a typology. In this chapter we have seen some of the implications of typological work for other areas of research.

Finally, returning to number: in §1.1, I mentioned surveys of linguistics where number seems to merit only a footnote. I trust that readers now believe that number deserves much more. This is true of many topics which barely squeeze into even the best surveys. Language is like that.

REFERENCES

Aikhenvald, Alexandra Y. 1994. Classifiers in Tariana. *Anthropological Linguistics* 36. 407–65.

— 1998. Warekena. In: Desmond C. Derbyshire and Geoffrey K. Pullum (eds.) *Handbook of Amazonian Languages* IV, 225–439. Berlin: Mouton de Gruyter.

Aikhenvald, Alexandra Y. and Dixon, R. M. W. 1998. Dependencies between grammatical systems. *Language* 74. 56–80.

Aissen, Judith L. 1989. Agreement controllers and Tzotzil comitatives. *Language* 65. 518–36.

Aitchison, Jean 1990. The missing link: the role of the lexicon. In: Jacek Fisiak (ed.) *Historical Linguistics and Philology* (Trends in Linguistics: Studies and Monographs 46), 11–28. Berlin: Mouton de Gruyter.

Alhoniemi, Alho 1993. *Grammatik des Tscheremissischen (Mari): Mit Texten und Glossar* (Aus dem Finnischen übersetzt von Hans-Hermann Bartens). Hamburg: Busske.

Allan, Edward J. 1976. Dizi. In: M. Lionel Bender (ed.) *The Non-Semitic Languages of Ethiopia*, 377–392. East Lansing: African Studies Center, Michigan State University.

Allan, Keith 1976. Collectivizing. *Archivum Linguisticum* 7. 99–117.

— 1980. Nouns and countability. *Language* 56. 541–67.

— 1986. *Linguistic Meaning* I. London: Routledge and Kegan Paul.

— 1987. Hierarchies and the choice of left conjuncts (with particular attention to English). *Journal of Linguistics* 23. 51–77.

Allen, Gerald N. 1987. *Halia Grammar* (Data Papers on Papua New Guinea Languages 32). Ukarumpa, Papua New Guinea: Summer Institute of Linguistics.

Amborn, Hermann; Minker, Gunter and Sasse, Hans-Jürgen 1980. *Das Dullay: Materialen zu einer ostkuschitischen Sprachgruppe* (Kölner Beiträge zur Afrikanistik 6). Berlin: Reimer.

Anderson, Gregory D. S. 1996. On redundancy and the Yeniseian [PL]. In: Lise M. Dobrin, Kora Singer and Lisa McNair (eds.) *CLS 32: the Main Session*, 1–10. Chicago: Chicago Linguistic Society.

Anderson, Stephen C. 1985. Animate and inanimate pronominal systems in Ngyebɔɔn-βamileke. *Journal of West African Languages* 15. 61–74.

Anderson, Stephen R. 1992. *A-Morphous Morphology* (Cambridge Studies in Linguistics 62). Cambridge: Cambridge University Press.

References

Andrade, Manuel 1933–38. Quileute. In: Franz Boas (ed.) *Handbook of American Indian Languages* III, 149–292. New York: Columbia University Press.

Andrzejewski, B. W. 1960. The categories of number in noun forms in the Borana dialect of Galla. *Africa* 30. 62–75.

Anisfeld, Moshe and Tucker, G. Richard 1967. English pluralization rules of six-year-old children. *Child Development* 38. 1201–17.

Anshen, Frank and Aronoff, Mark 1988. Producing morphologically complex words. *Linguistics* 26. 641–55.

Aoun, Joseph; Benmamoun, Elabbas and Sportiche, Dominique 1994. Agreement, word order and conjunction in some varieties of Arabic. *Linguistic Inquiry* 25. 195–220.

Appleyard, David L. 1987. A grammatical sketch of Khamtanga I. *Bulletin of the School of Oriental and African Studies, University of London* 50. 241–65.

Aquilina, Joseph 1965. *Teach Yourself Maltese.* Sevenoaks: Hodder and Stoughton.

Arbatskij, D. I. 1972. Množestvennoe čislo giperboličeskoe. *Russkij jazyk v škole* no. 5. 91–6.

Aronson, Howard I. 1982. *Georgian: a Reading Grammar.* Columbus, Ohio: Slavica.

Baayen, Harald; Burani, Christina and Schreuder, Robert 1997. Effects of semantic markedness in the processing of regular nominal singulars and plurals in Italian. In: Geert Booij and Jaap van Marle (eds.) *Yearbook of Morphology 1996*, 13–33. Dordrecht: Kluwer.

Baayen, Harald; Dijkstra, Ton and Schreuder, Robert 1997. Singulars and plurals in Dutch: evidence for a dual route model. *Journal of Memory and Language* 37. 94–119.

Baayen, R. Harald; Lieber, Rochelle and Schreuder, Robert 1997. The morphological complexity of simplex nouns. *Linguistics* 35. 861–77.

Bach, Emmon; Jelinek, Eloise; Kratzer, Angelika and Partee, Barbara (eds.) 1995. *Quantification in Natural Languages.* Dordrecht: Kluwer.

Bailey, Guy; Maynor, Natalie and Cukor-Avila, Patricia 1989. Variation in subject–verb concord in Early Modern English. *Language Variation and Change* 1. 285–300.

Banti, Giorgio 1988. 'Adjectives' in East Cushitic. In: Marianne Bechhaus-Gerst and Fritz Serzisko (eds.) *Cushitic-Omotic: Papers from the International Symposium on Cushitic and Omotic Languages: Cologne, January 6–9, 1986*, 203–59. Hamburg: Buske.

Barker, Chris 1992. Group terms in English: representing groups as atoms. *Journal of Semantics* 9. 69–93.

Barker, Muhammad A. R. 1964. *Klamath Grammar* (University of California Publications in Linguistics 31). Berkeley: University of California.

Barlow, Michael 1991. The Agreement Hierarchy and grammatical theory. In: Laurel A. Sutton, Christopher Johnson and Ruth Shields (eds.) *Seventeenth Annual Meeting of the Berkeley Linguistics Society, February 15–18, 1991: General Session and Parasession on the Grammar of Event Structure*, 30–40. Berkeley: Berkeley Linguistics Society, University of California.

1992. *A Situated Theory of Agreement.* New York: Garland.

Barnes, Janet 1990. Classifiers in Tuyuca. In: Doris L. Payne (ed.) *Amazonian Linguistics: Studies in Lowland South American Languages*, 273–92. Austin: University of Texas Press.

Bartke, Suzanne; Marcus, Gary F. and Clahsen, Harald 1995. Acquiring German noun plurals. In: Dawn MacLaughlin and Susan McEwen (eds.) *Proceedings of the 19th Annual Boston University Conference on Language Development* I, 60–9. Somerville, MA: Cascadilla.

Battistella, Edwin L. 1990. *Markedness: the Evaluative Superstructure of Language.* New York: State University of New York Press.

Bauer, Laurie 1988. Number agreement with collective nouns in New Zealand English. *Australian Journal of Linguistics* 8. 247–59.

Bauer, Winifred 1993. With William Parker and Te Kareongawai Evans. *Maori* (Descriptive grammars series). London: Routledge.

Bean, Susan S. 1975. The meanings of grammatical number in Kannada. *Anthropological Linguistics* 17. 33–41.

Beard, Robert 1982. The plural as a lexical derivation. *Glossa* 16. 133–48.

Beaumont, Clive H. 1976. Austronesian languages: New Ireland. In: Stephen A. Wurm (ed.) *Austronesian Languages: New Guinea Area Languages and Language Study* II (Pacific Linguistics, series C, no. 39), 387–97. Canberra: Department of Linguistics, Research School of Pacific Studies, Australian National University.

   1979. *The Tigak Language of New Ireland* (Pacific Linguistics, series B, no. 58). Canberra: Department of Linguistics, Research School of Pacific Studies, Australian National University.

Becker, A. L. and Oka, I. Gusti Ngurah 1974. Person in Kawi: exploration of an elementary semantic dimension. *Oceanic Linguistics* 13. 229–55.

Behrens, Leila 1995. The MASS/COUNT distinction in a cross-linguistic perspective. *Lexicology* 1. 1–112.

Belić, Aleksandar 1932. *O dvojini u slovenskim jezicima.* Beograd: Srpska kraljevska akademija.

Bell, Andrew J. 1923. *The Latin Dual and Poetic Diction: Studies in Numbers and Figures.* London: Oxford University Press.

Bell, C. R. V. 1953. *The Somali Language.* London: Longmans Green.

Belnap, R. Kirk 1991. Grammatical agreement variation in Cairene Arabic. PhD dissertation, University of Pennsylvania. [Distributed by University Microfilms International, Ann Arbor, reference NIR92–00311.]

   1993. The meaning of deflected/strict agreement variation in Cairene Arabic. In: Mushira Eid and Clive Holes (eds.) *Perspectives on Arabic Linguistics* V: *Papers from the Fifth Annual Symposium on Arabic Linguistics* (Amsterdam Studies in the Theory and History of Linguistic Science 101), 97–117. Amsterdam: John Benjamins.

   1999. A new perspective on the history of Arabic: variation in marking agreement with plural heads. *Folia Linguistica* 33. 169–85

Belnap, R. Kirk and Gee, John 1994. Classical Arabic in contact: the transition to near categorical agreement patterns. In: Mushira Eid, Vincente Cantarino and Keith Walters (eds.) *Perspectives on Arabic Linguistics* VI: *Papers from the Sixth Annual Symposium on Arabic Linguistics* (Amsterdam Studies in the Theory and History of Linguistic Science 115), 121–49. Amsterdam: John Benjamins.

References

Belnap, R. Kirk and Shabaneh, Osama 1992. Variable agreement and nonhuman plurals in Classical and Modern Standard Arabic. In: Ellen Broselow, Mushira Eid and Clive Holes (eds.) *Perspectives on Arabic Linguistics* IV: *Papers from the Fourth Annual Symposium on Arabic Linguistics* (Amsterdam Studies in the Theory and History of Linguistic Science 85), 245–62. Amsterdam: John Benjamins.

Bender, Byron W. 1969. *Spoken Marshallese: an Intensive Language Course with Grammatical Notes and Glossary.* Honolulu: University Press of Hawaii.

Benzing, Johannes 1955. *Lamutische Grammatik: mit Bibliographie, Sprachproben und Glossar* (Akademie der Wissenschaften und der Literatur: Veröffentlichungen der orientalischen Kommission 6). Wiesbaden: Franz Steiner.

Berg, Helma van den 1995. *A Grammar of Hunzib (with texts and lexicon)* (Lincom Studies in Caucasian Linguistics 1). Munich: Lincom Europa.

Berg, René van den 1989. *A Grammar of the Muna Language* (Verhandelingen van het Koninklijk Instituut voor Taal-, Land- en Volkenkunde 139). Dordrecht: Foris.

Berg, Thomas 1998. The resolution of number conflicts in English and German agreement patterns. *Linguistics* 36. 41–70.

Bergsland, M. Knut 1956. The Uralic half-eye in the light of Eskimo-Aleut. *Ural-Altaische Jahrbücher* 28. 165–73.

Berko, Jean 1958. The child's learning of English morphology. *Word* 14. 150–77.

Bhattacharya, Sudhibhushan 1976. Gender in the Munda languages. In: Philip N. Jenner, Laurence C. Thompson and Stanley Starosta (eds.) *Austroasiatic Studies: Part I* (Oceanic Linguistics Special Publication 13), 189–211. Honolulu: University Press of Hawaii.

Biermann, Anna 1982. Die grammatische Kategorie Numerus. In: Hansjakob Seiler and Christian Lehmann (eds.) *Apprehension: Das sprachliche Erfassen von Gegenständen* I: *Bereich und Ordnung der Phänomene*, 229–43. Tübingen: Narr.

Bisang, Walter 1996. Areal typology and grammaticalization: processes of grammaticalization based on nouns and verbs in East and mainland South East Asian languages. *Studies in Language* 20. 519–97.

Bjerrum, Anders 1949. Verbal number in the Jutlandic Law. *Travaux du cercle linguistique de Copenhague* 5 (Recherches structurales 1949), 157–76. Copenhagen: Nordisk Sprog- og Kulturforlag.

Blake, Barry J. 1979. *A Kalkatungu Grammar* (Pacific Linguistics, series B, no. 57). Canberra: Department of Linguistics, Research School of Pacific Studies, Australian National University.

Blanc, Haim 1970. Dual and pseudo-dual in the Arabic dialects. *Language* 46. 42–57.

Boas, Franz 1911a. Introduction. In: Franz Boas (ed.) *Handbook of American Indian Languages, Part I* (Bureau of American Ethnology Bulletin 40, part 1, part A), 1–83. Washington: Smithsonian Institution.

1911b. Kwakiutl. In: Franz Boas (ed.) *Handbook of American Indian Languages, Part I* (Bureau of American Ethnology Bulletin 40, part 1, part A), 423–557. Washington: Smithsonian Institution.

1947. *Kwakiutl Grammar: with a glossary of the suffixes.* Edited by Helene Boas

Yampolsky with the collaboration of Zellig S. Harris. (=Transactions of the American Philosophical Society, New Series, volume 37, part 3). Philadelphia: American Philosophical Society.

Bock, Kathryn and Miller, Carol A. 1991. Broken agreement. *Cognitive Psychology* 23. 45–93.

Bodomo, Adams B. 1997. *The Structure of Dagaare.* Stanford: Center for the Study of Language and Information, Stanford University.

Bogdanov, V. N. 1968. Osobyj slučaj dialektnogo soglasovanija skazuemogo s podležaščim po smyslu i kategorija predstavitel'nosti, *Naučnye doklady vysšej školy: filologičeskie nauki* no. 4. 68–75.

Bolling, George M. 1933. On the dual in Homer. *Language* 9. 298–308.

Booij, Geert 1996. Inherent versus contextual inflection and the split morphology hypothesis. In: Geert Booij and Jaap van Marle (eds.) *Yearbook of Morphology 1995*, 1–15. Dordrecht: Kluwer.

Booker, Karen M. 1978. On the origin of number marking in Mukogean. *Kansas Working Papers in Linguistics* 3. 100–12.

1982. Number suppletion in North American Indian languages. *Kansas Working Papers in Linguistics* 7. 15–29.

Borg, Albert J. 1981. *A Study of Aspect in Maltese.* Ann Arbor: Karoma.

Bragg, Lois 1989. Old English dual pronouns and their poetic uses. *Language and Style* 22. 337–49.

Brinton, Laurel J. 1991. The mass/count distinction and Aktionsart: the grammar of iteratives and habituals. *Belgian Journal of Linguistics* 6. 47–69.

Brooks, Bryan 1991. Pluractional verbs in African languages. *Afrikanistische Arbeitspapiere* (Cologne) 28. 157–68.

Brown, Dunstan; Corbett, Greville; Fraser, Norman; Hippisley, Andrew and Timberlake, Alan 1996. Russian noun stress and network morphology. *Linguistics* 34. 53–107.

Brown, Gordon D. A.; Preece, Tim and Hulme, Charles 2000. Ocillator-based memory for serial order. *Psychological Review* 107. 127–81.

Brown, Penelope and Levinson, Stephen C. 1987. *Politeness: some Universals in Language Usage* (Studies in Interactional Sociolinguistics 4). Cambridge: Cambridge University Press.

Brown, Roger 1973. *A First Language: the Early Stages.* London: George Allen and Unwin.

Bruce, Les 1984. *The Alamblak Language of Papua New Guinea (East Sepik)* (Pacific Linguistics, series C, no. 81). Canberra: Department of Linguistics, Research School of Pacific Studies, Australian National University.

Brunet, Jacqueline 1978. *Grammaire critique de l'italien* I. Vincennes: Université de Paris VIII.

Brusenskaja, L. A. 1992. *Kategorija čisla v russkom jazyke: strukturno-semantičeskij i kommunikativno-funkcional'nyj aspekty: učebnoe posobie k speckursu.* Rostov-na-Donu: Izdatel'stvo Rostovskogo gosudarstvennogo pedagogičeskogo instituta.

Bugenhagen, Robert D. 1994. The notion of non-singularity in Mangaaba-Mbula. Paper presented at the Seventh International Conference on Austronesian Linguistics, Leiden, August 1994. Unpublished.

Bukatevič, N. I.; Gricjutenko, I. E.; Miževskaja, G. M.; Pavljuk, N. V.; Savickaja, S. A. and Smaglenko, F. P. 1958. *Očerki po sravnitel'noj grammatike vostočnoslavjanskix jazykov.* Odessa: Odesskij gosudarstvennyj universitet im. I. I. Mečnikova. [Reprinted as Slavistic Printings and Reprintings no. 139, 1969, The Hague: Mouton.]

Bunn, Gordon 1974. *Golin Grammar* (Workpapers in Papua New Guinea Languages 5). Ukarumpa, Papua New Guinea: Summer Institute of Linguistics.

Bunt, Harry C. 1985. *Mass Terms and Model-Theoretic Semantics* (Cambridge Studies in Linguistics 42). Cambridge: Cambridge University Press.

Bybee, Joan 1985a. Diagrammatic iconicity in stem-inflection relations. In: John Haiman (ed.) *Iconicity in Syntax: Proceedings of a Symposium on Iconicity in Syntax, Stanford, June 24–6, 1983* (Typological Studies in Language 6), 13–47. Amsterdam: John Benjamins.

1985b. *Morphology: a Study of the Relation between Meaning and Form* (Typological Studies in Language 9). Amsterdam: John Benjamins.

1995. Regular morphology and the lexicon. *Language and Cognitive Processes* 10. 425–455.

Camarata, Stephen and Gandour, Jack 1985. Rule invention in the acquisition of morphology by a language-impaired child. *Journal of Speech and Hearing Disorders* 50. 40–5.

Campbell, Lyle 1985. *The Pipil Language of El Salvador* (Mouton Grammar Library 1). Berlin: Mouton.

Capell, Arthur 1971. The Austronesian languages of Australian New Guinea. In: Thomas A. Sebeok (ed.) *Current Trends in Linguistics* VIII: *Linguistics in Oceania*, 240–340. The Hague: Mouton.

1976. General picture of Austronesian languages, New Guinea area. In: Stephen A. Wurm (ed.) *Austronesian Languages: New Guinea Area Languages and Language Study* II (Pacific Linguistics, series C, no. 39), 5–52. Canberra: Department of Linguistics, Research School of Pacific Studies, Australian National University.

Carnochan, J. 1962. The category of number in Igbo grammar. *African Language Studies* 3. 110–15.

Carstairs-McCarthy, Andrew 1994. Inflection classes, gender, and the principle of contrast. *Language* 70. 737–88.

Chapman, Shirley and Derbyshire Desmond C. 1991. Paumarí. In: Desmond C. Derbyshire and Geoffrey K. Pullum (eds.) *Handbook of Amazonian Languages* III, 161–352. Berlin: Mouton de Gruyter.

Chappell, Hilary 1996. Inalienability and the personal domain in Mandarin Chinese discourse. In: Hilary Chappell and William McGregor (eds.) *The Grammar of Inalienability: a Typological Perspective on Body Parts and the Part–Whole Relation* (Empirical Approaches to Language Typology 14), 465–527. Berlin: Mouton de Gruyter.

Charney, Jean O. 1993. *A Grammar of Comanche*. Lincoln: University of Nebraska Press.

Chierchia, Gennaro 1998a. Reference to kinds across languages. *Natural Language Semantics* 6. 339–405.

1998b. Plurality of mass nouns and the notion of 'semantic parameter'. In: Susan Rothstein (ed.) *Events and Grammar* (Studies in Linguistics and Philosophy 70), 53–103. Dordrecht: Kluwer.

Choe, Jae-Woong 1987. A theory of distributivity. In: Jeroen Groenendijk, Martin Stokhof and Frank Veltman (eds.) *Proceedings of the Sixth Amsterdam Colloquium: April 13–16 1987*, 21–41. Amsterdam: University of Amsterdam, ITLI.

Clahsen, Harald 1999. Lexical entries and rules of language: a multidisciplinary study of German inflection. *Behavioral and Brain Sciences* 22. 991–1060.

Clahsen, Harald; Eisenbeiss, Sonja and Sonnenstuhl-Henning, Ingrid 1997. Morphological structure and the processing of inflected words. *Theoretical Linguistics* 23. 201–49.

Clahsen, Harald; Marcus, Gary F.; Bartke, Suzanne and Wiese, Richard 1996. Compounding and inflection in German child language. In: Geert Booij and Jaap van Marle (eds.) *Yearbook of Morphology 1995*, 115–42. Dordrecht: Kluwer.

Clahsen, Harald; Rothweiler, Monika; Woest, Andreas and Marcus, Gary F. 1992. Regular and irregular inflection in the acquisition of German noun plurals. *Cognition* 45. 225–55.

Claudi, Ulrike 1985. *Zur Entstehung von Genussystemen: Überlegungen zu einigen theoretischen Aspekten, verbunden mit einer Fallstudie des Zande: Mit einer Bibliographie und einer Karte*. Hamburg: Buske.

Členova, S. F. 1973. Kategorija čisla v ličnyx mestoimenijax. *Lingvotipologičeskie issledovanija*, vyp. 1, čast' 1. 164–201. (Publikacii Laboratorii vyčislitel'noj lingvistiki, Izdatel'stvo Moskovskogo universiteta.)

Coates, Richard 1980. Ethnoichthyology and noun morphology in English. *York Papers in Linguistics* 8. 193–6.

Cole, Desmond T. 1955. *An Introduction to Tswana Grammar*. London: Longmans Green.

Collins, Chris 1998. Plurality in ǂHòan. *Khoisan Forum, Working Papers* 9. Cologne: Institut für Afrikanistik, University of Cologne.

Comrie, Bernard 1975. Polite plurals and predicate agreement. *Language* 51. 406–18.

1981. Ergativity and grammatical relations in Kalaw Lagaw Ya (Saibai dialect). *Australian Journal of Linguistics* 1. 1–42.

1982. Grammatical relations in Huichol. In: Paul J. Hopper and Sandra A. Thompson (eds.) *Studies in Transitivity* (Syntax and Semantics 15), 95–115. New York: Academic Press.

1986. On delimiting cases. In: Richard D. Brecht and James S. Levine (eds.) *Case in Slavic*, 86–106. Columbus, OH: Slavica.

1989. *Language Universals and Linguistic Typology: Syntax and Morphology*. Oxford: Blackwell. [Second edition; First edition 1981.]

1991. Form and function in identifying cases. In: Frans Plank (ed.) *Paradigms: the Economy of Inflection* (Empirical Approaches to Language Typology 9), 41–55. Berlin: Mouton de Gruyter.

References

1998. Switch reference in Haruai: grammar and discourse. In: Mark Janse (ed.) *Productivity and Creativity: Studies in General and Descriptive Linguistics in Honor of E. M. Uhlenbeck* (Trends in Linguistics: Studies and Monographs 116), 421–32. Berlin: Mouton de Gruyter.

Comrie, Bernard and Corbett, Greville G. (eds.) 1993. *The Slavonic Languages.* London: Routledge.

Conklin, Harold C. 1962. Lexicographical treatment of folk taxonomies. In: Fred W. Householder and Sol Saporta (eds.) *Problems in Lexicography* (Publication of the Indiana University Research Center in Anthropology, Folklore, and Linguistics 21, =*International Journal of American Linguistics* 28, no. 2, pt. 4), 119–41. Bloomington: Indiana University. [Second edition 1967.]

Cook, Eung-Do 1974. Internal evidence for the evolution of number categories in Sarcee. In: John M. Anderson and Charles Jones (eds.) *Historical Linguistics* I: *Syntax, Morphology, Internal and Comparative Reconstruction. Proceedings of the First International Conference on Historical Linguistics, Edinburgh 2nd–7th September 1973*, 101–15. Amsterdam: North-Holland.

Corbett, Greville G. 1978. Universals in the syntax of cardinal numerals. *Lingua* 46. 355–68.

1979. The agreement hierarchy. *Journal of Linguistics* 15. 203–24.

1980. Neutral agreement. *Quinquereme – New Studies in Modern Languages* 3. 164–70.

1982. Gender in Russian: an account of gender specification and its relationship to declension. *Russian Linguistics*, 6. 197–232.

1983. *Hierarchies, Targets and Controllers: Agreement Patterns in Slavic.* London: Croom Helm.

1987. The morphology/syntax interface: evidence from possessive adjectives in Slavonic. *Language* 63. 299–345.

1988. Agreement: a partial specification, based on Slavonic data. In: Michael Barlow and Charles A. Ferguson (eds.) *Agreement in Natural Language: Approaches, Theories, Descriptions*, 23–53. Stanford: Center for the Study of Language and Information, Stanford University.

1991. *Gender.* Cambridge: Cambridge University Press.

1993. The head of Russian numeral expressions. In: Greville G. Corbett, Norman M. Fraser and Scott McGlashan (eds.) *Heads in Grammatical Theory*, 11–35. Cambridge: Cambridge University Press.

1996. Minor number and the plurality split. *Rivista di Linguistica* 8, 101–122.

1999. Prototypical inflection: implications for typology. In: Geert Booij and Jaap van Marle (eds.) *Yearbook of Morphology 1998*, 1–22. Dordrecht: Kluwer.

forthcoming a. Types of typology, illustrated from gender systems. To appear in: Frans Plank (ed.) *Noun Phrase Structure in the Languages of Europe* (EUROTYP volume 7). Berlin: Mouton de Gruyter.

forthcoming b. Agreement in Slavic. WWW document prepared for the workshop 'Morphosyntax in Slavic' available at: http://www.indiana.edu/~slavconf/linguistics/index.html [January 1998]. To appear in the *Proceedings*, ed. George Fowler. Bloomington, IN: Slavica.

Corbett, Greville G. and Fraser, Norman 1993. Network Morphology: a DATR account of Russian nominal inflection. *Journal of Linguistics* 29. 113–42.

Corbett, Greville G. and Hayward, Richard J. 1987. Gender and number in Bayso. *Lingua* 73. 1–28.

Corbett, Greville G.; Hippisley, Andrew; Brown, Dunstan and Marriott, Paul forthcoming. Frequency, regularity and the paradigm: a perspective from Russian on a complex relation. To appear in: Joan Bybee and Paul Hopper (eds.) *Frequency and the Emergence of Linguistic Structure*. Amsterdam: John Benjamins.

Corbett, Greville G. and Mithun, Marianne 1996. Associative forms in a typology of number systems: evidence from Yup'ik. *Journal of Linguistics* 32. 1–17.

Corbett, Greville G. and Mtenje, Alfred D. 1987. Gender agreement in Chichewa. *Studies in African Linguistics* 18. 1–38.

Cowell, Mark W. 1964. *A Reference Grammar of Syrian Arabic (based on the dialect of Damascus)* (Arabic series 7). Washington, DC: Georgetown University Press.

Croft, William 1990. *Typology and Universals.* Cambridge: Cambridge University Press.

Crowley, Terry 1982. *The Paamese Language of Vanuatu* (Pacific Linguistics, series B, no. 87). Canberra: Department of Linguistics, Research School of Pacific Studies, Australian National University.

Cruse, D. Alan 1994. Number and number systems. In: R. E. Asher (ed.) *Encyclopedia of Language and Linguistics* V, 2857–61. Oxford: Pergamon.

Cuny, Albert 1906. *Le nombre duel en grec.* Paris: Klincksieck.

Cusic, David D. 1981. Verbal plurality and aspect. PhD dissertation, Stanford University. [Distributed by University Microfilms International, Ann Arbor, reference 8124052.]

Cuzzolin, Pierluigi 1998. Sull'origine del singolativo in celtico, con particolare riferimento al medio gallese. *Archivio Glottologico Italiano* 83, 2. 121–49.

Daley, Fergus; Hand, David; Jones, Chris; Lunn, Daniel and McConway, Kevin 1995. *Elements of Statistics.* London: Addison-Wesley.

Dalrymple, Mary; Hayrapetian, Irene and King, Tracy Holloway 1998. The semantics of the Russian comitative construction. *Natural Language and Linguistic Theory* 16. 597–631.

Dalrymple, Mary and Kaplan, Ronald M. forthcoming. Feature indeterminacy and feature resolution. To appear in *Language*.

Danièl', M. A. 1999. Semantičeskie tipy associativnosti (na materiale bagvalinskogo jazyka). In: Ja. G. Testelets and E. V. Rakhilina (eds.) *Tipologija i teorija jazyka. Ot opisanija k ob''jasneniju. K 60-letiju Aleksandra Evgen'eviča Kibrika* [Typology and Linguistic Theory: from Description to Explanation. For the 60th Birthday of Aleksandr E. Kibrik], 362–82. Moscow: Jazyki russkoj kul'tury.

Davies, John 1981. *Kobon* (Lingua Descriptive Series 3). Amsterdam: North Holland.

DeBose, Charles E. 1974. Papiamento plurals. *Studies in African Linguistics*, Supplement 5, 67–73.

References

Degtjarev, Vladimir I. 1982. *Kategorija čisla v slavjanskix jazykax (istoriko-semantičeskoe issledovanie)*. Rostov-na-Donu: Izdatel'stvo Rostovskogo universiteta.

Delsing, Lars-Olof 1993. *The internal structure of noun phrases in the Scandinavian languages: a comparative study.* Lund: Department of Scandinavian Languages, University of Lund.

Dench, Alan 1987. Kinship and collective activity in the Ngayarda languages of Australia. *Language in Society* 16. 321–40.

— 1994. The historical development of pronoun paradigms in the Pilbara Region of Western Australia. *Australian Journal of Linguistics* 14. 155–91.

— 1995. *Martuthunira: a Language of the Pilbara Region of Western Australia.* (Pacific Linguistics, series C, no. 125). Canberra: Department of Linguistics, Research School of Pacific and Asian Studies, Australian National University.

Denez, Per and Urien, Jean-Yves 1980. Studiadenn war an niver-daou (Analyse semiologique du duel en breton). *Hor Yezh* 126. 3–26.

Derganc, Aleksandra 1988. On the history of the dual in Slovene and Russian. *Wiener Slawistischer Almanach* 22. 237–47.

— 1994. Some specific features in the development of the dual in Slovene as compared to other Slavic languages. *Linguistica* 34, 1 (=Mélanges Lucien Tesnière), 71–80. Ljubljana.

Derwing, Bruce L. 1980. English pluralization: a testing ground for rule evaluation. In: Gary D. Prideaux, Bruce L. Derwing and William J. Baker (eds.) *Experimental Linguistics: Integration of Theories and Applications* (Story-Scientia Linguistics Series 3), 81–112. Ghent: Story-Scientia.

Derwing, Bruce L. and Baker, William J. 1979. Recent research on the acquisition of English morphology. In: Paul Fletcher and Michael Garman (eds.) *Language Acquisition*, 209–24. Cambridge: Cambridge University Press.

— 1980. Rule learning and the English inflections (with special emphasis on the plural). In: Gary D. Prideaux, Bruce L. Derwing and William J. Baker (eds.) *Experimental Linguistics: Integration of Theories and Applications* (Story-Scientia Linguistics Series 3), 247–72. Ghent: Story-Scientia.

Dickens, Patrick J. 1992. Juǀ'hoan Grammar. Windhoek: Nyae Nyae Development Foundation. Unpublished manuscript.

Dijkhoff, Martha B. 1983. The process of pluralization in Papiamentu. In: Lawrence D. Carrington, Dennis R. Craig and Ramon Todd-Dandaré (eds.) *Studies in Caribbean Language*, 217–29. St Augustine, Trinidad: Society for Caribbean Linguistics, University of the West Indies.

Dimmendaal, G. J. 1983. *The Turkana Language* (Publications in African Languages and Linguistics 2). Dordrecht: Foris.

Diver, William 1987. The dual. *Columbia University Working Papers in Linguistics* 8. 100–14.

Dixon, R. M. W. 1972. *The Dyirbal Language of North Queensland.* Cambridge: Cambridge University Press.

— 1980. *The Languages of Australia.* Cambridge: Cambridge University Press.

1981. Wargamay. In: R. M. W. Dixon and Barry J. Blake (eds.) *The Handbook of Australian Languages* II: *Wargamay, the Mpakwithi Dialect of Anguthimri, Watjarri, Margany and Gunya, Tasmanian*, 1–144. Amsterdam: John Benjamins.

1988. *A Grammar of Boumaa Fijian*. Chicago: University of Chicago.

1995. Fusional development of gender marking in Jarawara possessed nouns. *International Journal of American Linguistics* 61. 263–94.

Dochartaigh, Cathair Ó. 1992. The Irish language. In: Donald MacAulay *The Celtic Languages*, 11–99. Cambridge: Cambridge University Press.

Doerfer, Gerhard 1963. *Der Numerus im Mandschu* (=Akademie der Wissenschaften und der Literatur in Mainz. Abhandlungen der Geistes- und Socialwissenschaftlichen Klasse. Jahrgang 1962. No. 4, 175–283). Wiesbaden: Franz Steiner.

Doke, Clement M. 1992. *Textbook of Zulu Grammar*. Cape Town: Maskew Miller Longman. [Sixth edition; First edition 1927.]

Dostál, Antonín 1954. *Vývoj duálu v slovanských jazycích, zvláště v polštině*. Prague: ČSAV.

Downing, Pamela A. 1996. *Numeral Classifier Systems: the Case of Japanese* (Studies in Discourse and Grammar 4). Amsterdam: John Benjamins.

Drabbe, P. 1955. *Spraakkunst von het Marind: Zuidkust Nederlands Nieuw-Guinea* (Studia Instituti Anthropos 11). Wien-Mödling: Drukkerij van het Missiehuis St. Gabriel.

Dressler, Wolfgang V. 1968. *Studien sur verbalen Pluralität: Iterativum, Distributivum, Durativum, Intensivum in der allgemeinen Grammatik, im Lateinischen und Hethitischen.* (Österreichische Akademie der Wissenschaften: Philosophisch-historische Klasse: Sitzungsberichte, 259 Band, 1. Abhandlung). Vienna: Hermann Böhlaus Nachf.

Driem, George van 1987. *A Grammar of Limbu* (Mouton Grammar library 4). Berlin: Mouton de Gruyter.

Drossard, Werner 1982. Nominalklassifikation in ostkaukasischen Sprachen. In: Hansjakob Seiler and Franz J. Stachowiak (eds.) *Apprehension: Das sprachliche Erfassen von Gegenständen* II: *Die Techniken und ihr Zusammenhang in Einzelsprachen*, 155–78. Tübingen: Narr.

Dryer, Matthew S. 1989. Plural words. *Linguistics* 27. 865–95.

1992. The Greenbergian word order correlations. *Language* 68. 81–138.

Du Feu, Veronica 1996. *Rapanui* (Descriptive grammars series). London: Routledge.

Dunaj, Bogusław 1993. Die Distribution der Endungen des Nominativus Pluralis männlicher Substantive im Polnischen. In: Gerd Hentschel and Roman Laskowski (eds.) *Studies in Polish Morphology and Syntax* (Specimina philologiae slavicae 99), 107–20. Munich: Otto Sagner.

Durie, Mark 1985. *A Grammar of Acehnese: on the Basis of a Dialect of North Aceh* (Verhandelingen van het Koninklijk Instituut voor Taal-, Land- en Volkenkunde 112). Dordrecht: Foris.

1986. The grammaticization of number as a verbal category. In: Vassiliki Nikiforidou, Mary VanClay, Mary Niepokuj and Deborah Feder (eds.) *Proceedings of the Twelfth Annual Meeting of the Berkeley Linguistics Society: February 15–17, 1986*, 355–70. Berkeley, CA: Berkeley Linguistics Society, University of California.

References

Dyła, Stefan 1988. Quasi-comitative coordination in Polish. *Linguistics* 26. 383–414.

Edgerton, Franklin 1910. Origin and development of the elliptic dual and of dvandva compounds. *Zeitschrift für vergleichende Sprachforschung auf dem Gebiete des Deutschen, Griechischen und Lateinischen* 43. 110–20.

El-Solami-Mewis, Catherine 1988. On classifying Somali nouns by their plural classes. In: Marianne Bechhaus-Gerst and Fritz Serzisko (eds.) *Cushitic-Omotic: Papers from the International Symposium on Cushitic and Omotic Languages: Cologne, January 6–9, 1986*, 553–63. Hamburg: Buske.

Elson, Ben 1960. Sierra Popoluca morphology. *International Journal of American Linguistics* 26. 206–23.

England, John 1976. 'Dixo Rachel e Vidas': subject–verb agreement in Old Spanish. *Modern Language Review* 71. 812–26.

Eri-Birk, Marijana 1976. Pogostnost in skladenjska vloga sklonov v besedilu Šeligovega Triptiha Agate Schwarzkobler. *Slavistična revija* 24. 119–26.

Eriksson, Olof 1979. Scandinavian gender agreement revisited. *Journal of Linguistics* 15. 93–105.

Ermakova, M. I. 1966. Dvojstvennoe čislo v serbolužickix jazykax na materiale pamjatnikov XVI–XVIII vekov. In: Helmut Faßke and Ronald Lötzsch (eds.) *Beiträge zur sorbischen Sprachwissenschaft*, 242–51. Bautzen: VEB Domowina Verlag.

Études linguistiques: Le problème du nombre 1965. = *Bulletin de la Faculté des Lettres de Strasbourg* 43.6, March 1965, 443–592.

Eulenberg, John B. 1971. Conjunction reduction and reduplication in African languages. In: Chin-Wu Kim and Herbert Stahlke (eds.) *Papers in African Linguistics* (Current Inquiry into Language and Linguistics 1), 71–80. Edmonton: Linguistic Research.

Evans, Barrie 1994. *Draft Grammar of Pular.* Conakry: Mission Protestante Réformée.

Evans, Nicholas 1995. A-quantifiers and scope in Mayali. In: Emmon Bach, Eloise Jelenek, Angelika Kratzer and Barbara Partee (eds.) *Quantification in Natural Languages* I (Studies in Linguistics and Philosophy 54), 207–70. Dordrecht: Kluwer.

forthcoming. *Bininj Gun-wok: a pan-dialectal grammar of Mayali, Kunwinjku and Kune.*

Everett, Daniel 1986. Pirahã. In: Desmond C. Derbyshire and Geoffrey K. Pullum (eds.) *Handbook of Amazonian Languages* I, 200–325. Berlin: Mouton de Gruyter.

1997. Pirahã. (ESRC Research Seminar Series 'Challenges for Inflectional Description' – III, University of Surrey, 13.5.1997). Unpublished.

Faarlund, Jan Terje 1977. Embedded clause reduction and Scandinavian gender agreement. *Journal of Linguistics* 13. 239–57.

Fabri, Ray 1993. *Kongruenz und die Grammatik des Maltesischen* (Linguistische Arbeiten 292). Tübingen: Niemeyer.

Fabricius, Anne H. 1998. *A Comparative Survey of Reduplication in Australian Languages* (Lincom Studies in Australian Languages 2). Munich: Lincom Europa.

Faraclas, Nicholas 1984. *A Grammar of Obolo* (Studies in African Grammatical Systems 1). Bloomington, IN: Indiana University Linguistics Club.

Farkas, Donka and Ojeda, Almerindo 1983. Agreement and coordinate NPs. *Linguistics* 21. 659–73.

Farrell, Patrick 1996. Categories of number in Brazilian Portuguese. In: Patrick Farrell, Debra Ochhi and Alison Rukeyser (eds.) *Topics in Language, Culture, and Cognition* (= *Davis Working Papers in Linguistics* 5). Electronic document: http://philo.ucdavis.edu/LINGUISTICS/linghp 36.html

Faßke, Helmut 1981. *Grammatik der obersorbischen Schriftsprache der Gegenwart: Morphologie.* Bautzen: VEB Domowina Verlag.

Fenech, Edward 1996. Functions of the dual suffix in Maltese. *Rivista di Linguistica* 8. 89–99.

Fennell, Trevor G. and Gelsen, Henrik 1980. *A Grammar of Modern Latvian* I (Slavistic Printings and Reprintings, 304). The Hague: Mouton.

Ferguson, Charles A. 1959. The Arabic Koine. *Language* 35. 616–30.

1989. Grammatical agreement in Classical Arabic and the modern dialects: a response to Versteegh's pidginization hypothesis. *Al-ᶜArabiyya* 22. 5–17.

Findreng, Ådne 1976. *Zur Kongruenz in Person und Numerus zwischen Subjekt und finitem Verb im modernen Deutsch.* Oslo: Universitetsforlaget.

Fischer, Wolfdietrich 1980. Die arabische Pluralbildung. *Zeitschrift für arabische Linguistik* 8. 70–88.

Foley, William A. 1986. *The Papuan Languages of New Guinea.* Cambridge: Cambridge University Press.

1991. *The Yimas Language of New Guinea.* Stanford: Stanford University Press.

Fontinoy, Charles 1969. *Le duel dans les langues sémitiques* (Bibliothèque de la Faculté de Philosophie et Lettres de l'Université de Liège 179). Paris: Les Belles Lettres.

Forchheimer, Paul 1953. *The Category of Person in Language.* Berlin: de Gruyter.

Fortescue, Michael 1984. *West Greenlandic.* London: Croom Helm.

Fortescue, Michael; Jacobson, Steven A. and Kaplan, Lawrence D. 1994. *Comparative Eskimo Dictionary: with Aleut Cognates.* Fairbanks: Alaska Native Language Center, University of Alaska.

Fortune, Reo F. 1942. *Arapesh.* (Publications of the American Ethnological Society 19). New York: J. J. Augustin. [Reprinted 1977, New York: AMS.]

Fradkin, Robert A. 1991. Marking, markedness, and person–gender–number patterning in the Arabic tenses and moods. *Folia Linguistica* 25. 609–64.

Frajzyngier, Zygmunt 1985. Ergativity, number, and agreement. In: Mary Niepokuj, Mary Van Clay, Vassiliki Nikiforidou, and Deborah Feder (eds.), *Proceedings of the Eleventh Annual Meeting of the Berkeley Linguistics Society, February 16–18, 1985,* 96–106. Berkeley, CA: Berkeley Linguistics Society, University of California.

1997. Grammaticalization of number: from demonstratives to nominal and verbal plural. *Journal of Linguistic Typology* 1. 193–242.

Fraser, Norman M. and Corbett, Greville G. 1997. Defaults in Arapesh. *Lingua* 103. 25–57.

Friedman, Victor A. 1993. Macedonian. In: Bernard Comrie and Greville G. Corbett (eds.), *The Slavonic Languages,* 249–305. London: Routledge.

Furukawa, Naoyo 1977. *Le nombre grammatical en français contemporain.* Tokyo: France Tosho.

References

Gathercole, Virginia 1985. 'He has too much hard questions': the acquisition of the linguistic mass–count distinction in *much* and *many*. *Journal of Child Language* 12. 395–415.

1986. Evaluating competing linguistic theories with child language data: the case of the mass–count distinction. *Linguistics and Philosophy* 9. 151–90.

Gauthiot, Robert. 1912. Du nombre duel. In: Ernst Kuhn (ed.) *Festschrift Vilhelm Thomsen zur Vollendung des siebzigsten Lebensjahres am 25. Januar 1912 dargebracht von Freunden und Schülern*, 127–33. Leipzig: Otto Harrassowitz.

Gawełko, Marek 1985. Analyse fonctionnelle de la catégorie du nombre dans les langues française, roumaine et polonaise. *Cahiers Ferdinand de Saussure* 39. 131–42.

Genetti, Carol 1994. *A Descriptive and Historical Account of the Dolakha Newari Dialect* (Monumenta Serindica 24). Tokyo: Institute for the Study of Languages and Cultures of Asia and Africa, Tokyo University of Foreign Studies.

Giancarli, Pierre-Don 1999. Discontinu: fonctionnement, formations et emplois du pluriel nominal homogène externe chez des enfrants unilingues et bilingues. *Cycnos* 16, 2. 111–34.

Gibson, Lorna and Bartholomew, Doris 1979. Pame noun inflection. *International Journal of American Linguistics* 45. 309–22.

Gil, David 1987. Definiteness, noun-phrase configurationality, and the count–mass distinction. In: E. J. Reuland and A. G. B. ter Meulen (eds.) *The Representation of (In)definiteness*, 254–69. Cambridge, MA: MIT Press.

1988. Georgian reduplication and the domain of distributivity. *Linguistics* 26. 1039–65.

1993. Nominal and verbal quantification. *Sprachtypologie und Universalienforschung* 46. 275–317.

1995. Universal quantifiers and distributivity. In: Emmon Bach, Eloise Jelenek, Angelika Kratzer and Barbara Partee (eds.) *Quantification in Natural Languages* I (Studies in Linguistics and Philosophy 54), 321–62. Dordrecht: Kluwer.

1996. Maltese 'collective nouns': a typological perspective. *Rivista di Linguistica* 8. 53–87.

forthcoming. English goes Asian: number and (in)definiteness in the Singlish noun phrase. To appear in: Frans Plank (ed.) *Noun Phrase Structure in the Languages of Europe* (EUROTYP volume 7). Berlin: Mouton de Gruyter.

Gilley, Leoma G. 1992. *An Autosegmental Approach to Shilluk Phonology* (Summer Institute of Linguistics and the University of Texas at Arlington Publications in Linguistics 103). Dallas: International Academic Bookstore.

Givón, Talmy 1970. The resolution of gender conflicts in Bantu conjunction: when syntax and semantics clash. *Papers from the Sixth Regional Meeting, Chicago Linguistic Society*, 250–61. Chicago: Chicago Linguistic Society.

Glasgow, Kathleen 1964. Four principal contrasts in Burera personal pronouns. In: Richard Pittman and Harland Kerr (eds.) *Papers in the Languages of Australian Aborigines* (Occasional Papers in Aboriginal Studies 3), 109–17. Canberra: Australian Institute of Aboriginal Studies.

Goddard, Cliff 1995. Who are *We*? The natural semantics of pronouns. *Language Sciences* 17. 99–121.

Golston, Chris and Wiese, Richard 1996. Zero morphology and constraint interaction: subtraction and epenthesis in German dialects. In: Geert Booij and Jaap van Marle (eds.) *Yearbook of Morphology 1995*, 143–59. Dordrecht: Kluwer.

Gonda, J. 1942. The functions of word duplication in Indonesian languages. *Lingua* 2. 170–97.

1974. *The Dual Deities in the Religion of the Veda* (Verhandelingen der Koninklijke Nederlandse Akademie van Wetenschappen, afd. Letterkunde, Nieuwe Reeks, deel 81). Amsterdam: North-Holland.

Gordon, Peter 1985a. Evaluating the semantic categories hypothesis: the case of the count/mass distinction. *Cognition* 20. 209–42.

1985b. Level-ordering in lexical development. *Cognition* 21. 73–93.

1988. Count/mass category acquisition: distributional distinctions in children's speech. *Journal of Child Language* 15. 109–28.

Goulden, Rick 1996. The Maleu and Bariai languages of West New Britain. In: Malcolm D. Ross (ed.) *Studies in Languages of New Britain and New Ireland* I: *Austronesian Languages of the North New Guinea Cluster in Northwestern New Britain* (Pacific Linguistics Series C, no. 135), 63–144. Canberra: Research School of Pacific and Asian Studies, Australian National University.

Grapow, Hermann 1939. Zum Dualis a potiori. *Zeitschrift für Ägyptische Sprache und Altertumskunde* 75. 134–5.

Grasserie, Raoul de la 1886–87. Études de grammaire comparée: de la catégorie du nombre. *Revue de linguistique et de philologie comparée* 19 (1886), 87–105, 113–46, 232–53; and 20 (1887), 57–67.

Graudina, L. K.; Ickovič, V. A. and Katlinskaja, L. P. 1976. *Grammatičeskaja pravil'nost' russkoj reči: opyt častotno-stilističeskogo slovarja variantov.* Moscow: Nauka.

Green, Ian 1989. Marrithiyel, a language of the Daly River region of Australia's Northern Territory. PhD thesis, Australian National University.

1993. The Daly language family: a reassessment. Unpublished monograph, Canberra: Department of Linguistics, Australian National University.

Green, Tom 1992. Covert clause structure in the Miskitu noun phrase. Unpublished paper, Cambridge, MA: Massachusetts Institute of Technology.

Greenberg, Joseph H. 1963. Some universals of grammar with particular reference to the order of meaningful elements. In: Joseph H. Greenberg (ed.) *Universals of Language,* 73–113. Cambridge, MA: MIT Press. [Paperback edition published 1966; page references to this edition.] [Reprinted in Keith Denning and Suzanne Kemmer (eds.) 1990. *On Language: Selected Writings of Joseph H. Greenberg*, 40–70. Stanford: Stanford University Press.]

1966. *Language Universals: with Special Reference to Feature Hierarchies.* The Hague: Mouton.

1972. Numeral classifiers and substantival number: problems in the genesis of a linguistic type. *Working Papers on Language Universals* (Stanford University) 9. 1–39. [Reprinted in Keith Denning and Suzanne Kemmer (eds.) 1990. *On Language: Selected Writings of Joseph H. Greenberg*, 166–93. Stanford: Stanford University Press.]

References

1988. The first person inclusive dual as an ambiguous category. *Studies in Language* 12. 1–18. [Reprinted in Keith Denning and Suzanne Kemmer (eds.) 1990. *On Language: Selected Writings of Joseph H. Greenberg*, 344–58. Stanford: Stanford University Press.]

1989. On a metalanguage for pronominal systems: a reply to McGregor. *Studies in Language* 13. 452–8.

1991. The Semitic 'intensive' as verbal plurality. In: Alan S. Kaye (ed.) *Semitic Studies in Honor of Wolf Leslau: on the Occasion of his Eighty-fifth Birthday, November 14th, 1991* I, 577–87. Wiesbaden: Otto Harrassowitz.

Gregores, Emma and Suárez, Jorge A. 1967. *A Description of Colloquial Guaraní* (Janua linguarum, Series practica 27). The Hague: Mouton.

Gruber, Jeffrey S. 1975. Plural predicates in ǂHòã. In: Anthony Trail (ed.) *Bushman and Hottentot Linguistics Studies* (= ASI Communication no. 2), 1–50. Johannesburg: African Studies Institute, University of the Witwatersrand.

Guðmundsson, Helgi 1972. *The Pronominal Dual in Icelandic* (University of Iceland Publications in Linguistics 2). Reykjavik: Institute of Nordic Linguistics.

Güldemann, Tom 1999. Noun categorization in Non-Khoe lineages of Khoisan. Paper read at the Max Planck Institute for Evolutionary Anthropology, May 1999. Unpublished.

Guthrie, Malcolm 1948. Gender, number and person in Bantu languages. *Bulletin of the School of Oriental and African Studies, University of London* 12. 847–56.

Haas, Mary R. 1948. Classificatory verbs in Muskogee. *International Journal of American Linguistics* 14. 244–6.

Haeberlin, Herman K. 1918. Types of reduplication in the Salish dialects. *International Journal of American Linguistics* 1. 154–74.

Haiman, John 1980. *Hua: a Papuan Language of the Eastern Highlands of New Guinea* (Studies in Language Companion Series 5). Amsterdam: John Benjamins.

Hakulinen, Lauri 1961. *The Structure and Development of the Finnish Language* (translated by John Atkinson) (= Research and studies in Uralic and Altaic Languages, Project no. 50). Bloomington, IN: Indiana University.

1968. *Suomen kielen rakenne ja kehitys. Kolmas, korjattu ja lisätty painos* [The structure and development of the Finnish language]. Helsinki: Otava. (3rd Edition.)

Hale, Kenneth 1956–57. Notes on Jemez grammar. Unpublished fieldnotes.

1997. Some observations on the contributions of local languages to linguistic science. *Lingua* 100. 71–89.

Hale, Kenneth; Jeanne, LaVerne M. and Pranka, Paula M. 1991. On suppletion, selection, and agreement. In: Carol Georgopoulos and Roberta Ishihara (eds.) *Interdisciplinary Approaches to Language: Essays in Honor of S.-Y. Kuroda*, 255–70. Dordrecht: Kluwer.

Hall, Robert A. 1968. Neuters, mass-nouns, and the ablative in Romance. *Language* 44. 480–6.

Hammerich, L. L. 1959. Wenn der Dualis lebendig ist. *Die Sprache* 5. 16–26.

Hammond, Michael 1988. Templatic transfer in Arabic broken plurals. *Natural Language and Linguistic Theory* 6. 247–70.

Hao, Cao Xuan 1988. The count/mass distinction in Vietnamese and the concept of 'classifier'. *Zeitschrift für Phonetik Sprachwissenschaft und Kommunikationsforschung* 41. 38–47.

Harris, James W. 1992. The form classes of Spanish substantives. In: Geert Booij and Jaap van Marle (eds.) *Yearbook of Morphology 1991*, 65–88. Dordrecht: Kluwer.

Harrison, Sheldon P. 1976. With the assistance of Salich Y. Albert. *Mokilese Reference Grammar.* Honolulu: University Press of Hawaii.

Haspelmath, Martin 1989. Schemas in Hausa plural formation: product-orientation and motivation vs. source-orientation and generation. *Buffalo Working Papers in Linguistics* 89–01. 32–74.

1993. *A Grammar of Lezgian* (Mouton Grammar Library 9). Berlin: Mouton de Gruyter.

Haugen, Einar 1975. Pronominal address in Icelandic: from you-two to you-all. *Language in Society* 4. 323–39.

Hawkins, John A. and Cutler, Anne 1988. Psycholinguistic factors and morphological asymmetry. In: John A. Hawkins (ed.) *Explaining Language Universals*, 280–317. Oxford: Blackwell.

Hayes, Bruce and Abad, May 1989. Reduplication and syllabification in Ilokano. *Lingua* 77. 331–74.

Hayward, Katrina 1998. The verbal auxiliary *padha* in contemporary Javanese. In: Mark Janse (ed.) *Productivity and Creativity: Studies in General and Descriptive Linguistics in Honor of E. M. Uhlenbeck* (Trends in Linguistics: Studies and Monographs 116), 317–35. Berlin: Mouton de Gruyter.

Hayward, Richard J. 1979. Bayso revisited: some preliminary linguistic observations II. *Bulletin of the School of Oriental and African Studies, University of London* 42. 101–32.

1984. *The Arbore Language: a First Investigation: Including a Vocabulary.* (Cushitic Language Studies 2). Hamburg: Buske.

1990. Notes on the Aari language. In: Richard J. Hayward (ed.) *Omotic Language Studies*, 425–93. London: School of Oriental and African Studies.

1998. Qafar (East Cushitic). In: Andrew Spencer and Arnold M. Zwicky (eds.) *The Handbook of Morphology*, 624–47. Oxford: Blackwell.

Hayward, Richard J. and Corbett, Greville G. 1988. Resolution rules in Qafar. *Linguistics* 26. 259–79.

Head, Brian F. 1978. Respect degrees in pronominal reference. In: Joseph H. Greenberg, Charles A. Ferguson and Edith A. Moravcsik (eds.) *Universals of Human Language* III: *Word Structure*, 151–211. Stanford: Stanford University Press.

Hedlund, Cecilia 1992. *On participles.* PhD dissertation, Department of Linguistics, University of Stockholm. Distributed by Akademitryck AB, Edsbruk.

Hellan, Lars 1977. X̄-syntax, categorial syntax and logical form. In: Thorstein Freitheim and Lars Hellan (eds.) *Papers from the Trondheim Syntax Symposium 1977*, 85–135. Trondheim: University of Trondheim, Department of Linguistics.

Hemon, Roparz 1975. *A Historical Morphology and Syntax of Breton* (Mediaeval and Mordern Breton Series III). Dublin: Dublin Institute for Advanced Studies.

References

Henderson, John 1990. Morpho-syntactic strategies in Arrernte verb morphology. Paper presented to the Australian Linguistic Society Annual Conference, Macquarie University, September 1990. Unpublished.

Hercus, Louise A. 1966. Some aspects of the form and use of the trial number in Victorian languages and in Arabana. *Mankind* 6. 335–7.

Herweg, Michael 1991. Perfective and imperfective aspect and the theory of events and states. *Linguistics* 29. 969–1010.

Hetzron, Robert 1972. Phonology in syntax. *Journal of Linguistics* 8. 251–65.

1973. Conjoining and comitativization in Hungarian: a study of rule ordering. *Foundations of Language* 10. 493–507.

Higginbotham, James 1995. Mass and count quantifiers. In: Emmon Bach, Eloise Jelenek, Angelika Kratzer and Barbara Partee (eds.) *Quantification in Natural Languages* II (Studies in Linguistics and Philosophy 54), 383–419. Dordrecht: Kluwer.

Hill, Deborah 1992. Longgu grammar. PhD thesis, Australian National University, Canberra.

Hill, Jane H. and Hill, Kenneth C. 1996. Marked and unmarked plural nouns in Uto-Aztecan. Paper presented at the Friends of Uto-Aztecan Conference 1996. Unpublished.

Hill, Jane H. and Zepeda, Ofelia 1998. Tohono O'odham (Papago) plurals. *Anthropological Linguistics* 40. 1–42.

Hirtle, Walter H. 1982. *Number and Inner Space: a Study of Grammatical Number in English* (Cahiers du pychoméchanique du langage). Québec: Les Presses de l'Université Laval.

Hoeksema, Jack 1983. Plurality and conjunction. In: Alice G. B. ter Meulen (ed.) *Studies in Modeltheoretic Semantics* (Groningen–Amsterdam studies in semantics 1), 63–83. Dordrecht: Foris.

Hoijer, Harry 1933–38. Tonkawa: an Indian language of Texas. In: Franz Boas (ed.) *Handbook of American Indian Languages* III, 1–148. New York: Columbia University Press.

Holisky, Dee Ann 1985. A stone's throw from aspect to number in Tsova-Tush. *International Journal of American Linguistics* 51. 453–5.

Holm, John 1990. Features in the noun phrase common to the Atlantic creoles. *Linguistics* 28. 867–81.

Holsinger, David J. and Houseman, Paul D. 1999. Lenition in Hessian: cluster reduction and 'subtractive plurals'. In: Geert Booij and Jaap van Marle (eds.) *Yearbook of Morphology 1998*, 159–74. Dordrecht: Kluwer.

Honti, László 1995. Wieviel Augen haben die Uralier? (Zu Funktionen der Numeri im Uralischen). In: Ago Künnap (ed.) *Minor Uralic Languages: Grammar and Lexis*, 73–87. Tartu-Groningen: University of Tartu and University of Groningen.

1997. Numerusprobleme (Ein Erkundungszug durch den Dschungel der uralischen Numeri). *Finnisch-Ugrische Forschungen (Zeitschrift für finnisch-ugrische Sprach- und Volkskunde)* 54. 1–126.

Hualde, José Ignacio 1992. Metaphony and count/mass morphology in Asturian and Cantabrian dialects. In: Christiane Laeufer and Terrell A. Morgan (eds.) *Theoretical*

Analyses in Romance Linguistics: Selected Papers from the Nineteenth Linguistic Symposium on Romance Languages (LSRL XIX): the Ohio State University, 21–23 April 1989 (Current Issues in Linguistic Theory 74), 99–114. Amsterdam: John Benjamins.

Humboldt, Wilhelm von 1830. Über den Dualis. *Abhandlungen der historisch-philologischen Klasse der Königlichen Akademie der Wissenschaften zu Berlin aus dem Jahre 1827*, 161–87. [Reprinted 1907 in *Wilhelm von Humboldts Gesammelte Schriften* edited by Königlich Preussische Akademie der Wissenschaften, VI, 4–30. Berlin: B. Behr.]

Huntley, David 1989. Grammatical and lexical features in number and gender agreement in Old Bulgarian. *Palaeobulgarica* 13, 4. 21–32.

Hurford, James R. forthcoming. Numeral noun interaction. To appear in: Frans Plank (ed.) *Noun Phrase Structure in the Languages of Europe*. Berlin: Mouton de Gruyter.

Hutchisson, Don. 1986. Sursurunga pronouns and the special uses of quadral number. In: Ursula Wiesemann (ed.) *Pronominal Systems* (Continuum 5), 217–55. Tübingen: Narr.

Hyman, Larry M. and Comrie, Bernard 1981. Logophoric reference in Gokana. *Journal of African Languages and Linguistics* 3. 19–37.

Ibragimov, G. X. 1974. O mnogoformantnosti množestvennogo čisla imen suščestvitel′nyx v vostočnokavakazskix jazykax (Na materiale rutul′skogo, caxurskogo, kryzskogo i buduxskogo jazykov). *Voprosy jazykoznanija* no. 3: 82–93.

Idrissi, Ali 1997. Plural formation in Arabic. In: Mushira Eid and Robert T. Ratcliffe (eds.) *Perspectives on Arabic Linguistics* X: *Papers from the Tenth Annual Symposium on Arabic Linguistics* (= Amsterdam Studies in the Theory and History of Linguistic Science, Series IV, Current Issues in Linguistic Theory 153), 123–45. Amsterdam: John Benjamins.

Ikari, Osamu 1989. Pluralization: Japanese and Tagalog. *Philippine Journal of Linguistics* 20. 45–54.

Iljic, Robert 1994. Quantification in Mandarin Chinese: two markers of plurality. *Linguistics* 32. 91–116.

Iordanskij, A. M. 1960. *Istorija dvojstvennogo čisla v russkom jazyke*. Vladimir.

Isačenko, Aleksandr V. 1941/1976. Dvojstvennoe čislo vъ 'Slově o pъlku Igorevě' In *Zametki k Slovu o polku Igoreve*, 34–48. Belgrade. [Reprinted in Alexander V. Isačenko 1976. *Opera Selecta: Russische Gegenwartssprache, russische Sprachgeschichte, Probleme der slavischen Sprachwissenschaft* (Forum Slavicum 45), 34–48. Munich: Fink Verlag.]

   1962. *Die russische Sprache der Gegenwart* I: *Formenlehre*. Halle (Saale): Max Niemeyer.

Ivens, W. G. 1927. A study of the Oroha Language, Mala, Solomon Islands. *Bulletin of the School of African and Oriental Studies, University of London* 4. 587–610.

Ivić, Milka 1982. Slavic fruit and vegetable names and countability. *International Journal of Slavic Linguistics and Poetics* 25–6 (= Kenneth E. Naylor, Howard I. Aronson, Bill J. Darden and Alexander M. Schenker eds *Slavic Linguistics and Poetics: Studies for Edward Stankiewicz on his 60th Birthday, 17 November 1980)*, 209–11. Columbus, OH: Slavica.

References

Jackendoff, Ray 1991. Parts and boundaries. *Cognition* 41. 9–45.

Jacobson, Steven A. 1995. *A Practical Grammar of the Central Alaskan Yup'ik Eskimo language* (with Yup'ik readings written by Anna W. Jacobson). Fairbanks: Alaska Native Language Center, University of Alaska.

Jakobson, Roman 1932. Zur Struktur des russischen Verbums. In: *Charisteria Gvilelmo Mathesio qvinqvagenario a discipulis et Circuli Lingvistici Pragensis sodalibus oblata*, 74–84. Prague: Pražký Lingvistický Kroužek. [Reprinted in *Jakobson's Selected Writings* II, 3–15. The Hague: Mouton.]

Jamison, Stephanie W. 1988. Vāyav Indraś ca revisited. *Münchener Studien zur Sprachwissenschaft* 49. 13–59.

Janaš, Pětr 1984. *Niedersorbische Grammatik*. Bautzen: Domowina Verlag. [Second edition; First edition 1976.]

Janda, Laura A. 1996. *Back from the Brink: a Study of how Relic Forms in Languages Serve as Source Material for Analogical Extension* (Lincom Studies in Slavic Linguistics 1). Munich: Lincom Europa.

— 1998. Linguistic innovation from defunct morphology: old dual endings in Polish and Russian. In: Robert A. Maguire and Alan Timberlake (eds.) *American Contributions to the Twelfth International Congress of Slavists, Cracow, August–September 1998*, 431–43. Bloomington, IN: Slavica.

Janda, Richard D. 1991. Frequency, markedness, and morphological change: on predicting the spread of noun-plural -*s* in Modern High German and West Germanic. In: Yongkyoon No and Mark Libucha (eds.) *ESCOL '90: Proceedings of the Seventh Eastern States Conference on Linguistics*, 136–53. Columbus: Ohio State University.

Jarvis, Donald K. 1986. Some problems with noun number choice. *Slavic and East European Journal* 30. 262–70.

Jenč, Rudolf 1966. Wo woznamjenjenju porowosće w hornjoserbšćinje. In: Helmut Faßke and Ronald Lötzsch (eds.) *Beiträge zur sorbischen Sprachwissenschaft*, 214–41. Bautzen: VEB Domowina Verlag.

Jensen, Hans 1952. Die sprachliche Kategorie des Numerus. *Wissenschaftliche Zeitschrift der Universität Rostock, Reihe Gesellschafts- und Sprachwissenschaften* 1, 2. 1–21.

Jespersen, Otto 1924. *The Philosophy of Grammar*. London: Allen and Unwin.

Johansson, Stig 1979. American and British English grammar: an elicitation experiment. *English Studies* 60. 195–215.

Juul, Arne 1975. *On Concord of Number in Modern English* (Publications of the Department of English, University of Copenhagen 1). Copenhagen: Nova.

Källström, Roger 1993. *Kongruens i svenskan* (Nordistica Gothoburgensia 16). Göteborg: Acta Universitatis Gothoburgensis.

Kang, Beom-Mo 1994. Plurality and other semantic aspects of common nouns in Korean. *Journal of East Asian Linguistics* 3. 1–24.

Karlsson, Göran 1959a. Suomen kielen numeruksesta kardinaalilukusanan ollessa subjektina [The number of the verb in Finnish when the subject is a cardinal numeral]. *Virittäjästä* 3. 356–68.

1959b. Suomen kielen monikko likimääräisyyden ilmaisukeinona [The plural in Finnish as a means of expressing approximation]. In: Pertti Virtaranta, Terho Itkonen and Paavo Pulkkinen (eds.) *Verba docent: Juhlakirja Lauri Hakulisen 60–vuotispäiväksi 6.10.1959* (*Suomalaisen Kirjallisuuden Seuran Toimituksia* 263), 330–42. Helsinki: Suomalaisen Kirjallisuuden Seura.

Kehayia, Eva; Jarema, Gonia and Kądziela, Danuta 1990. Cross-linguistic study of morphological errors in aphasia: evidence from English, Greek, and Polish. In: Jean-Luc Nespoulous and Pierre Villiard (eds.) *Morphology, Phonology and Aphasia*, 140–55. New York: Springer.

Kemmer, Suzanne 1993. Marking oppositions in verbal and nominal collectives. *Faits de langues 2: Le nombre*, 84–95. Evry Cedex: Presses Universitaires de France.

Kibrik, Aleksandr E. 1991. Organising principles for nominal paradigms in Daghestanian languages: comparative and typological observations. In: Frans Plank (ed.) *Paradigms: the Economy of Inflection* (Empirical Approaches to Language Typology 9), 255–74. Berlin: Mouton de Gruyter.

1992. Defective paradigms: number in Daghestanian. European Science Foundation Programme in Language Typology: Theme 7, Noun Phrase Structure: Working Paper no. 16. (EUROTYP Working Papers VII/16) 18pp.

(ed.) 1999. [Co-editor Jakov G. Testelec.] *Èlementy grammatiki caxurskogo jazyka v tipologičeskom osveščenii*. Moscow: Nasledie.

forthcoming. Nominal inflection in Daghestanian languages. To appear in: Frans Plank (ed.) *Noun Phrase Structure in the Languages of Europe*. Berlin: Mouton de Gruyter.

Kibrik, Aleksandr E. and Kodzasov, Sandro V. 1990. *Sopostavitel'noe izučenie dagestanskix jazykov: Imja, fonetika*. Moscow: Izdatel'stvo Moskovskogo universiteta.

Kim, Yookyung 1994. A non-spurious account of 'spurious' Korean plurals. In: Young-Key Kim-Renaud (ed.) *Theoretical Issues in Korean Linguistics*, 303–23. Stanford: Center for the Study of Language and Information.

Kimball, Geoffrey 1990. Noun pluralization in Eastern Huasteca Nahuatl. *International Journal of American Linguistics* 56. 196–216.

1991. *Koasati Grammar*. Lincoln: University of Nebraska.

1993. Two hunters, two wives, two dogs, and two clawed witches: the use of the dual in a Koasati narrative. *International Journal of American Linguistics* 59. 473–88.

Kinkade, M. Dale 1981. Singular vs. plural roots in Salish. *Anthropological Linguistics* 23. 262–9.

1995. A plethora of plurals: inflection for number in Upper Chehalis. *Anthropological Linguistics* 37. 347–65.

Kiparsky, Paul 1982. From cyclic phonology to lexical phonology. In: Harry van der Hulst and Norval Smith (eds.) *The Structure of Phonological Representations* I (Linguistic Models 2), 131–75. Dordrecht: Foris.

Kiyomi, Setsuko 1995. A new approach to reduplication: a semantic study of noun and verb reduplication in the Malayo-Polynesian languages. *Linguistics* 33. 1145–67.

Klamer, Marian 1998. *A Grammar of Kambera* (Mouton Grammar Library 18). Berlin: Mouton de Gruyter.

References

Klein, Flora 1980. Pragmatic and sociolinguistic bias in semantic change. In: Elizabeth C. Traugott, Rebecca Labrum and Susan Shephard (eds.) *Papers from the Fourth International Conference on Historical Linguistics* (Current Issues in Linguistic Theory 14), 61–74. Amsterdam: John Benjamins.

Klein-Andreu, Flora 1996. Anaphora, deixis, and the evolution of Latin *ille*. In: Barbara Fox (ed.) *Studies in Anaphora* (Typological Studies in Language 33), 305–31. Amsterdam: John Benjamins.

Klobukov, Evgenij V. 1998. Čislo i kommunikativnaja tipologija grammatičeskix značenij. In: A. A. Kiklevič, A. A. Kožinova, I. V. Kožinova, N. B. Mečkovskaja, B. Ju. Norman and B. A. Plotnikov (eds.) *Čislo–jazyk–tekst: Sbornik statej k 70-letiju Adama Evgeňeviča Supruna*, 127–36. Minsk: Belorusskij Gosudarstvennyj Universitet.

Koch, Grace and Koch, Harold 1993. *Kaytetye Country: an Aboriginal History of the Barrow Creek Area.* Alice Springs: Institute for Aboriginal Development.

Koch, Harold 1990. Do Australian languages really have morphemes? Issues in Kaytej morphology. In: Peter Austin, R. M. W. Dixon, Tom Dutton and Isobel White (eds.) *Language and History: Essays in Honour of Luise A. Hercus* (Pacific Linguistics, series C, no. 116), 193–208. Canberra: Department of Linguistics, Research School of Pacific Studies, Australian National University.

Koehn, C. 1994. The acquisition of gender and number morphology within NP. In: Jürgen Meisel (ed.) *Bilingual First Language Acquisition: French and German Grammatical Development* (Language acquisition and language disorders 7), 53–88. Amsterdam: John Benjamins.

Kohnen, B. 1933. *Shilluk Grammar, with a Little English–Shilluk Dictionary.* Verona: Missioni Africane.

Koneski, Blaže 1967. *Gramatika na makedonskiot literaturen jazik* I and II. Skopje: Kultura.

Köpcke, Klaus-Michael 1988. Schemas in German plural formation. *Lingua* 74. 303–35.

1993. *Schemata bei der Pluralbildung des Deutschen: Versuch einer kognitiven Morphologie* (Studien zur deutschen Grammatik 47). Tübingen: Narr.

1994. Zur Rolle von Schemata bei der Pluralbildung monosyllabischer Maskulina. In: Klaus-Michael Köpcke (ed.) *Funktionale Untersuchungen zur deutschen Nominal- und Verbalmorphologie* (Linguistische Arbeiten 319), 81–95. Tübingen: Niemeyer.

1998. The acquisition of plural marking in English and German revisited: schemata versus rules. *Journal of Child Language* 25. 293–319.

Kornfilt, Jaklin 1997. *Turkish* (Descriptive grammars series). London: Routledge.

Koval', A. I. 1979. O značenii morfologičeskogo pokazatelja klassa v fula. In: N. V. Oxotina (ed.) *Morfonologija i morfologija klassov slov v jazykax Afriki*, 5–100. Moscow: Nauka.

1997. Imennye kategorii v pular-ful'ful'de. In: V. A. Vinogradov (ed.) *Osnovy afrikanskogo jazykoznanija: Imennye kategorii*, 92–220. Moscow: Aspekt.

Krámský, Jiři 1972. *The article and the concept of definiteness in language.* The Hague: Mouton.

Krasil'nikova, E. V. 1990. *Imja suščestvitel'noe v russkoj razgovornoj reči: Funkcional'nyj aspekt.* Moscow: Nauka.

Kraus, Hedwig 1977. *Das Numerus-System des Englischen.* (Linguistische Arbeiten 44). Tübingen: Niemeyer.

Krauss, Michael 1992. The world's languages in crisis. *Language* 68. 4–10.

1993. The language extinction catastrophe just ahead: should linguists care? In: André Crochetière, Jean-Claude Boulanger and Conrad Ouellon (eds.) *Proceedings of the XVth International Congress of Linguists, Québec, Université Laval 9–14 August 1992: Endangered Languages* 1: *Endangered Languages,* 43–6. Sainte-Foy: Les Presses de l'Université Laval.

Krifka, Manfred 1991. Massennomina. In: Arnim von Stechow and Dieter Wunderlich (eds.) *Semantik: Ein internationales Handbuch der zeitgenössischen Forschung* (Handbücher zur Sprach- und Kommunikationswissenschaft 6), 399–417. Berlin: de Gruyter.

1995. Common nouns: a contrastive analysis of Chinese and English. In: Gregory N. Carlson and Francis J. Pelletier (eds.) *The Generic Book,* 398–411. Chicago: University of Chicago Press.

Kuh, Hakan 1987. Plural copying in Korean. *Harvard Studies in Korean Linguistics* 2. 239–50.

Kuhn, Wilfried 1982. Kollektiva und die Technik KOLLEKTION am Beispiel des Deutschen. In: Hansjakob Seiler and Christian Lehmann (eds.) *Apprehension: Das sprachliche Erfassen von Gegenständen: I: Bereich und Ordnung der Phänomene,* 84–97. Tübingen: Narr.

Kühner, Raphael and Stegmann, Carl 1955. *Ausführliche Grammatik der lateinischen Sprache: Satzlehre* I. Leverkusen: Gottschalksche Verlagsbuchhandlung. (Third edition.)

Kulick, Don and Stroud, Christopher 1992. The structure of the Taiap (Gapun) Language. In: Tom Dutton, Malcolm Ross and Darrell Tryon (eds.) *The Language Game: Papers in Memory of Donald C. Laycock* (Pacific Linguistics, series C, no. 110), 203–26. Canberra: Department of Linguistics, Research School of Pacific Studies, Australian National University.

Kumaxov, M. A. 1969. Čislo i grammatika. *Voprosy jazykoznanija* 4. 65–74.

Kunene, Euphrasia. C. L. 1986. Acquisition of siSwati noun classes. *South African Journal of African Languages* 6. 34–7.

Kwak, Eun-Joo 1996. The ambiguity of plurals and distributives. In: Marek Przezdziecki and Lindsay Whaley (eds.) *ESCOL '95: Proceedings of the Twelfth Eastern States Conference on Linguistics,* 149–60. Ithaca: Field of Linguistics, Cornell University.

Lafitte, Pierre 1962. *Grammaire Basque (Navarro-Labourdin littéraire).* Donostia: Elkar.

Laidig, Wyn D. and Laidig, Carol J. 1990. Larike pronouns: duals and trials in a Central Moluccan language. *Oceanic Linguistics* 29. 87–109.

Langacker, Ronald W. 1987. Nouns and verbs. *Language* 63. 53–94.

1991. *Foundations of Cognitive Grammar* II: *Descriptive Application.* Stanford: Stanford University Press.

References

Langdon, Margaret 1988. Number suppletion in Yuman. In: William Shipley (ed.) *In Honor of Mary Haas: from the Haas Festival Conference on Native American Linguistics*, 483–96. Berlin: Mouton de Gruyter.

1992. Yuman plurals: from derivation to inflection to noun agreement. *International Journal of American Linguistics* 58. 405–24.

Lasersohn, Peter 1990. Group action and spatio-temporal proximity. *Linguistics and Philosophy* 13. 179–206.

1995. *Plurality, Conjunction and Events* (Studies in Linguistics and Philosophy 55). Dordrecht: Kluwer.

Le Nombre 1993. = *Faits de langues 2/ 1993: Le nombre.* Evry Cedex: Presses Universitaires de France.

Lee, Han-Gyu 1991. Plural marker copying in Korean. *Studies in the Linguistic Sciences* 21, 1. 81–105.

Leeding, Velma J. 1989. Anindilyakwa Phonology and Morphology. Unpublished PhD dissertation, University of Sydney. [Available through AIATSIS, Canberra.]

Leer, Jeff 1991. Evidence for a Northern Northwest Coast language area: promiscuous number marking and periphrastic possessive constructions in Haida, Eyak, and Aleut. *International Journal of American Linguistics* 57. 158–93.

Lefebvre, Claire 1981. Variation in plural marking: the case of Cuzco Quechua. In: David Sankoff and Henrietta Cedergren (eds.) *Variation Omnibus* (Current Inquiry into Language, Linguistics and Human Communication 40), 73–84. Edmonton: Linguistic Research.

Lehmann, Christian 1995. *Thoughts on Grammaticalization.* (Lincom studies in theoretical linguistics 1). Munich: Lincom Europa. [Revised and expanded version: previous edition: Cologne: Institut für Sprachwissenschaft der Universität, 1982.]

Lenček, Rado L. 1972. O zaznamovanosti in nevtralizaciji slovnične kategorije spola v slovenskem knjižnem jeziku. *Slavistična revija* 20. 55–63.

1982. On poetic functions of the grammatical category of dual. *South Slavic and Balkan Linguistics* (Studies in Slavic and General Linguistics 2), 193–214. Amsterdam: Rodopi.

Levelt, Willem J. M.; Roelofs, Ardi and Meyer, Antje S. 1999. A theory of lexical access in speech production. *Behavioral and Brain Sciences* 22. 1–75.

Levy, Yonata 1983. The acquisition of Hebrew plurals: the case of the missing gender category. *Journal of Child Language* 10. 107–21.

1988. On the early learning of formal grammar systems: evidence from studies of the acquisition of gender and countability. *Journal of Child Language* 15. 179–87.

Lewis, Geoffrey L. 1967. *Turkish Grammar.* London: Oxford University Press.

Lichtenberk, Frantisek 1983. *A Grammar of Manam* (Oceanic Linguistics Special Publication 18). Honolulu: University of Hawaii Press.

Liclan, Patsy A. and Marlett, Stephen 1990. Madija noun morphology. *International Journal of American Linguistics* 56. 102–20.

Link, Godehard 1991. Quantity and number. In: Dietmar Zaefferer (ed.) *Semantic Universals and Universal Semantics* (GRASS series, no. 12), 133–49. Dordrecht: Foris.

1998. Ten years of research on plurals: where do we stand? In: Fritz Hamm and Erhard Hinrichs (eds.) *Plurality and Quantification* (Studies in Linguistics and Philosophy 69), 19–54. Dordrecht: Kluwer.

Löbel, Elizabeth 1993. On the parametrization of lexical properties. In: Gisbert Fanselow (ed.) *The Parametrization of Universal Grammar* (Linguistik Aktuell 8), 183–99. Amsterdam: John Benjamins.

2000. Classifiers versus genders and noun classes: a case study in Vietnamese. In: Barbara Unterbeck and Matti Rissanen (eds.) *Gender in Grammar and Cognition* (Trends in Linguistics: Studies and Monographs 124), 259–319. Berlin: Mouton de Gruyter.

Löfstedt, Einar 1928. *Syntactica: Studien und Beiträge zur historischen Syntax des Lateins* I: *Über einige Grundfragen der lateinischen Nominalsyntax.* Lund: Gleerup.

Lönngren, Lennart 1993. *Častotnyj slovar' sovremennogo russkogo jazyka.* (= Acta Universitatis Upsaliensis, Studia Slavica Upsaliensis 33). Uppsala.

Lötzsch, Ronald 1965. *Die spezifischen Neuerungen der sorbischen Dualflexion* (Spisy Instituta za serbski ludospyt 28). Bautzen: VEB Domowina Verlag.

Lucy, John A. 1992a. *Grammatical Categories and Cognition: a Case Study of the Linguistic Relativity Hypothesis* (Studies in the Social and Cultural Foundations of Language 13). Cambridge: Cambridge University Press.

1992b. *Language Diversity and Thought: a Reformulation of the Linguistic Relativity Hypothesis* (Studies in the Social and Cultural Foundations of Language 12). Cambridge: Cambridge University Press.

Luong, Hy V. 1987. Plural markers and personal pronouns in Vietnamese: an analysis of pragmatic ambiguity and native models. *Anthropological Linguistics* 29. 49–70.

Luutonen, Jorma 1997. *The Variation of Morpheme Order in Mari Declension* (Mémoires de la société finno-ougrienne 226). Helsinki: Soumalais-Ugrilainen Seura.

1999. The history of Permic, Mari and Chuvash plural suffixes in the light of Indo-Aryan parallels. *Journal de la société finno-ougrienne* 88. 73–101.

Lydall, Jean 1976. Hamer. In: M. Lionel Bender (ed.) *The Non-Semitic Languages of Ethiopia*, 393–438. East Lansing: African Studies Center, Michigan State University.

1988. Gender, number, and size in Hamar. In: Marianne Bechhaus-Gerst and Fritz Serzisko (eds.) *Cushitic–Omotic: Papers from the International Symposium on Cushitic and Omotic Languages: Cologne, January 6–9, 1986*, 75–90. Hamburg: Buske.

Lynch, John 1977. On the history of the Tanna numerals and number-markers. *Te Reo* 20. 3–28.

1986. The Proto-Southern Vanuatu pronominal system. In: Paul Geraghty, Lois Carrington and Stephen A. Wurm (eds.) *FOCAL II: Papers from the Fourth International Conference on Austronesian Linguistics* (Pacific Linguistics, series C, no. 94), 259–87. Canberra: Department of Linguistics, Research School of Pacific Studies, Australian National University.

Lyons, John 1968. *Introduction to Theoretical Linguistics*. Cambridge: Cambridge University Press.

MacAulay, Donald 1992. The Scottish Gaelic Language. In: Donald MacAulay *The Celtic Languages*, 137–248. Cambridge: Cambridge University Press.

References

Macaulay, Monica 1989. The plural word in Chalcatongo Mixtec. In: Caroline Wiltshire, Randolf Graczyk and Bradley Music (eds.) *CLS 25: Papers from the 25th Annual Regional Meeting of the Chicago Linguistic Society Part I: The General Session*, 288–99. Chicago: Chicago Linguistic Society.

McCarthy, John 1982. Prosodic templates, morphemic templates, and morphemic tiers. Harry van der Hulst and Norval Smith (eds.) *The Structure of Phonological Representations* I (Linguistic Models 2), 191–224. Dordrecht: Foris.

    1983. A prosodic account of Arabic broken plurals. In: Ivan Dihoff (ed.) *Current Trends in African Linguistics* I, 289–320. Dordrecht: Foris.

McCarthy, John and Prince, Alan 1990. Foot and word in prosodic morphology: the Arabic broken plural. *Natural Language and Linguistic Theory* 8. 209–83.

    1995. Prosodic morphology. In: John A. Goldsmith (ed.) *The Handbook of Phonological Theory*, 318–66. Oxford: Blackwell.

McCawley, James D. 1968. Review of Thomas A. Sebeok (ed.) 'Current trends in linguistics, vol. 3: theoretical foundations'. *Language* 44. 556–93.

    1975. Lexicography and the count–mass distinction. In: Cathy Cogen, Henry Thompson, Graham Thurgood, Kenneth Whistler and James Wright (eds.) *Proceedings of the First Annual Meeting of the Berkeley Linguistics Society*, 314–321. Berkeley, CA: University of California.

MacDonell, Arthur A. 1916. *A Vedic Grammar for Students*. London: Oxford University Press.

    1927. *A Sanskrit Grammar for Students*. London: Oxford University Press. [Third edition.]

McGregor, William B. 1989. Greenberg on the first person inclusive dual: evidence from some Australian languages. *Studies in Language* 13. 437–58.

    1996. Dyadic and polyadic kin terms in Gooniyandi. *Anthropological Linguistics* 38. 216–47.

McKay, Graham R. 1978. Pronominal person and number categories in Rembarrnga and Djeebbana. *Oceanic Linguistics* 17. 27–37.

    1979. Gender and the category *unit augmented*. *Oceanic Linguistics* 18. 203–10.

    1984. Ndjébbana (Kunibidji) grammar: miscellaneous morphological and syntactic notes. *Papers in Australian linguistics no. 16* (Pacific Linguistics, series A, no. 68), 119–51. Canberra: Department of Linguistics, Research School of Pacific Studies, Australian National University.

    1990. The addressee: or is the second person singular? *Studies in Language* 14. 429–32.

McNally, Louise 1993. Comitative coordination: a case study in group formation. *Natural Language and Linguistic Theory* 11. 347–79.

Maiden, Martin 1990. *Interactive Morphonology: Metaphony in Italy.* London: Routledge.

Malsch, Derry L. 1987. The grammaticalization of social relationship: the origin of number to encode deference. In: Anna Giacalone Ramat, Onofrio Carruba and Giuliano Bernini (eds.) *Papers from the 7th International Conference on Historical Linguistics* (Current Issues in Linguistic Theory 48), 401–18. Amsterdam: John Benjamins.

Maltshukov, Andreij L. 1992. Distributive constructions and verbal valence in Even. *Languages of the World* 3. 4–10.

Manessy, G. 1968. La catégorie du nombre dans les langues de l'Afrique occidentale. *Bulletin de la Société de linguistique de Paris* 63. 197–217.

Marchese, Lynell 1986. The pronominal system of Godié. In: Ursula Wiesemann (ed.) *Pronominal Systems* (Continuum 5), 217–55. Tübingen: Narr.

   1988. Nouns classes and agreement systems in Kru: a historical approach. In: Michael Barlow and Charles A. Ferguson (eds.) *Agreement in Natural Language: Approaches, Theories, Descriptions*, 323–41. Stanford: Center for the Study of Language and Information, Stanford University.

Marcus, Gary F.; Brinkmann, Ursula; Clahsen, Harald; Wiese, Richard and Pinker, Steven 1995. German inflection: the exception that proves the rule. *Cognitive Psychology* 29. 189–256.

Markman, Ellen M. 1985. Why superordinate category terms can be mass nouns. *Cognition* 19. 31–53.

   1989. *Categorization and Naming in Children*. Cambridge, MA: MIT Press.

Marle, Jaap van 1993. Morphological adaptation. In: Geert Booij and Jaap van Marle (eds.) *Yearbook of Morphology 1993*, 255–65. Dordrecht: Kluwer.

   1996. The unity of morphology: on the interwovenness of the derivational and inflectional dimension of the word. In: Geert Booij and Jaap van Marle (eds.) *Yearbook of Morphology 1995*, 67–82. Dordrecht: Kluwer.

Marlett, Stephen A. 1990. Person and number inflection in Seri. *International Journal of American Linguistics* 56. 503–41.

Martin, Jack 1988. Subtractive morphology as dissociation. In: Hagit Borer (ed.) *Proceedings of the Seventh West Coast Conference on Formal Linguistics*, 229–40. Stanford: Center for the Study of Language and Information, Stanford University.

Martin, Samuel 1975. *A Reference Grammar of Japanese*. New Haven: Yale University Press.

Masica, Colin P. 1991. *The Indo-Aryan Languages*. Cambridge: Cambridge University Press.

Mathiot, Madeleine 1973. *A Dictionary of Papago Usage* I: *B–K*. (Indiana University Publications: Language Science Monographs 8/1). Bloomington: Indiana University.

Matthews, Peter H. 1991. *Morphology*. Cambridge: Cambridge University Press. [Second edition; first edition 1974.]

Maurer, H. 1966. *Grammatik der Tangga-Sprache (Melanesien)*. (Micro-Bibliotheca Anthropos 40). Bonn: Anthropos Institut.

Megaard, John 1976. Predikatets kongruens i serbokroatisk i setninger med koordinerte subjektsnominalfraser. Unpublished dissertation, University of Oslo.

Mehlig, Hans Robert 1996. Some analogies between the morphology of nouns and the morphology of aspect in Russian. *Folia Linguistica* 30. 87–109.

Mel'čuk, Igor' A. 1979. Countability vs. non-countability. In: Paul R. Clyne, William F. Hanks and Carol L. Hofbauer (eds.) *Papers from the Fifteenth Regional Meeting,*

References

Chicago Linguistic Society, April 19–20, 1970, 220–7. Chicago: Chicago Linguistic Society.

1985. *Poverxnostnyj sintaksis russkix čislovyx vyraženij* (Wiener Slawistischer Almanach: Sonderband 16). Vienna: Institut für Slawistik der Universität Wien.

1994. Suppletion: toward a logical analysis of the concept. *Studies in Language* 18, 2. 339–410.

Merlan, Francesca 1982. *Mangarayi* (Lingua Descriptive Series 4). Amsterdam: North-Holland.

1983. *Ngalakan Grammar, Texts and Vocabulary* (Pacific Linguistics, series B, no. 89). Canberra: Department of Linguistics, Research School of Pacific Studies, Australian National University.

Merrifield, William R. 1959. Classification of Kiowa nouns. *International Journal of American Linguistics* 25. 269–71.

Mey, Jacob L. 1960. *La catégorie du nombre en finnois moderne* (= Travaux du cercle linguistique de Copenhague 13). Copenhagen: Nordisk Sprog- og Kulturforlag.

Mifsud, Manwel 1996. The collective in Maltese. *Rivista di Linguistica* 8. 29–51.

Milner, G. B. 1956. *Fijian Grammar.* Suva, Fiji: Government Press.

Mithun, Marianne 1988a. Lexical categories and the evolution of number marking. In: Michael Hammond and Michael Noonan (eds.) *Theoretical Morphology: Approaches in Modern Linguistics,* 211–34. San Diego: Academic Press.

1988b. Lexical categories and number in Central Pomo. In: William Shipley (ed.) *In Honor of Mary Haas: from the Haas Festival Conference on Native American Linguistics,* 517–37. Berlin: Mouton de Gruyter.

1990. Language obsolescence and grammatical description. *International Journal of American Linguistics* 56, 1. 1–26.

1991. The development of bound pronominal paradigms. In: Winfred P. Lehmann and Helen-Jo Jakusz Hewitt (eds.) *Language Typology 1988: Typological Models in Reconstruction* (Current Issues in Linguistic Theory 81), 85–104. Amsterdam: John Benjamins.

1993. Reconstructing the unidentified. In: Henk Aertsen and Robert J. Jeffers (eds.) *Historical Linguistics 1989: Papers from the 9th International Conference on Historical Linguistics* (Current Issues in Linguistic Theory 106), 329–47. Amsterdam: John Benjamins.

1999. *The Languages of Native North America.* Cambridge: Cambridge University Press.

Mithun, Marianne and Corbett, Greville G. 1995. Distributives, collectives, and number in the world's languages. Paper presented at the Inaugural Meeting of the Association for Linguistic Typology (ALT), K. Mitxelena I. Ihardunaldiak, Vitoria-Gasteiz, 7–10 September, 1995. Unpublished.

Molčanova, E. K. 1975. Kategorija čisla. In: V. S. Rastorgueva (ed.) *Opyt istoriko-tipologičeskogo issledovanija iranskix jazykov* II: *Èvoljucija grammatičeskix kategorij,* 200–49. Moscow: Nauka.

Molen, Hugo van der and Morton, John 1979. Remembering plurals: unit of coding and form of coding during serial recall. *Cognition* 7. 35–47.

Montler, Timothy 1986. *An Outline of the Morphology and Phonology of Saanich, North Straits Salish* (University of Montana Occasional Papers in Linguistics 4). Missoula, MT: University of Montana.

Moravcsik, Edith A. 1978. Reduplicative constructions. In: Joseph H. Greenberg, Charles A. Ferguson and Edith A. Moravcsik (eds.) *Universals of Human Language* III: *Word Structure*, 297–334. Stanford: Stanford University Press.

1991. Review article on Anna Wierzbicka 'The semantics of grammar'. *Studies in Language* 15. 129–48.

1994. Group plural: associative plural or cohort plural. Email document, LINGUIST List: Vol-5–681. 11 June 1994. ISSN: 1068–4875.

1998. Classifiers and plural marking. Email document, 9 November 1998, Discussion List for The Association for Linguistic Typology <lingtyp@linguist.ldc.upenn.edu>.

forthcoming. Inflectional morphology in the Hungarian noun phrase: a typological assessment. To appear in: Frans Plank (ed.) *Noun Phrase Structure in the Languages of Europe*. Berlin: Mouton de Gruyter.

Morgan, Jerry L. 1984. Some problems of determination in English number agreement. In: Gloria Alvarez, Belinda Brodie and Terry McCoy (eds.) *ESCOL '84: Proceedings of the First Eastern States Conference on Linguistics*, 69–78. Columbus, OH: Ohio State University.

Mosel, Ulrike 1982. Number, collection and mass in Tolai. In: Hansjakob Seiler and Franz J. Stachowiak (eds.) *Apprehension: Das sprachliche Erfassen von Gegenständen* II: *Die Techniken und ihre zusammenhang in Einzelsprachen*, 123–54. Tübingen: Narr.

1984. *Tolai Syntax and its Historical Development* (Pacific Linguistics, series B, no. 92). Canberra: Department of Linguistics, Research School of Pacific Studies, Australian National University.

Mosel, Ulrike and Hovdhaugen, Even 1992. *Samoan Reference Grammar.* Oslo: Scandinavian University Press.

Mosel, Ulrike and Spriggs, Ruth 1993. *A Sketch Grammar of Teop.* Draft, Canberra: Department of Linguistics, Arts Faculty, Australian National University.

2000. Gender in Teop (Bougainville, Papua New Guinea). In: Barbara Unterbeck and Matti Rissanen (eds.) *Gender in Grammar and Cognition* (Trends in Linguistics: Studies and Monographs 124), 321–49. Berlin: Mouton de Gruyter.

Moser, Edward and Moser, Mary 1976. Seri noun pluralization classes. In: Margaret Langdon and Shirley Silver (eds.) *Hokan Studies: Papers from the First Conference on Hokan Languages held in San Diego, California, April 23–25, 1970* (Janua Linguarum, Series Practica 181), 285–96. The Hague: Mouton.

Moszyński, Leszek 1985. Czy w języku staro-cerkiewno-słowianskim była kategoria *duale tantum*. *Slavica Hierosolymitana: Slavic Studies of the Hebrew University* 7. 107–18.

Mufwene, Salikoko S. 1980. Number, countability, and markedness in Lingala LI-/MA-noun class. *Linguistics* 18. 1019–52.

References

1981. Non-individuation and the count/mass distinction. In: Roberta A. Hendrick, Carrie A. Masek and Mary F. Miller (eds.) *Papers from the Seventeenth Regional Meeting, Chicago Linguistic Society*, 221–38. Chicago: Chicago Linguistic Society.

1984. The count/mass distinction and the English lexicon. In: David Testen, Veena Mishra and Joseph Drogo (eds.) *Papers from the Parasession on Lexical Semantics*, 200–21. Chicago: Chicago Linguistic Society.

1986. Number delimitation in Gullah. *American Speech* 61. 33–60.

1995. Review of John A. Lucy 'Language Diversity and Thought: A Reformulation of the Linguistic Relativity Hypothesis' and 'Grammatical Categories and Cognition: A Case Study of the Linguistic Relativity Hypothesis'. *Languages of the World* 9. 65–74.

Mugdan, Joachim 1994. Morphological units. In: R. E. Asher (ed.) *Encyclopedia of Language and Linguistics* V, 2543–53. Oxford: Pergamon.

Mühlhäusler, Peter 1981. The development of the category of number in Tok Pisin. In: Pieter Muysken (ed.) *Generative Studies on Creole Languages* (Studies in Generative Grammar 6), 35–84. Dordrecht: Foris.

Mühlhäusler, Peter and Harré, Rom 1990. *Pronouns and People: the Linguistic Construction of Social and Personal Identity.* Oxford: Blackwell.

Müller, Natascha 1994. Gender and number agreement within DP. In: Jürgen Meisel (ed.) *Bilingual First Language Acquisition: French and German Grammatical Development* (Language Acquisition and Language Disorders 7), 53–88. Amsterdam: John Benjamins.

Munro, Pamela 1976. *Mojave Syntax.* New York: Garland.

Murtonen, A. 1964. *Broken Plurals: Origin and Development of the System.* Leiden: Brill.

Myksvoll, Mari 1995. Number marked on verbs in Tokelauan: a study of the meaning of number in a Polynesian language. Cand. Philol. dissertation, Department of Linguistics, University of Oslo.

Myrkin, V. Ja. 1964. Tipologija ličnogo mestoimenija i voprosy rekonstrukcii ego v indoevropejskom aspekte. *Voprosy jazykoznanija* no. 5. 78–86.

Naylor, Kenneth E. 1972. On some developments of the dual in Slavic. *International Journal of Slavic Linguistics and Poetics* 15. 1–8.

Neira Martínez, Jesús 1955. *El habla de Lena.* Oviedo: Disputación de Oviedo.

1982. *Bables y castellano en Asturias.* Madrid: Silverio Cañadas.

Neweklowsky, Gerhard 1984. Die Häufigkeit grammatikalischer Kategorien in slowenischen Zeitungstexten. In: *Didaktische Reflexion und Wussenschaft in einer sich ändernden Welt: Forschungsperspektiven '84*, 383–400. Klagenfurt: Forschungskommission der Universität für Bildungswissenschaften.

1988. Zur Häufigkeit morphologischer Kategorien in slowenischen Prosatexten. In: Boris Paternu and Franc Jakopin (eds.) *Sodobni slovenski jezik, književnost in kultura: mednarodni simpozij v Ljubljani od 1. do 3. julija 1986 (= Obdobja 8)*, 337–49. Ljubljana: Univerza Edvarda Kardelja v Ljubljani, Filozofska fakulteta.

Newman, Michael 1992. Pronominal disagreements: the stubborn problem of singular epicene antecedents. *Language in Society* 21. 447–75.

Newman, Paul 1980. *The Classification of Chadic within Afroasiatic.* Leiden: Universitaire Pers Leiden.

 1990. *Nominal and Verbal Plurality in Chadic* (Publications in African Languages and Linguistics 12). Dordrecht: Foris.

Nichols, Johanna 1992. *Linguistic Diversity in Space and Time.* Chicago: University of Chicago Press.

Nichols, Johanna; Rappaport, Gilbert and Timberlake, Alan 1980. Subject, topic and control in Russian. *Proceedings of the Sixth Annual Meeting of the Berkeley Linguistics Society*, 372–86. Berkeley: Berkeley Linguistics Society, University of California.

Nikolaeva, Irina A. 1995. *Obdorskij dialekt chantyjskogo jazyka* (Mitteilungen der Societas Uralo-Altaica 15). Hamburg: Finnisch-Ugrisches Seminar der Universität Hamburg.

 1999. A grammar of Udihe. PhD dissertation, University of Leiden.

Nilsson, Kim 1979. Concerning number and gender in a non-congruent construction. *Studia Linguistica* 33. 79–88.

Nixon, Graham 1972. Corporate-concord phenomena in English. *Studia Neophilologica: a Journal of Germanic and Romance Philology* 44. 120–6.

Noonan, Michael P. 1992. *A Grammar of Lango* (Mouton Grammar Library 7). Berlin: Mouton de Gruyter.

Nordlinger, Rachel 1998. *A Grammar of Wambaya, Northern Territory (Australia)* (Pacific Linguistics, series C, no. 140). Canberra: Pacific Linguistics, Research School of Pacific and Asian Studies, Australian National University.

Norman, Jerry 1988. *Chinese.* Cambridge: Cambridge University Press.

Noyer, Rolf 1997. *Features, Positions and Affixes in Autonomous Morphological Structure.* New York: Garland.

Nuessel, Frank 1984. (Dis)agreement in Spanish. *Papers in Linguistics* 17. 267–81.

Ojeda, Almerindo E. 1992a. The semantics of number in Arabic. In: Chris Barker and David Dowty (eds.) *Proceedings of the Second Conference on Linguistics and Semantic Theory, held at the Ohio State University May 1–3, 1992* (= The Ohio State University Working Papers in Linguistics 40), 303–25. Columbus, OH: The Ohio State University Department of Linguistics.

 1992b. The 'mass neuter' in Hispano-Romance dialects. *Hispanic Linguistics* 5. 245–77.

 1992c. The markedness of plurality. In: Diane Brentari, Gary N. Larson and Lynn A. MacLeod (eds.) *The Joy of Grammar: a Festschrift in Honor of James D. McCawley*, 275–88. Amsterdam: John Benjamins.

 1993. *Linguistic Individuals* (CSLI Lecture Notes 31). Stanford: Center for the Study of Language and Information, Stanford University.

 1995. The semantics of the Italian double plural. *Journal of Semantics* 12. 213–37.

Omar, Margaret K. 1973. *The Acquisition of Egyptian Arabic as a Native Language.* The Hague: Mouton.

Ozbalt, Marija A. I. 1973. Case frequency in Modern Slovene noun declension. MA thesis, McGill University.

References

Padučeva, E. V. 1967. Dva podxoda k semantičeskomu analizu kategorii čisla. In: *To Honor Roman Jakobson: Essays on the Occasion of his Seventieth Birthday, 11. October 1966, II,* 1474–88. The Hague: Mouton.

Palmer, F. R. 1955. The 'broken plurals' of Tigrinya. *Bulletin of the School of Oriental and African Studies, University of London* 17. 548–66. [Reprinted in: Eric Hamp, Fred Householder and Robert Austerlitz (eds.) 1966. *Readings in Linguistics* II, 341–58. Chicago: University of Chicago Press.]

    1962. *The Morphology of the Tigre Noun* (London Oriental Series 13). London: Oxford University Press.

    1990. The semantics of grammar. *Journal of Linguistics* 26. 223–33.

Panfilov, V. Z. 1958. Grammatičeskoe čislo suščestvitel´nyx v nivxskom jazyke. *Doklady i soobščenija Instituta jazykoznanija AN SSSR* 11. 46–61.

    1976. Tipologija grammatičeskoj kategorii čisla i nekotorye voprosy ee istoričeskogo razvitija. *Voprosy jazykoznanija* no. 4: 18–38.

Panov, M. V. (ed.) 1968. *Morfologija i sintaksis sovremennogo russkogo literaturnogo jazyka (Russkij jazyk i sovetskoe obščestvo: Sociologo-lingvističeskoe issledovanie III).* Moscow: Nauka.

Park, Tschang-Zin 1978. Plurals in child speech. *Journal of Child Language* 5. 237–50.

Parker, Enid M. and Hayward, Richard J. 1985. *An Afar–English–French Dictionary (with Grammatical Notes in English).* London: School of Oriental and African Studies, University of London.

Parker, Frank 1983. Number in indefinite pronouns and correlatives. *University of South Florida Language Quarterly* 22, 1–2. 13–16.

Parodi, Theresa; Schwartz, Bonnie D. and Clahsen, Harald 1997. On the L2 acquisition of the morphosyntax of German nominals. *Essex Research Reports in Linguistics* 15. 1–43.

Paton, W. F. 1971. *Ambrym (Lonwolwol) Grammar* (Pacific Linguistics, series B, no. 19). Canberra: Department of Linguistics, Research School of Pacific Studies, Australian National University.

Pawley, Andrew 1977. The development of determining pronouns in Oceanic, or, why change a system that works? Paper presented at the Austronesian Symposium, 1977. Unpublished.

Pawley, Andrew and Sayaba, Timoci 1990. Possessive-marking in Wayan, a Western Fijian language: noun class or relational system? In: Jeremy H. C. S. Davidson (ed.) *Pacific Island Languages: Essays in Honour of G. B. Milner,* 147–71. London: School of Oriental and African Studies, University of London and Honolulu: University of Hawaii Press.

Pelletier, Francis J. (ed.) 1979. *Mass Terms: some Philosophical Problems* (Synthese Language Library 6). Dordrecht: Reidel.

Penny, Ralph 1970. Mass nouns and metaphony in the dialects of north-western Spain. *Archivum Linguisticum* n.s. 1. 21–30.

Perlmutter, David M. 1988. The split morphology hypothesis: evidence from Yiddish. In: Michael Hammond and Michael Noonan (eds.) *Theoretical Morphology: Approaches in Modern Linguistics,* 79–100. San Diego: Academic Press.

References

Peterson, Peter G. 1986. Establishing verb agreement with disjunctively conjoined subjects: strategies vs principles. *Australian Journal of Linguistics* 6. 231–49.

Phillips, Betty S. and Bouma, Lowell 1980. The acquisition of German plurals in native children and non-native adults. *International Review of Applied Linguistics* 18. 21–9.

Piau, J. 1985. The verbal syntax of Kuman. MA thesis, Australian National University [Cited from Foley 1986.]

Piper, Nick 1989. A sketch grammar of Meryam Mir. MA thesis, Australian National University.

Plank, Frans 1985. On the reapplication of morphological rules after phonological rules and other resolutions of functional conflicts between morphology and phonology. *Linguistics* 23. 45–82.

1987. Number neutralization in Old English: failure of functionalism? In: Willem Koopman, Frederike van der Leek, Olga Fischer and Roger Eaton (eds.) *Explanation and Linguistic Change* (Current Issues in Linguistic Theory 45), 177–238. Amsterdam: John Benjamins.

1989. On Humboldt on the Dual. In: Roberta Corrigan, Fred Eckman and Michael Noonan (eds.) *Linguistic Categorization* (Amsterdam Studies in the Theory and History of Linguistic Science 61), 293–333. Amsterdam: John Benjamins.

1996. Domains of the dual, in Maltese and in general. *Rivista di Linguistica* 8. 123–40.

Plank, Frans and Schellinger, Wolfgang 1997. The uneven distribution of genders over numbers: Greenberg nos. 37 and 45. *Linguistic Typology* 1. 53–101.

Plungian, Vladimir A. 1995. *Dogon* (Languages of the world: Materials 64). Munich: Lincom Europa.

Plungjan [Plungian], Vladimir A. 1997. *Vremja i vremena:* k voposu o kategorija čisla. In: N. D. Arutjunova and T. E. Janko (eds.) *Logičeskij analiz jazyka: jazyk i vremja,* 158–69. Moscow: Indrik.

Plungjan [Plungian], Vladimir A. and Raxilina, Ekaterina V. 1995. Semantičeskie tipy predmetnyx imen: grammatika, leksika i kognitivnaja interpretacija. In: R. G. Buxaraev, A. S. Narim'jani and V. D. Solov'ev (eds.) *Trudy Meždunarodnogo seminara 'Dialog '95': komp'juternaja lingvistikea i ee priloženija,* 252–8. Kazan'.

Plunkett, Kim and Nakisa, Ramin Charles 1997. A connectionist model of the Arabic plural system. *Language and Cognitive Processes* 12. 807–36.

Polivanova, A. K. 1983. Vybor čislovyx form suščestvitel'nogo v russkom jazyke. In: V. P. Grigor'ev (ed.) *Problemy strukturnoj lingvistiki,* 130–45. Moscow: Nauka.

Pollard, Carl and Sag, Ivan A. 1994. *Head-Driven Phrase Structure Grammar.* Chicago: University of Chicago Press.

Popjes, Jack and Popjes, Jo 1986. Canela-Krahô. In: Desmond C. Derbyshire and Geoffrey K. Pullum (eds.) *Handbook of Amazonian Languages* I, 128–99. Berlin: Mouton de Gruyter.

Poplack, Shana 1980. Deletion and disambiguation in Puerto Rican Spanish. *Language* 56. 371–85.

1981. Mortal phonemes as plural morphemes. In: David Sankoff and Henrietta

Cedergren (eds.) *Variation Omnibus* (Current Inquiry into Language, Linguistics and Human Communication 40), 59–71. Edmonton: Linguistic Research.

Poplack, Shana and Tagliamonte, Sali 1989. There's no tense like the present: verbal -*s* inflection in Early Black English. *Language Variation and Change* 1. 47–84.

1994. -*S* or nothing: marking the plural in the African American diaspora. *American Speech* 69. 227–59.

Poplack, Shana; Tagliamonte, Sali and Eze, Ejike 1999. Reconstructing the source of Early African American English plural marking: a comparative study of English and Creole. In: Shana Poplack (ed.) *The English History of African American English*, 73–105. Oxford: Blackwell.

Prasada, Sandeep 1996. Knowledge of the count/mass noun distinction: the relation of syntactic, semantic and conceptual structure. In: Marek Przezdziecki and Lindsay Whaley (eds.) *ESCOL '95: Proceedings of the Twelfth Eastern States Conference on Linguistics*, 256–66. Ithaca: Field of Linguistics, Cornell University.

Premper, Waldfried 1986. *Kollektion im Arabischen.* (Arbeitspapier 49). Cologne: Institut für Sprachwissenschaft, University of Cologne.

Press, Margaret L. 1979. *Chemehuevi: a Grammar and Lexicon.* (University of California Publications in Linguistics 92). Berkeley: University of California Press.

Priestly, Tom M. S. 1993. Slovene. In: Bernard Comrie and Greville G. Corbett (eds.), *The Slavonic Languages*, 388–451. London: Routledge.

forthcoming. Gender change, local markedness, and speculations on the dual. To appear in: Ron Smyth (ed.) *A Festschrift for Bruce Derwing.*

Prost, Martine 1992. Pluralité en coréen: deux fonctions de *TUL. Cahiers de Linguistique Asie Orientale* 21. 37–70.

Pullum, Geoffrey K. 1984. How complex could an agreement system be? In: Gloria Alvarez, Belinda Brodie and Terry McCoy (eds.) *ESCOL '84: Proceedings of the First Eastern States Conference on Linguistics*, 79–103. Columbus, OH: Ohio State University.

Pullum, Geoffrey K. and Zwicky, Arnold M. 1986. Phonological resolution of syntactic feature conflict. *Language* 62. 751–73.

Quirk, Randolph; Greenbaum, Sidney; Leech, Geoffrey and Svartvik, Jan 1985. *A Comprehensive Grammar of the English Language.* London: Longman.

Ratcliffe, Robert R. 1998, *The 'Broken' Plural Problem in Arabic and Comparative Semitic: Allomorphy and Analogy in Non-concatenative Morphology.* (Current Issues in Linguistic Theory 168). Amsterdam: John Benjamins.

Ravila, Paavo 1941. Über die Verwendung der Numeruszeichen in den uralischen Sprachen. *Finnisch-Ugrische Forschungen (Zeitschrift für finnisch-ugrische Sprach- und Volkskunde)* 27. 1–136.

Redden, James E. 1966. Walapai II: morphology. *International Journal of American Linguistics* 32. 141–63.

Reed, Judy and Payne, David L. 1986. Asheninca (Campa) pronominals. In: Ursula Wiesemann (ed.) *Pronominal Systems* (Continuum 5), 323–31. Tübingen: Narr.

Reesink, Ger P. 1987. *Structures and their Functions in Usan: a Papuan Language of Papua New Guinea* (Studies in Language Companion Series 13). Amsterdam: John Benjamins.

Refsing, Kirsten 1986. *The Ainu Language: the Morphology and Syntax of the Shizunai Dialect*. Århus: Aarhus University Press.

Reid, Nicholas J. 1990. Ngan'gityemerri: a language of the Daly River region, Northern Territory of Australia. PhD thesis, Australian National University.

Reid, Wallis 1991. *Verb and Noun Number in English: a Functional Explanation*. London: Longman.

Remneva, M. L. and Kijanova, O. N. 1991. Iz istorii ispol'zovanija form dvojstvennogo čisla v knižno-slavjanskoj i delovoj piśmennosti XII–XVII vv. *Vestnik Moskovskogo universiteta: Filologija* 46, 9, no. 1. 23–33.

Rhodes, Richard 1990. Lexical hierarchies and Ojibwa noun derivation. In: S. L. Tsohatzidis (ed.) *Meanings and Prototypes: Studies in Linguistic Categorization*, 151–8. London: Routledge.

Rice, Keren 1989. *A Grammar of Slave* (Mouton Grammar Library 5). Berlin: Mouton de Gruyter.

Rickford, John R. 1986. Some principles for the study of black and white speech in the South. In: Michael B. Montgomery and Guy Bailey (eds.) *Language Variety in the South: Perspectives in Black and White*, 38–62. University, AL: University of Alabama Press.

1990. Number delimitation in Gullah: a response to Mufwene. *American Speech* 65. 148–63.

Rigsby, Bruce 1996. *Gitksan Grammar*. Unpublished manuscript, Department of Anthropology and Sociology, University of Queensland.

Rijkhoff, Jan N. M. 1992. The noun phrase: a typological study of its form and structure. PhD dissertation, University of Antwerp.

Ritter, Elizabeth 1995. On the syntactic category of pronouns and agreement. *Natural Language and Linguistic Theory* 13. 403–43.

Roberts, Craige 1987. Distributivity. In: Jeroen Groenendijk, Martin Stokhof and Frank Veltman (eds.) *Proceedings of the Sixth Amsterdam Colloquium: April 13–16 1987*, 291–309. Amsterdam: University of Amsterdam, ITLI.

Roberts, John R. 1987. *Amele*. London: Croom Helm.

1997. Switch reference in Papua New Guinea: a preliminary survey. In: Andrew Pawley (ed.) *Papers in Papuan Linguistics 3*, 101–241. Canberra: Australian National University, Department of Linguistics, Research School of Pacific and Asian Studies.

Rocchetti, A. 1968. Les pluriels doubles de l'italien: une interférence de la sémantique et de la morphologie du nom. *Les langues modernes* 62. 351–9.

Rogers, Margaret 1997. Synonymy and equivalence in special-language texts: a case study in German and English texts on genetic engineering. In: Anna Trosborg (ed.) *Text Typology and Translation* (Benjamins Translation Library 26), 217–45. Amsterdam: John Benjamins.

Rombandeeva, E. I. 1973. *Mansijskij (vogul'skij) jazyk*. Moscow: Nauka.

References

Ross, Malcolm D. 1988. *Proto Oceanic and the Austronesian Languages of Western Melanesia* (Pacific Linguistics, series C, no. 98). Canberra: Department of Linguistics, Research School of Pacific Studies, Australian National University.

Rukeyser, Alison 1997. *A Typology of the Nominal Dual: Evidence from Indo-European, Finno-Ugric, Semitic and Australian Languages* (= *Davis Working Papers in Linguistics* 6). Electronic document: http://linguistics.ucdavis.edu/Ruk00.html

Rumsey, A. 1982. *An Intra-sentence Grammar of Ungarinjin North-Western Australia* (Pacific Linguistics, series B, no. 86). Canberra: Department of Linguistics, Research School of Pacific Studies, Australian National University.

Rusiecki, Jan 1991. Generic sentences, classes of predicate, and definite generic noun phrases. In: Maciej Grochowski and Daniel Weiss (eds.) '*Words are Physicians for an Ailing Mind*' (Sagners Slavistische Sammlung 17), 363–70. Munich: Otto Sagner.

Saeed, John I. 1987. *Somali Reference Grammar.* Wheaton, MD: Dunwoody.

Sag, Ivan A.; Gazdar, Gerald; Wasow, Thomas and Weisler, Steven 1985. Coordination and how to distinguish categories. *Natural Language and Linguistic Theory* 3. 117–71.

Salmons, Joseph C. 1994. Umlaut and plurality in Old High German: some problems with a Natural Morphology account. *Diachronica* 11. 213–29.

Samarin, William J. 1967. *A Grammar of Sango.* The Hague: Mouton.

Sand, Diane E. Z. 1971. Agreement of the Predicate with Quantitative Subjects in Serbo-Croatian. PhD dissertation, University of Pennsylvania. [Distributed by University Microfilms, Ann Arbor, reference 72–17, 420.]

Santangelo, Annamaria 1981. I plurali italiani del tipo 'le braccia'. *Archivio Glottologico Italiano* 66. 95–153.

Sapir, Edward 1917. *The position of Yana in the Hokan stock* (University of California Publications in American Archaeology and Ethnology 13.1). Berkeley: University of California.

——— 1930–31. *The Southern Paiute Language* I: *Southern Paiute, a Shoshonean Language;* II: *Texts of the Kaibab Paiutes and Uintah Utes*; III: *Southern Paiute Dictionary* (Proceedings of the American Academy of Arts and Sciences vol. 65, nos. 1–3). Boston: American Academy of Arts and Sciences. [Reprinted as Edward Sapir 1992. *The Collected Works* X*: Southern Paiute and Ute Linguistics and Ethnography*, edited by William Bright. Berlin: Mouton de Gruyter.]

Sapir, Edward and Swadesh, Morris 1960. *Yana dictionary* (University of California Publications in Linguistics 22). Berkeley: University of California Press.

Saussure, Ferdinand de 1916/1971. *Cours de linguistique générale* (publié par Charles Bally et Albert Sechehaye avec la collaboration de Albert Riedlinger). Paris: Payot. [Third edition; First edition 1916.]

Sauvageot, Serge 1967. Sur la classification nominale en baïnouk. *La classification nominale dans les langues négro-africaines*, 225–35. Paris: Centre national de la recherche scientifique.

Scha, Remko 1981. Distributive, collective and cumulative quantification. In: Jeroen

Groenendijk, Theo M. V. Janssen and Martin Stokhof (eds.) *Formal Methods in the Study of Language*, 483–512. Amsterdam: Mathematical Centre.

Schein, Barry 1993. *Plurals and events* (Current Studies in Linguistics 23). Cambridge, MA: MIT Press.

Schmidt, Annette 1988. Language in a Fijian village: an ethnolinguistic study. PhD thesis, Australian National University.

Schroeder, Christoph 1999. *The Turkish Nominal Phrase in Spoken Discourse* (Turcologica 40). Wiesbaden: Harrassowitz.

Schuh, Russell G. 1989. Number and gender in Miya. In: Zygmunt Frajzyngier (ed.) *Current Progress in Chadic Linguistics: Proceedings of the International Symposium on Chadic Linguistics: Boulder, Colorado, 1–2 May, 1987* (Current Issues in Linguistic Theory 62), 171–81. Amsterdam: John Benjamins.

1998. *A Grammar of Miya* (University of California Publications in Linguistics 130). Berkeley: University of California Press.

Schupbach, Richard D. 1984. *Lexical Specialization in Russian* (= UCLA Slavic Studies 8). Columbus, OH: Slavica.

Schütz, Albert J. 1985. *The Fijian Language*. Honolulu: University of Hawaii Press.

Schwartz, Linda 1988a. Conditions for verb-coded coordinations. In: Michael T. Hammond, Edith A. Moravcsik and Jessica R. Wirth (eds.) *Studies in Syntactic Typology* (Typological Studies in Language 17), 53–73. Amsterdam: John Benjamins.

1988b. Asymmetric feature distribution in pronominal 'coordinations'. In: Michael Barlow and Charles A. Ferguson (eds.) *Agreement in Natural Language: Approaches, Theories, Descriptions*, 237–49. Stanford: Center for the Study of Language and Information, Stanford University.

Schwartz, Linda; Newman, Paul and Sani, Sammani 1988. Agreement and scope of modification in Hausa coordinate structures. In: Diane Brentari, Gary N. Larson and Lynn A. MacLeod (eds.) *CLS 24: Papers from the 24th Annual Regional Meeting of the Chicago Linguistic Society Part II: Parasession on Agreement in Grammatical Theory*, 278–90. Chicago: Chicago Linguistic Society.

Schwarzschild, Roger S. 1996. *Pluralities* (Studies in Linguistics and Philosophy 61). Dordrecht: Kluwer.

Schwarzwald, Ora R. 1991. Grammatical vs. lexical plural formation in Hebrew. *Folia Linguistica* 25. 577–608.

Scollon, Ron and Scollon, Suzie 1991. Mass and count nouns in Chinese and English: a few further Whorfian considerations. In: Robert Blust (ed.) *Currents in Pacific Linguistics: Papers on Austronesian Languages and Ethnolinguistics in Honour of George W. Grace* (Pacific Linguistics, series C, no. 117), 465–75. Canberra: Department of Linguistics, Research School of Pacific Studies, Australian National University.

Scott, Graham 1978. *The Fore Language of Papua New Guinea* (Pacific Linguistics, series B, no. 47). Canberra: Department of Linguistics, Research School of Pacific Studies, Australian National University.

References

Serzisko, Fritz 1982. Numerus/Genus-Kongruenz und das Phänomen der Polarität am Beispiel einiger ostkuschitischer Sprachen. In: Hansjakob Seiler and Franz J. Stachowiak (eds.) *Apprehension: Das sprachliche Erfassen von Gegenständen* II: *Die Techniken und ihr Zusammenhang in Einzelsprachen*, 179–200. Tübingen: Gunter Narr.

— 1992. Collective and transnumeral nouns in Somali. In: Hussein M. Adam and Charles L. Geshekter (eds.) *Proceedings of the First International Congress of Somali Studies* (Scholars Press Occasional Papers and Proceedings 2), 513–25. Atlanta, GA: Scholars Press.

Shibatani, Masayoshi 1990. *The Languages of Japan*. Cambridge: Cambridge University Press.

Shields, Kenneth 1991–92. The emergence of the non-singular category in Indo-European. *Lingua Posnaniensis* 34. 75–82.

Sigler, Michele 1992. Number agreement and specificity in Armenian. In: Costas P. Canakis, Grace P. Chan and Jeanette Marshall Denton (eds.) *Papers from the 28th Regional Meeting of the Chicago Linguistic Society 1992* I: *The Main Session*, 499–514. Chicago: Chicago Linguistic Society.

Silverstein, Michael 1976. Hierarchy of features and ergativity. In: R. M. W. Dixon (ed.) *Grammatical Categories in Australian Languages*, 112–71. (Linguistic Series 22). Canberra: Australian Institute of Aboriginal Studies.

Simmons, Donald C. 1956. Oron verb morphology. *Africa* 26. 250–64.

— 1957. Ibibio verb morphology. *African Studies* 16. 1–19.

Simons, Linda 1986. The pronouns of To'abaita (Solomon Islands). In: Ursula Wiesemann (ed.) *Pronominal Systems* (Continuum 5), 21–35. Tübingen: Narr.

Singler, John V. 1991. Social and linguistic constraints on plural marking in Liberian English. In: Jennifer Cheshire (ed.) *English around the World: Sociolinguistic Perspectives*, 545–61. Cambridge: Cambridge University Press.

Smirnova, I. A. 1981. Kategorija čisla v jazykax s nemarkirovannym imenem (na materiale iranskix jazykov). *Voprosy jazykoznanija* no. 2. 77–87.

Smith, Lawrence R. 1979. Labrador Inuttut inverted number marking, exchange rules and morphological markedness. *Linguistics* 17. 153–67.

Smith-Stark, T. Cedric 1974. The plurality split. In: Michael W. La Galy, Robert A. Fox and Anthony Bruck (eds.) *Papers from the Tenth Regional Meeting, Chicago Linguistic Society, April 19–21, 1974*, 657–71. Chicago: Chicago Linguistic Society.

Sobolevskij, S. I. 1960. Istorija dvojstvennogo čisla v drevnegrečeskom jazyke, preimuščestvenno po komedijam Aristofana. In: *Voprosy grammatiki: Sbornik statej k 75-letiju A. I. Meščaninova*, 401–8. Moscow/Leningrad: Izdatel'stvo Akademii Nauk, AN SSSR.

Soja, Nancy; Carey, Susan and Spelke, Elizabeth S. 1991. Ontological categories guide young children's induction of word meaning: object terms and substance terms. *Cognition* 38. 179–211.

Solomon, Martha Bellamy 1972. Stem endings and the acquisition of inflections. *Language Learning* 22. 43–50.

Song, Jae Jung 1997. The so-called plural copy in Korean as a marker of distribution and focus. *Journal of Pragmatics* 27. 203–24.

Song, Seok Choong 1975. Rare plural marking and ubiquitous plural marker in Korean. In: Robin E. Grossman, L. James San and Timothy J. Vance (eds.) *Papers from the Eleventh Regional Meeting, Chicago Linguistic Society, April 18–20, 1975*, 536–46. Chicago: Chicago Linguistic Society.

Sonnenstuhl, Ingrid; Eisenbeiss, Sonja and Clahsen, Harald 1999. Morphological priming in the German mental lexicon. *Cognition* 72. 203–36.

Speirs, Randall H. 1972. Number in Tewa. In: M. Estellie Smith (ed.) *Studies in Linguistics in Honor of George L. Trager*, 479–86. The Hague: Mouton.

Speiser, E. A. 1938. The pitfalls of polarity. *Language* 14. 187–202.

Spencer, Andrew 1991. *Morphological Theory*. Oxford: Blackwell.

Sridhar, S. N. 1990. *Kannada* (Descriptive grammars series). London: Routledge.

Stebbins, Tonya 1997. Asymmetrical nominal number marking: a functional account. *Sprachtypologie und Universalienforschung* 50. 5–47.

Steever, Sanford B. 1987. The roots of the plural action verb in the Dravidian languages. *Journal of the American Oriental Society* 107. 581–604.

Štejnfel′dt, È. A. 1963. *Častotnyj slovar′ sovremennogo russkogo literaturnogo jazyka: 2500 naibolee upotrebitel′nyx slov: Posobie dlja prepodavatelej russkogo jazyka*. Tallin: Naučno-issledovatel′skij institut pedagogiki Èstonskoj SSR.

Sten, Holger 1949. Le nombre grammatical. *Travaux du cercle linguistique de Copenhague* 4. 47–59. Copenhagen: Einar Munksgaard.

Stone, Gerald 1993a. Sorbian (Upper and Lower). In: Bernard Comrie and Greville G. Corbett (eds.) *The Slavonic Languages*, 593–685. London: Routledge.

  1993b. Cassubian. In: Bernard Comrie and Greville G. Corbett (eds.) *The Slavonic Languages*, 759–94. London: Routledge.

Street, Chester S. 1987. *An Introduction to the Language and Culture of the Murrinh-patha*. Darwin: Summer Institute of Linguistics, Australian Aborigines Branch.

Stump, Gregory T. 1989. A note on Breton pluralization and the elsewhere condition. *Natural Language and Linguistic Theory* 7. 261–75.

  1990. Breton inflection and the split morphology hypothesis. In: Randall Hendrick (ed.) *The Syntax of the Modern Celtic Languages* (Syntax and Semantics 20), 97–119. San Diego: Academic Press.

  1991. A paradigm-based theory of morphosemantic mismatches. *Language* 67. 675–725.

  1996. Two types of mismatch between morphology and semantics. In: Eric Schiller, Elisa Steinberg and Barbara Need (eds.) *Autolexical Theory: Ideas and Methods* (Trends in Linguistics Studies and Monographs 85), 291–318. Berlin: Mouton de Gruyter.

Sugamoto, Nobuko 1989. Pronominality: a noun–pronoun continuum. In: Roberta Corrigan, Fred Eckman and Michael Noonan (eds.) *Linguistic Categorization* (Amsterdam Studies in the Theory and History of Linguistic Science 61), 267–91. Amsterdam: John Benjamins.

Sulejmanov, Ja. G. 1985. O formax ograničennogo i neograničennogo množestvennogo

References

čisla imen suščestvitel'nyx v avarskom jazyke. In: K. Š. Mikailov (ed.) *Kategorija čisla v dagestanskix jazykax: sbornik statej*, 114–19. Maxačkala: Dagestanskij filial AN SSSR.

Sunik, O. P. 1997. Mańčžurskij jazyk. In: V. M. Alpatov, I. V. Kormušin, G. C. Pjurbeev and O. I. Romanova (eds.) *Mongol'skie jazyki, Tunguso-man'čžurskie jazyki, Japonskij jazyk, Korejskij jazyk*, 162–73. Moscow: Indrik.

Suprun, A. E. 1959. *O russkix čislitel'nyx*. Frunze: Kirghiz State University.

1961. *Staroslavjanskie čislitel'nye*. Frunze: Kirghiz State University.

1963a. O soglasovanii skazuemogo s podležaščim, vključajuščim količestvennye čislitel'nye v serbo-lužickix jazykax. *Serbo-lužickij lingvističeskij sbornik*, 138–53. Moscow.

1963b. Zametki po sintaksisu pol'skix čislitel'nyx. *Pytannja slovjans'koho movoznavstva* (L'vov) 7–8. 135–45

1969. *Slavjanskie čislitel'nye (stanovlenie čislitel'nyx kak osoboj časti reči)*. Minsk: Belorussian State University.

Sutcliffe, Edmund F. 1936. *A Grammar of the Maltese Language: with Chrestomathy and Vocabulary*. Valletta: Progress.

Švedova, N. Ju. 1980. *Russkaja grammatika* I: *Fonetika, fonologija, udarenie, intonacija, slovoobrazovanie, morfologija*. Moscow: Nauka.

Szupryczyńska, Maria 1991. Związki składniowe w konstrukcjach z tzw. 'podmiotem towarzyszącym'. In: Maciej Grochowski and Daniel Weiss (eds.) *'Words are Physicians for an Ailing Mind'* (Sagners Slavistische Sammlung 17), 415–20. Munich: Otto Sagner.

Tagliamonte, Sali; Poplack, Shana and Eze, Ejike 1997. Plural marking patterns in Nigerian Pidgin English. *Journal of Pidgin and Creole Languages* 12. 103–29.

Takatori, Yuki and Schwanenfulgel, Paula J. 1992. Superordinate category terms and mass–count noun status. *Journal of Linguistic Anthropology* 2. 199–209.

Tauli, Valter 1973. *Standard Estonian Grammar* I: *Phonology, morphology, word-formation* (Acta Universitatis Upsaliensis, Studia Uralica et Altaica Upsaliensia 8). Uppsala: Almqvist and Wiksell.

Tembiné, Issiaka 1986. Kategorial'naja sistema mladopis'mennogo jazyka (na materiale dogon). Doctoral thesis. Moscow: Institute of Linguistics.

Tereščenko, N. M. 1973. *Sintaksis samodijskix jazykov: prostoe predloženie*. Leningrad: Nauka.

Ternes, Elmar 1970. *Grammaire structurale du breton de l'Ile de Groix (dialecte occidental)*. Heidelberg: Carl Winter Universitätsverlag.

1992. The Breton Language. In: Donald MacAulay (ed.) *The Celtic Languages*, 371–452. Cambridge: Cambridge University Press.

Tesnière, Lucien 1925a. *Les formes du duel en slovène*. Paris: Champion.

1925b. *Atlas linguistique pour servir à l'étude du duel en slovène*. Paris: Champion.

1951. Le duel sylleptique en français et en slave. *Bulletin de la Société de Linguistique de Paris* 47, 1. 57–63.

Thomas, David 1955. Three analyses of the Ilocano pronoun system. *Word* 11. 204–8.

338

Thomson, Robert L. 1992. The Manx Language. In: Donald MacAulay (ed.) *The Celtic Languages*, 100–36. Cambridge: Cambridge University Press.

Tiersma, Peter M. 1982. Local and general markedness. *Language* 58. 832–49.

Tiffou, Étienne and Patry, Richard 1995. La notion de pluralité verbale: le cas du bourouchaski du Yasin. *Journal asiatique* 282. 407–44.

Timberlake, Alan 1993. Russian. In: Bernard Comrie and Greville G. Corbett (eds.) *The Slavonic Languages*, 827–86. London: Routledge.

Tobin, Yishai 1988. Sign: context: text – theoretical and methodological implications for translation: the dual number in Modern Hebrew: a case in point. In: Reiner Arntz (ed.) *Textlinguistik und Fachsprache: Akten des Internationalen übersetzungswissenschaftlichen AILA-Symposions: Hildesheim, 13.–16. April 1987* (Studien zu Sprache und Technik 1), 449–68. Hildesheim: Georg Olms.

1990. *Semiotics and Linguistics.* London: Longman.

Todd, Evelyn M. 1978. A sketch of Nissan (Nehan) Grammar. In: Stephen A. Wurm and Lois Carrington (eds.) *Second International Conference on Austronesian Linguistics: Proceedings: Fascicle 2* (Pacific Linguistics, series C, no. 61), 1181–239. Canberra: Department of Linguistics, Research School of Pacific Studies, Australian National University.

Tomić, Olga Mišeska (ed.) 1989. *Markedness in Synchrony and Diachrony* (Trends in Linguistics: Studies and Monographs 39). Berlin: Mouton de Gruyter.

Trager, George 1961. Taos IV: Morphemics, Syntax and Semology in nouns and in pronominal reference. *International Journal of American Linguistics* 27. 211–22.

Trépos, Pierre 1957. *Le Pluriel breton.* Brest: Emgleo Breiz.

1980. *La Grammaire bretonne.* Brest: Imprimerie Simon.

Tsunoda, Tasaku 1981. *The Djaru Language of Kimberley, Western Australia* (Pacific Linguistics, series B, no. 78). Canberra: Department of Linguistics, Research School of Pacific Studies, Australian National University.

Tuite, Kevin 1992. The category of number in Common Kartvelian. In: Howard I. Aronson (ed.) *The Non-Slavic Languages of the USSR: Linguistic Studies: New Series*, 245–83. Chicago: Chicago Linguistic Society, University of Chicago.

Turner, Paul R. 1976. Pluralization of nouns in Seri and Chontal. In: Margaret Langdon and Shirley Silver (eds.) *Hokan Studies: Papers from the First Conference on Hokan Languages held in San Diego, California, April 23–25, 1970* (Janua Linguarum, Series Practica 181), 297–303. The Hague: Mouton.

Unterbeck, Barbara 1993. *Kollektion, Numeralklassifikation und Transnumerus: Eine typologische Studie zum Koreanischen* (Continuum 9). Frankfurt am Main: Lang.

Urban, Greg 1985. Ergativity and accusativity in Sholkeng (Gê). *International Journal of American Linguistics* 51. 164–87.

Večerka, R. 1960. K sintaksisu imen čislitel'nyx v staroslavjanskom jazyke. In: V. Georgiev (ed.) *Ezikovedsko-etnografski izsledvanija v pamet na akademik Stojan Romanski*, 195–208. Sofia: Bulgarian Academy of Sciences.

Veksler, Bunim X. and Jurik, Vladimir A. 1978. *Latyšskij jazyk (samoučitel').* Riga: Zvajgzne. [Third edition.]

References

Vidal, Alejandra 1997. Noun classification in Pilagá (Guaykuruan). *Journal of Amazonian Languages* 1. 58–111.

Vigliocco, Gabriella; Butterworth, Brian and Semenza, Carlo 1995. Constructing subject–verb agreement in speech: the role of semantic and morphological factors. *Journal of Memory and Language* 34. 186–215.

Vincenot, C. 1975. *Essai de grammaire slovène.* Ljubljana: Mladinska knjiga.

Vincent, Nigel 1988. Italian. In: Martin Harris and Nigel Vincent (eds.) *The Romance Languages*, 279–313. London: Croom Helm/Routledge.

Voorhoeve, Clemens L. 1965. *The Flamingo Bay Dialect of the Asmat Language* (Verhandelingen van het Koninklijk Instituut voor Taal-, Land- en Volkenkunde 46). 's-Gravenhage: M. Nijhoff.

Wallace, Constance V. 1988. Broken and double plural formations in the Hebrew Bible. PhD dissertation, New York University. [Distributed by University Microfilms International, Ann Arbor, reference NIA89–10613.]

Walsh, Michael J. 1976. The Murinypata Language of North-West Australia. PhD thesis, Australian National University.

War, Badaplin 1992. The personal pronouns and their related clitics in six Khasi dialects: a grammatical and sociolinguistic study. PhD thesis, School of Oriental and African Studies, University of London.

Warner, Anthony R. 1988. Feature percolation, unary features, and the coordination of English NPs. *Natural Language and Linguistic Theory* 6. 39–54.

Watkins, Laurel J. 1976. Position in grammar: sit, stand, lie. *Kansas Working Papers in Linguistics* 1. 16–41.

1984. *A Grammar of Kiowa.* Lincoln and London: University of Nebraska Press.

1995. Noun classification in Kiowa-Tanoan. Paper presented at the meeting of the Society for the Study of the Indigenous Languages of the Americas, Albuquerque, University of New Mexico, July 8–9, 1995. Unpublished.

Watson, Bruce 1979. The singularity and plurality of collective nouns: a case study. *Melbourne Working Papers in Linguistics* 5. 42–9.

Wegener, Heide 1995. The German plural and its acquisition in the light of markedness theory. In: Hanna Pishwa and Karl Maroldt (eds.) *The Development of Morphological Systematicity: a Cross-Linguistic Perspective* (Tübinger Beiträge zur Linguistik 399), 247–61. Tübingen: Gunter Narr.

Welmers, William E. 1973. *African Language Structures.* Berkeley: University of California Press.

1976. *A Grammar of Vai* (University of California Publications in Linguistics 84). Berkeley: University of California Press.

Westermann, Diedrich 1945–46. Pluralbildung und Nominalklassen in einigen afrikanischen Sprachen. *Abhandlungen der Deutschen Akademie der Wissenschafte zu Berlin: Philosophisch-Historische Klasse* 1. 1–27. Berlin: Akademie-Verlag.

Westrum, Peter N. and Wiesemann, Ursula 1986. Berik pronouns. In: Ursula Wiesemann (ed.) *Pronominal Systems* (Continuum 5), 37–46. Tübingen: Narr.

Whitney, Arthur H. 1956 *Teach Yourself Finnish.* London: English Universities Press. [Quoted from 11th impression 1989.]

Wickens, Mark A. 1992. *Grammatical Number in English Nouns: an Empirical and Theoretical Account* (Current Issues in Linguistic Theory 76). Amsterdam: John Benjamins.

Wierzbicka, Anna 1988. *The Semantics of Grammar* (Studies in Language Companion Series 18). Amsterdam: John Benjamins.

  1991a. The semantics of grammar: a reply to Professor Palmer. *Journal of Linguistics* 27. 495–8.

  1991b. Semantic rules know no exceptions. *Studies in Language* 15. 371–98.

Wiesemann, Ursula 1986. The pronoun system of some Jê and Macro-Jê languages. In: Ursula Wiesemann (ed.) *Pronominal Systems* (Continuum 5), 359–80. Tübingen: Narr.

Wilkins, David P. 1984. Nominal reduplication in Mparntwe Arrernte. *Language in Central Australia* 1. 16–22.

  1989. Mparntwe Arrernte (Aranda): studies in the structure and semantics of grammar. PhD thesis, Australian National University.

Witherspoon, Gary J. 1971. Navajo categories of objects at rest. *American Anthropologist* 73. 110–27.

Wolfart, H. Christoph and Carroll, Janet F. 1981. *Meet Cree: a Guide to the Cree Language.* Lincoln: University of Nebraska Press. [Second edition; First edition 1973.]

Wonderly, William; Gibson, Lorna F. and Kirk, Paul L. 1954. Number in Kiowa: nouns, demonstratives, and adjectives. *International Journal of American Linguistics* 20. 1–7.

Woodbury, Anthony 1981. Study of the Chevak dialect of Central Yup'ik Eskimo. PhD dissertation, University of California, Berkeley.

Wright, William. 1967. *A Grammar of the Arabic Language, Translated from the German of Caspari and Edited with Numerous Additions and Corrections* I, third edition revised by W. Robertson Smith and M. J. de Goeje. Cambridge: Cambridge University Press. [First edition 1859.]

Xalilov, M. Š. 1985. Ob ograničennom množestvennom čisle suščestvitel´nyx bežtinskogo jazyka. In: K. Š. Mikailov (ed.) *Kategorija čisla v dagestanskix jazykax: sbornik statej*, 136–43. Maxačkala: Dagestanskij filial AN SSSR.

  1995. *Bežtinsko-russkij slovar´.* Maxačkala: Dagestanskij naučnyj centr Rossijskoj akademii nauk.

Xolodovič, A. A. 1979. Kategorija množestva v japonskom jazyke v svete obščej teorii množestva v jazyke. In: A. A. Xolodovič: *Problemy grammatičeskoj teorii*, 173–95. Leningrad: Nauka.

Xrakovskij, Viktor S. (ed.) 1997. *Typology of Iterative Constructions* (Lincom Studies in Theoretical Linguistics 4). Munich: Lincom Europa.

Yli-Vakkuri, Valma 1986. *Suomen kieliopillisten muotojen toissijainen käyttö* [Secondary use of grammatical forms in Finnish] (Publications of the Department of Finnish and General Linguistics of the University of Turku 28). Turku: Department of Finnish and General Linguistics.

Zaliznjak, A. A. 1977. *Grammatičeskij slovar' russkogo jazyka: slovoizmenenie.* Moscow: Russkij jazyk.

Zemskaja, E. A. and Kapanadze, L. A. (eds.) 1978. *Russkaja razgovornaja reč': teksty.* Moscow: Nauka.

Zigmond, Maurice L.; Booth, Curtis G. and Munro, Pamela 1991. *Kawaiisu: a Grammar and Dictionary with Texts* (University of California Publications in Linguistics 119). Berkeley: University of California Press.

Žolobov, Oleg F. 1998. *Symbolik und historische Dynamik des slavischen Duals = Simvolika i istoričeskaja dinamika slavjanskogo dvojstvennogo čisla* (Beiträge zur Slavistik 35). Frankfurt am Main: Peter Lang.

Žukova, A. N. 1972. *Grammatika korjakskoga jazyka: Fonetika, morfologija.* Leningrad: Nauka.

Zwicky, Arnold M. 1978. On markedness in morphology. *Die Sprache* 24. 129–43.

Zwicky, Arnold M. and Pullum, Geoffrey K. 1983. Phonology in syntax: the Somali optional agreement rule. *Natural Language and Linguistic Theory* 1. 385–402.

AUTHOR INDEX

Author index

Urien, Jean-Yves 36

Veksler, Bunix X. 276, 276n10
Večerka, R. 215n34
Vidal, Alejandra 22n16
Vigliocco, Gabriella 178n1
Vincenot, C. 215n34
Vincent, Nigel 153n21
Voorhoeve, Clemens L. 64

Wallace, Constance V. 150n17
Walsh, Michael J. 25
War, Badaplin 221
Warner, Anthony R. 198n20
Wasow, Thomas, (Sag et al.) 198n20
Watkins, Laurel J. 159–60, 160n28, 186, 261
Watson, Bruce 189
Wegener, Heide 295
Weisler, Steven, (Sag et al.) 198n20
Welmers, William E. 15, 74, 156n26
Westermann, Diedrich 135n3
Westrum, Peter N. 65n6
Whitney, Arthur H. 234
Wickens, Mark A. 174
Wierzbicka, Anna 80, 144n10, 173, 175

Wiese, Richard 150–1; (Clahsen et al.)
    295n29; (Marcus et al.) 296
Wiesemann, Ursula 22n17, 65n6
Wilkins, David P. 149n16, 220
Witherspoon, Gary J. 249n9
Woest, Andreas (Clahsen et al.) 295
Wolfart, H. Christoph 277
Wonderly, William 159
Woodbury, Anthony 108n22
Wright, William 32, 37n31, 209

Xalilov, M. Š. 97n10
Xolodovič, A. A. 74
Xrakovskij, Viktor S. 245

Yli-Vakkuri, Valma 231
Yngve, Victor 81n22

Zaliznjak, A. A. 145n11
Zemskaja, E. A. 231
Zepeda, Ofelia 78
Zigmond, Maurice L. 171
Žolobov, Oleg F. 269n7
Žukova, A. N., 238 279
Zwicky, Arnold M. 153, 166, 198n19

LANGUAGE INDEX

SUBJECT INDEX

9 780521 649704